The
Institutional
Construction
Of
Organizations

The Institutional Construction Of Organizations

International and Longitudinal Studies

W. Richard Scott
Søren Christensen
Editors

SAGE Publications
International Educational and Professional Publisher
Thousand Oaks   London   New Delhi

For information address:

SAGE Publications, Inc.
2455 Teller Road
Thousand Oaks, California 91320
E-mail: order@sagepub.com

SAGE Publications Ltd.
6 Bonhill Street
London EC2A 4PU
United Kingdom

SAGE Publications India Pvt. Ltd.
M-32 Market
Greater Kailash I
New Delhi 110 048 India

Library of Congress Cataloging-in-Publication Data

The institutional construction of organizations : international and
    longitudinal studies / edited by W. Richard Scott, Søren
Christensen.
        p. cm.
    Includes bibliographical references and index.
    ISBN 0-8039-7070-6 (alk. paper). — ISBN 0-8039-7071-4 (pbk. :
alk. paper)
    1. Organization. 2. Social institutions. I. Scott, W. Richard.
II. Christensen, Søren, 1940–   .
HM131.I5275   1995
302.3′5—dc20   95-9039

This book is printed on acid-free paper.

95 96 97 98 99 10 9 8 7 6 5 4 3 2 1

Sage Project Editor: Susan McElroy   Typesetter: Christina Hill

Contents

Preface

ALL OF US ASSOCIATED WITH THIS VENTURE are, of course, glad to celebrate the publication of the volume that you are now holding in your hands, but many of us are equally pleased by the process that produced the publication. The development of this volume is the result of a genuinely collaborative, collegial process, one which initiated and cemented our friendships, increased our appreciation for research styles different from our own, and improved the quality of each of the chapters here assembled. Permit us to provide a brief, thumbnail sketch of this process.

During the spring of 1992, a set of colleagues engaged in a variety of collaborative research projects from the Institute of Organization and Industrial Sociology, Copenhagen Business School (CBS), decided that it would be helpful to discuss their work in progress with colleagues in the United States. Because most of the projects drew on institutional theory, and also because of an existing network of collegial and friendship ties, colleagues at two universities, New York University and Stanford University, were contacted to determine if a visit might be scheduled. The Copenhagen group wanted not only to discuss their own research—Have papers; will travel!—but also to hear about related research under way on the host campuses—Have interest; will listen!—so the agenda was broadened to allow for two-way exchange. The visits took place in June of 1992.

Copenhagen travelers participating in both the New York and Stanford seminars included Ib Andersen, Finn Borum, Søren Christensen, James Hopner, Peter Karnøe, Jan Molin, Jesper Strandgaard Pedersen, Marianne Risberg, and Ann Westenholz. At New York University, the host group consisted of Charles Fombrun, Raghu Garud, Theresa Lant, and Steven

Mezias. At Stanford, the local participants included Jim March, John Meyer, Dick Scott, Mark Suchman, Pat Thornton, and Mark Ventresca.

The 1-day meetings at the two universities proved to be sufficiently helpful and stimulating that several members of the group determined to find ways to continue the dialogue. Søren Christensen, convener of the Copenhagen group, invited Dick Scott to spend a week in Copenhagen on his way home from Tromsø, Norway, where Dick was completing a part-time, 2-year stint as an Adjunct Professor associated with the Institute of Social Science, University of Tromsø. A workshop on institutional theory and research was arranged to include the participation of Christian Knudsen of the Institute of Industrial Research and Social Development, CBS, and of Jan Mouritsen and Peter Skærbæk of the Institute of Informatics and Management Accounting, CBS. This September workshop advanced the process by providing a deadline to encourage Copenhagen researchers to turn their June verbal presentations into hard copy first drafts. In November the CBS groups held a 2-day workshop that included Peter Abell of the London School of Economics and Political Science.

During the September visit, Søren suggested to Dick the possibility of holding a 3-day conference during the coming summer to bring together current participants, along with others having similar interests, to present and discuss completed papers on institutional research. The possibility of a resulting publication was also discussed. Dick was invited to serve as a Visiting Professor at CBS and in that capacity to provide feedback to authors on early drafts of their papers prior to the conference.

During the next few months, Søren and Dick settled on the final list of invitees and made preparations for the conference. Invitations were issued during the fall, with abstracts due in mid-January and feedback to be received by March 1993. Final papers were due May 1 so that copies could be sent to all participants before the conference. The conference itself was scheduled for June 16-19 at the Praestekilde Kro and Hotel on the beautiful island of Møn, south of Copenhagen.

At the conference, each paper was summarized and then thoroughly discussed. The atmosphere was civil, supportive, and thoughtful. Unlike many conferences where time is limited and the pace is too fast, the format here permitted sufficient time to discuss the strengths and weaknesses of each paper. The food was superb and breaks were included to allow the group to enjoy the 14th-century frescoes in nearby Keldby Church and to hike down the chalk cliffs of Møn's Klint. Dinners involved the most serious competition witnessed during the conference: singing contests.

At the conclusion of the conference, Dick Scott made summary comments and led the discussion concerning whether a publication was to be prepared. Buoyed by the group's enthusiasm and level of commitment to the venture, participants devised further steps to improve the papers. A minimum of two conference participants agreed to provide written comments on each of the papers as the author prepared a penultimate draft for the editors. These drafts, due in December 1993, were then reviewed and final changes were suggested by either Søren or Dick. Final manuscripts were to be received in June of 1994. The editors met at Stanford in August to deal with the remaining problems and to discuss the contents of the introductory and final chapters. Both of us believe that the quality of all of the papers was improved by this rather elaborate review process.

During such a prolonged process, numerous social debts and obligations are incurred. We would like to thank, first and foremost, our colleagues and contributors. They put up with a good deal of editorial harassment and, without exception, remained cool, calm, and committed to the completion of the project. Marianne Risberg, Research Secretary, CBS, provided expert administrative support for the entire undertaking, from the earliest visits and workshops to the final editorial stages. Lisa Hellrich, administrator of the Stanford Center for Organizations Research, assisted on many of the multiple tasks associated with a project involving so many collaborators. Special thanks are also due to Jim March, head of the Scandinavian Consortium for Organizational Research located at Stanford University, and to his administrator Barbara Beuche, who together provided intellectual, spiritual, and logistic support throughout the project.

As we began to move more into a production mode, our efforts were greatly aided by Pamela Vergun, a doctoral student in the Department of Sociology at Stanford, who provided expert assistance in editing and smoothing the English of the Copenhagen papers and in compiling the bibliography and helping to prepare the index for the volume. We are also indebted to Harry M. Briggs, Editorial Director of Sage Publications, who had the good judgment to offer us a book contract, and who provided assistance and encouragement throughout the publication process.

Financial support for the project was provided by grants from the Danish Social Science Research Council, The Basic Research Foundation of the Copenhagen Business School, The Institute of Organization and Industrial Sociology of CBS, and the Danish Society for the Advancement of Business Education.

It is our fond hope that this completed volume shows some evidence of the gestation and birthing process, which, in our minds, was natural, healthy, and conducive to the production of additional offspring.

Dick Scott
Søren Christensen

Introduction

Institutional Theory and Organizations

W. RICHARD SCOTT

INSTITUTIONAL THEORY IS ON THE RISE. Perhaps it takes a period of rapid and momentous change to make us aware of the importance of the social and cultural context surrounding and supporting organizational forms. We are assuredly in such a period now.

- The Soviet Union has been dismantled and its former parts and appendages are struggling to create a new order. Consultants and advisers rush in with blueprints of market-based organizations, only to discover that stable enterprises cannot be constructed in the absence of wider social structures supporting social institutions and that markets themselves are not natural entities but must be socially constructed.

- Within Europe an initial attempt to reduce national barriers to economic exchange has led to extensive, often unexpected changes in institutional rules regarding capital and labor markets, competition, and property rights as the interdependence of politics and markets, and of states and firms, is redefined.

- Many students of organizations have long believed in the superior nature of Western-style organizations. Our models of rational organizational forms have been derived from a distillation of the characteristics of the more successful varieties of organizations operating in the Western world, but these assumptions have been severely challenged of late by the superior productivity and efficiencies attained by industrial enterprises in Asia exhibiting substantially different characteristics from their Western counterparts. Can it be that there is more than one way to rationally organize?

• For many decades, organizational analysts have operated under the assumption that managers were the primary agents in organizations and that their preference for growth and security in their environment would continue to dominate stockholders' interests in higher returns on their investments. A decade of turbulence in financial markets, with many of America's largest corporations being confronted by and succumbing to hostile takeover attempts, suggests that the old assumptions undergirding managerialism have been challenged if not replaced by a different institutional order favoring owners and financial intermediaries. How do such basic beliefs and understandings change? Does the safety and stability of our most powerful corporations really depend on the ephemeral backing of ideas and beliefs?

Living as we do in the midst of so much change and turmoil, it is difficult for students of organizations to continue assuming the existence of stable organizational forms and to focus our energies on examining routine organizational operations and decisions. How can we continue to scrutinize the figure and ignore the ground when shifts in the ground dislodge and reshape the figures we are attempting to study, explain, and understand?

During the past three decades, organizational studies has witnessed a succession of theoretical perspectives that focus attention on one or another aspect of organizations, including contingency theory, resource dependency, and population ecology. Although all of these approaches emphasize that organizations are open systems, affected by and affecting the environments in which they exist (see Scott, 1992), only institutional theory highlights the importance of the wider social and cultural environment as the ground in which organizations are rooted. Though some versions of institutional theory can be seen as offering simply another selective and specialized perspective, in the hands of its boldest practitioners, institutional theory provides a context or frame within which earlier approaches can find their place, and by which they are conditionalized.

As is so often the case in the history of ideas, the development of institutional theory involves, in part, a recapturing of earlier insights: Institutional approaches were strong, if not dominant, in economics, in political science, and in sociology early in the 20th century. (Note that this period, during the height of industrialization, was also marked by extensive and rapid changes in social structures.) The current revival of institutional theory also brings with it different emphases and novel insights.

I begin with a brief description of institutional theory in organizational studies and then comment on some of the distinctive features of this collection of papers.

Institutional Theory

I propose the following definition of institutions:

Institutions consist of cognitive, normative, and regulative structures and activities that provide stability and meaning to social behavior. Institutions are transported by various carriers—cultures, structures, and routines—and they operate at multiple levels of jurisdiction. (Scott, 1995, p. 33)

To assume an institutional perspective is to emphasize the importance of psychological, social, and political elements in the study of social phenomena generally and organizations specifically. In contrast to most of the earlier perspectives, which emphasize the importance of materialist forces—technology, resources, production systems—institutionalists call attention to the role of ideational forces—of knowledge systems, beliefs, and rules in the structure and operation of organizations. Much of the stability and order we associate with the world of organizations is seen to flow from the existence of belief systems and regulatory structures, both formal and informal.

Further, an institutional perspective privileges the role of cognitive processes and symbol systems. Following Weber (1968), action is viewed as social only to the extent that actors attach meaning to it. Environmental stimuli must be cognitively processed by actors—interpreted by individuals employing socially constructed symbol systems—before they can respond by taking action.

Whereas there is substantial agreement on these common elements by institutional analysts, differences in emphasis exist which give rise to important disagreements and misunderstandings. Table I.1 cross-classifies the three elements and the three types of carriers of institutions. Analysts vary in the extent to which they emphasize the cognitive, normative, or regulative facets of institutions as well as where they situate these elements—whether cultures, structures, or routines are viewed as the primary carriers.

TABLE I.1 Institutional Elements and Carriers

	Elements		
Carriers	Regulative	Normative	Cognitive
Cultures	rules laws	values expectations	categories typifications
Structures	governance systems power systems	regimes authority systems	structural isomorphism identities
Routines	compliance obedience	conformity performance of duty	performance programs scripts

SOURCE: Adapted from Scott (forthcoming, Table 3.2).

Institutions as Regulatory Systems

Analysts who view institutions primarily as regulatory systems are more likely to be social realists in their ontology. "For the realist, the social world exists independently of an individual's appreciation of it. . . . It is not something which the individual creates—it exists 'out there' " (Burrell & Morgan, 1979, p. 4). Individual and collective actors (such as organizations) are assumed to have interests which they pursue in an intended rational manner. Because sometimes interests conflict and differences must be resolved, rules and laws are formulated to which regulatory machinery is attached. Actors obey these rules primarily out of self-interest, out of expedience, in order to avoid sanctions. The primary institutional control mechanism, employing DiMaggio and Powell's (1983) typology, is that of coercion. Institutions are often established by a powerful actor or coalition of actors, who enforce rules that favor their interests. Institutions can also arise in situations in which it is in the interests of all actors to develop and enforce rules that bind their own behavior in certain respects. However, rules which, if enacted, would benefit all may fail to be established. Need does not necessarily lead to existence.

Economists, including economic historians, and political scientists are most likely to take a regulative view of institutions. Economic historians, such as North (1990), tend to focus on the development of rules and laws embedded primarily in cultural carriers. They examine how property rights vary over time and place, what processes give rise to them, and how they affect economic forms and processes.

The new institutional economists, including agency theorists and transactions cost analysts, also adopt a primarily regulative view of institutions. For these theorists, however, structures are viewed as the primary carriers of institutional rules. Agency theorists attempt to ascertain how control systems, including monitoring and sanctioning machinery, vary according to the nature of the work being performed, including its visibility and interdependence (see Alchian & Demsetz, 1972; Jensen & Meckling, 1976). Williamson (1975, 1985) and colleagues have developed and tested numerous arguments regarding how organizational governance systems vary in scope and complexity as designers attempt to reduce transactions costs. As Williamson (1991a, p. 269) points out, although economic historians emphasize the broader "institutional rules of the game: customs, laws, politics," transactions cost economics "focuses on the comparative efficacy with which alternative generic forms of governance—markets, hybrids, hierarchies—economize on transaction costs." The "institutions" that these theorists are attempting to explain are differences in the governance structures of organizations. Although normative elements, such as the level of trust among participants, sometimes enter into the arguments of institutional economists, they are treated as "environmental" conditions affecting institutional design, not as institutional elements themselves.

Similarly, a number of political scientists and political sociologists focus on the creation of regimes—systems of rules and surveillance mechanisms operating, for example, at the international or industry level—intended to curb destructive conflicts or competitive behavior among nation-states or firms (see Krasner, 1983; Schmitter, 1990). In some cases, these institutional forms are primarily rule systems and negotiated multilateral arrangements that operate primarily at the cultural level. In other cases, they are embodied in specific structures, such as the United Nations at the international level, or a trade association at the industry level. Still other political scientists focus on the development of specific political institutions—congressional committees or bureaucratic agencies—attempting to account for the development of particular rules or practices embedded in structures or routines (see Shepsle & Weingast, 1987).

Institutions as Normative Systems

To emphasize the normative aspects of institutions is to give priority to moral beliefs and internalized obligations as the basis for social meaning and social order. In this conception, behavior is guided not primarily by self-interest and expedience, but by an awareness of one's role in a social situation and a concern to behave appropriately, in accordance with others' expectations and internalized standards of conduct. Employing DiMaggio and Powell's (1983) typology, the institutional mechanisms at work are not coercive but normative processes.

Like the analysts stressing the regulative aspects of institutions, those emphasizing the normative elements also tend to be social realists, but they embrace a different conception of the "natural" state of man. In particular, they are more likely to take a collectivist rather than individualist conception of human nature, emphasizing the power of social patterns to shape individual beliefs and behavior, and to conceive of individual actions as determined more by nonrational than rational forces (see Alexander, 1987). Individuals are strongly influenced by collective norms and values that impose social obligations on them, constraining their choices. March (1981a, p. 221) provides a useful description of the difference between a normative conception and one emphasizing rational choice: "To describe behavior as driven by rules is to see action as a matching of behavior with a position or situation. The criterion is appropriateness rather than consequential optimality. The terminology is one of duties and roles rather than anticipatory decision making."

From the founding fathers up to the recent past, sociologists have championed the view of institutions as fundamentally normative systems—as systems of normative expectations and internalized obligations. From Durkheim and Weber to Parsons and Selznick, sociologists have focused attention on the normative aspects of institutional forms. Durkheim (1961) stressed the importance of collective representations and normative frameworks in stabilizing social life, and Weber (1968) noted how varying types of normative systems legitimized regulatory and administrative structures—traditional norms and beliefs underlying patrimonial systems, and rational-legal norms underlying bureaucratic structures. In his general theoretical framework, Parsons (1951) proposed that a system of action was institutionalized to the extent that actors in ongoing relations oriented their actions to a common set of normative standards and values. In his work on organizations, Parsons (1960) developed his *cultural-institutional* approach by examining the ways in which the value system of the organization was legitimated by its connection to the wider societal institutional norms and values. Selznick (1949, 1957) examined the ways in which individuals developed normative commitments to procedures, structures, and social relations both within and outside the organization.

Durkheim, Weber, and Parsons located institutions primarily in wider, societal belief systems—in cultural carriers. Selznick viewed some institutional processes as carried by cultures—for example, organizational ideologies—but viewed others as embedded in structures, in informal ties and cooptative relations within and among organizations.

Among political scientists, March and Olsen (1984, 1989) have given priority to a normative conception of institutions in their analysis of political structures. They argue that much behavior in organizational situations is governed by rules and routines, noting that, "Much of the behavior we observe in political institutions reflects the routine way in which people do what they are supposed to do" (1989, p. 22). They also insist, however, that to conclude that behavior is oriented to and governed by rules does not imply that behavior is mindless or automatic. Actors must determine which rules apply to which cases and must interpret their meaning in particular situations. To argue that behavior is not "rational" in the utility-maximizing sense is not to argue that it is not reasonable or intelligent.

Institutions as Cognitive Systems

The newest conception of institutions sees them as composed primarily of cognitive elements. In its more fully developed versions, a cognitive view of institutions replaces social realist assumptions with a social constructionist vision of the social world. In this view, people don't discover reality; they create it. Actors don't naturally exhibit capacities or utilities or interests; these are social constructions that vary by time and place. The characteristics of actors, both individual and collective, are defined by cultural rules.

This cognitive conception of institutions has multiple roots: in social psychology, anthropology, political science, and sociology. Briefly, the cognitive revolution in psychology, ushered in by the early work of Lewin (1951) and Bruner (1951), focuses on the ways in which individual behavior in situations is governed by schema, frames, or scripts (see Markus & Zajonc, 1985). In anthropology, scholars such as Geertz and D'Andrade have redefined the concept of culture, from its earlier broad reference to the full range of customs, usages, and traditions, to emphasize its symbolic role: "Culture consists of socially established structures of meaning" (Geertz, 1973, p. 12). Political scientists March and Simon (March & Simon, 1958; Simon, 1957) were among the first to emphasize the extent to which the order observed in organizations was a cognitive order, based on shared premises, rules, and performance programs. Sociologists Berger and Luckmann (1967), along with ethnomethodologists such as Garfinkel (1967), pointed to the ways in which shared conceptions of the situation were produced in interaction but, having been produced, were perceived as objective and external to the actors: not as man-made but a natural and factual order.

Anthropologists and sociologists give particular emphasis to the "constitutive rules" that are part of the cultural system. These rules are employed to construct actors and actions. The clearest examples are provided by games in which a set of rules and definitions creates, in the example of baseball, actors such as pitchers and catchers and actions such as base stealing and bunting. Specific roles (pitcher) are often identified with specific activities (pitching) so that the relation between actor and actor is often "socially tautological." "Both social actors and the patterns of action they engage in are institutionally anchored" (Meyer, Boli, & Thomas, 1987, p. 22). Other rule systems create doctors and patients, supervisors and workers, and lawyers and clients, but these institutionalized systems are not viewed as "games," and the actors and their actions are less likely to be viewed as socially constructed. Not only individual but also collective actors are socially constituted. Cultural systems provide models for how to construct corporations and schools and hospitals. These entities are granted rights and assumed to have certain characteristics and capacities to the extent that they conform to these cultural templates. (See D'Andrade, 1984; Meyer et al., 1987.)

Thus, from a cognitive perspective, institutions are not so much bundles of regulations or collections of norms, but knowledge systems. Cognitive systems control behavior by controlling our conception of what the world is and what kinds of action can be taken by what types of actors. Social categories and typifications help us to determine what things and people are similar, and thus to be treated according to one set of rules, and what other things and people are different and are thus to be treated differently. As DiMaggio and Powell (1983) emphasize, there is great pressure on organizations engaged in the same types of activities to look and act alike, to become isomorphic. It is this cognitive emphasis that distinguishes the "new" institutionalism in the sociological study of organizations from the earlier institutionalism associated with Parsons and Selznick and their students (see Powell & DiMaggio, 1991).

Meyer and Rowan (1977) were the first theorists to apply a cognitive conception of institutions to the creation and legitimation of organizational forms. Subsequently these arguments have been further elaborated by DiMaggio and Powell (1983) and Meyer and Scott (1983). Zucker (1977) has developed a similar formulation and examined cognitive processes at the micro (intraorganizational) level. All of these scholars regard institutions as primarily carried by cultural systems, whether at the level of the world system, the society, the organizational field, or a particular organization (corporate culture). By contrast, a related approach known as evolutionary economics, developed by Nelson and Winter (1982), also emphasizes the importance of cultural conceptions for the functioning of organizations but locates these elements primarily in the habits and routines of workers and work groups. For these analysts, the tacit knowledge embedded in skills and work routines is the carrier of institutional rules.

We see then that within the framework of institutional analysis, quite different assumptions and arguments are made. Economists tend to emphasize the more regulative aspects of institutions, as do many political scientists. Early sociologists stressed the normative elements, but more recent sociologists and social psychologists have given more attention to their cognitive features. Anthropologists and sociologists, along with economic historians, tend to view these institutional elements as primarily carried by cultural rules and beliefs. By contrast, institutional economists tend to locate institutions in social structures, and evolutionary economists emphasize the importance of organizational routines as institutional carriers.[1]

Many of these divergent conceptions, as well as others yet to be described, are reflected in the collection of papers brought together in this volume. I will discuss some of the areas of divergence, but only after I first identify some unifying features that distinguish this work from previous efforts in the institutional analysis of organizations.

Distinctive Features of This Volume

All of the papers in this volume deal with some aspect of the institutional analysis of organizations. Although the collection contains much diversity, to be discussed subsequently, there are several common strands exhibited by most if not all the chapters. These common elements represent, I believe, important strengths of the collection.

COMMON INTERESTS AND THEMES

First, virtually all of the papers are *empirical*, dealing with some topic or problem concerning which systematic observations have been made. This emphasis contrasts with much contemporary work on institutions and organizations, which literature consists of more than its share of speculative and discursive pieces, the argument relying on illustrations, speculations, or "stylized facts" rather than on empirical observations. The fact that much of the work reported here is empirical does not mean that it is devoid of or unconnected to theoretical arguments. In some cases, the arguments are more deductive and treated as hypotheses to be tested; in others they are inductive, as theoretical questions arise from the information assembled. In all the empirical papers, theoretical arguments are explicitly recognized to be at work.

Second, a great many of the papers involve *longitudinal* analyses. In some papers (e.g., Christensen & Molin; Mouritsen & Skærbæk; Borum &

Westenholz), single organizations are followed as they change and develop over long periods of time. In other cases (e.g., Dobbin, Karnøe, Mezias, Thornton), industries or collections of organizations are followed over a period of several years. Longitudinal studies are particularly suited to institutional arguments, because institutionalization is both a condition and a process: Regulations, norms, and cognitive systems do not appear instantaneously but develop over time; the diffusion of common activity patterns and structures through time is viewed as important evidence for the developing strength of an institutional pattern. Thus theory drives design. Conversely, when data are gathered on organizational forms over time, analysts are often compelled to resort to institutional arguments in order to explain the types of changes observed. Design often drives theory.

Third, unlike previous volumes dealing with institutional arguments and organizations, a sizable proportion of the organizations examined here are *market-based forms*. Institutional arguments regarding organizations first emerged in the study of nonmarket organizational forms, in particular educational and other public organizations (see, e.g., Meyer & Scott, 1983; Zucker, 1988). Although the current volume reports on nonmarket organizations such as the Red Cross and the Danish theater, it also includes analyses of a variety of market organizations: semiconductor firms, computing companies, hotels, publishing houses, railroads, and wind energy companies. This volume should help to correct the mistaken impression that institutional arguments are only relevant in the absence of markets.

Fourth, a substantial proportion of the papers in this volume also attempt to correct another type of problem besetting the earlier institutional studies: the neglect of *agency* and *strategy*. Many early studies seemed to assume that organizations were primarily passive systems, conforming readily to the rules and requirements of their environments. A sense of agency (individuals acting purposefully) was often missing: Actors were often invisible and, if present, were assumed to be slavishly following their social scripts (see DiMaggio, 1988). Institutional effects were often observed, but the processes or mechanisms by which they were achieved were not uncovered. Moreover, many studies seemed to assume that the only action open to organizations was to conform to the cognitive and normative demands made upon them (see Oliver, 1991). By contrast, in many of the studies contained in this volume, actors are accorded careful attention. They are seen, variously, as adopting but also adapting the belief systems, selecting among the relevant rule systems, interpreting and modifying the meanings applicable to the situation. For example, Suchman describes the actions of lawyers and venture capitalists as they codified and spread selected institutional practices among Silicon Valley semiconductor firms.

In this and other studies reported in this volume, actors are also seen as having interests—albeit often institutionally shaped preferences—and as having powers—often institutionally constructed rights and capacities. They also are seen to behave strategically, sometime conforming but often negotiating, protesting, resisting, and hiding from the dictates of regulatory or symbolic systems. Agency is attended to along with structure; conformity is studied but not to the neglect of conflict.

DIVERGENT INTERESTS AND THEMES

In the review of institutional theory above, I noted two important sources of divergence among institutional analysts: which institutional elements are emphasized and which carriers are presumed to operate. Most of our authors focus attention on either the cognitive or the normative aspects of institutions, and there is a rather even split between those who stress culture and those stressing structure as carrier. By focusing on the "competence view of the firm," however, Knudsen contributes to our understanding of routines as institutional carriers.

For some analysts, institutions are the dependent variable, but for others they are the independent variable. Most of the authors in our volume treat institutions as the independent variable, asking how differences in institutional arrangements give rise to differences in organizational arrangements or practices. However, a few of our contributors—Abell, Lant and Baum, and Suchman—attempt to seek the determinants of institutions (see Part I). Abell points out that there are more likely to be disagreements between rational choice theorists and others over the origins than the consequences of institutional forms. Lant and Baum, along with Suchman, describe processes by which actors in an organizational field develop common conceptions of the field and common rules or models of appropriate organizational forms.

Although the remaining authors focus attention on the consequences of institutional arrangements, they differ greatly in the level of analysis employed to define the dependent variables of interest. A number of analysts focus on differences created at the industry level. Dobbin, for example, reports how differing cultural beliefs (both over time and between the United States and Britain) created varying policies structuring the organization of the railroad industry. Karnøe examines how differences in institutional context between Denmark and the United States affected the development of wind energy technology and practice. Thornton examines changes over time occurring among firms in the U.S. educational publishing industry as growth-by-acquisition strategies were adopted by an increasing proportion of firms. Garud and Kumaraswamy examine how changes over time in both the technical and institutional environments of computer companies shape the competitive strategies pursued by component and system manufacturers in this "network" industry (see Part IV).

Mezias's study at first appears to focus on changes occurring in a diverse collection of organizations. He examines factors affecting the adoption by firms of new accounting practices by a sample of firms drawn from the 200 largest nonfinancial corporations in the United States. Although such firms are not members of a single industry, they can be treated as members of the same organizational field in the sense that the largest multidivisional companies increasingly compare themselves to one another and take each other into account as they develop their structures and strategies. As Fligstein (1990, p. 19) argues, the definition of organizational field has shifted for these companies from boundaries "based on product lines to industry to the population of the largest firms."

Knudsen's chapter provides an interesting examination of how Selznick's early institutional arguments can be employed to help current analysts better understand how firms manage to set and pursue objectives, even though confronted by (a) conflicting priorities among participants and (b) changes over time in participants and priorities. Although Mezias focuses attention on factors affecting institutional controls exercised over firms at the organizational field level, Knudsen attends to the processes by which firms create institutional controls, via the construction of "constitutions" at the firm level (see Part III).

Other studies in this volume focus on changes in the structure of individual organizations. Thus, Christensen and Molin trace the development of the Danish Red Cross as it transforms itself from era to era, as varying demands are made and opportunities are presented. Mouritsen and Skærbæk, as well as Borum and Westenholz, each examine organizations—the Royal Danish Theater and the Copenhagen Business School—attempting to locate themselves on active fault lines—in the one case between cultural and business criteria and in the other between public and private funding and control (see Part II).

As described in the preface, this volume brings together work from two different research traditions—the United States and Europe, in particular, Danish researchers. Although these research traditions share many common elements, they differ predictably in the style of study undertaken. Although many exceptions can be found, U.S. research is more likely to be theory driven, deductive, and quantitative, usually based on data collected from multiple organizations. By contrast, European/Danish studies are more likely to be problem driven, with more attention to context. They are more often inductive and qualitative, and they are often based on the examination of one or a few cases. Both of these traditions have strengths, and each has its limitations. We hope that bringing representative instances of each tradition together in a single volume allows us to capture the best of both worlds.

Note

1. For a fuller discussion of the many varieties of institutional theorizing in organizations, see Powell and DiMaggio (1991) and Scott (1994b; 1995). For reviews of the new institutionalism in economics, see Hodgson (1988), Langlois (1986), and Mäki, Gustafsson, and Knudsen (1993). For discussions of the new institutionalism in political science, see March and Olsen (1984), Moe (1984), and Thelen and Steinmo (1992).

I. ACCOUNTING
FOR INSTITUTIONS

1

The New Institutionalism
and Rational Choice Theory

PETER ABELL

THE NEW INSTITUTIONALISM DOES NOT APPEAR to be an entirely homogeneous body of thought, but Powell and DiMaggio (1991, p. 8) give a flavor of what it is all about, at least in organization theory and sociology:

> The new institutionalism in organization theory and sociology comprises a rejection of rational actor models, an interest in institutions as independent variables, a turn toward cognition and cultural explanations and an interest in properties of supra-individual units of analysis that cannot be reduced to aggregations or direct consequences of individuals' attributes or motives.

Although a statement of this sort invites a variety of interpretations, one thing stands out, namely an explicit *rejection of rational actor models*. I shall in this essay concentrate upon this rejection and argue an almost contrary position. That is to say, I shall urge that the explanatory claims of any form of institutionalism, new or old, are severely incomplete without resort to some sort of purposive action theory and, in this respect, rational actor models should hold our first attention. To put it succinctly, such models provide our rational choice of theoretical framework (Abell, 1991).

I am, however, anxious not to overstate the case and also particularly not to encourage any division into competing camps, each with claims to irreconcilable legitimacy. Despite my advocacy of rational choice theory (RCT), I am by no means sanguine about all of its more exclusive ambitions. I merely believe it is our best bet at this moment.

In order to furnish the argument, I need a working definition of the "new institutionalism." This is not an easy task, given the varied offerings that appear to attract the label, ranging from transactions cost theory (Coase, 1960; North, 1990; Williamson, 1985), where the framework of the rational actor is substantially preserved in the face of uncertainty, incomplete contracts, individual cognitive limitations, and opportunism, to what we might term radical institutionalism, partially captured in the above quotation from Powell and DiMaggio. Here, we are apparently invited to engage in an exercise where *individual-level analysis (choice) largely disappears and institutions (i.e., supra-individual units) are explained by the presence of prior institutions*, perhaps conjoined with some exogenous constraint or shock. Insofar as individuals enter the picture, they do so with their actions propelled without reflection (taken for granted) by institutions, which serve as "independent variables." Lying between this radical perspective and the more accommodating claims of North are a variety of positions, but the one of greatest significance is a form of evolutionary functionalism (e.g., Nelson & Winter, 1982). Here, institutions, though straining toward optimality, are not pictured as products of efficient foresight but arise, and are explained, as a consequence of random variation, environmental selection, and reproduction in human populations. In general, we may speak of adaptive models, but again these can take on a "rational" (in the sense of optimally chosen) character, to the degree that the postulated selection mechanism is calculative or not.

It is important to appreciate where the tensions do and do not lie between RCT and any form of new institutionalism. First, let it be noted that RC theorists do not deny that human actions and interactions are sometimes (even often) determined (partially or wholly) by institutions (i.e., sets of rules or norms), so the institution in question might be described, if you wish, as an independent variable. There may be some considerable grounds for disagreement as to how frequently this is the case and, if it is, to what extent the dictates of the institution are followed without reflection—but adjudication here should ultimately be an empirical matter. RC theorists could in principle be perfectly welcoming to the idea that at some point in time all human actions are institutionally shaped. Differences arise when we come to interpret the *fact* that actions are so shaped. Then this is, if you will, a matter of institutions as the dependent (endogenous) rather than the independent variable. Institutionalists appear either to accept institutions as given (exogenous) or to explain their occurrence by reference to prior institutions. In the latter case, the approach is heavily Durkheimian, because institutions are clearly properties of the social system, and the explanatory precepts invoked amount to a plea whereby social facts are to be explained in terms of other such facts—thus Powell and DiMaggio's rejection of reductionism. Also consider Durkheim's (1982) authoritative pronouncement: "One may term an *institution* all the beliefs and modes of behavior instituted by the collectivity; sociology can then be defined as the science of institutions, their genesis and their functioning" (p. 45).

Rational choice theorists reject much of this. First, institutions are never taken as exogenous. If, in fact, actions or interactions are wholly or in part determined by institutions, then their genesis and persistence (equilibrium characteristics) must be accounted for. Second, any such account/explanation will necessarily be at the individual level and formulated according to the precepts of RCT. Thus, it is on matters of the explanation of the genesis and persistence of institutions that the two perspectives most fundamentally diverge. Rational choice theorists are quite happy to theoretically embrace the full panoply of taken-for-granted assumptions and expectations, social and individual norms, rules of thumb, copying behavior, other-regarding utilities, and so on, if they occur—how could they do otherwise? They need, however, to demonstrate that they can be explained in terms of RCT precepts. It is this which institutionalists resist.

In order to grasp the differences between the new institutionalist and rational choice theorists, it will perhaps prove helpful to make explicit their respective assumptions.

The Assumptions of the New Institutionalism

1. An institution comprises a set of more-or-less-agreed-upon rules which carry meaning for and determine the actions (or interactions) of a population of actors.

2. The rules are of two essential types:

> *Constitutive rules* which take the form: In a situation with characteristics C, X is to count as a Y (Schotter, 1981; Scott, 1994b). Social identities are a particularly important example (White, 1992).

> *Regulative rules* (normative expectations) which take the form: In situations with characteristics C, Y ought/ought not to do Z.

3. The level of agreement about the appropriateness of the rules in a population of actors is usually given exogenously.

4. The rules are to a degree (level of institutionalization) *taken for granted*. (Various other terms are used as well.) Thus, once the situation is recognized as one where the dictates of the institution are deemed appropriate (a constitutive rule), actors will (a) tend not to reflect upon available alternatives; (b) therefore, tend not to seek available alternatives; and (c) to a degree, come to have preferences (beliefs and affects) that identify

with the obligations of the institution (internalization). This internalization opens the door to ritualization.

5. Following rules (institutional actions) becomes to a degree separated from the possible reasoning about their purpose and from the outcomes that might be realized. Actors *enact* rather than act. Further, only rarely will the rules in any sense of the term be optimal with respect to self-regarding interests.

6. The genesis or persistence of institutions (sets of rules) cannot be deduced from assumptions or observations about individual motives (design, purposes, intentions, choices, etc.) taken independently or interactively or in aggregate. Thus, the explanation of their genesis, if sought, will be in terms of prior institutions, (random?) shocks, nonoptimal selection, and reproduction.

As with any framework, it is possible to relax some of the assumptions without fatal consequences and in so doing arrive at a "thinner" institutionalism. I would regard assumptions 1 and 4 as providing the sine qua non of institutionalism.

The Assumptions of Rational Choice Theory

There are many ways of characterizing RCT, ranging from the very technical to the more discursive. I shall here take the latter route for it helps to link into sociological ways of thinking more expeditiously (Abell, 1991; Elster, 1989).

I. Individualism
    a. Individual human beings are the sole source of purposive motor energy and thus of action and interaction.
    b. Events in the social world must in principle (not necessarily in practice) be explained in terms of (deducible from, supervenient upon) individual actions/interactions.

II. Optimality
    – Individual actions are deemed to be optimally chosen with respect to an individual's preferences.
    – Preferences over actions are optimally formed with respect to beliefs about the outcomes of actions.
    – Beliefs are optimally formed with respect to information (gathered/available).

- Information (gathered/available) is optimal with respect to affects (wants).
- Affects (if consistent with IV) are exogenous.

III. Consistency
- Preferences are transitive over actions.

IV. Self-regard
- Affects range over the actor's own welfare/interests only.

It is worth noting here that these assumptions are extremely demanding; however, some of them may be relaxed while still staying within the spirit of RCT. For instance, those who enthusiastically embrace one of the many interpretations of "bounded rationality" only require of an RCT approach that it conform to a statement along the following lines: Individuals, given their circumstances as they see them, do the best they can to satisfy whatever their wants might be. Here, wants may range over an unlimited domain, and, insofar as optimality may be said to be involved, it is unreservedly subjective in nature. Nevertheless, the assumption is still made that individuals circumstantially act reasonably and further, would, if required, be able to proffer reasons for their chosen course of action. The challenging nature of radical institutionalism is thereby brought into relief, for it asks us to dispense with even this watered-down version of RCT. There is no sense in which individuals even "do the best they can," unless of course they want to be institutional puppets.

A Confrontation

I shall now consider in turn each of the assumptions of the new institutionalism and see how they clash with RCT and, if they do so, seek a resolution.

Assumptions 1 and 2: The definition of an institution is entirely acceptable to RC theorists. This is equally true of the constitutive and regulative components. Further, the attribution of "meaning" causes no problem either. Both schools should be careful to speak of actions and interactions and not of behaviors.

Assumption 3: Rational choice theorists will not accept "agreement" as exogenous, which, in effect, is part of accepting the existence and persistence of an institution as exogenous. Insofar as an institution rests upon regulative and constitutive rules, an explanation for the extent of agreement (scope) of both components is called for. I will consider the nature of these sorts of explanations in a moment.

Assumption 4: This assumption and its attendant parts apparently come into conflict with the RCT assumption of optimality, but matters are not quite as straightforward as this. Rational choice theorists could hardly deny that actions sometimes (often?) take on a taken-for-granted appearance where it would be *empirically* wrong to assume that the full panoply of optimality holds sway, action by action. The important point here is that this observation is an empirical one, not a theoretical precept, as is apparently urged by many institutionalists. Thus, the taken-for-granted nature of actions becomes the explicandum for rational choice theorists. Parallel reasoning applies to Assumption 5, which in practice is an extension of Assumption 4.

Assumption 6: Rational choice theorists reject this assumption by virtue of Assumption I(a). Institutions are to be explained from RCT precepts.

The key points of dispute appear to be about neither the nature of institutions nor their ubiquity, but about how their genesis and persistence are to be explained.

The Explanation of the
Genesis and Persistence of Institutions

It is manifestly clear what RC theorists need to achieve. The origins and persistence of the various ingredients (regulative and constitutive rules and scope of agreement) of any institution must be shown to be "rational" in the sense of the above-outlined assumptions. However, before we proceed to show how this objective might be approached, it is important to sound a certain word of caution. It would be wrong to expect that all institutions could be brought satisfactorily under the explanatory auspices of a strict RCT. Rather, we should, as with any general theory, only seek paradigmatic privilege for it (Abell, 1993a). By this I mean: first, wide but most likely not universal applicability; second, yet wider applicability by a judicious relaxation of assumptions; and third, a baseline role whereby it is departures from the precepts of the paradigm which need special explanation, if and when they occur. In this last respect, if we were to adopt the most relaxed version of RCT, then we should have to ask why it is that people do not circumstantially do the best they can, given their wants and beliefs. Presumably, institutionalists see institutions as having this sort of consequence.

Let us start with persistence—even if we could furnish a rational account of the origins of an institution, the observation is made that they often continue to hold sway in changed circumstances where their continued rationality is highly questionable. Institutionalists make the telling point that most institutionally governed action is clearly not optimal but, nevertheless, persists and is even transmitted across generations. That is to say, the constitutive and regulative rules followed can, by no stretch of the imagination, be seen as the best thing under the circumstances for the actor to do (or one of a number of equally good things to do, in the fact of multiple equilibria). Note here in passing that the analyst is implicitly comparing what transpires with some externally imposed criterion (rational action). Rational choice theorists cannot, I think, deny that institutions often have this property. So, how do they accommodate the fact?

Perhaps the first thing to observe is that, for rational choice theorists, such persistence is regarded as theoretically problematic, whereas institutionalists are able to treat it with a certain equanimity, merely as a fact of social life. When it is asserted that persistent institutions do not lead to optimal individual actions, it is important to be clear about what is being claimed. I assume it is not being claimed that people act against their dominant preference, but that their preferences are not optimally formed (see the assumptions of RCT). This can be accounted for by any number of reasons associated with lack of information, restricted search, copying, or, more generally, the taken-for-granted status of the action. Alternatively, the dictates of the institution can be internalized and/or ritualized in the mind (conscious or unconscious) of the actor. When any of these things occur, then rational choice theorists need an explanation of the occurrence consistent with their own precepts.

Most of the RCT models purporting to account for the persistence and transmission of institutions rely upon ideas of economizing on search and thinking, where both sorts of activity are assumed to be relatively costly (optimizing costs). We all know there is a logical conundrum (self-reference, see Knudsen, 1993a) at the foundation of any search model—not being able to know in advance what search will reveal, and therefore to place a utility upon the possible outcome. This conundrum aside, the general approach is one whereby the apparent suboptimality of the persistent institution is dissolved by an appeal to optimizing costs of one sort or another.

What institutionalists implicitly assert, however, is that if actors were to search, to think, and not to copy (i.e., more generally not to take a course of action for granted), then they would act differently (i.e., more rationally). It is perhaps a little ironic that the truth of this counterfactual in practice implicitly empowers RCT assumptions. What could be a more graphic demonstration of paradigmatic privilege?

Rational choice theorists have a number of other ripostes to claims of suboptimal persistence. First, as many economists no doubt would, they deny the suboptimality, at least in the long run, suggesting that institutions always approximate optimality if they survive in a competitive environment. I think this may be true, but we rarely encounter perfectly competitive environments. Nevertheless, there is here the makings of a refutable theory, which suggests that the more competitive the environment, the closer persistent institutions will approximate optimality (see, however, Steuer, 1989).

In the absence of such denials, however, the rational choice theorist will always initially try to interpret persistence as a sign of a nonoptimal (Nash) equilibrium; it is precisely this idea that gives RCT a theoretical cutting edge, something which seems to me is rather absent from the various types of institutionalism. The various types of institutionalism are essentially descriptive, despite their claim to theoretical denomination. Thus, persistence invites a search for the reasons why nobody has an incentive to be the first mover in deserting the institution despite the conjectured fact that each has an interest in others doing so. Note that framing the question this way already separates the institution in focus from a Pareto-efficient, conventional equilibrium where all have no incentive to want others to change. One can reason that the costs of search and thinking are greater than the benefits that would be realized for each individual; thus, there are no individual incentives. On the other hand, with cheap copying, there is a clear public goods disincentive.

I suspect many institutionalists will nevertheless feel this whole approach misses the essential point about taken-for-grantedness. It is not, they will aver, that people do not have an incentive to move to a Pareto-superior action; it is that they do not even think of, or search for, such an action, regardless of whether there are incentives. Of course, this may be because the actors have internalized the rules of the institution (i.e., made following the rules their optimal preference). Here, the action is rational, but rational choice theorists would always seek an explanation for internalization (see below).

In the absence of such attachment, taken-for-grantedness does pose severe problems for RCT. Note, however, that once again the counterfactual world is regulated by an appeal to an RCT idea—individuals would act more rationally if they were to relinquish taken-for-grantedness. I think it is open to question how ubiquitous such taken-for-granted, non-Pareto equilibria are, especially where the potential gains to be had are significant. Institutionalists are nevertheless confident about their ubiquity, but the issue is not so much a conceptual as an empirical one. Rational choice theorists would at least regard any such equilibria as only quasi-stable.

Certainly, at the aggregate level where nobody recognizes an easily obtainable, attractive alternative, the equilibrium will be labile. Turning briefly to the genesis of institutions, I can find no compelling theory of institutional genesis within the framework of institutionalism. The claims seem to be essentially negative with respect to RCT, namely that:

1. institutional genesis cannot be accounted for rationally (i.e., in terms of optimal self-interested actions);
2. institutional genesis is not derivable from individually motivated behavior.

The truth of the first statement would appear to be an empirical matter. Certainly, there are now at our disposal quite powerful RCT theories concerning the origins of norms (e.g., the Arrow-Coleman theory of externalities); we would, in my opinion, have to be sure these do not fit the bill before searching elsewhere. A number of anthropologists (e.g., Popkin, 1979) have recently shown considerable skill in adapting RCT to explain the origins of what might initially appear as rather unyielding institutions. Further multiple-self models open the way for explanations of the genesis of personal norms. It may be that RCT will not always work and alternative theories will have to be sought. Be this as it may, it is not at all clear to me what positive theoretical ideas institutionalism has to offer in this respect.

In the context of both the persistence and genesis of institutions, institutionalists believe, rightly, in my view, a number of social mechanisms frequently occur, namely:

- typifying contexts or situations,
- comparing oneself with others,
- copying or mimetic action, and
- learning by adaptation.

I do not believe that RC theorists can deny the wide occurrence of these mechanisms (though some try), because they are, after all, the very stuff of social life; rather, they should show how they have at least a relaxed RCT interpretation. Out-and-out RC theorists would have us model individuals as case-by-case optimizers who face each situation anew and optimally analyze it. Individuals are not only blessed of foresight and the ability to calculate in abundance, but are also largely innocent of their own and others' histories. All of this seems to me just factually false, though it may sometimes prove analytically sensible to proceed as though much of it were true.

In practice, a great deal of day-to-day decision making and consequent action takes place in contexts where the actor deems certain actions (often previously resorted to) as appropriate, regardless of whether apparently optimal. Clearly, both the constitutive and regulative components of institutions fit into this way of thinking rather well. RC theorists must ask when it might be optimal to resort to and persist with typification. We might postulate that typification (as opposed to full-blooded calculation) will be found in situations that are variously (a) relatively complex, (b) relatively uncertain, and (c) of relatively little consequence. Certainly, as cognitivists have taught us, all action is predicated upon an imposition of equivalence upon the world, and such equivalences may be deemed institutionalized insofar as they are widespread (see the definition of an institution). RC theorists and institutionalists should not fall out over this point. A hard-line RC theorist would no doubt wish to interpret any typification as resulting from an optimal cognitive encounter with the world (e.g., scientific method), but I suspect the modern philosophy of science would bring him or her little comfort in this respect. It is, however, important for social theorists not to get overtrammeled by debates of this sort, which are ultimately rooted in intractable epistemological matters. The issues at stake are altogether more mundane: Should we model everyday human actions (net of some fundamental epistemological considerations) as characteristically calculative or as unreflectively institutionalized? I am sure the empirical answer is both, and it may be useful to take the degree of calculation (optimal search) as a fundamental variable. I can see how this may be achieved within a relaxed RCT framework, where, as a special case, institutionalized rule following becomes the best way of proceeding. I find it more difficult, however, to conceive of operating the other way around. Copying and comparing are allied to this way of thinking. I shall deal with the latter presently.

Institutions are manifestly mimetically transmitted in human populations. Indeed, culture and socialization are preponderantly mimetic phenomena by their very nature (Steuer, 1989). When would it be optimal to copy others? Again, it might be useful to distinguish, by the scale of the degree of calculation involved between models, where individuals reflectively copy and where copying is thoroughly institutionalized. RC theorists have developed models whereby individuals act on the basis of observing the average actions of others, some of whom are themselves imitators and some of whom are optimizers (Conlisk, 1980). It is relatively easy to use standard evolutionary models to study the equilibrium behavior of such systems. Indeed, I believe that evolutionary epistemology, with the admixture of either imperfect copying or limited adaptive learning (variety), and a relaxed RCT component comprises our best bet for developing a theory of socialization and preference acquisition. This leads me to the second point.

The second point above is, I think, a plea for a Durkheimian-type priority of the collective level in determining individual preferences. RCT's reaction to this claim is complicated. As a theoretical framework, it is more impressive when preferences are modeled over generalized means to specific ends (e.g., income). So, a preference for personal income is postulated exogenously, and any further inquiry as to why individuals prefer more to less income is hardly thought worrying about as long as it is directed to self-regarding ends (see below). More generally still, individuals are assumed to maximize utility. RCT is distinctly less impressive when trying to account for the consumption of particular goods, or equivalently why certain goods bring utility whereas others do not. Orthodox rational choice theorists are still inclined to postulate fixed preferences (across individuals and within individuals across time) and account for variations in behavior by variations in constraints. In practice this permits an avoidance of any serious questions about the origins of preferences by the agency of the collectivity or otherwise. This stratagem is clearly not going to work if RCT is to extend its province to situations where we want to know about the source of particular preferences, or where preferences might reasonably be thought to change. RCT has no convincing theory of preference formation, though the current preoccupation with learning theory and how it might be attached to game theory holds out some hope. RCT is not alone in this respect; I know of no other significant theories in this area.

I find it difficult to attach clear meaning to the second point, but possible interpretations are either (a) that institutions are the unintended consequences of individual actions or (b) that institutional genesis requires assumptions of group/collectivity (more generally other-regarding) oriented preferences. RCT can live with (a) though is inclined to see it as rare.

Finally, I should like to comment upon the self-regard assumption of RCT. RCT always encourages us to start with an assumption of self-regard and then to deduce the emergence of norms and institutions. It is not infrequently argued that such an assumption is ultimately based in (evolutionary) biology and/or comprises a median assumption, perched innocuously midway between malign and benign other-regard. Furthermore, other-regarding sentiments are themselves seen as internalized norms or institutions, and thus not to be taken as exogenous but in need of explanation. My own view, however, is that relative utilities (i.e., utility functions containing arguments about an individual's relative standing vis-à-vis others including possibly social groups) are both ubiquitous and compatible with evolutionary arguments in an uncertain world. I am happy, therefore, to take such utilities as exogenous. Doing so often opens up easier theoretical routes to puzzling facts about social life (Abell, 1993b; Frank, 1985).

In fact, it is rather easy to deduce both copying and its opposite from assumptions about the form of comparative or relative utilities (Abell, 1993b; Oswald, 1993). Assume the utility of an individual depends, at least in part, upon the relative level of his or her utility-delivering activity compared with the level of some specified reference group or individual (e.g., a group mean). Then, if the relationship between utility and the comparative measure is concave, a rise (fall) in the activity of the reference group will lead to a rise (fall) in the action of the individual mimetic action. So, those who are risk averse will copy. Conversely, with convex functions (i.e., risk embracing) the effects are in the opposite direction. Armed with these ideas, we can easily introduce complications like hysteresis, for example: a concave function on the upside and a convex one on the down. Individuals will then follow up but not down. If we care to entertain relative utilities, then a wide range of following behavior becomes easily explicable in RCT terms.

Concluding Remarks

I think it would be a mistake to propose institutionalism, new or old, as a general theoretic paradigm in sociology or organization theory. It would be to compound this mistake if, in addition, it were to be framed in antipathy to RCT. RCT does not deny the significance of institutions in social life, rather it offers a wide range of theoretical perspectives on their origins and persistence. It would, though, be surprising if these were to prove exclusively successful in answering all the theoretical problems we might pose.

It would seem sensible to me, when faced with clear evidence of institutionally governed action, to pose the following questions: To what extent is the institution followed in an unreflective manner? Is it almost autonomous or is there an element of calculation in it? If the latter, does the action conform to the weakest form of RCT or a stronger version? Is there evidence for relative utilities from which mimetic action can be deduced? If the former, could we still find an RCT version of its origin? If we can and the institution persists in changed circumstances that render it manifestly suboptimal, is this because of search and thinking costs in an uncertain and complex world? Or, is it because in fact little is at stake? Is the once rationally constructed guide to action now the thing to do?

If all this fails, then and only then look elsewhere.

2

Cognitive Sources of Socially Constructed Competitive Groups

Examples From the Manhattan Hotel Industry

THERESA K. LANT

JOEL A. C. BAUM

THE ROLES OF INDIVIDUAL AND COLLECTIVE COGNITION in the institutionalization of organizational beliefs and actions have a long history (Selznick, 1957; Zucker, 1977). However, much of the recent work in institutional theory has emphasized the macrosociological foundations of institutionalization. "There has been little effort to make neoinstitutionalism's microfoundations explicit. . . . Most institutionalists prefer to focus on the structure of environments, macro- to microlevel effects, and the analytic autonomy of macrostructures" (DiMaggio & Powell, 1991, p. 16). Recent work, however, has called for a reemergence of the role that microprocesses have in creating macro-level phenomena. "Yet it is important, we believe, to develop a social psychological underpinning in order to highlight both gross differences between institutional and rational-actor models, and more subtle departures from established traditions in sociology and from such approaches to organizational analysis as resource

AUTHORS' NOTE: We are grateful to Søren Christensen, Charles Fombrun, Dick Scott, Larry Van Horn, and the participants at the Workshop on Institutional Organizational Analysis at Møn, Denmark, for helpful comments on an earlier version of this chapter. We also thank Julie Harris and Helaine Korn for their assistance with data collection.

dependence and strategic contingency theories" (DiMaggio & Powell, 1991, p. 16).

Institutional theory is not the only research domain in which the importance of micro-level processes for macro-level outcomes has been recognized. The literature on competitive groups, for example, has argued that the cognitions of managers can determine membership in competitive groups and responses to competition (Baum & Lant, 1993; Fombrun & Zajac, 1987; Porac, Thomas, & Baden-Fuller, 1989; Reger & Huff, 1993). The growing body of literature on the role of managerial cognition in strategic decision making takes as its very premise the importance of the linkage between micro and macro phenomena (Huff, 1990). The reintegration of cognitive and institutional theories provides a means of exploring how institutionalized beliefs and activities evolve over time.

This chapter explores the role of managerial cognition in the evolution of institutionalized behavior in a competitive environment. The institutional literature has demonstrated that institutionalization processes, such as the adoption of common organizational structures and practices, occur among for-profit firms in competitive industries as well as among non-profit organizations (Amburgey & Lippert, 1989; Burns & Wholey, 1993; Fligstein, 1985; Galaskiewicz & Wasserman, 1989; Levitt & Nass, 1989; Mezias, 1990; Oliver, 1991; Tolbert, 1988). Even industrial economics suggests that firms in competitive industries recognize their mutual interdependence and develop "rules of the game" that guide and constrain firms' strategic choices (Chamberlin, 1962; Edwards, 1955; Porter, 1979; Scherer & Ross, 1990).

Our exploration of the role of cognition in creating institutionalized behavior among competing firms focuses on two ideas highlighted by the new institutionalism (Powell & DiMaggio, 1991). The first is the idea of isomorphism, or how groups of firms develop shared beliefs, structures, practices, strategies, and networks of relations (DiMaggio & Powell, 1983; Meyer & Rowan, 1977). The second is the idea that the cognitions and interactions of organizational members may be an important source of this isomorphism. Institutionalized behaviors depend on individuals and collectives within institutionalized contexts sharing similar beliefs about the meaning of their actions (Pfeffer, 1981; Zucker, 1977). Although these shared beliefs and behaviors can develop through mutual interaction (Porac et al., 1989), they can also develop even when direct interaction among actors is minimal and understanding of the social network of which the actors are a part is limited (Rabinowitz, Kelley, & Rosenblatt, 1966; Wallace, 1961; Weick, 1979). These institutionalized patterns of behavior may evolve through a reciprocal process of cognition and enactment; that is, organizations both *respond to* and *create* their environment (Weick, 1979).

This chapter explores the role of institutionalized beliefs in an industry by analyzing one of the most critical decisions that organizational strategists must make: deciding on a *competitive set*, the relevant set of firms in the environment that constitutes the competition. The selection of a competitive set requires managers to categorize other firms as *relevant to my strategic decisions* or *not relevant to my strategic decisions*. Porac and Thomas (1990) argue that managers make these decisions by comparing the attributes of firms to determine which are most similar to themselves. Given that such comparisons potentially constitute a large information-processing task, they suggest that managers simplify the task by using cognitive categories. In this chapter, we explore whether managers' competitive sets aggregate to form competitive groups of mutually interacting firms (Reger & Huff, 1993), and whether firms within these groups tend to be more similar in form, practice, strategy, and managerial beliefs than firms in different competitive groups.

The Role of Managerial Cognitions in the Formation of Competitive Sets

The idea that managerial cognition is important in strategic decision making has been gaining support (Daft & Weick, 1984; Dutton & Jackson, 1987). Research in this area suggests that managers' mental models of their environment are influenced by their interpretations of incidents in their environment, and that these interpretations influence their strategic choices (Barr, Stimpert, & Huff, 1992; Huff & Schwenk, 1990). Two types of interpretations that managers make are key: To determine (a) who their relevant competitors are and (b) how their firms can best compete with their set of competitors.

The literature on strategic groups suggests that firms within an industry may not all compete with one another; competition will be most intense within groups of firms that are similar to one another on key structural or strategic dimensions (Dess & Davis, 1984; McGee & Thomas, 1986). As summarized by Porter (1979):

[A]n industry can . . . be viewed as composed of clusters or groups of firms, where each group consists of firms following similar strategies in terms of the key decision variables. . . . Firms within a strategic group resemble one another closely and, therefore, are likely to respond in the same way to disturbances, to recognize their mutual dependence quite closely, and to be able to anticipate each other's reactions quite accurately. (p. 215)

This perspective has been criticized for its lack of attention to the role of managers' perceptions and decisions in the creation of strategic groups. Fombrun and Zajac (1987) argue that attempting to describe the stratification of firms within an industry by using only structural factors fails to recognize the critical role of managerial perceptions, and thus managers' posture toward the environment, in determining the groupings of firms that emerge. They found that managers' perceptions about their competitive environment were important predictors of strategic group membership. More recently, Reger and Huff (1993, p. 118) proposed that "the groups managers perceive will have real effects on strategy reformulation, strategic action, and subsequently on industry structure."

Cognitive Categories and
Managers' Conceptions of Competitive Sets

The determination of a firm's set of competitors requires managers to compare a large number of organizations on numerous attributes. However, managers are limited in their ability to make such comparisons by time and cost constraints and by cognitive limitations (March & Simon, 1958; Simon, 1957). There is substantial evidence that decision makers, faced with complex information-processing tasks, will use a variety of heuristics to simplify information processing (Kahneman, Slovic, & Tversky, 1982; Payne, 1976). Cognitive categorization is an information-processing and -storage strategy that enables decision makers to simplify their efforts to assess the characteristics of a complex environment (Porac & Thomas, 1990). There is substantial research in the psychology literature about cognitive categorization. This research suggests that decision makers develop cognitive categories by assessing the similarities and differences among the objects or events being classified (Holland, Holyoak, Nisbett, & Thagard, 1986; Neisser, 1987; Rosch, 1978). Cognitive categories develop as the decision maker determines sets of attributes that distinguish groups of objects from one another. Once these categories have been formed in the decision maker's mind, further classification is a relatively simple task of assessing a few key attributes, rather than the whole set of attributes that an object may exhibit.

Strategic groups researchers suggest that industries are composed of competitive groups within which firms share several key objective attributes, such as firm strategy or structure (Dess & Davis, 1984; McGee &

Thomas, 1986; Porter, 1979). If there are organizational attributes that effectively distinguish between firms in different competitive groups, then this industry structure should be reflected in the cognitive categories of managers working in the industry. However, it is possible that managers' cognitive categorizations of who are relevant competitors may not only *reflect* the attributes of firms within competitive groups, but that managers' actions based on these beliefs may actually *create* these groups. This suggests a reciprocal process, where managers *categorize* competitive sets based on the attributes and actions of these firms, and simultaneously, managers take *action* that is consistent with these categorizations, thus *enacting* a structure of strategic groups. Thus, managers both *respond to* and *create* their competitive environment (Weick, 1979).

Porac and his colleagues have made a forceful argument for this possibility. They suggest that membership in competitive groups is socially constructed (Porac & Thomas, 1990; Porac et al., 1989). They argue that the structure of an industry not only influences managers' cognitions, but that the structure of an industry is determined by managers' cognitions. The characteristics of an industry, or group of firms, and phenomena at the firm level are linked by the mental models of key decision makers. "A crucial linking mechanism is the creation of socially-shared beliefs which define the relevant set of rivals and guide strategic choices about how to compete within this set. These shared beliefs establish the identity of individual firms and help to create a stable transactional network in which the actions of rivals are at least somewhat predictable" (Porac et al., 1989, p. 400). That is, certain groups of competitors will come to see and respond to one another as the relevant players in one anothers' environment, and in so doing, actually create competitive groups.

This idea is consistent with Weick's (1979) notion that organizations enact their environments; by acting on their beliefs, they create conditions consistent with them. Through this enactment process firms may come to share similar conceptualizations or social constructions. Firms within a competitive set may eventually enact similar "realities" through direct and indirect interaction, such as trade association membership, industry news-letters, trade conferences, informal interaction, and monitoring day-to-day activities (Porac & Thomas, 1990; Reger & Huff, 1993). Further, "because of both indirect and direct imitative tendencies over time, the mental models of competing strategists become similar, thereby creating 'group level' beliefs about the marketplace" (Porac et al., 1989, p. 400). Porac et al. (1989) refer to such groups as *cognitive communities*.

The development of shared cognitions and knowledge structures among competing firms is a potential source of the institutional isomorphism that often is observed among groups of firms within industries. These shared beliefs can contribute to the development of similar causal attributions, similar conceptions of managerial roles, and similar strategic choices. Thus, work on managerial cognition may have relevance for the study of the development of institutional environments in competitive organizational fields. This paper follows the work of Porac, Thomas, and Baden-Fuller (1989, p. 401), who state that: ". . . an interpretive account of competition extends the work of institutional theorists and cognitively oriented strategy researchers who have argued that consensual socially constructed beliefs influence the actions of competing organizations."

Research Questions

This chapter explores several research questions regarding the role of managerial cognitions in the development of shared beliefs among sets of competing firms. We address these questions by assessing managers' cognitive categories of competitors within the Manhattan hotel industry, and comparing these categories with the actual characteristics of the hotels in the industry.

Our first research question concerns the issue of whether sets of firms in an industry develop shared beliefs about which firms are members of competitive sets. In their study of bank holding companies, Reger and Huff (1993) found support for the proposition that managers in different firms perceived similar groupings of firms in their industry. Porac and Thomas (1994, p. 9) suggest that, "When a particular business definition is a shared cognitive category held by managers from several organizations, the joint focus on each other creates a competitive community of firms that are engaged in reciprocal monitoring and mutual adjustments. In this way, competitive boundaries are psychologically defined by managerial minds and sustained via self-reinforcing cognitive categorizations." Our first proposition predicts that we will find evidence of competitive groups in the Manhattan hotel industry, based on an examination of the subsets of hotels identified as relevant competitors by a sample of hotel managers.

Proposition 1: Managers' categorizations of hotels into *competitive sets* will reveal the cognitive substructure of the industry, or competitive subgroups of hotels that tend to identify one another as relevant competitors.

The literature on competitive groups has suggested that there will be a higher degree of similarity among firms within a group than between firms in different competitive groups (Fombrun & Zajac, 1987; Porter, 1979).

That is, managers will perceive *similar others* to be members of their competitive set (Porac & Thomas, 1990). Baum and Mezias (1992) argued that size, price, and location were key variables influencing the intensity of competition among firms in the hotel industry. Supporting this conclusion, they found that the risk of hotel failure was a function of how similar a hotel was to other hotels in terms of size, price, and location. Hotels that were more similar to one another on these dimensions tended to compete more intensely and had larger influences on one another's survival chances. In this study, we predict that hotels with similarities on these dimensions will be more likely to identify one another as competitors. Thus, we expect that hotels within the competitive groups identified in Proposition 1 will be more similar in terms of size, price, and location than hotels from different clusters.

Proposition 2: Hotels within competitive groups will be more similar on dimensions of size, location, and price than hotels in different groups.

Our second research question concerns (a) the exploration of additional strategic or perceptual attributes that may be relevant to managers' categorization of hotels and (b) whether the cognitions of managers within competitive groups are homogeneous, as well as different from the cognitions of managers in other competitive groups. Based on prior research in the hotel industry, Proposition 2 suggests that size, price, and location are categorization attributes that are universally relevant to all hotels in the industry. Other strategic variables that distinguish among hotels may also be relevant attributes to managers, such as the type of client typically served by the hotel or the type of facilities offered by the hotel (Ellerbrock & Wells, 1983; Wyckoff & Sasser, 1981).

Proposition 3: Hotels within competitive groups will have more similar strategies than hotels in different clusters.

The isomorphism of competitive strategies that we expect to see within competitive groups may evolve from managers' conceptualizations of their strategic identity. In the case of hotels, cues about a firm's strategic identity, and thus appropriate strategies, may come from several sources: the monitoring of the actions of firms perceived to be relevant competitors (*mimetic isomorphism*); a parent company, if the hotel is the member of a hotel chain; and agents in the institutional environment which spread information, such as travel agents, hotel or travel associations, industry consultants, and institutions of higher education (*normative isomorphism*).

We predict that these forms of direct and indirect interaction will create similarities in the perceptions and attributions of managers within competitive sets.

> **Proposition 4:** The perceptions and attributions of managers within competitive groups will be more similar than the perceptions and attributions of managers from different groups.

Sample and Method

We explore these research questions in a study of the Manhattan hotel industry. We define the hotel industry as transient hotels that cater to short-term visitors, as opposed to residential hotels, which serve long-term or permanent tenants (Baum & Mezias, 1992). We use three data sources. The first type of data is gathered from a series of competitive mapping exercises conducted with general managers and sales/marketing managers from 43 of the 167 hotels operating in Manhattan as of the autumn of 1992. Of the 70 hotels that we selected randomly, 43 managers agreed to participate in our study (61% participation rate). The competitive mapping exercise is designed to tap the managers' beliefs about who they consider to be their relevant competitors, and their relationships with these key competitors. The details of these exercises are described below.

The managers are first given a list of all the hotels in Manhattan and asked to identify those hotels that they consider to be relevant competitors. That is, they are asked to identify those hotels that they consider when making strategic decisions for their hotel. They are then given a set of Post-It™ notes with their chosen hotels' names, and are asked to represent, on a large sheet of paper, the relationships between these hotels and themselves on any dimensions that they think are important. When managers complete this task, they explain the meaning of their map. For the purposes of this chapter, the information of interest is the list of hotels that each manager identifies as his or her hotel's *relevant competitors*; that is, the competitive set identified by each manager. Using this information, we created a matrix of competitor identifications for all hotels in Manhattan. Each cell in the matrix was coded "1" if the hotel on the vertical axis identified the hotel on the horizontal axis, and "0" otherwise.

The second data source is a database of hotel-level characteristics for all the hotels in Manhattan, based on five archival sources: *Directory of the Hotel Association of New York City*, *New York Hotel Guide*, *New York City Tour Package Guide*, *Hotel and Motel Redbook*, and the *Manhattan Classified Directory* (*Yellow Pages*). These data include information on the geographic location, size, and price of each hotel in the city. Size was measured as the number of guest rooms operated by the hotel. This is the standard measure of size used in the hotel industry (Wyckoff & Sasser, 1981). Location was indicated by the closest street and avenue to the hotel, based on the Manhattan street-avenue grid (Baum & Mezias, 1992). Price was measured using the average advertised daily rate for a double room during the observation period. For several hotels for which size or price data were not available in the archival sources, we obtained this information directly from the hotels.

The third data source is a questionnaire administered to the managers of the 43 participating hotels. Following the competitive mapping exercise, managers completed a questionnaire that provided information on the hotel's market segment, the manager's role and interpretations of the environment, and the hotel's performance.[1]

The empirical analysis in this chapter will focus on analyzing managers' competitive sets. By combining these data with information about the actual characteristics of hotels and with the questionnaire data, we are able to explore whether competitive sets aggregate to form competitive groups (Proposition 1), whether the actual characteristics of hotels within these groups are more similar than those in different groups (Propositions 2 and 3), and whether managers' perceptions are more similar within clusters than between clusters (Proposition 4).

Analysis and Results

METHOD OF ANALYSIS

We used the managers' selection of competitors as the raw data from which to map a network of linkages among the hotels. We refer to a categorization of one hotel as a competitor by another as a *linkage*. When we aggregate across managers' competitive sets, we expect to find subgroups of hotels that are more *densely linked* with one another than with hotels in other subgroups, that is, competitive groups. We included in the analysis the 134 hotels that either were in our sample or were mentioned by managers in the sample. Thus, the network includes hotels that we did not study directly. Network researchers frequently analyze networks using direct information from a subset of the network members (Knoke, 1990; Moore, 1979). The advantage of this approach is that all industry members potentially can be included in the network analysis, even though it is not possible to obtain competitive set information from all industry members. A linkage is defined as present when one manager identifies another hotel.

Given the tendency toward reciprocal categorization among our sample members (61% of the linkages that exist among our 43 sample hotels were reciprocal), we believe that this approach is appropriate. In addition, given the asymmetries that often occur in competitive interactions (Brittain & Wholey, 1988), there may still be competition in the absence of reciprocation, so it makes sense to include unreciprocated categorizations as well.

We used *UCINET IV* (Borgatti, Everett, & Freeman, 1992) to analyze this network information. We used the *CLIQUE* procedure to identify cliques in the network and overlaps among the cliques. Cliques are groupings of three or more hotels with at least a single linkage between hotels. Each entry in the matrix of clique overlaps represents the number of common cliques in which two hotels have membership. For example, in our data there is a total of 207 cliques of three or more hotels. Assume that Hotel Gamma and Hotel Omega have common membership in 20 of these cliques; the overlap matrix entry for these two hotels would be 20.

The matrix of overlaps among cliques is transformed into a correlation matrix and then used as the input for a cluster analysis. We used cluster analysis to assign the hotels to relatively homogenous groupings based on their patterns of clique membership. Previously, cluster analysis has been used to identify strategic groups based on perceptual data by Dess and Davis (1984) and Fombrun and Zajac (1987). In the cluster analysis we performed, hotels are agglomerated into small groups on the basis of similarity in clique membership, then the small groups are joined into larger groups. This agglomeration is repeated until all hotels are joined in one large group. A hierarchy of clusters results. A variety of clustering algorithms is available, but most researchers use one or more of the three common techniques: single linkage, complete linkage, or group average method. We use the group average method, which is recommended by several organizations researchers (McKelvey, 1982; Ulrich & McKelvey, 1990).

Results of Cluster Analysis

The results of the cluster analysis are illustrated by the dendogram in Figure 2.1.[2] The dendogram presents a hierarchical clustering of hotels; the distances between hotels are scaled to a range from 0 to 25. The dendogram is read from left to right. Vertical lines denote joined clusters. The position of the vertical line on the scale indicates the distance at which clusters were joined (Norusis, 1990, pp. 348-363). The closer a vertical line is to 0 on the scale, the more homogeneous is that cluster. Because we based our analysis on information from only a subset of the network members, we assessed the robustness of these cluster results. We did this by comparing the cluster results in Figure 2.1 with the results for separate analyses in which network data for 4 (9%) of the 43 sample hotels were removed randomly. We used cophenetic correlation coefficients (Sneath & Sokal, 1973) to assess the similarity of cluster patterns. The average cophenetic correlation between the cluster results in Figure 2.1 and five randomly reduced cluster results was .894. Thus, the clustering results in Figure 2.1 are robust.

This cluster analysis addresses our first proposition that distinctive competitive groups of hotels would emerge from the data on competitor identification. We have interpreted the cluster analysis as representing 14 competitive groups of hotels; we have chosen to examine clusters that formed at a distance of approximately 15 on the distance scale. One indication of the distinctness of these competitive groups is a comparison of the mean correlation among clique overlaps for the whole set of hotels ($r = .08$) to the mean correlation among clique overlaps for hotels within groups ($r = .57$). The correlations among clique overlaps for hotels within groups varied from .34 to 1.0. These correlation patterns indicate that hotels within clusters are more densely linked than hotels in different clusters.

Notably, the competitive groups in Figure 2.1 vary in their size, homogeneity, and distinctness. Group 14, for example, is a 5-member group of small, economy hotels on the westside of Manhattan. This group is extremely homogeneous in its clique membership; the formation of the group occurs very close to the 0 point on the dendogram scale, and its group correlation of clique overlaps is 1.0. It can also be seen that this group is very distinct from any other group; it is not joined to any other group until almost the top of the hierarchical clustering, at about a distance of 20 on the dendogram scale. On the other hand, Group 12 is a 13-member group of large, luxury hotels. It is much more heterogeneous than Group 14. Its within-group correlation of clique overlaps is only .34. Thus, as predicted in Proposition 1, distinct groups of hotels can be identified simply by analyzing the decisions of hotel managers regarding whom they classify as competitors. The aggregate of managers' competitive sets reveals groups of hotels whose managers tend to regard one another as relevant competitors.

Within-Group Versus Between-Group
Similarity on Size, Price, and Location

The second question we were concerned with was whether the strategic characteristics of hotels within groups were more similar than those of

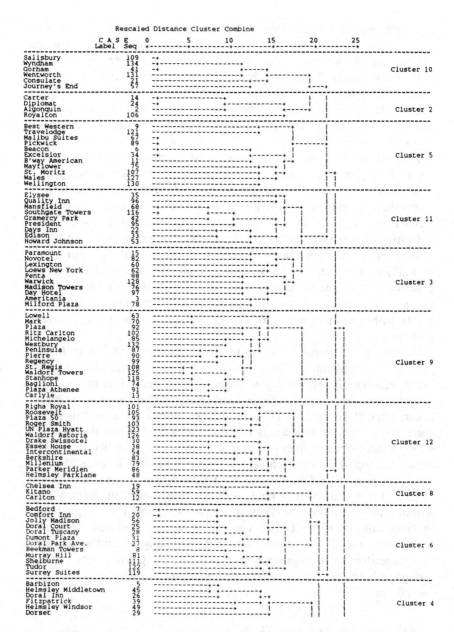

Figure 2.1 Manhattan Hotel Industry Dendrogram Using Average Linkage (Between Groups)

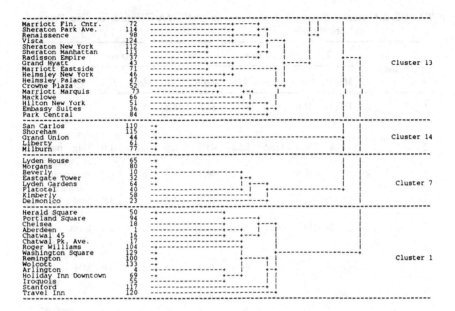

Figure 2.1 (Continued)

hotels in different groups. In the hotel industry, the attributes of size, price, and geographic location are considered to be key characteristics that distinguish between firms and influence their relative success (Baum & Mezias, 1992). Proposition 2 suggested that hotels within groups would be more similar on the dimensions of size, price, and location than hotels in different groups. We had information on size, price, and location for all the hotels in the industry. We conducted four one-way analyses of variance to examine whether there were significant differences in mean size, price, and location (street and avenue) among the hotels comprising the 14 groups. Tables 2.1 and 2.2 present the results of this analysis.

Table 2.1 displays the means and standard deviations of each dependent variable for each competitive group. The significant F ratios show that there are significant differences between competitive groups on size, price, and location, indicating that the aggregation of managers' competitive sets reveals relatively homogeneous groups of hotels. For each group, we have also given a qualitative description of the type of hotels within each group. In terms of size, hotels are classified as small, mid-size, large, or very large. In terms of price, the hotels are classified as economy, moderate,

TABLE 2.1 Means, Standard Deviations, and ANOVA F Ratios for Size, Price, and Location

Description Group	N	Size Mean	Size S.D.	Price Mean	Price S.D.	Street Mean	Street S.D.	Avenue Mean	Avenue S.D.	Qualitative
1	16	160.4	81.6	98.1	41.2	31.9	14.8	5.5	1.6	Mid-size, economy, downtown
2	4	316.8	256.4	128.5	82.2	43.5	0.6	6.5	1.0	Large, moderate, westside
3	10	651.8	479.9	161.7	31.8	46.3	8.4	6.3	1.7	Very large, 1st class, westside
4	6	320.7	191.3	171.7	31.0	55.0	5.5	4.3	1.0	Large, 1st class, midtown
5	11	245.2	213.8	108.8	31.4	69.3	18.1	6.7	3.1	Large, economy, upper westside
6	12	172.0	78.9	189.8	66.3	40.2	13.9	3.9	1.0	Mid-size, 1st class, eastside
7	7	185.1	100.8	247.1	69.5	50.8	9.7	3.6	1.5	Mid-size, luxury, eastside
8	3	109.0	94.5	116.0	51.8	28.0	10.5	4.7	0.6	Small, economy, downtown
9	15	279.3	178.9	326.0	60.0	63.1	9.2	4.9	0.8	Large, deluxe, upper eastside
10	6	203.8	64.6	130.7	25.4	50.8	7.1	6.2	0.8	Mid-size, moderate, westside
11	9	394.8	250.6	130.8	36.0	43.8	13.4	6.6	1.9	Large, moderate, westside
12	13	616.5	337.9	250.0	57.2	44.4	21.5	4.6	1.5	Very large, luxury, mid-town-down-town
13	17	901.8	565.8	219.3	41.4	40.1	25.3	6.0	1.7	Very large, luxury, westside-downtown
14	5	71.6	41.8	102.0	27.9	52.8	15.7	6.9	3.4	Small, economy, westside
Total	134	383.0	383.4	183.8	86.0	47.2	18.7	5.4	1.9	
F ratio			7.75		22.47		5.07	3.58			
d.f.			13		13		13		13		
p-level			.001		.001		.001		.001		

TABLE 2.2 Scheffé Multiple Range Tests for Group Differences in Size, Price, and Location

Group													
	1	2	3	4	5	6	7	8	9	10	11	12	13
1													
2													
3													
4													
5	L												
6	P												
7	P			P									
8	1												
9	PL	P	P	P	P	P		P					
10									P				
11						p			P				
12	P				P					P	P		
13	SP				SPl	S	S	s	SP	S			
14	S						P		P			P	p

NOTE: Size differences: S = $p < .05$, s = $p < .10$; Price differences: P = $p < .05$, p = $p < .10$; Location differences (street or avenue): L = $p < .05$, l = $p < .10$.

first-class, luxury, and deluxe. Location is indicated by the standard references used to refer to different geographic regions of Manhattan: uptown, midtown, downtown, eastside, and westside.

Table 2.2 displays comparisons between pairs of groups, using Scheffé's Multiple Range Test. These tests indicate where there were significant differences between specific cluster pairs in terms of size, price, or location. The Scheffé test is considered to be a conservative test of differences between pairs of means, and it can be applied to groups of unequal sizes (Dess & Davis, 1984; Neter & Wasserman, 1974, pp. 479-480). Not all groups were significantly different from each other on all dimensions, but overall there were significant differences among a number of groups on these attributes. Price appears to be the attribute that varied the most between groups. Groups of hotels that were either far uptown or downtown or that were made up of very small or very large hotels also tended to be significantly different from other groups on these attributes.

To determine more precisely the relative importance of size, price, and location in distinguishing among groups, we conducted a discriminant analysis.[3] The results of the discriminant analysis are reported in Table 2.3, which presents the rotated varimax standardized discriminant function coefficients for the four functions resulting from the analysis. Each function corresponds to one of the discriminating variables. Discriminant analysis chooses the first function based on the variable or variables that

TABLE 2.3 Rotated (Varimax) Standardized Discriminant Function
Coefficients for Size, Price, and Geographic Location, 134 Hotels

Variable	Function 1	Function 2	Function 3	Function 4
Price	1.009*	−.018	.044	.004
Size	−.005	1.004*	−.002	−.018
Street	.098	−.017	1.010*	−.081
Avenue	.005	−.071	−.044	1.008*
% Variance	58.69	18.88	13.70	8.72

NOTE: 50.0% of cases correctly classified. * indicates significant variable in each function.

produce the largest ratio of between-groups to within-groups sums of squares. A second function is chosen that also maximizes this ratio, but subject to the constraint that it must be uncorrelated with the first function. Each function must be uncorrelated with other functions.

The discriminant analysis demonstrates that of the characteristics examined, price is the most important in discriminating between the groups. The percentage of the total between-groups variance explained by price is 59%. Size, street location, and avenue location are also important, but together they explain less variance than price [size = 19%, street location (i.e., uptown-downtown) = 14%, avenue location (i.e., eastside-westside) = 9%]. Classification of hotels into groups using the functions in Table 2.3 yielded only partial success. Overall, only 50% of our cases are classified correctly. Thus, although these key strategic variables are important, it is apparent that managers' categorization of competitors into competitive sets is more complex than assigning membership based only on a simple scan of obvious attributes.

Within-Group Versus Between-Group Similarity
on Market Segment, Perception, and Attribution

Propositions 3 and 4 predicted that the hotel strategies and managerial beliefs and perceptions within groups would be more similar than those of hotels from different groups. Thus, we examined additional factors that might help us differentiate hotels in the different groups more accurately. We conducted analyses of variance and discriminant analyses that included additional strategic, managerial, and perceptual variables. The discriminant analysis allows us to examine the homogeneity of configurations of these variables within groups. Definitions of these variables are given in Table 2.4. Information on these additional factors were only available for the sample of 43 hotels that we studied directly.

TABLE 2.4 Variable Definitions

Percentage Business Travelers
  What percentage of your hotel's clients are business travelers?

Performance Attributions
  How much has each of the following factors influenced your hotel's performance:
    1. Market position
    2. Strategic decisions
    3. Actions by other hotels
    4. Internal operations

Predictability Perceptions
  To what extent are you able to predict accurately:
    1. Strategic decision outcomes
    2. Impact of environmental change

Managerial Roles
  Indicate the extent of your involvement in the following types of activities:
    1. Monitoring environmental trends
    2. Staffing
    3. Setting hotel policy

First, we examined the impact of an additional strategic variable that was available for our sample of hotels. The managers provided us with an estimate of the percentage of the hotel's clients who were business travelers. This variable represents information on the market segment served by the hotel.[4] Column 1 in Table 2.5 lists the means and standard deviations of each group on this variable. The *F* test from the analysis of variance indicates that there is a significant difference among groups in terms of the market segment served by the hotels.[5] In order to determine the relative importance of market segment versus our size, price, and location variables, we conducted a discriminant analysis on our 43 sample firms, using all five strategic variables. The results of this analysis are presented in Table 2.6. These results indicate that market segment served is a very important variable in discriminating between groups. The analysis yielded four functions, each representing one of the strategic variables. Price remains the most important variable and explains 43% of the total between-groups variance. The percentage of business travelers is the second-most-important variable and explains about 34% of the variance. Size and street location remain important discriminating variables (15% and 8% variance explained, respectively), but avenue location is no longer an important discriminator once information on market segment is included. The inclu-

TABLE 2.5 Means, Standard Deviations, and ANOVA *F* Ratios for Percent Business Travelers, Performance Attribution, Predictability Perception, and Managerial Role Variables

Group	N	Percentage Business Travelers Mean (S.D.)	Market Position Mean (S.D.)	Strategic Decisions Mean (S.D.)	Actions by Others Mean (S.D.)	Internal Operations Mean (S.D.)	Strategic Decision Outcomes Mean (S.D.)	Impact of Environ. Change Mean (S.D.)	Monitor Environ. Trends Mean (S.D.)	Staffing Mean (S.D.)	Setting Hotel Policy Mean (S.D.)
1	4	32.5 (15.0)	5.8 (0.5)	2.0 (6.1)	-0.3 (5.0)	6.0 (1.4)	5.0 (0.0)	3.5 (1.7)	5.8 (1.9)	6.8 (0.5)	6.5 (0.6)
3	5	27.0 (9.8)	3.0 (5.1)	5.6 (0.5)	-5.4 (1.3)	1.2 (5.7)	5.2 (0.8)	5.4 (0.5)	5.2 (1.9)	5.8 (1.6)	4.2 (2.4)
4	1	80.0 (0.0)	7.0 (0.0)	7.0 (0.0)	-5.0 (0.0)	7.0 (0.0)	6.0 (0.0)	3.0 (0.0)	7.0 (0.0)	7.0 (0.0)	7.0 (0.0)
5	2	20.0 (0.0)	5.0 (0.0)	5.5 (0.7)	-4.0 (2.8)	6.5 (0.7)	5.0 (0.0)	5.0 (0.0)	5.5 (2.1)	5.5 (2.1)	7.0 (0.0)
6	2	75.0 (21.1)	5.5 (0.7)	5.5 (0.7)	-0.5 (3.5)	5.0 (1.4)	5.0 (1.4)	5.5 (0.7)	5.5 (2.1)	6.5 (0.7)	6.5 (0.7)
7	2	50.0 (42.4)	0.5 (6.3)	6.0 (0.0)	-5.5 (0.7)	5.5 (2.1)	5.5 (0.7)	5.5 (0.7)	6.0 (2.1)	7.0 (0.7)	4.5 (2.1)
9	4	75.0 (12.9)	3.0 (6.0)	5.0 (0.8)	0.3 (4.3)	4.8 (2.5)	5.0 (0.0)	4.0 (1.4)	6.3 (0.5)	6.5 (0.6)	6.5 (0.6)
10	2	70.0 (14.4)	6.5 (0.7)	6.0 (0.0)	-6.0 (1.4)	6.0 (0.0)	6.0 (1.4)	5.0 (0.0)	6.5 (0.7)	3.5 (3.5)	3.5 (3.5)
11	2	12.5 (3.5)	6.0 (1.4)	5.5 (0.7)	-5.0 (1.4)	5.0 (1.4)	6.5 (0.7)	6.0 (0.0)	6.0 (0.0)	7.0 (0.0)	7.0 (0.0)
12	5	79.0 (11.4)	3.8 (6.1)	6.8 (0.4)	-0.2 (5.8)	6.2 (1.1)	5.4 (0.5)	5.2 (0.8)	6.4 (1.3)	6.4 (1.3)	6.6 (0.9)
13	11	52.7 (22.3)	5.5 (3.6)	3.3 (5.8)	-3.7 (4.3)	5.9 (1.3)	5.3 (1.0)	5.0 (0.8)	6.6 (0.7)	6.4 (0.8)	5.8 (1.4)
14	3	33.3 (5.8)	0.7 (6.8)	4.7 (2.1)	1.3 (3.8)	5.0 (1.7)	3.7 (1.2)	3.7 (1.2)	4.7 (2.1)	7.0 (0.0)	6.7 (0.6)
Total	43	50.6 (26.1)	4.3 (4.3)	4.7 (3.6)	-2.6 (4.2)	5.2 (2.6)	5.2 (0.9)	4.8 (1.1)	6.1 (1.4)	6.3 (1.3)	5.9 (1.6)
F ratio		5.61	0.61	0.57	1.39	1.50	1.71	2.40	0.90	1.50	1.88
d.f.		11	11	11	11	11	11	11	11	11	11
p-level		.001	.806	.836	.225	.182	.117	.027	.552	.182	.083

NOTE: None of the sample hotels were members of groups 2 or 8.

TABLE 2.6 Rotated (Varimax) Standardized Discriminant Function
Coefficients for Size, Price, Geographic Location, and Percentage
Business Travelers, 43 Sample Hotels

Variable	Function 1	Function 2	Function 3	Function 4
Price	1.076*	.070	.084	.227
% Business	−.082	1.091*	.241	.073
Size	.104	.256	1.094*	−.044
Street	.203	.054	−.030	1.077*
% Variance	43.08	33.69	14.94	8.29

sion of the market segment variable increases our overall correct classification rate to 67%.[6]

In addition to the strategic variables that emerged as important in Table
2.6, we also explored the impact of three types of variables that are distinct
from objective attributes of the hotels. These are managers' performance
attributions, managers' perceptions of environmental predictability, and
perceived managerial roles (see Table 2.4). Information about the roles and
cognitions of other hotel managers would not be easy for a manager to
obtain from simple environmental scanning. Cues about these sorts of
variables would be obtained only through direct interaction among hotels,
or indirect interaction via institutionalizing agents, such as industry consultants, travel agents, or parent companies. A finding that these variables
influence group formation would help us to identify some possible mechanisms by which shared cognitions emerge. The means and standard deviations of these variables for each group are shown in Table 2.5. The *F* tests
suggest that only the predictability of environmental change and setting
hotel policy were significantly different across the groups. However, a
discriminant analysis indicated that many of these variables did contribute
to our ability to classify hotels into groups. This analysis produced five
discriminant functions, as displayed in Table 2.7.

The first discriminant function contains variables that represent both
strategic information and managers' perceptions regarding external factors. It explains 50% of the between-groups variance. The objective strategy variables that emerge in this function are price, street location, and
size; these represent three of the objective strategy variables that emerged
in the analysis presented in Table 2.6. The variable *strategic decisions*
represents managers' assessment of the impact of the hotel's strategic
decisions on the hotel's performance; as such, it represents a nonobjective
indicator of strategy. The remaining variables in the first function represent

TABLE 2.7 Rotated (Varimax) Standardized Discriminant Function Coefficients for Performance Attribution, Predictability Perception, and Managerial Role Variables, 43 Sample Hotels

Variable	Function 1	Function 2	Function 3	Function 4	Function 5
Strategic decisions	1.898*	.069	.072	.431	−.192
Impact of environmental change	−1.512*	.445	−.333	−.413	.039
Street	1.322*	.139	.119	−.337	−.234
Price	1.219*	.232	.934	.117	.361
Actions by other hotels	1.021*	−.178	−.159	.012	.376
Size	−.977*	.684	−.070	.244	.838
Monitoring environmental trends	−.760*	.677	.378	−.587	−.185
% Business travelers	.049	1.329*	−.054	.039	−.116
Staffing	.563	.049	1.418*	.277	−.363
Internal operations	−.485	.110	1.118*	.647	−.045
Market position	−.071	.037	.420	1.475*	−.090
Strategic decision outcomes	.059	−.568	.542	.800*	−.113
Setting hotel policy	−.066	−.450	.211	−.618	1.168*
% Variance	50.53	24.95	11.88	6.42	6.22

NOTE: 95.4% of cases correctly classified. * indicates significant variable in each function.

managers' stances toward the environment. The variable *impact of environmental change* represents managers' assessments of how accurately they are able to predict the impact that environmental changes will have on their hotels. The variable *actions by other hotels* represents managers' assessments of the impact that actions by other hotels have on their hotels' performance. The variable *monitoring environmental trends* represents the extent to which the manager is involved in this activity.

The second discriminant function consists of only the market segment variable, the percentage of clients that are business travelers. Thus, this strategic variable forms its own function, which explains almost 25% of the between-groups variance. The third discriminant function explains almost 12% of the variance and consists of managers' stances toward internal factors. The variable *staffing* represents the extent to which a manager is involved in making staffing decisions. The variable *internal operations* represents the managers' assessments of the impact that internal operations have on their hotels' performance. The fourth discriminant function explains 6% of the variance and represents two aspects of managers' stances toward the relationship between their strategies and the external environment. The variable *market position* represents managers' assessment of the impact that their hotels' market position has on their hotels' performance. The variable *strategic decision outcomes* represents managers' assessments of how well they can predict the outcomes of their strategic decisions. The fifth discriminant function consists of only one variable that represents managers' decision-making responsibility; it explains 6% of the variance. The variable *setting hotel policy* represents the extent of the managers' involvement in setting policies for their hotel.

The addition of the perceptual, attribution, and managerial role variables raised our overall classification rate to 95%. This indicates that although strategic variables are important in discriminating among the members of competitive groups, the cognitions and roles of managers are also important. This analysis provides support for both Propositions 3 and 4. Not only are the strategies of hotels more similar within groups than between groups, but the cognitions and enacted roles of managers are also more similar within groups than between groups.

Discussion and Future Directions

This chapter set out to explore the role of managerial cognitions in the development of institutionalized beliefs and practices among competing organizations. We have done so by investigating two general questions: (a) Do managers' categorizations of firms in their industry into competitive sets result in the formation of competitive groups and (b) do firms within competitive groups tend to be more similar in form, practice, strategy, and belief than firms in different competitive groups? Taken together, our evidence lends support to the four propositions that we set out to test in this chapter. We believe this study has provided several intriguing insights into the possible role of managerial cognitions in the development of competitive groups within industries, and the existence of shared beliefs and isomorphic practices within these sets of firms.

First, our findings suggest that managers do engage in a cognitive categorization task in order to determine the relevant group of firms that they should consider to be their competition. We saw that firms could be arranged into groups, based solely on managers' categorizations of subsets of firms in the industry. This approach to identifying strategic groups of firms within an industry differs distinctly from approaches used in prior research. We identify strategic groups solely by using information about managers' beliefs about who their competitors are. Most empirical work on strategic groups has been based on the measurement of objective financial, strategic, or structural variables (McGee & Thomas, 1986). With several noteworthy exceptions (Dess & Davis, 1984; Fombrun & Zajac, 1987; Porac et al., 1989; Reger & Huff, 1983), most studies have ignored the role that managerial cognition and choice might play in the determination of strategic groups. Our premise in this study has been that homogeneous firms, typically identified post hoc as strategic groups based on objective measures, may exhibit institutionalized behavior in their causal attributions and choices of strategies and practices, as a result of the development of shared cognitions about who are members of these strategic groups and which attributes distinguish members from nonmembers.

Second, based on the fact that we used managers' beliefs to uncover the existence of competitive groups, we have demonstrated support for the argument that competitive groups are socially constructed. There appear to be a number of strategic factors that managers use to categorize firms as *relevant to my strategic choices* or *not relevant to my strategic choices*. We found that the groups of hotels that emerged in our analysis were fairly homogeneous with respect to the strategic variables of size, price, location, and market segment served.

Third, our findings regarding the homogeneity of strategies and cognitions within groups suggest that cognitive communities that evolve within industries tend toward isomorphism both in their practices and in their beliefs. We observed evidence of a convergence of perceptions and beliefs among firms within competitive groups. This lends credence to the argument that competitive groups are socially constructed cognitive communities (Porac et al., 1989). Overall, these results highlight the importance of managerial cognitions for patterns of competitive interaction among organizations, the production of isomorphism in competitive fields, and the formation of competitive substructures.

The findings of this study suggest a number of future directions that research in this area might take. First, we need to understand better the mental models that managers use in categorizing firms as competitors. We can derive some insights from this study, but we need a richer understanding of how managers make these choices. Second, we need to understand whether managers' categorizations of competitors are predictive of strategic actions that they may take. At this point, we have only very indirect associations between the characteristics of a firm's strategy and its manager's cognitions. It would be worth exploring whether competitor categorizations influence day-to-day decisions as well as long-term strategic decisions. If these cognitions do drive behavior, then it is easy to see how shared mental models can result in relatively stable industry substructures if industry actors are all behaving in ways consistent with their mental models.

Finally, we focused on managers' categorizations of hotels to derive a macrostructure of managers' cognitions about sets of competing firms within their industry. However, we do not have an understanding of how managers' cognitions about competitors form. That is, how does convergence of cognition within a competitive group evolve? We speculate that this process is reciprocal, with factors such as managerial education, interactions among group members, and the diffusion of information by trade associations and industry consultants resulting in movement toward collective mental models of the industry, as well as the actual substructures of an industry being reflected in the mental models of managers. Such a continuous, reciprocal process has been described by Neisser (1976, p. 112) in his discussion of schema-driven perception, and by Weick (1979) in his discussion of enactment. In these discussions, beliefs are developed through a continuous process of schema-driven information processing, where both existing beliefs and objective reality combine to create a cognitive map of one's world. This process is probably occurring at many levels that can influence the competitive maps of hotel managers. More insight into this process could be obtained by studying the process during time of change in an industry, where managers' beliefs and the positions and strategies of their firms will be in a state of flux (Baum & Lant, 1993).

Managers arrive in their positions with certain schemas about "doing business in the hotel industry" already "in residence" in their minds. These schemas may develop from their education (many hotel managers have enrolled in hospitality programs, such as the Cornell School of Hotel Management), their experience in the industry (many have extensive experience in the hotel industry, beyond their current position), and their cultural experience (e.g., about 90% of the managers of the deluxe hotels in Manhattan are European; these hotels form a competitive group).

Individual hotels may also have their own schemas in place which influence the mental model of the individual hotel manager. These schemas may arise from the hotel's relationship with a parent company (e.g., member of a hotel chain) or from the hotel's identification with a certain style of accommodation or type of client (e.g., a "French" hotel or an "Irish" hotel).

Information about the industry that can influence the development and modification of mental models is provided not only by active scanning by a manager but also by many institutions that diffuse information and opinion throughout the industry. These include travel agents, the hotel association, and consultants specializing in the Manhattan hotel industry. These actors engage in industry analysis and diffuse their findings to hotel managers.

In this chapter, we demonstrated how Manhattan hotel managers use organizational characteristics as cues to impose cognitive boundaries on their competitive environment. As Weick (1979) and others (e.g., Porac & Thomas, 1990; Porac et al., 1989) have argued, organizations create their environments by constructing interpretations and then acting on them as if they were true. Also, we have shown that an aggregation of managers' competitive sets within an industry reveals groups of organizations that have similar strategies. In addition, we found that managers within competitive groups also shared similar perceptions and attributions about their world. We have taken these findings as evidence that the cognitions of managers within an industry might be an important source of the isomorphism often seen among firms in competitive environments. We have speculated about the ways in which competing firms can interact, directly or indirectly, and in so doing, develop shared beliefs about the structure of their industry and their appropriate position within that structure. Future research should examine some of these institutionalization mechanisms more directly.

Notes

1. The variables used in the analysis are described in the analysis and results sections. A complete description of the questionnaire and variables is available from the authors.

2. The dendogram in Figure 2.1 lists the hotels in Manhattan by name. The 43 participating hotels are not identified for reasons of confidentiality.

3. Although discriminant analysis assumes that the independent variables have a multivariate normal distribution and equal covariances within groups, it is quite robust to violations of these assumptions (Klecka, 1980).

4. We also had information on the ownership of each hotel in the sample, for example, independent versus chain ownership. We had speculated that ownership might also influence competitive group membership, but this was not the case. There are two primary explanations. First, chain hotels are typically very large, and so this variable was very highly correlated with our size variable. Thus, any impact of ownership may be absorbed by size. Second, the relationship between a Manhattan hotel and its chain is quite different from that of other hotels in a chain. Because of the idiosyncrasies of the Manhattan hotel industry and the popularity of independent, unique hotels, members of hotel chains are often operated quite independently of the chain in terms of strategic positioning, advertising, and strategic identity.

5. These analyses are based on our sample of 43 hotels. None of our sample were members of clusters 2 or 8; thus, these clusters are excluded from this analysis. Further, the F tests must be interpreted with caution, given the relatively small sample size and large number of clusters.

6. The correct classification rate for the 43 sample hotels is 53.5% when the information on the percentage of business travelers is not included in the analysis, which is comparable to the 50% correct classification for the 134 hotels.

3

Localism and
Globalism in Institutional Analysis

The Emergence of
Contractual Norms in Venture Finance

MARK C. SUCHMAN

IN A RECENT WIDE-RANGING REVIEW of the new institutionalism in anthropology, economics, political science, psychology, and sociology, Scott (1994b) notes that one of the most persistent debates among institutionalists centers on the distinction between top-down and bottom-up models of the institution-building process. At the core of this debate lies a disagreement over whether governance structures (including norms, organizations, and regimes) rise up from the active planning, strategy, and negotiation of those who will be subject to them, or precipitate down from exogenous authoritative models lodged in the larger cultural environment. Although often caricatured (perhaps fairly) as a dispute between sociologists and economists (Scott, 1994b), this difference of opinion appears within disciplines as well as between them.[1] One possible explanation for this state of affairs is simply that such debates are metatheoretical, and that the riven disciplines are multiparadigmatic (Ritzer, 1975). For the time being, however, such a conclusion remains premature: To date, few researchers have examined the equally plausible possibility that distinctions between bottom-up and top-down institutionalization may reflect relatively modest differences in context and focus, rather than irreconcilable divergences in foundational assumptions.

39

In a preliminary effort to explore this optimistic alternative, the following pages develop a number of arguments about various factors that may
affect the localism or globalism of the institutionalization process. This
analysis rests firmly on the assumption that individuals actively collaborate in constructing institutions to resolve pressing practical problems;
however, it rests equally firmly on the assumption that foremost among
these problems are the challenges of articulating new routines with preexisting institutions and with the definitional systems that give those institutions meaning. The resulting account depicts the locus of institutionalization as a highly contingent phenomenon, determined by the interplay of
information sources and communication channels, of institutions and enforcement mechanisms, and of normative models and cognitive definitions.

Adopting this perspective, this chapter posits a number of theoretical
considerations that may affect the likelihood that institutionalization will
be driven by dynamics at various levels of analysis. It then examines data
on the development of high-technology venture capital financing practices
in the United States in the 1980s, to determine the extent to which these
were institutionalized at the level of individual firms, at the level of a
geographically localized organizational community, and at the level of a
nationwide societal sector. The empirical analysis focuses, in particular,
on historical patterns of divergence and convergence between California's
Silicon Valley and other geographic regions.

Theorizing the Locus of Institutionalization

Organizations theory recognizes that institutionalization can occur at a
number of levels of analysis, including, but not limited to interpersonal
interactions in the workplace (Zucker, 1977), geographically localized
organizational communities (Galaskiewicz, 1991), functionally differenti-
ated societal sectors or organizational fields (DiMaggio, 1991; DiMaggio
& Powell, 1983; Scott & Meyer, 1983), society-wide political and cultural
systems (Friedland & Alford, 1991; Meyer & Rowan, 1977; Zucker, 1983),
and international regimes (Krasner, 1983). This recognition does not,
however, imply that institutionalization will necessarily occur uniformly
across all levels. In particular, the pace at which shared understandings
develop depends on the elaboration of a social infrastructure capable of
supporting such sharing, and the elaboration of such an infrastructure
depends, in turn, both on the idiosyncratic histories of individual collectivities and on the progress of the institutionalization project itself.

Whatever one may feel about the metatheoretical assumptions embodied
in top-down versus bottom-up models of institutionalization, a strong case

can be made that the fundamental *empirically adjudicable* distinction between these camps revolves around the question of where in the social structure particular shared understandings arise. In any system encompassing multiple levels of social organization, most institutions will reflect both top-down processes, such as socialization, social control, and cultural hegemony, and bottom-up processes, such as coordination, integration, and mimesis. Thus, the relative importance of top-down versus bottom-up effects is likely to depend primarily on how high in the system the initial locus of institutionalization lies. This question is at once both historically specific, in any given instance, and also capable of theorization, in the abstract. This section will outline a rudimentary theoretical account of several abstract factors affecting the locus of institutionalization; the following section will demonstrate the possibility of examining the locus of institutionalization in one historical instance. Although the empirical analysis will not formally test the proposed theory, it may illuminate important dynamics and suggest potential avenues for future research.

THE MODEL

Because the elements of social systems rarely enjoy perfect articulation with one another, various problems will inevitably arise from time to time. These may be technical, political, or hermeneutic in nature, and they may vary substantially in their novelty, that is, in the degree to which they depart from expected patterns and established models. Often, problems will be so obviously congruent with preexisting models (according to some cultural standard of congruence) and so easily resolved within those models (according to some cultural standard of satisfactory resolution) that entities experiencing the problems will simply extrapolate the prior institutional scheme to cover the new data points. When this happens, the primary dynamic of the institutionalization process remains located at the level of the larger system, and a top-down account would seem to be the only appropriate explanation.[2] Thus, for example, a new university department is likely to simply borrow the model of departments in related fields at the same university, or of departments in the same field at related universities.

Occasionally, however, a novel problem may arise which does not fit well within any preexisting model or, at least, which does not fit well within any model known to the entities experiencing the problem. When this occurs, the troubled entities may either ignore the problem, or what is the same, treat it inadequately as though it were something else (cf. Kuhn, 1962); or they may acknowledge the problem and search for an appropriate response (Cyert & March, 1963). Although a full analysis of this process of *problem cognition* lies beyond the scope of the present discussion, it seems likely that entities will most readily acknowledge problems (a) when these problems are large or recurrent, (b) when these problems affect central or vocal constituencies, and (c) when these problems arise in arenas that have been culturally designated as problematic. In any case, it is only when problems are cognized that an institutional resolution can begin.

Several hurdles, however, stand between the identification of an isolated problem and the institutionalization of a standardized solution. First, the entities experiencing the problem must come to the conclusion that it is not unique; otherwise, they will be far more likely to normalize the problem or to resolve it in an ad hoc manner than to address it institutionally (cf. Scott & Lyman, 1968). This "problem naming" activity represents a limited typification of the problem, linking it with other problems and, perhaps, with previous ad hoc resolutions (cf. Felstiner, Abel, & Sarat, 1980; Berger & Luckmann, 1967). Naming also situates problems within a larger institutional discourse; however, there is no guarantee that naming, alone, will allow the adoption of a ready-made top-down solution. Indeed, unless the entities experiencing such problems occupy particularly central locations in the larger system, there is a good chance that naming will simply reveal a problem to be a recurrent dilemma, a Hobson's choice, or a Catch-22—in other words, one of the plethora of annoyances that arise from gaps or contradictions in the institutional order and are resolved in an ad hoc manner every day, but that are too "unimportant" to merit a more lasting institutional response.

Still, the naming process does link the problem with others, and, if certain associated responses are sufficiently common, they may actually support a second stage of typification: the identification of a limited number of standard responses or solutions. This process of *response categorization* allows entities to develop a cognitively tractable repertoire of alternative strategies, and it facilitates the otherwise prohibitive task of *response comparison*—the evaluation of solutions with respect to various standards of desirability. Here again, it is important to note that both the categorization of observed responses and the selection of standards of desirability often incorporate or mimic preexisting, top-down definitional structures. Indeed, one might argue that the entire categorization and comparison process is merely a subset of the more generic phenomenon of "retrospective rationality," in which actors adopt institutionalized "vocabularies of motive" in order to make their ad hoc actions appear sensible in hindsight (Mills, 1940). It is equally noteworthy, however, that although general organizing principles may enter this response-categorization process from the top down, these principles serve primarily to structure a preexisting set of ad hoc responses, which enter from the bottom up.

Once ad hoc responses have been generalized into solutions, and once these solutions have been mapped onto some criterion of evaluation (profit, efficiency, equity, comprehensibility, etc.), it often becomes possible for actors to engage in a more thoroughgoing "theorization" of the situation—in other words, to formulate general accounts of how the system works and, in particular, of which solutions are appropriate in which contexts. Occasionally, the data may support multiple accounts, but this is usually an unstable equilibrium, easily disrupted either by further data or by more elaborate accounts (cf. Arthur, 1989, David, 1986). As a single account emerges, the choice of solutions tends to become prescriptive or even definitional. In this way, the prevailing model moves toward reification, and the preferred solutions toward institutionalization.

Finally, through a process of diffusion, solutions generated and reified in one segment of the social structure may begin to spread outward (or upward or downward) from their initial locus of institutionalization. Articulating these new models with the larger institutional structure often proves to be quite easy, because they thoroughly embody its organizing assumptions, if not its specific prescriptions. Ultimately, the new models may become fully integrated elements of the global institutional scheme, enforced coercively (or simply taken for granted) even in realms remote from those that gave them birth.[3] Figure 3.1 illustrates this model in the form of a simplified flowchart.

THEORETICAL HYPOTHESES

Despite a sensitivity to DiMaggio's countervailing injunction (1988), the preceding account intentionally employs the passive voice, defocalizing the agents of institutionalization and obscuring their location. This reflects the fact that, within the proposed model, one cannot identify these agents in the abstract. First, problems may arise at any level of analysis, from the individual to the societal.[4] Second, multiple entities at multiple levels may be equally capable of recognizing these frictions, with the actual locus of problem cognition depending in part on historically specific definitions of relevance, responsibility, and competence. Third, once an entity has become aware of a problem, that entity may attempt to name the problem on its own, or it may refer the problem to the chartered label-giving institutions of a higher-order collectivity (e.g., professions, think tanks, regulatory agencies, and the like). Finally, depending on the rate at which similarly labeled problems arise, an entity may or may not have enough experience with ad hoc responses to allow it to single-handedly formulate solution categories; if local experience is lacking, entities may rely on the compiled experience of higher-level agents who benefit from

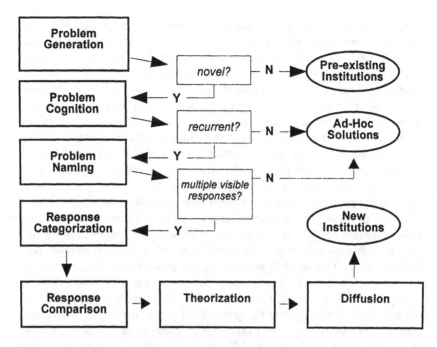

Figure 3.1. A Multistage Model of Institutionalization

a broader purview. In short, there is no single "necessary" locus of institutionalization. Rather, numerous historical circumstances act probabilistically (Lieberson, 1992) to focus institutional dynamics either locally or globally—or to shift dynamics across several levels as the institutionalization process unfolds.

The particularistic nature of this sequence in any given setting does not, however, preclude the formulation of theoretical propositions regarding the determinants of localism or globalism in general. A number of such propositions appear below. The underlying theoretical considerations focus on (a) experiences and interpretive schema, (b) communication channels and barriers, (c) articulation of new models with preexisting institutions, (d) resilience of new models against deviance and dissensus, and (e) institutionalized definitions of agency and competence.[5]

The first group of hypotheses addresses the incidence of problematic experiences. Because problems generally do not arise with equal frequency in all parts of a social system, the likelihood that a given entity will theorize a given set of problems and solutions depends on the extent of that entity's relevant experience, either direct or vicarious. Problems are unlikely to become visible within a given social unit until they have been cognized and named *by that unit*, and they are unlikely to be cognized and named until they interfere with the operations of that unit or its constituent entities[6] and, particularly, until they do so within the context of cognitive schema that make such disruptions appear interrelated and systematic:

> **Hypothesis 1:** The probability that institutional theorization will occur at a given level is proportional to the number of problems and responses cognized by social units at that level.[7]

> **Hypothesis 1a:** The number of problems and responses cognized by a social unit is proportional to the rate of disruptions in the activities of that unit.

> **Hypothesis 1b:** The number of problems cognized by a social unit is proportional to the salience of disruptions in the activities of that unit.

> **Hypothesis 1c:** The number of problems cognized by a social unit is proportional to the availability within that unit of cognitive schema defining disruptions as systematic and interrelated.

These hypotheses suggest that when problems remain confined to a single social location, theorization is likely to occur locally—at least as long as the local entities are not so overwhelmed that the problems accumulate into broader disruptions.

The second set of hypotheses focuses on the fact that institutional theorization is a *social* product, emerging through the communication of shared experience. Consequently, the locus of institutionalization often depends on the structure of communication networks. In particular, theorization seems most likely to occur within social settings characterized by an intense and comprehensive discourse—that is, a discourse capable of constructing accounts and typifications without extensive input from external actors. These conditions most often pertain when the communication channels *within* a given social setting are broad and numerous, and the channels *between* that setting and others (either coordinate or superordinate) are narrow and scarce:

> **Hypothesis 2:** The probability that institutional theorization will occur at a given level is proportional to the intensity and comprehensiveness of discourse within social units at that level.

> **Hypothesis 2a:** The intensity of discourse in a social unit is proportional both to the number of communication channels among the constituent entities of that unit and to the number of communication channels between those entities and subordinate units.

> **Hypothesis 2b:** The comprehensiveness of discourse in a social unit is proportional to the number of communication channels among the constitu-

ent entities of that unit and is inversely proportional to the number of communication channels between those entities and coordinate or superordinate units.

Unlike the first set of hypotheses, this second group does not clearly favor either localism or globalism. For certain issues, communication networks may facilitate institution-building discourse only in fairly immediate settings, but for other issues, the only viable discourse may be one of national or even international scale. To further complicate matters, some of the settings capable of sustaining discourse on a given topic may not experience relevant problems with sufficient frequency to initiate such discourse—and other settings with more salient experiences may nonetheless lack adequate communication structures.

The third cluster of hypotheses addresses the relationship between new models and preexisting institutions. Although an intricate prior structure may occasionally hide the existence of problems, institutionalization generally tends to breed further institutionalization, with well-elaborated regimes providing numerous "handles" on which to hang new extensions. This is particularly true when the existing institutional structure is both coherent in its articulation and comprehensive in its scope, offering strong analogies, metaphors, and models for the resolution of novel problems. Unfortunately, these two desiderata often pull in opposite directions: Institutional regimes encompassing widely disparate activities tend to become diffuse and platitudinous, and regimes focusing on narrow specialties tend to allow few easy extensions or extrapolations. New institutions are thus most likely to arise when coherence and comprehensiveness stand in relative balance:

> **Hypothesis 3:** The probability that institutional theorization will occur at a given level is proportional to the coherence and comprehensiveness of institutional structure within social units at that level.
>
> **Hypothesis 3a:** The coherence of institutional structure in a social unit is inversely proportional to the diversity of experience encompassed by the constituent entities of that unit.
>
> **Hypothesis 3b:** The comprehensiveness of institutional structure in a social unit is directly proportional to the number of different activities institutionalized in that unit.

These propositions slightly favor globalism—at least within a modern world order characterized by strong, relatively coherent institutional structures at the level of the nation-state (Thomas & Meyer, 1984). At the same time, however, this group of hypotheses also helps to shed some light on the oft-noted institutionalizing power of the professions, because professional ideologies generally offer coherent and comprehensive models of broad areas of potentially problematic social experience.

The fourth set of hypotheses focuses on the resilience of new institutions to the deinstitutionalizing effects of deviance and dissent. Because institutionalization requires a certain degree of taken-for-grantedness (cf. Jepperson, 1991), the emergence of new institutions often depends on the existence of adequate mechanisms to (a) preserve the coherence of new models and accounts and (b) hold actors to new routines long enough for these practices to become habitual. The former task is easiest when neither subordinate nor superordinate social units are promulgating competing models; the latter task is easiest when constituent entities are well integrated with one another and coordinate units are well regulated by superordinates (cf. Durkheim, 1966; Hirschi, 1969; Merton, 1938):

Hypothesis 4: The probability that institutional theorization will occur at a given level is inversely proportional to the degree of deviance and dissensus within social units at that level.

Hypothesis 4a: The degree of dissensus in a social unit is proportional to the number of activities institutionalized at subordinate levels and to the degree of institutional contradiction at superordinate levels.

Hypothesis 4b: The degree of deviance in a social unit is proportional to the degree of disorganization among constituents and to the degree of overlap among coordinates and is inversely proportional to the degree of institutionalization at superordinate levels.

In general, these propositions slightly favor localism, because they suggest that institutions are most likely to arise within close, densely interconnected communities in stable environments. Such communities often rely on face-to-face contacts and informal social controls, and as a result, they can prove difficult to maintain as the number of participants rises and as geographic distances increase.

The final group of hypotheses focuses less on social structure and more on culture. These propositions recognize that cultural regimes often implicitly allocate institution-building power to specific loci by promulgating socially constructed assumptions that some entities are inherently more capable of generating models and formulating practices than are others. These "assumptions of agency" fall broadly into three groups: (a) the willingness of superordinate units to delegate discretion, (b) the willingness of coordinate units to extend comity, and (c) the willingness of subordinate units to embrace commonality:

Hypothesis 5: The probability that institutional theorization will occur at a given level is proportional to the degree of agency accorded to social units at that level by the general institutional discourse.

Hypothesis 5a: The agency of a social unit is proportional to the autonomy and competence accorded to that unit by superordinate units.

Hypothesis 5b: The agency of a social unit is proportional to the authority and credibility accorded to that unit by coordinate units.

Hypothesis 5c: The agency of a social unit is proportional to the collective identity and allegiance accorded to that unit by subordinate units.

For obvious reasons, these hypotheses suggest globalism in some circumstances and localism in others. In general, for example, the modern Western order tends to attribute agency primarily to individuals, formal organizations, and the state, and to deny agency to informal groups, communities, and international regimes. These attributions increase the likelihood of institutionalization in the former loci and decrease it in the latter.

A Preliminary Empirical Investigation

To demonstrate the empirical accessibility of the issues outlined above, the following pages present an exploratory analysis of the institutionalization of venture capital financing practices in California's Silicon Valley during the period 1975–1990. This setting is relevant to the foregoing model for a number of reasons. First, Silicon Valley in the late 1970s and early 1980s faced precisely the sort of recurring problems highlighted above. In a span of barely two decades, the region witnessed the emergence of a new industrial community built around new physical and social technologies with few precedents elsewhere in American industry. The microprocessor revolution of the 1970s created the technological basis for the formation of several new industries, but the fate of these industries remained largely contingent on the development of a social infrastructure capable of integrating their activities in a mutually complementary manner. Initially, the primary obstacle to commercial development was the difficulty of obtaining funding for innovative ventures from traditional institutional investors and other corporate entities. This failure of the capital markets (coupled with subsequent modifications in capital-gains tax laws) created an opportunity for wealthy and/or well-connected individuals to provide initial infusions of venture capital. The scope of venture capital financing, however, was severely limited by the absence of institutionalized understandings of this novel funding process and of the new industrial activities it was sponsoring. Only after the challenges of venture capital finance had become cognized, named, categorized, evaluated, and theorized could the high-tech start-up process take on the highly institutionalized, almost routine character that it increasingly displays today. Thus, Silicon Valley is relevant to the present discussion in part because it represents an industrial community that has clearly experienced and benefited from institutionalization.

A second, equally important, motive for examining Silicon Valley venture financing lies in the way it exemplifies a number of the determinants of institutional localism/globalism identified above. Three potential loci of institutionalization present themselves in this instance: (a) Institutions could have developed at a national level and diffused (either coercively or mimetically) down to the local Silicon Valley setting; (b) institutions could have developed locally, as a "collective product" of the Silicon Valley community as a whole; or (c) institutions could have developed at certain sites within Silicon Valley and then diffused outward, first to the rest of the community and then to the nation at large.

Taken together, the foregoing hypotheses suggest that venture financing practices were unlikely to have been theorized at a national level: Relative to the national economy, the problems of financing high-tech start-ups were relatively peripheral, sporadic, and unimportant (Hypothesis 1). Further, although numerous communication channels existed at this superordinate level of analysis, in the early days of Silicon Valley, these channels were only weakly connected to the discourse of what was then just another small suburban region of Northern California. Moreover, issues of small-company finance were easily overwhelmed by more significant concerns, such as Third World debt, corporate takeovers, and the federal budget deficit. Consequently, the national discourse on venture finance was neither comprehensive nor intense (Hypothesis 2). This state of affairs effectively eliminated any advantages that might have otherwise accrued to national actors by virtue of the extensive elaboration of national regulatory institutions (Hypothesis 3) (Scott & Meyer, 1983), the disciplinary potential of national financial hegemony (Hypothesis 4) (Glasberg & Schwartz, 1983), or the legitimated agency of the nation-state (Hypothesis 5) (Meyer et al., 1987). If the national discourse had attended to the problems of venture finance in the 1970s, national actors could easily have preempted the field, but it did not, and this created room for the emergence of more local institutions.

The prospects for theorizing venture capital finance at the level of the Silicon Valley community were somewhat more promising: As an initially isolated industrial enclave with an unusually high rate of corporate foundings, Silicon Valley experienced the problems of start-up company finance far more frequently than did most geographic regions and industrial sectors. At the same time, the technological promise of the fledgling micro-computer industry and the make-or-break character of venture finance for entrepreneurs and financiers alike ensured that problematic start-up financings enjoyed significantly higher salience than would have been the case in more established communities (Hypothesis 1). Furthermore, Silicon Valley's isolation and its "small town" character facilitated a relatively intense and comprehensive discourse with regard to these pressing business concerns (Hypotheses 2). In counterbalance against these advantages, however, institutionalization at the level of the Silicon Valley community was hampered by (a) the absence of coherent and comprehensive community-level institutions (Hypotheses 3), (b) the existence of substantial (although unsystematic) deviance and dissensus (Hypothesis 4), and (c) the reluctance of American culture to accord any significant degree of agency to diffuse collectivities such as industrial communities (Hypothesis 5). Consequently, although financing norms certainly could have formed at this community-wide level, their emergence and persistence would have been difficult.

Finally, rather than developing uniformly throughout the Silicon Valley community, standardized venture financing practices could have initially coalesced within specific Silicon Valley organizations, which could then have served as "pollinators" in the subsequent diffusion process. In other words, it is possible that venture financing practices originally achieved institutionalization within a number of local "information intermediaries" (Suchman, 1991), whose structural positions allowed them to see large numbers of start-ups facing similar sets of transactional challenges. Among the potential candidates for this role were Silicon Valley's corporate law firms, which drafted many of the region's early financing agreements. These law firms were well situated to drawn upon their experiences with multiple clients in order to cognize, name, categorize, and evaluate recurring problems and solutions—and then to promulgate coherently theorized models to the community at large. Even if different firms initially propounded different solutions, it seems likely that the collective impact of these efforts over time would have been to reduce the diversity of accounts to cognitively manageable proportions. Thus, law firms benefited from a fairly broad experience base (Hypothesis 1), within the context of well-developed organizational communication structures and well-institutionalized professional roles (Hypotheses 2 and 3). Further, being unitary formal organizations, these firms were able to sustain relatively low levels of internal deviance and dissensus (Hypothesis 4) (cf. Zucker, 1977), and they enjoyed high degrees of socially constructed competence, credibility, identity, and agency (Hypothesis 5) (Zucker, 1983).

RESEARCH HYPOTHESES

This brief overview suggests a number of testable predictions regarding the institutionalization of venture capital financing practices in Silicon Valley. First, if institutionalization has occurred at all, one would expect to find evidence that venture capital financings have, indeed, become more routine over time. Second, it seems likely that this routinization arose from within the Silicon Valley community, rather than being imposed from without. In particular, based on the foregoing analysis, one might predict that the initial locus of institutionalization lay within a few central "intermediary" organizations, which coupled (a) a broad base of vicarious experience with (b) strong internal communication structures and (c) shared normative and cognitive orientations. The most plausible candidates in this regard are the community's indigenous law firms. Finally, one might hypothesize that, over time, standardized financing practices gradually diffused outward beyond the community's boundaries, producing a curvilinear pattern in the association between community membership and contractual standardization: In early years, community membership presumably bore little relationship to standardization because standards were weak even within the community. In later years, community membership presumably bore little relationship to standardization because standards were strong even outside the community. Only during the intermediate "diffusion phase" should standardization have been significantly higher within the community than outside.

DATA AND MEASURES

To test these hypotheses, the following analyses employ content-analytic data on 108 venture capital financing contracts obtained from two leading Silicon Valley venture capital funds (Suchman, 1994). These agreements represent the full population of the funds' recorded first-round high-technology investments during the period 1975–1990. Because venture capital financing agreements are formally confidential business documents, the structure of this sample largely reflects issues of data accessibility. Nonetheless, every effort was made to construct as comprehensive a data set as possible: The two funds under consideration are widely recognized leaders in the industry, yet they do not maintain particularly close ties with each other; the coded agreements cover a wide range of industry segments, including semiconductors, computer systems, software, telecommunications, and biotechnology; the sampling frame does not exclude agreements on the basis of transaction size, geographic focus, legal representation, or contractual structure; the time period extends from the early years of Silicon Valley almost to the present. Although none of these precautions can entirely eliminate the possibility that the observed contracts were in some ways atypical, substantial exploratory analysis has failed to uncover any evidence that the reported results constitute mere artifacts of the data collection procedures. Rather, the data seem to represent a reasonable cross-section of the state of the art in venture capital finance during the period under consideration.

Each of the observed agreements was coded on more than 400 items, spanning 16 general dimensions: (1) company information, (2) law firm information, (3) investor information, (4) valuation and ownership, (5) control structure, (6) dividend provisions, (7) liquidation rights, (8) stock redemption provisions, (9) conversion/antidilution rules, (10) class voting requirements, (11) representations and warranties, (12) restrictive covenants, (13) financial reporting requirements, (14) stock sale restrictions, (15) stock registration rights, and (16) documentation. Background research (including numerous field interviews, review of several legal formbooks, and extensive pretesting) suggests that these dimensions capture virtually the entire range of formal and substantive variation in venture financing agreements during the observation period.

THE DEPENDENT VARIABLE

In addition to coding venture capital financing agreements on the specific aspects listed above, the data set also provides two summary measures of contractual standardization/idiosyncrasy: (a) an *uncodability* score, indicating the number of terms departing from the canonical alternatives identified in interviews, formbooks, and pretesting, and (b) a *rarity* score, indicating the number of terms shared with fewer than 5% of the other sampled agreements. From these indices, a combined *idiosyncrasy* score can be computed by (a) logging the uncodability and rarity counts, (b) standardizing the logged scores, and (c) summing the standardized values. Despite minor distributional differences (see Figure 3.2), all three of these measures yield broadly similar statistical results. Consequently, for brevity's sake, the models reported below employ only the more comprehensive *combined idiosyncrasy score* as their dependent variable. This score provides a rough index of the degree to which a given contract contains *nonstandard*, *counternormative*, or *deviant* terms—unusual provisions absent both from prescriptive models and from other observed financing agreements. In the current data, idiosyncrasy ranges from −3.621 to 3.703, with a mean of 0.02 and a standard deviation of 1.534.[8]

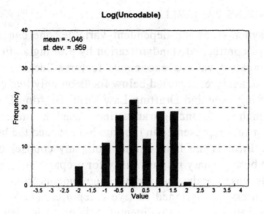

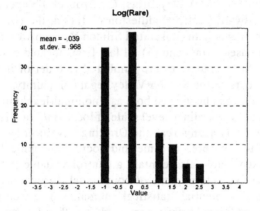

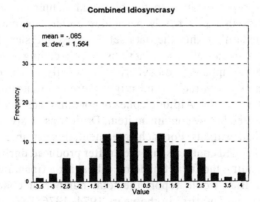

Figure 3.2. Distributions of Idiosyncrasy Measures

THE INDEPENDENT VARIABLES

Using idiosyncrasy as the dependent variable, one can examine the determinants of contractual standardization by plotting and/or regressing this measure against various exogenous factors. Because of the small sample size, the analyses reported below focus on only two central determinants: Drafting Date and Drafting Law Firm. Drafting Date is simply the year in which the financing transaction closed; as indicated in Table 3.1, the earliest year represented in the data is 1976, and the latest is 1990. Drafting Law Firm is the firm—either company counsel or investors' counsel—that bore primary responsibility for preparing contractual documentation.[9] Because the data set includes agreements from more than 30 law firms, drafters are assigned to five categories: (1) Wilson Sonsini Goodrich & Rosati, the largest indigenous Silicon Valley law firm; (2) all other indigenous Silicon Valley firms; (3) Brobeck Phleger & Harrison, and Cooley Godward Castro Huddleston & Tatum, the two leading San Francisco-based firms with substantial Silicon Valley offices; (4) all other San Francisco-based firms; and (5) all law firms located outside the Bay Area. Because these categories are numbered in order of increasing distance from the core of the Silicon Valley legal community,[10] the Drafting Law Firm variable can be viewed both as a nominal-level indicator of law firm identity and as an ordinal-level scale of localism/globalism. Table 3.1 cross-tabulates the Drafting Year and Drafting Law Firm variables.

In addition to measures of time and socio-geographic location, the analyses reported below also contain a control variable intended not to address substantive determinants of contractual idiosyncrasy, but rather to compensate for potential statistical anomalies produced by the data-collection scheme. Stated briefly, the problem is this: If a certain law firm contributes disproportionately to the observed sample of contracts, the possibility arises that this firm's particular boilerplate may, in effect, define the "standard" within the data set. Because the sampling scheme overrepresents Silicon Valley transactions, such a coding bias might artificially reduce the apparent idiosyncrasy of locally produced contracts relative to nonlocal contracts—and might thereby inflate the ostensible impact of drafter location. Although one cannot eliminate this risk entirely, the models reported below contain an item, Draft Bias, designed to control for such statistical artifacts. For each agreement, this variable indicates the total number of coded contracts that the drafter produced during the 3-year window surrounding the focal financing. Thus, for a financing conducted in 1985, Draft Bias would report the total number of coded contracts drafted by the same law firm in the years 1974–1976. Presumably, if the overrepresentation of a particular law firm during a particular time period

TABLE 3.1 Joint Distribution of Drafting Year and Drafting Law Firm

Drafting Year	Drafting Law Firm					
	Wilson (1)	Other SV (2)	SF in SV (3)	Other SF (4)	Other (5)	Total
1976	2	0	0	0	0	2
1977	0	0	0	0	0	0
1978	1	0	0	0	0	1
1979	2	1	0	1	1	5
1980	7	1	3	1	2	14
1981	4	2	2	1	1	10
1982	4	1	4	1	3	13
1983	3	0	4	0	1	8
1984	1	0	4	0	2	7
1985	2	0	0	0	1	3
1986	1	2	1	0	1	5
1987	1	1	6	1	0	9
1988	2	0	6	1	0	9
1989	7	0	4	0	2	13
1990	7	0	0	0	1	8
Total:	44	8	34	6	15	107

is making other firms' contracts appear excessively idiosyncratic, this control variable will reflect and correct that distortion.[11]

RESULTS AND DISCUSSION

Figure 3.3 depicts *3-year moving averages* of contractual idiosyncrasy for each of the five drafter categories identified above. The height of a given curve in a given year represents the mean idiosyncrasy level for all contracts drafted by that firm in that year, the year before, and the year after.[12] Although the limited sample size renders a few of the coordinates in this graph unstable, the overall pattern emerges fairly clearly: In general, idiosyncrasy levels decline with time and increase with distance from the core of Silicon Valley. This configuration accords well with the theoretical predictions outlined above. As hypothesized, venture capital financing practices do, indeed, become substantially more standardized between 1975 and 1990, and at each time point, the level of institutionalization is greater within Silicon Valley than outside.

Figure 3.3 also offers preliminary support for the assertion that individual information intermediaries contributed significantly to the routiniza-

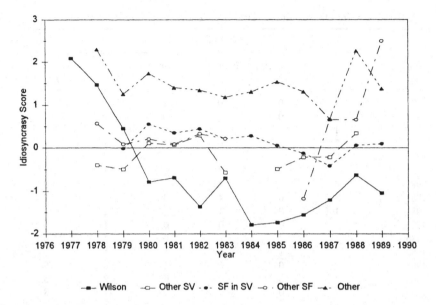

Figure 3.3. Contractual Idiosyncrasy, by Law Firm (3-year moving average)

tion process: If routinization were occurring primarily at the community level, one would expect to find similar (low) levels of idiosyncrasy among all local firms and similar (high) levels of idiosyncrasy among all nonlocal firms. This does not appear to be the case. Instead, throughout most of the 1980s, the leading indigenous law firm—Wilson Sonsini—shows consistently lower levels of idiosyncrasy than any other drafter, including other members of the Silicon Valley community. This suggests that the financing practices that eventually became Silicon Valley standards may have initially arisen largely within this particular firm, rather than within the community as a whole.

In addition to indicating that contractual idiosyncrasy declines with time and with proximity to Silicon Valley, Figure 3.3 also highlights two further points. First, this graph provides suggestive, if tentative, evidence of the hypothesized pattern of outward diffusion: Until roughly 1980, idiosyncrasy is high both within Silicon Valley and outside—indeed, in this early period, contracts from more established regions are often *less* idiosyncratic than those from Silicon Valley. Then, in the early 1980s, Wilson Sonsini draws ahead of the other local firms, but the differences between these other firms and the nonlocal drafters remain less marked.[13] In the mid-1980s, however, the other Silicon Valley law offices begin to catch up with

Wilson Sonsini and, in the process, begin to increase the standardization gap between themselves and the non-Silicon Valley contingent. Finally, in the closing years of the observation period, the idiosyncrasy of nonlocal contracts begins to decline, and the gap between all firms starts to narrow—although it never entirely closes.

The second noteworthy feature of Figure 3.3 is a bit more puzzling: Contrary to expectations, the curve for Wilson Sonsini appears *not* to decrease monotonically, instead rising gradually from about 1984 onward. A similar rise also appears to have occurred among the Silicon Valley-oriented San Francisco firms (Brobeck and Cooley) near the end of the observation period. The source of these increases is hard to determine from the present data. Possibly, as core contractual terms become increasingly routinized and increasingly cognitively tractable, drafters and negotiators begin to experience more opportunity (and, perhaps, more professional pressure) to fine-tune previously peripheral aspects of their agreements. Alternatively, however, the observed up-tick in idiosyncrasy might reflect changes in other structural factors not captured by these essentially bivariate plots.

Table 3.2 reports an alternative, multivariate approach to this data. Here, contractual idiosyncrasy is regressed against a series of time-period dummies, as well as against Drafting Law Firm (treated as an ordinal measure of social/geographic distance from the core of Silicon Valley) and the Draft Bias control variable.[14] Model 1 incorporates these terms simply as independent linear effects; Model 2 includes a set of two-way interactions between time period and drafter location.

The regression results in Table 3.2 strongly support the hypothesized theoretical account. Although Model 1 employs information on only two substantive independent variables (year and drafter location), this regression achieves a high level of significance ($p < .0001$), explaining more than one quarter of the entire variance in contractual idiosyncrasy ($R^2 = .27$). Moreover, the individual parameter estimates reconfirm the geographic and temporal patterns described above: Proximity to Silicon Valley significantly reduces contractual idiosyncrasy ($p < .05$), and idiosyncrasy levels also decrease through time except during the 1988–1990 period, when the incidence of nonstandard contractual terms rebounds somewhat.

Model 2 further expands this analysis by incorporating a set of two-way interactions between time period and drafter location. With the addition of four interaction terms, the level of explained variance rises to roughly one third ($R^2 > .33$), and the model remains highly significant ($p < .0001$). Substantively, the inclusion of time distance interactions does little to alter the previous conclusions. Two aspects of Model 2 merit further comment, however: First, in contrast to the *main effects* model (Model 1), the

TABLE 3.2 Temporal and Socio-Geographic Determinants of Contractual
Idiosyncrasy, 1976–1990

	MODEL 1 Main Effects	MODEL 2 Interaction Effects
TIME PERIOD[a]:		
1981–1982	−.437	−1.622**
	(.428)	(.790)
1983–1985	−.932**	−3.049***
	(.451)	(.878)
1986–1987	−1.031**	−1.802
	(.486)	(1.099)
1988–1990	−.434	−1.516**
	(.428)	(.750)
Drafter Proximity	.305**	−.168
to Silicon Valley	(.143)	(.226)
INTERACTION EFFECTS[a]:		
Drafter × 1981–1982		.535*
		(.277)
Drafter × 1983–1985		.859***
		(.300)
Drafter × 1986–1987		.364
		(.394)
Drafter × 1988–1990		.512*
		(.272)
Draft Bias	−.079**	−.087*
	(.143)	(.044)
Intercept	.286*	1.373*
	(.611)	(.739)
R^2	.267	.330
F Test	p < .0001	p < .0001
N	106	106

NOTE: Figures in parentheses are standard errors.
a. Reference time period is 1976–1980.
*p < .10; **p < .05; ***p < .01.

interaction effects model (Model 2) shows the rebound in contractual
idiosyncrasy to begin in 1986, rather than in 1988. This suggests that law
firms closer to the core of Silicon Valley may have experienced this
rebound slightly earlier than more remote entities. Second, the interaction-
effects model reveals the influence of drafter location to be statistically in-
significant in both 1975–1980 and 1986–1987, and only marginally significant in 1981–1982 and 1988–1990. Indeed, Drafting Law Firm only

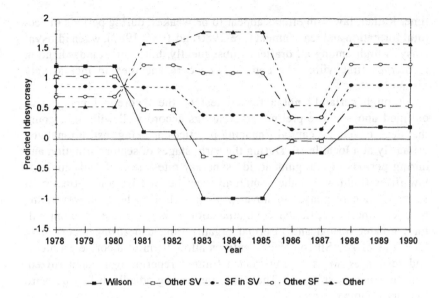

Figure 3.4. Predicted Idiosyncrasy, by Law Firm (time interactions)

exhibits an unambiguously significant effect in the period 1983–1985, although during these middle years, the impact is quite substantial.

Figure 3.4 illustrates these patterns by plotting the predicted values of contractual idiosyncrasy over time, for each of the five law firm categories. The graph reveals a large but short-lived gap among drafters in the early 1980s, as local Silicon Valley firms pull ahead of their external counterparts. This separation closes by 1986, in part because of a rebound in Wilson Sonsini's idiosyncrasy rate; however, the spread increases again during the final years of the decade, as more remote law firms experience idiosyncrasy rebounds of their own.

Although these findings can support multiple interpretations, perhaps the most plausible explanation is that the middle to late 1980s witnessed some shake-up in Silicon Valley's institutional order—with this disruption acting to elevate overall idiosyncrasy levels and to reduce the effects of geographic/cultural centrality. Although the nature of this shake-up is hardly self-evident, it may be noteworthy that (a) the computer industry underwent a painful bloodletting in 1984–1985, (b) the venture capital market retrenched in 1985–1986, and (c) Brobeck overtook Cooley, in 1987, as the least idiosyncratic nonindigenous law firm in Silicon Valley. In any case, Table 3.2 and Figure 3.4 clearly illustrate that the relationship between drafter location and contractual idiosyncrasy is not constant over

time. Rather, law firm effects appear to be weakest during periods of sec-
toral formation and realignment (pre-1980 and 1986–1987), when idiosyncrasy is high among all drafters; subsequently, however, standardization
reemerges first within the community's core and then in increasingly
distant locales.

Although certainly not a formal test of the theoretical perspective
outlined above, these preliminary findings accord well with an account
that depicts venture capital financing practices as being institutionalized
primarily at a local level. During the early stages of sector formation and
during periods of realignment, idiosyncrasy rates are uniformly high, as
law firms (both within the community and beyond its boundaries) construct ad hoc responses to novel problems. Before long, however, the
broader experience, tighter communication linkages, more coherent culture, greater formal and informal organization, and stronger collective
identities of key Silicon Valley entities allow them to theorize problems
and responses so as to construct a limited repertoire of standardized,
nonidiosyncratic solutions. These solutions then gradually diffuse outward
to more remote regions.

Conclusion

The results outlined above offer important empirical insights into the
development of standardized venture capital financing practices in Silicon
Valley. The foregoing data analysis illustrates Silicon Valley's transition
from being a relatively inchoate organizational community, situated on the
periphery of the national financial scene; to being a rapidly developing
high-tech enclave, in which a few key entities struggle to formulate coherent solutions to the recurrent problems of new-company finance; to
ultimately being a national exemplar whose business practices are increasingly widely emulated, even well beyond the community's borders. This
preliminary investigation broadly supports the theoretical predictions that
(a) venture capital financing agreements become more routinized over
time; (b) for most time periods, routinization declines with distance from
the core of Silicon Valley; and (c) the disparity in routinization between
local and nonlocal contracts is greatest during the early 1980s, when the
pace of community structuration is at its peak.

Rather than judging the foregoing data analysis as a test of the theoretical propositions introduced at the start of this chapter, however, readers
might do better to accept it in the spirit in which it is intended: as a limited
demonstration of one potentially fruitful strategy for shedding empirical
light on previously elusive debates over localism and globalism in institu-

tional analysis. In the preceding pages, I have attempted to lay out an abstract and general model of several factors affecting the locus of theorization in institutional dynamics; I have also attempted to demonstrate how these abstract factors translate into the realities of a concrete setting, and to reveal how the process of institutionalization in such a real-world context may leave empirical traces that researchers can observe, quantify, and analyze. Although this exploration has focused on Silicon Valley, presumably such analytic techniques could be applied to other sites as well. If so, the possibility of a more rigorous and comprehensive test of the underlying theoretical scheme may emerge in the not-too-distant future.

All of this having been said, however, it is also important to note that a full understanding of any historical instance of institutionalization is likely to require something more than statistical analysis, no matter how rigorous and comprehensive that statistical analysis may be. The model of localism/globalism posited above revolves around fundamentally cognitive constructs: problem visibility, discursive intensity, institutional coherence, cultural dissensus, and presumptive agency. All of these exist only in the minds of individuals and in the patterned symbols of collectivities. As this chapter demonstrates, one can often count symbolic displays, such as contractual terms, and regress them against other quantified symbols, such as time and location, but in order to make sense of the results, one must also grapple with the hermeneutics of the symbols themselves. One cannot comprehend the development of venture financing without understanding the cultural meaning of ventures and of financings, and one cannot examine localism and globalism without exploring the cultural meaning of the proximate and the remote. In the end, taking symbolic processes seriously implies taking them seriously both as processes and as symbols. For all its power and rigor, statistical analysis seems far better suited to the former task than to the latter.

Notes

1. Indeed, on occasion it even emerges within the collected works of individual theorists (e.g., compare Coleman, 1974, with Coleman, 1990).

2. It is perhaps worth noting that an accumulation of individual extrapolations may create strains that ultimately destabilize the larger institutional structure. This is certainly an important way in which local settings may affect global institutions, but if the strains are ultimately resolved at the global level, the crucial dynamic remains top-down.

3. Although theorists have commonly used the phrase *institutionalization* to refer to both institutional theorization and institutional diffusion, the two processes are conceptually distinct—at least with regard to their loci. Thus, for example, entities located at one level of a social system often embrace and promulgate models initially theorized at a subordinate

level. At the extreme, superordinate entities may even coercively impose models derived from one subordinate setting onto other subordinate settings far removed from the original sector.

Indeed, it is quite possible that this distinction between the center of theorization and the center of diffusion explains the recurrent empirical finding (Suchman & Eyre, 1992; Tolbert & Zucker, 1983) that early adopters of new organizational forms tend to do so for "instrumental" reasons (i.e., to solve novel practical dilemmas), and later adopters tend to do so for "institutional" reasons (i.e., to obtain legitimacy). Most early adopters reside at or near the locus of theorization and may, in fact, have served as the data points on which the theory was built. Late adopters, in contrast, are more likely to reside in remote sectors, where the only problems that the new model solves are problems of meaning and legitimation.

Rather than pursuing a futile debate over whether theorization or diffusion represents the true essence of institutionalization, the present discussion simply treats the two as distinct stages of an integrated whole. Most of the analysis, however, focuses on theorization, because it is here that the confrontation between top-down and bottom-up models seems most pointed.

4. Indeed, institutional contradictions and lacunae often take the form of poor articulation between levels, producing manifestations in several places at once.

5. Although these propositions are potentially testable, here they serve more to clarify the foregoing theoretical account than to guide the subsequent data analysis. Though the empirical findings presented below broadly comport with the theoretical model outlined above, the specific results are not designed to provide formal tests of the model's more abstract propositions.

6. If social structure consists of multiple nested units, then each unit at a given level of analysis (a) resides within one or more *superordinate* units at higher levels, (b) parallels one or more *coordinate* units at the same level, and (c) contains one or more *subordinate* units at lower levels. Those subordinate units that participate directly in the social life of a given level can be referred to as that level's *constituent entities*.

7. Here, and below, propositions will be stated in terms of processes *at a given level of analysis*. This phrasing, although parsimonious, is somewhat misleading. At any particular level of analysis, it is, of course, possible for practices to become institutionalized in some coordinate units but not in others—or for different practices to become institutionalized in different coordinate units. Thus, propositions about the probability of institutionalization at a given level of analysis are, more properly, propositions about the probability of institutionalization *within similar coordinate units at a given level of analysis*. Thus, for example, if favorable conditions for institutionalization exist within some (but not all) of the organizations in an industry, we might expect work practices to be institutionalized *at the organizational level in those firms*; firms lacking such conditions either might experience poorly institutionalized work practices or might adopt work practices institutionalized at some subordinate or superordinate level (say, the work group or the industry).

8. This methodology defines *idiosyncrasy* in fundamentally retrospective terms: A contractual provision is considered idiosyncratic if it fails to achieve either widespread usage or normative endorsement during the observation period, *taken as a whole*. Consequently, a contractual form might conceivably be both standardized and normatively endorsed by a limited number of firms (or during a limited period of time) without ever achieving enough acceptance to avoid the idiosyncratic label. Thus, the idiosyncrasy measure employed here reflects institutionalization or lack thereof, rather than irrationality or quirkiness. From this perspective, lost innovations and careless mistakes look pretty much the same, and high idiosyncrasy scores do not necessarily imply failures of draftership.

9. Somewhat surprisingly, exploratory analysis suggests that secondary law firms (e.g., investors' counsel in an agreement drafted primarily by company counsel) generally exert

little impact on the overall level of contractual idiosyncrasy; consequently, only the primary drafter is included in the analyses reported below.

For each contract, coders determined the primary drafter based on a number of factors, including cover letters, memoranda of closing, and contractual clauses detailing legal expenses. In a handful of cases, drafting responsibility appeared to have been shared between both company counsel and investors' counsel. In these instances, the primary drafter was initially assumed to be the company counsel, as preferred by Silicon Valley tradition. Exploratory analyses were then conducted to investigate the effects of "flipping" the primary and secondary law firms. In cases where a transposition was clearly indicated, the drafter was accordingly reassigned. Ultimately, of the 17 cases where drafting responsibility appeared to have been shared, 11 were assigned to the investors' counsel, and the remaining 6 were assigned to the company counsel.

10. Exploratory analyses employing other classification schemes (ranging from three to six categories) yielded results almost identical to those reported here.

11. In this regard, it is also reassuring that the reported effects remain relatively invariant under multiple definitions of idiosyncrasy: In preliminary exploratory analyses, the findings did not change substantially when idiosyncrasy was defined (a) as the number of uncodable items, (b) as the number of codable but uncommon values, or (c) as a combination of the two. Further, if observed levels of standardization were purely artifactual, it would be hard to explain the secular trend of rising standardization across all drafters and investors, which is reported below.

12. This procedure enhances the presentational clarity of Figure 3.3 by "smoothing out" random year-by-year fluctuations that would otherwise make this graph difficult to read.

13. Interestingly, Figure 3.3 provides some evidence that idiosyncrasy levels for other Silicon Valley law firms actually rise during the early 1980s. Based on the theoretical arguments outlined above, one might speculate that this rise reflects unsuccessful attempts to propound alternative models. Unfortunately, the current data are insufficient to either confirm or refute this speculation.

14. The regressions in Table 3.2 employ dummy variables in order to allow for curvilinearities in the relationship between idiosyncrasy and time—a possibility made particularly salient by the graphical evidence of Figure 3.3. Equivalent regressions were also calculated using linear and quadratic time terms, with much the same results as the models reported here.

II. ORGANIZATIONAL ADAPTATION TO CONFLICTING AND SHIFTING INSTITUTIONAL AND TECHNICAL ENVIRONMENTS

4

Origin and
Transformation of Organizations

Institutional Analysis of the Danish Red Cross

SØREN CHRISTENSEN

JAN MOLIN

OUR AIM IN THIS CHAPTER is to examine the origin and transformation of organizations. The empirical basis for our discussion is a study of the Danish Red Cross (DRC) over a period of more than 125 years. We trace the origin of the organization to 1864, when Denmark (along with other nations) signed the Geneva Treaty and agreed to establish local Red Cross organizations. The founding of the Danish Red Cross organization was, however, not easily achieved. It took 12 years before the local organization was established.

Rather than understanding the creation of the Red Cross organizations as the mobilization of particular interests (Brint & Karabel, 1991), we claim it to be a dramatization by the environment. Scott (1994c, p. 208) talks of such a process as the "enactment of an organization by the environment." The creation of the Danish Red Cross became a symbol of

AUTHORS' NOTE: We would like to thank the other contributors to this book for their high spirits during the Møn workshop in June 1993, and for their constructive comments. Special thanks to Asmund Born, Frank Dobbin, James G. March, W. Richard Scott, and Pamela Vergun for detailed comments on earlier versions of this manuscript.

Denmark's status as a civilized nation, and the institutional form of the Red Cross was a sort of celebration of the newly won democratic rights of citizens to participate in public life. The approach of this chapter draws attention to the symbolic aspects of organizations and environments, and to participants as carriers of cultural beliefs created at the societal level (Friedland & Alford, 1991).

From its founding in 1876 to the present day, the Danish Red Cross has undergone substantial changes in tasks, in leadership, and in its member base, adapting to changing demands and opportunities in its environment. In spite of these changes, the basic organizational form—a democratic structure—has been retained throughout the history of the organization.

The central thesis of population ecology, "that environments differentially select organizations for survival on the basis of fit between organizational forms and environmental characteristics" (Scott, 1992, p. 113), does not apply to our case. The organizational form has been retained, and, at the same time, the organization has adapted to changing environments. The resilience of this organization makes a case for a key argument of new institutionalism: Organizations that devise structures that conform closely to institutional requirements "maximize their legitimacy and increase their resources and survival capabilities" (Meyer & Rowan, 1977, p. 352).

It has been argued that new institutionalism "is more applicable to the study of institutional form and functioning than to the equally important topics of institutional origin and transformations" (Brint & Karabel, 1991, p. 338), and that the process of creating and transforming organizations is profoundly a political process that "reflects the power of organized interests and the actors that mobilize around them" (DiMaggio, 1988).

In this chapter, we try to demonstrate that the new institutionalism is applicable to origin and transformations of organizations, and that interests should not be conceived as naturally occurring groups with transparent and primordial interests, as pluralist and neo-Marxist theorists tend to conceive them, but rather as institutionally defined and shaped. This calls for "three (nested) levels of analysis—individuals competing and negotiating, organizations in conflict and coordination, and institutions in contradiction and interdependency" (Friedland & Alford, 1991, p. 241).

Models of organizational change often use organizational goals as a key variable. In Powell and Friedkin's (1987) study of change in nonprofit organizations, they discuss change in terms of the achievement, subversion, or supplanting of goals. Rather than postulating the importance of goals, we view the Danish Red Cross as an "empty vessel" which acts as a recipient of institutionally defined and shaped interests. In our analysis, we use the model of an "organized anarchy" (Cohen, March, & Olsen, 1972), viewing the organization as an opportunity structure that, through time, accommodates shifting problems, solutions, and participants. The tasks taken on by the Danish Red Cross at a given period in time depend on the mix of the streams of participants, problems to be dealt with, and available solutions that flow past the organization. However, the way the tasks are performed is in part determined by the identity, structure, and activity pattern (Meyer, 1994) that is established in the organization over time.

The approach in this chapter is inductive. We think it is important to separate data from the subsequent theoretical analysis of the data to make it possible for the reader to develop his or her own understanding of the material before we present our interpretation, so we begin by summarizing the history of the DRC, and then we examine the founding and subsequent transformations of the organization, discussing the founding of the organization as a case of dramatization by the environment, and the transformations of the organization as a case of adaptation to changing conditions in the environment. We discuss the loose coupling between the organization form and governance system, and the effects of sediments (or early established ways of doing things). We also treat the impact of symbolism on the origin of the DRC and discuss the impact of participants, problems, and solutions on the organization's transformation.

Our main theoretical points will be summarized in the analysis section. In the conclusion we develop the more general implications of our analysis for organizations in institutionalized environments.

History[1]

1864–1876: THE FOUNDING OF THE DANISH RED CROSS

In 1876 "The Society for the Improvement of the Conditions for the Sick and Wounded during War" was founded in the "King's Club" Restaurant in Copenhagen. General Thomsen, former Minister of War, became president of the society. The other members of the executive committee were men drawn from the nobility and the military establishment. Although the society was formally organized as a voluntary association, with open membership and election of the leadership, the founding members were drawn from very conservative circles in Copenhagen, the capital of Denmark, and the leadership of the society reflected this. The executive committee assumed power and got concessions from the board, allowing it to increase its size and replace members as it saw fit.

Nevertheless, the actual founding of the society took place a full 12 years after Denmark had committed itself to creating a local Red Cross-type organization based on guidelines set out in the Geneva Treaty. In 1864 Denmark, along with 12 other European countries, had responded to the initiative of a committee headed by Henri Dunant to participate in a conference in Geneva on aid to the sick and wounded in war situations. The conference resulted in the signing of the first Geneva Convention.

At this same point in time (1864), Denmark was at war with Prussia. The Geneva Committee sent delegates to the Danish side as well as to the Prussian side. This was not looked upon favorably by the Danish government, which questioned the impartiality of the delegates. Nor did the Danish army view the committee favorably; it felt criticized for not being able to adequately prevent and care for wounded soldiers. Denmark lost the war in 1864.

The military establishment, however, was reluctant to have civilians involved in military affairs. Apart from various measures concerning the treatment of the wounded and the neutrality of Red Cross personnel and materials (e.g., ambulances), the Geneva Treaty stipulated some kind of cooperation between the (civilian) Red Cross Committee and the military establishment. The national governments that signed the treaty were supposed to accept the role of a civilian organization in assisting the army in caring for the sick and wounded on the battlefield.

During the period from 1864 to 1876, the Red Cross Committee in Geneva tried several times to establish contact with Denmark. Its inquiries were not answered. In 1876 the Red Cross Committee once again asked why Denmark—having signed the Geneva Convention—offered no assistance to the wounded in the French-Prussian War taking place at the time. This time Denmark was criticized in public, and the story was published in the International Bulletin of The Red Cross Committee in Geneva.

And so, finally, the pressure on Denmark bore fruit.

1876–1917: SUPPORTING THE DANISH ARMY

The charter of the Society—which later changed its name to The Danish Red Cross—was to organize private individuals to provide assistance to the sick and wounded during wartime and, in peacetime, to prepare such help and to encourage interest and skill in voluntary (as distinguished from military) nursing. However, for a long period of time, the goal that was primarily pursued by the society was the more narrow one of supporting the Danish army; this was a reflection of the primary interests of the society's leadership. The society collected money for preparing military sanitary depots and later organized the training of nurses and first aid volunteers.

In 1881 the name was changed to The Red Cross. This reflects the fact that the society wanted to be considered a part of the international movement. Although it was supposed to be part of the International Red Cross, the many appeals in the period from 1876 to 1917 to the Danish Society from other societies and from the International Red Cross Committee were not answered. The society was very reluctant to get involved. Only in three cases did the society respond favorably: during the Turkish-Russian War in 1877–1878, in 1897 when the Red Cross sent 12 nurses to Greece during the war with Turkey, and again in 1912 during the Greek-Turkish War. In all three cases, the Danish royal family had put pressure on the Red Cross to assist, and in all cases there were family ties between the royal family and the courts of Greece and Russia. Not until the outbreak of the First World War in 1914 did the Danish Red Cross engage in major relief work abroad.

From 1886 the society received a small contribution from the government, but the major part of the funding was still membership fees, philanthropic gifts, and voluntary work aimed at supplementing the Danish army. The society was still tightly controlled by the executive committee, which in this period made no attempt to consult the general assembly, nor did it consider trying to transform the Danish Red Cross into a popular movement. On the contrary, during the first 20 years of its history, even though the society had difficulty building its membership and getting donations, it still firmly believed that private initiative and charity were the key to dealing with the sick and wounded in the battlefields.[2]

To expand the capacity of the society to organize field hospitals, the executive committee decided, in 1899, to introduce "Ladies' Circles," which had been a success for Red Cross societies in other countries. The executive committee used its connections with the best circles in Copenhagen, and a Copenhagen Ladies' Circle was founded. In 1900 the executive committee asked Crown Princess Louise to become the patroness of the Ladies' Circles. She accepted and asked prominent ladies all over the country who numbered among her friends to organize such circles. (These women were drawn primarily from the nobility.) Two years later, some 5,000 ladies recruited from the upper class were busy collecting donations and organizing field hospitals.

Another task of the Red Cross was the training of nurses and first aid volunteers to work in war zones. However, in the years before the First World War, the board, beginning in 1910, tied the need for training in first aid to the issue of workplace safety, which at this time was a growing problem in the major industrial plants in Copenhagen. As a result of this strategy, many young workers were recruited as first aid volunteers, but they never came to join the organization as members. Concerns over worker safety caused the trade union movement to establish its own organization to provide first aid training for the workplace. In 1912, with a view to the threat of war, the Trade Union First Aid Organization joined the Red Cross and got a representative on the executive committee. When the war broke out in 1914, Denmark did not become involved. Although the first aid volunteers were not members of the Danish Red Cross, they had organized themselves informally and now wanted to have a say in the decisions of the society. Nevertheless, the issues that concerned them had to do with uniforms, stretchers, and badges, rather than with the policies pursued by the executive committee.

1917–1976: FROM MILITARY SUPPORT TO VOLUNTARY RELIEF

By 1917 it was clear that Denmark would not get involved in the war. The growing pressure from the first aid volunteers resulted in a reorganization of the society. At this point the society consisted of three parts: the society, with some 400 members, the Ladies' Circles, with some 4,000 members, and the first aid volunteers, with some 2,000 members.

The military establishment, which had totally dominated the central committee until 1917, now completely withdrew. At a meeting of the central committee in 1919, it was decided that because the army was now apparently very reluctant to make a contract with the Red Cross for support, maybe, "instead of servicing the army as an appendix, the Red Cross should change to become a voluntary relief organization primarily concerned with civilian tasks."[3]

Although the organization of the society until 1917 had formally included a general assembly, this body had never exercised its formal influence: The executive committee had been in total control. Now the general assembly passed a new constitution that gave the society a federated structure with local branches. According to the new constitution, a central committee would be elected by delegates from the local branches. The central committee appointed an executive committee, and a university professor from the University of Copenhagen was elected as the new president. The executive committee consisted of medical doctors and other prominent citizens. This executive committee, for all practical purposes, took control of the organization. Therefore, although there was a change of formal structure in 1917, the control of the organization was still in the hands of a small group of people at the executive level. Even so, the federated structure—the outcome of the reorganization in 1917—became a major source of change in the society.

Because the majority of the members belonged to Ladies' Circles throughout the country, it would have been an obvious move to take these as the starting point for establishing local branches. However, Louise (who had become Queen of Denmark) insisted that she alone, as had been the case since 1900, was to appoint the presidents of the local Ladies' Circles. She also insisted that the Ladies' Circles could not be part of the local branches. Consequently, it became very difficult to establish local branches, partly because of local rivalry and partly because the ladies with the time and resources needed for the task had already been recruited to the circles. It took some 10 years until the society had national coverage with its local branches. Until the Ladies' Circles disappeared in 1948 with the death of Louise, you could still find a local branch and a Ladies' Circle in the same town, although in the 1930s and the 1940s, some of the Ladies' Circles did merge with local branches, in spite of the queen's dictate.

In 1919 the League of Red Cross and Red Crescent Societies was established, and the Danish Red Cross became a member. As a consequence, the name was changed from the Red Cross to the Danish Red Cross.

From an organization originally intended to support the Danish army, the Red Cross became primarily involved after the First World War in helping prisoners of war. It established offices in St. Petersburg, Berlin, Vienna, and Paris. This was its first major international effort, but the effort ended in 1920. From 1920 until the outbreak of the Second World War, its international involvement virtually disappeared. Instead, the efforts of the DRC were concentrated in Denmark, and the tasks engaged in were related to the furthering of health and the prevention of illness and need, in accordance with the league's charter.

In the period from 1920 to 1940, the local branches became very important in the organization. Local initiatives flourished, and the DRC became dependent on its local branches for its activities. The fate of the organization depended on local initiative. The tasks undertaken by the organization during this period can be described as supporting and supplementing the welfare state; these included care and assistance to young mothers, infants, and those in old folks' homes, as well as blood donor services, sanatoriums, first aid training, and so on.

During the Second World War, Denmark was occupied by Germany from 1940 to 1945. During the war and in the years afterward (1939–1951), the activities of the DRC were concentrated on tasks related to the war—relief assistance to Danish prisoners in German concentration camps and to families particularly affected by the war. Following the war, the DRC established and administered some 1,000 war refugee camps and provided assistance to Holland, Belgium, and France. This was done primarily through donations from the government.

The DRC continued its work in international relief and disaster operations throughout the period from 1952 to 1976, for example, providing assistance to victims and cities affected by flooding in the Netherlands in 1956. The financing of these operations came from donations and gifts, as well as funds collected by the local branches through activities such as organizing lotteries. At the same time, the branches continued to develop their local activities as well, organizing first aid guards at local sporting events, providing safety equipment at beaches, and so on. Even so, the activity level of the Danish Red Cross, in the period from 1952 to 1976, was far below that following the Second World War (1945–1951). Also, the number of members dropped dramatically: In 1948, there were 160,000 members; in 1976, the figure was 80,000.

1976–1992: ACCOMMODATING THE PROFESSIONALS: DEVELOPMENT AID AND REFUGEE SERVICES

In 1976 a series of meetings of the central committee of the DRC were held to find ways of expanding and revitalizing the organization. The committee decided to professionalize and internationalize the organization; its decision was confirmed by the general assembly in 1978. Two years later, a new secretary general was hired—a civil servant from the Ministry of Foreign Affairs, with a network of contacts in the public sector, international development agencies, and Third World countries. The organization thus shifted from a primarily volunteer-run to a professionally run operation, and with the change came greater access to resources.

Meanwhile, the branches still maintained their local activities, though the activities had changed from previous periods: The welfare state was now well developed; local municipalities had assumed many of the social responsibilities that the local Red Cross branches had previously tried to shoulder. The consequence for the organization was that new members became more difficult to attract.

The society as a whole came to be characterized by growing internationalism. The Danish International Development Agency (DANIDA), which is part of the Ministry of Foreign Affairs, began to look for nongovernmental organizations (NGOs) through which to channel the increasing public commitment to disaster relief and development work in the Third World.

Around this time, other NGOs became professionalized as well. The NGOs recruited from the same group of professionals as DANIDA, held regular meetings, and kept in close contact with their colleagues at DANIDA. A number of Danish NGOs became involved in government-funded relief and development work in the Third World. The DRC figured prominently among them. Normally, 10% of the project funding is pro-vided by the NGO, and the remaining 90% comes from DANIDA. The government agencies involved required accurate accounting standards and budgeting procedures: During the late 1980s, government consultants conducted studies of the organizational setups of the NGOs to make sure that these organizations were accountable.

The DRC became involved in other types of international relief efforts as well. In 1984 the Ministry of Justice subcontracted with the DRC to establish and run camps for political refugees seeking asylum in Denmark. These developments changed the DRC dramatically. In 1980 the DRC employed 50 persons and had an annual operational budget of some 50 million Danish Kroner (DKK). In 1991 the staff at the head office num-bered 150, there were 100 delegates abroad, and 500 people were em-ployed at the refugee centers (a 15-fold growth in personnel). The opera-tional budget in 1991 was 500 million DKK, 10 times that of 1980.

Around 1990 the organization was split between its volunteer part (which now numbered some 75,000 members) and its professional part. The branches operated as self-contained units and were only loosely coupled to the head office, and the refugee operations were decoupled from the rest of the organization. The volunteer part of the Danish Red Cross—consisting of 17 regional and 250 local branches—performed activities such as first aid training and visitors' service for elderly, disabled, and lonely people, and for prisoners. Its first aid groups provided services at local sporting events, concerts, and so on. Sewing and needlework groups made baby and children's clothes for Third World countries. Funds for international disaster and relief operations were generated at the local level through the sale of secondhand clothing and through local fund-raising. But only 8% of the operating budget of the organization was now generated locally. The rest of the operating budget was generated by the DRC professional operations. At the head office, the professional part of the DRC worked with international disaster and aid programs primarily di-rected toward the Third World. This operation involved a professional staff and was financed primarily through governmental funding; 42% of the DRC's operational budget stemmed from support of these activities. The administration of the refugee programs was financed entirely through a subcontracting arrangement with the Ministry of Justice; this activity generated 50% of the DRC's operating budget.

These different parts were tied together by the formal structure of the organization; this structure had remained unchanged since the reorganiza-tion in 1917. The general assembly, composed of delegates from local and regional branches, met biannually and was responsible for electing the regular members of the central committee. The central committee in turn was responsible for electing the executive committee, the president, and the three vice presidents. Although appointed formally by the central committee, another group of individuals who were special members of the committee, called "the King's elect," were chosen by the president and the secretary general. The phrase *the King's elect* reflects the history of the organization. In practical terms, people who were believed to have special knowledge useful to the central committee were asked to join it.

The executive committee was in control of decision making, a reality that was very much consistent with the history and traditions of the organization. Nevertheless, the secretary general, the president, and the professional staff felt that the elected decision makers were not qualified to deal with the increasingly complicated issues involved in aid and disaster operations. They held the opinion that a more professionalized decision structure was needed.

The idea of modernizing the decision structure had been advocated by the professional staff, and especially by the secretary general during the expansion in the 1980s. In 1986 the general assembly decided to appoint a committee to suggest a new structure for the organization. However, the suggestion offered by the committee was rejected at the assembly meeting in 1988. At the next general assembly, in 1990, the president threatened to resign if a new structure was not devised, and the general assembly decided to ask for an independent analysis by outside consultants. The analysis would address the overall, federated structure of the organization and the quality of decision making at the executive level.

The consultants submitted their report in October of 1991. They did not recommend a single model but suggested that the organization discuss three alternative models. Model one suggested completely separating the voluntary organization from the professional organization, whereas models two and three involved modifications of the existing structure. All three models, however, suggested that the governing structure should be simplified.

In October 1992, after a year during which the report was discussed widely throughout the organization, the general assembly decided to make the changes suggested by the consultants and chose to maintain a simplified democratic structure of the organization (i.e., to not separate the volunteer organization from the professional organization). The biannual general assembly was replaced with an annual council consisting of the chairs of the branch and regional offices.

In April 1993 the newly formulated council met for the first time. It has been given responsibility for electing a slimmed down central committee, now consisting of the president, the vice president for international affairs, the vice president for national affairs, and 12 other members.

Analysis

THE ORIGIN OF THE DANISH RED CROSS

It took 12 years from the signing of the first Geneva Treaty in 1864 before the Danish Red Cross society was created in 1876. How can we understand the obvious delay in its founding? Why did Denmark sign the Geneva Treaty and commit itself to establish a local society if it was so very reluctant to implement that decision? And why was the DRC eventually founded anyway?

The Symbolic Nature of Environments

In their analysis of the founding of the American community colleges, Brint and Karabel (1991) identify organizational elites ready to take on the creation of a new organization, in order to further their own interests, as well as those that the new organization is overtly designed to serve. The claim is that " . . . the determination of organizational interests can be read with a high degree of probability out of the power structure and opportunity fields faced by new organizations trying to become established" (Brint & Karabel, p. 346). In the case of the Danish Red Cross, powerful interests such as the Danish government and the military establishment were trying to prevent the creation of the organization. As we shall discuss below, there were citizens who wanted Denmark to have a Red Cross Committee. However, the interests of many such citizens in there being a DRC Committee had to do with the symbols involved rather than the substance of such an organization.

It should be kept in mind during the following discussion that Denmark's first democratic constitution came into being in 1849 (only 15 years before the signing of the Geneva Treaty). To understand the process of the founding of the Danish Red Cross, we will look at three levels of analysis: individuals, organizations, and institutions. The founding of the DRC was a highly symbolic event. In important ways it reflected the shaping of a modern, civilized, and democratic society (Friedland & Alford, 1991; Meyer et al., 1987).

In particular, we need to address the question of why the Red Cross Committee was established when it was (in 1876), and why it was established at all, and we need to look at the role of the military and the bourgeoisie in this process. The answer to the question of why the committee was founded at all comes in two parts. First, we need to understand the forces that created the Red Cross Committee, and, second, we need to understand why the military establishment took control of the organization once it was established—and why it was able to do this successfully.

Although the Red Cross may have been full of positive symbolism to those interested in democracy, to the military establishment (and perhaps the ruling class from which the military elite came), it was heavy with foreboding symbolism. In the year that Denmark signed the agreement supporting the founding of the Red Cross, the army lost the war, and Denmark lost part of its territory to Prussia. In consequence, efforts to make good on the promise of Geneva faced a stalemate in the years that followed. The army was especially sensitive to the criticism implied in establishing a Red Cross Committee to care for those injured or made sick by war. Furthermore, the Danish government had questioned the impartiality of the delegates ever since its experience with Red Cross delegates during the Danish-Prussian War. The military establishment had its reservations as well. Would the creation of an organization to cater to the sick and wounded during wartime not question the ability of the military forces to do its job? Establishing a Red Cross Committee in Denmark to take care of the sick and wounded on the battlefields would bring up the issue of the military. After 1864 the issue of the military had become a political issue in parliament as well, where the up-and-coming Farmers' party tried to use it in a power play with the ruling conservative party.

Nevertheless, the pressure from 1864 to 1876 from the Red Cross Committee in Geneva made the difference—the Danish government gave up its resistance. As we will see further in the next section, the symbolism contained within the social construction of this organization facilitated the enactment of the DRC by its environment. The logic behind the government's giving in to international pressure had to do with Denmark's quest for international recognition and legitimacy, and a need to demonstrate that Denmark was a modern civilized nation. The structuration of civilization was an ongoing process in Europe at this time, and it resembles what Scott (1987, p. 504) terms "acquisition at the organizational level." Powerful interests in the Danish society and in government chose to "acquire" the Red Cross Committee as a building block to be used in the construction of a civilized nation.

The audiences of this acquisition were other civilized countries, with whom Denmark would like to be compared, as well as the Danish public themselves. Although highly symbolic, the signing of the treaty was an important act. At the founding of the society in 1876, it was argued that "the most important thing is to establish an organization. . . . It does not look good if our country is the only one among civilized nations that is not part of this movement" (Zalewski, 1992, p. 21). Thus, it was not so much interests in founding such an organization that caused it to come about, but rather it was the environment that pushed (dramatized) the organization within Denmark.

THE DRAMATIZATION OF THE DANISH RED CROSS

It was in 1874, with the visit of Hans Suenson from Copenhagen to Geneva, that the pressure on Denmark began to increase. Suenson learned from Gustave Moynier, the president of the Geneva Red Cross Committee, that Denmark had not replied to the numerous appeals from Geneva, and he started writing about this in Danish newspapers, thus creating pressure to establish a local organization. He succeeded in getting a group of people—primarily officers and medical doctors—to send an invitation to a group of people from all classes of society (among whom were several from the provinces who were in the capital as members of parliament) to discuss establishing a local Red Cross Committee affiliated with the international organization (Zalewski, 1992, p. 12). Thus, pressure from the outside brought about the Danish Red Cross through a process of dramatization—or in Scott's (1994c, p. 208) terms, there are "multiple ways in which environments operate to enact [to socially construct] organizations."

The organizational structure chosen for the "Society for the Improvement of the Conditions for the Sick and Wounded during War" was that of a voluntary association, with a democratic structure, based upon open membership and the secret election of leadership.

Following the first democratic constitution in Denmark, in 1849, voluntary associations became institutionalized as an organizational form in such disparate fields as political parties, farmers' cooperatives (dairies, slaughter houses, stores), folk high schools, savings banks, and trade unions. The pressure toward structural isomorphism can clearly be seen at the societal level in this period (see DiMaggio & Powell, 1983; Meyer & Rowan, 1977). We suggest that voluntary associations can be understood as symbolic manifestations of the larger project of constituting the individual as an abstract legal entity with rights to assemble and to vote (which was also going on at this time) (Boli, 1987; Friedland & Alford, 1991, p. 240; Thomas & Meyer, 1984). "The wider setting contains prescriptions regarding types of organizational actors that are socially possible and how they conceivably can be structured. Collectivities are thus as much the embodiment of the prescriptions available for constructing cultural forms as they are the aggregation of lower-level units and interests" (Meyer et al., 1987, p. 19).

Voluntary associations were an organizational form that carried important messages of a political, economic, and cultural nature. They became
a symbol of the newly won democratic rights (Gundelach, 1988, p. 94).

Loose Coupling of the Governance System and the Organizational Form

The governance system of the society, however, was far from the democratic structure of its organizational form (that of a voluntary association
with free membership and popular control). The governance system resem-
bled that of elite associations, which had been the dominant organizational
form prior to the democratic constitution of 1849.

On a formal level, the organization of the DRC was open and was
controlled by leaders elected by the members. In fact, an elite composed
of prominent citizens took full control of the organization. They constituted the governing body, which was headed by the former Minister of War,
General C.A.F. Thomsen.

Also, decisions were made and steps were taken by the governing body
without consultation with the rank-and-file members. Although, officially,
membership was open, comparatively high membership fees prevented the
ordinary citizen from joining.

Loose coupling between governance systems and organizational forms
is repeatedly found in studies of organizations (e.g., March & Olsen, 1976;
Orton & Weick, 1990; Weick, 1979). One of the basic assertions in new
institutionalism is that formal structures "must be taken for granted as
legitimate, apart from evaluations on their impact on work outcomes"
(Meyer & Rowan, 1977, p. 344). Organizational forms are important for
demonstrating legitimacy, not only to the environment but also to participants, who may sometimes value the procedures themselves more highly
than the results they generate, as in the case of a free school committed to
direct democracy (one person, one vote). In this school, decision makers
strongly supported the organizational form, although they were dissatis-
fied with the results generated by this organizational form (S. Christensen,
1976).

Sediments

As we have pointed out, the DRC at its founding imported competing
values and normative structures. On one hand, the organization was structured on the basis of the ideals of representative democracy. The charter
of the organization and the very nature of this civilizing project reflected
democratic values and humanitarianism. On the other, its actual governance was based on an elitist model of autocracy and on military principles

of discipline, loyalty, authority, and control. To a large extent, these seemingly antagonistic ideals and structures present at its founding became organizational components that were integrated into the organization. Despite the many institutional waves flooding the DRC over the following decades, these components or sediments that were introduced early on are still significant forces in the organization, even 125 years later.

This is in line with Stinchcombe's (1965) classic paper on founding processes, which suggests that the basic features of organizations vary systematically by the time of the organization's founding and remain fairly constant over time.

THE TRANSFORMATION OF THE ORGANIZATION

It has been argued that institutional theory tends to defocalize interests and agency in the analysis of organizational transformations (DiMaggio, 1988; DiMaggio & Powell, 1991). As we noted above, Brint and Karabel (1991) claim similarly that institutional theory is more applicable to the study of organizational form and function than to the study of organizational origin and transformation. These authors take a utilitarian position on interests and argue that actors pursue some form of primordial interests. In the case of the transformation of the American community colleges, an organizational elite is seen to take advantage of the environment to further their own interests as well as those of their organizations (Brint & Karabel, p. 345).

If, as in our analysis, we understand the interests of actors as institutionally defined and shaped (Friedland & Alford, 1991, p. 245), we would want to demonstrate the collective and cultural character of the development of a rationalized environment (Meyer, 1994). This position leads us to also question the concept of organizational goals so prominent in studies of organizations and change. Rather than postulating the importance of goals (e.g., Powell & Friedkin, 1987), we see the organization as a "recipient" of the evolving set of patterns, models, and cultural schemes of its rationalized environment (Meyer & Scott, 1983).

Viewing the organization as a recipient or an empty vessel is similar to the view of decisions as choice opportunities, as put forth in the garbage can model of decision making in organized anarchies (Cohen, March, & Olsen, 1972). In organized anarchies, preferences are seen as inconsistent and ill defined, technologies are unclear, and participation is fluid. In organized anarchies, a choice situation becomes a "meeting place for issues and feelings looking for decision situations in which they may be aired, solutions looking for issues to which they may be an answer, and participants looking for problems or pleasure" (Cohen, March, & Olsen, 1976, p. 25).

In studying the transformation of an organization over a long period of time, as in our case study of the DRC over a period of 125 years, the conditions surrounding an organization are seen as similar to those of an organized anarchy. In important ways, the DRC reflects the development of the Danish nation-state. We want to understand the resilience of this organization, and what allowed it to survive in the face of great changes and challenges. We suggest that the DRC is truly an institutionalized organization, in the sense that keeping old forms and even old names has allowed the organization to survive. We believe that what has happened in this organization is a reflection of changing conditions in the wider society.

We will use a modified version of the garbage can model to understand the transformation of the DRC. In our version, the organization is an opportunity structure that connects problems, solutions, and participants over time. In organized anarchies, the meaning of choice changes over time as a reflection of the participants, problems, and solutions that are connected to the choice opportunity. In our analysis of the DRC, the nature of the organization changes as a reflection of the streams of participants, problems, and solutions that are connected with the organization over time.

The Empty Vessel Model

The view of the organization (or the opportunity structure) as an empty vessel suggests that it is open to all available participants, problems, and solutions. In principle, there are no restrictions on access to the organization as long as participants, problems, or solutions are conceived as legitimate for this type of humanitarian, nonprofit organization. With this broad definition, we see the structure as unsegmented, with respect to both participation and access of problems and solutions (Cohen et al., 1972).

Participants join an organization for different reasons. Their motivation to participate is a reflection of the interests that they bring to the organization. These interests are, as we noted earlier, created and shaped by the institutional environment and may be either symbolic or material. Such individuals may be looking for work or for a professional career, or for the status attached to a leadership position in the organization. They may join for ideal (humanitarian) reasons, or to further particular (material) interests.

Problems are, like the roles and interests of participants, created and shaped in the institutional environment. We see the DRC as a major, although not the only, recent recipient for a number of humanitarian problems that have arisen in Danish society over the years. These problems may be defined in the organization itself (e.g., when the DRC took the initiative of supplementing welfare in the 1930s), or they may be defined in the environment (e.g., in 1984, when the government decided to ask the DRC to establish and handle the camps for political refugees seeking asylum in Denmark). Solutions may be generated in the organization (e.g., when the professional staff wanted to expand from relief and disaster work to development work in Third World countries in the 1980s) or in the environment (e.g., the decision in the 1980s by the government to increase the NGOs' share of the Danish international development budget).

PARTICIPANTS

In 1899 the Executive Committee of the DRC decided to introduce Ladies' Circles to expand the capacity of the organization with respect to organizing field hospitals. This had been done successfully in Red Cross Societies in other countries and is a very early case of international diffusion of models, as discussed by Meyer (1994).

The military/bourgeoisie domination of the DRC ended in 1917, when this group withdrew from the organization. Their attempts to protect military interests from civilian intervention were no longer relevant, and the protection of the old institution of autocratic rule was no longer possible. Denmark had come out of the First World War without having been involved, and the old autocratic rule was, from an institutional perspective, outdated. The bourgeoisie were vanishing or finding themselves supporting the democratic movement in society. The process of industrialization had changed the class structure and had given rise to trade unions, the social democratic party, and the liberal Farmers' party. After 1917 the new governing elite of the DRC reflected the modern class structure, and recruitment to the governing elite was based on academic standing rather than social class. We do not mean to suggest, of course, that these are not to some degree correlated. The leadership of the organization was and still is mostly composed of doctors and lawyers.

In 1917 the structure was changed from a unitary to a federated structure, and this made room for new members and new local elites. In the local branches, the governing bodies were recruited from the middle class. Both liberal and conservative individuals joined the DRC through their local social networks. This recruitment pattern is still dominant in the organization. In general, all members take pride in the international work of the DRC while at the same time focusing on local activities. The same type of people can be found in other humanitarian organizations like the Lion's Club, or even the Rotary Club.

The professional employees have, for good reasons, a somewhat shorter history in the DRC. They entered the organization at the time when the DRC expanded as a consequence of the growing Danish commitment to international development aid. Today they constitute a specialized category of NGO professionals. Their careers normally involve working in different NGOs in Denmark, as well as in Third World countries. Their focus is primarily international and professional, with only a little respect for the rank-and-file members of the DRC, and they pay little attention to the work performed at the local level of the organization.

The member base of the organization has changed over time. In general, the issues at hand have had a different appeal to the population at different times. In 1948 there were 160,000 members; in 1976 the figure was only half of that. The difference between the rulers and the ruled that we observed at the founding of the organization is a pattern that not only continued after 1917 but also exists today. In general, members are recruited from the lower classes and are not at all active in the leadership of the organization. Members have different motivations for joining the organization, which vary over time and by social class.

As we have seen, participants have different motives for joining the organization; these include status, work, and professional careers. The number of participants changes with changing conditions in society. The number and composition of participants in the organization have changed over time and across categories. Each of the groups has a profile of interests, which has formed the basis for the involvement in the organization. These institutionalized interests are then applied, transformed, and developed, even as they are employed in the everyday activities of the organization.

PROBLEMS AND SOLUTIONS

It is difficult to separate problems from solutions, but we argue that the changing tasks of the DRC are a reflection of problems and solutions generated in the institutionalized environment, national as well as international, and in the organization itself.

The main point of this analysis is to understand how problems and solutions are generated in the wider environment, thus reflecting the development of society. With the broad humanitarian charter of the DRC, the organization functions as a recipient of a diverse pool of problems and solutions arising in society over time. The following list shows the diversity of tasks taken up by the DRC and suggests how new tasks are added to the list, rather than replacing previous activities:

1876–1917	Support of the army's sanitary corp
1920–1940	Support of welfare development at the local (branch) level
1940–1950	Aid to prisoners of war and war refugees
1950–	International disaster and relief operations
1980–	International development aid to Third World countries
1984–	Refugee centers for political refugees seeking asylum

The basic argument here is that macrosociological processes occurring in society affect the development of problems and solutions that have become defined as relevant tasks for nonprofit organizations such as the DRC. This is a reflection of the development of the nation-state, of citizens, and of professions.

As we have demonstrated in this analysis, the DRC has been a recipient of developments in the wider environment, leading to a continuous evolution of both the activities carried out and the organization's identity. This organization has changed from having a primary goal of supporting the army to being a humanitarian organization with national as well as international activities. Since the early 1980s, part of the organization has become highly professionalized. However, the formal structure of the organization has not changed, and we have argued that the democratic structure has been a carrier of important values, such as democracy, values which were important to the members and, during the past decade, important to the government as well. Popular control, as it is formalized in the democratic structure, has legitimized the use of the DRC and other NGOs to channel still larger public funds to developing countries.

Loose Coupling

Beginning with the founding of the DRC, we observe that governance was decoupled from the formal democratic structure. The organization has always been dominated by an elite. This pattern has persisted throughout the history of the organization and has also been replicated in the local branches. We also observe a decoupling between structure and activities.

We observe, like Zald and Denton (1963), that the federated structure, occurring through the loose coupling (Orton & Weick, 1990) of the local branches from each other and from the head office, has made room for organizational development through local adaptation, and thus the federated structure is important in explaining the resilience of the organization.

Sediments

Organizations are meaning systems that develop normative rules to define values and activity scripts that are important mechanisms for producing stability (Scott, 1994b). The humanitarian values of the DRC provide a strong basis for organizational resilience. Many of the problems in society (welfare, aid, disasters, refugees, etc.) have been channeled into the organization. However, we also observe that the discipline and loyalty dominant in the early years of the organization, when the military was in control, still dominate the organization. The authority structure—with officers in command and private soldiers performing the work—is now translated into an elite governing the organization at central and local levels, and the rank-and-file members doing the everyday work. The activity scripts have also been influenced by the early years of military support. The technology of sanitary work developed in military situations was later applied to disaster operations in civilian settings. Early tasks, such as preparing sanitary depots, were transformed into others, such as knitting and other types of handicraft manufacturing in the local branches. The training of first aid volunteers and nurses to assist at the battlefields has likewise evolved. Nurses were used to assist young mothers and the poor in the early years of the welfare state (1920–1940), and the first aid volunteers are now attending sport events, outdoor concerts, and the like. The work with refugees after the Second World War is now being continued in the camps providing asylum for political refugees. Such phenomena are also observed by March and Olsen (1994): "Institutional routines seem to endure far beyond the historical settings in which they developed as plausible responses and after it is forgotten what made them meaningful."

Adaptation

Metaphorically speaking, we have suggested understanding the organization as an empty vessel that was and still is dramatized (or "filled") by the environment. Participants, problems, and solutions have dramatized the organization and the tasks of the DRC; they reflect the interests that have developed in society at different times. These processes are not unlike the findings of Selznick in his study of the TVA (1949), Zald and Denton's study of the YMCA (1963), and Clark's (1956) study of community colleges. All of these studies emphasize organizations adapting to changing environments. In the early years, supporting the military establishment was the primary task of the DRC; in the period from 1920 to 1950, supplementing the emerging welfare state dominated the Danish Red Cross. Beginning around 1950 the local municipalities gradually took over these welfare tasks, and the DRC adopted a more international perspective. In fact, the DRC continued supporting welfare programs, now in Third World countries rather than in Denmark, moving where the need was greatest.

From around 1980 the Danish Red Cross and similar humanitarian organizations were dramatized by the Danish International Aid Agency (a branch of the Danish Ministry of Foreign Affairs). The Danish government adopted a policy of channeling a growing amount of Danish aid to Third World countries through NGOs. A similar story could be told about the camps for political refugees seeking asylum in Denmark. With the fluctuating number of refugees coming to Denmark, the government decided to employ a private humanitarian organization to take care of this task. The choice was the DRC, whose neutrality and good public image made this choice a feasible one.

The three variables employed in this analysis—decoupling, sediments, and dramatization—help explain how the organization has developed a robustness that has made it possible to accommodate a diversity of tasks and participants—in a reflection of the development of society.

Conclusion

Because our main theoretical points have been summarized in the previous sections, we will now use these insights and discuss the more general implications for organizations in institutionalized environments.

In our analysis of the origin and transformation of the Danish Red Cross, we have stressed the macrosociological processes in the wider society as the source of the origin and transformation of this organization. The development of a modern society has created and transformed the rationalized environment. Stemming from this environment, changing institutional orders have, over time, shaped and defined not only the problems, solutions, and participants, but also the interests that have determined the evolving shape of the organization. We have viewed the organization as an empty vessel or a recipient of these macrosociological streams of change.

Organizational structure is the product of the institutional order at that point in time when the organization was founded. It is important not only for legitimating the organization in the wider environment but also as a meaning system to the participants. Although we have observed decoupling between the structure and the governance of the organization, and between structure and activities, and loose coupling between organizational units, the organizational structure has been maintained since the organization's founding. The DRC has survived and been able to adapt to rather dramatically changing conditions in the environment. As March and Olsen (1994) have suggested: "Institutional survival depends not only on satisfying current environmental and political conditions but also on an institution's origin and history."

Although in our analysis of the Danish Red Cross we have used a version of new institutionalism rather than old institutionalism as an explanatory frame, we will now use a term of Selznick's (1949) and argue that the resilience of the organization is due to the fact that the structure and identity of the organization have been "infused with value." We want to speculate about the conditions under which organizations show such resilience. In an early formulation of new institutionalism, Meyer and Rowan (1977) argued that organizations that devise structures that conform closely to institutional requirements "maximize their legitimacy and increase their resource and survival capabilities" (p. 352). The democratic structure dramatized at the founding of the Danish Red Cross is a case in point. However, not only structure but also identity and activity scripts add to survival capabilities. In our case, the identity of the organization as a prestigious, humanitarian, nonprofit organization has appealed to shifting groups of participants. These participants have used the organization as a platform for very different activities, within the broad definition of humanitarianism, and for different purposes: status, career, prestige, work, social relationships, and so on. In the long history of the DRC, activity scripts have been sedimented in the organization and have been readily available to participants, as well as to problems and solutions. These scripts have been defined and shaped by society and by the larger cultural environment.

We have argued that the founding of the organization, in 1876, was highly symbolic and came about as a dramatization by the environment. The organization came to symbolize Denmark's status both as a civilized nation and as a democracy in which the citizens could exercise their individual rights to elect their leadership. We believe that these values are important cornerstones of the resilience shown by the DRC. They have made it possible for the organization to change with the shifting and even contradicting institutional demands of the wider environment (those of both Danish society and the increasingly important international community). The more central the values are to the institutional demands faced by the organization (i.e., democracy and humanitarianism in the case of the DRC), the greater the organization's resilience, and the broader these values are, the easier it is for them to be interpreted favorably by different participants. In Danish society, it is difficult if not impossible to be *against* democracy and humanitarianism. In the same way as the federated structure allows the organization to adapt to local environments, the broad values of democracy and humanitarianism allow for local interpretations within the same organizational form.

The main threat to the organization would be if the organizational form (democracy) and core identity (humanitarianism) were seriously questioned. In recent times, there are examples of two such threats, both of which questioned the "central (institutional) logic—i.e., a set of material practices and symbolic constructions—which constitutes the organizing principles and which is available to organizations and individuals to elaborate" (Friedland & Alford, 1991, p. 248).

The first of these threats was the questioning of whether the organization was truly democratic. In the 1960s the development of grassroots movements led to a questioning of whether the representative democratic structure of organizations like the DRC was *truly* democratic. The grassroots movements were organized on a more ad hoc activity basis and subscribed to direct forms of democracy. This did cause some problems for the DRC. The member base decreased, and it was difficult for the organization to recruit young people, in spite of the fact that a separate Young People's Red Cross division was created in 1973.

However, the endorsement of the organization by the government in the 1980s, through the increased use of the DRC (and other NGOs) as partners for government-financed development work in the Third World, renewed the DRC's legitimacy. This was especially true because the government designated the organizational form of the NGOs (the democratic structure) to be an assurance of popular control.

The other major threat questioned whether the "institutional logic" (Friedland & Alford, 1991, p. 248) of the organization should be participatory and democratic rather than bureaucratic and hierarchical. This attack was launched around 1990 by the professionals in the organization who questioned the feasibility of the democratic structure (although, as we have noted earlier, the governance of the organization is only loosely coupled to the structure), in view of the complicated and highly professionalized work with refugee camps in Denmark and the development and relief work in the Third World countries.

The resilience of an organization is increased if the organizational form conforms closely to institutional requirements, and if its governance and activities are decoupled from the structure. It is further increased if the values of the organization (its identity) are consonant with the institutional logic of the organizational form, but are ambiguous enough to allow for a diversity of potential resources (participant, problems, and solutions) to get connected to the organization.

Notes

1. The history of the Danish Red Cross presented here draws heavily on an unpublished manuscript prepared for a doctoral dissertation by Barbara Zalewski. Her cooperation is acknowledged and greatly appreciated.

2. Barbara Zalewski: Hattedamer—Dameafdelingernes Historie 1899–1948. DRK's uge-brev 1991.

3. Minutes from the central committee meeting, 1919.

5

Civilization, Art, and Accounting

The Royal Danish Theater— An Enterprise Straddling Two Institutions

JAN MOURITSEN

PETER SKÆRBÆK

Neo-Institutional and Structuration Theory

The neo-institutionalist approach to social analysis pays attention to "the ways in which institutions incorporate historical experience into their rules and organizing logic" (DiMaggio & Powell, 1991, p. 33). The neo-institutional approach is diverse; different strains of it lie within political science, economics, sociology, and organizational theory (Knudsen, 1989; March & Olsen, 1989; Powell & DiMaggio, 1991). Yet, the common reference to "institutions" reflects a space of human conduct, reproduced as a social rule, that has developed in and through history (Berger & Luckmann, 1967; Jepperson, 1991). Institutional analysis is thus concerned with the modes of social conduct that extend across time and space (Giddens, 1979, 1984).

Neo-institutional analysis rejects the classical rational and naively evolutionist approaches to social analysis which stress coherence and integra-

AUTHORS' NOTE: We gratefully acknowledge comments from David Cooper, the participants at the EAA conference, Turku, 1993, and the participants at the Institutional Theory workshop, Møn, 1993.

tion of human systems (Krasner, 1988). Although neo-institutional analysis would not deny that social systems come in particular forms, it would question, or at least open the discussion of, their optimality and desirability. Neo-institutional analysis is not concerned with justifying particular social arrangements. Rather, it is concerned with the mechanisms that *legitimate* social practices, with the *social embeddedness* of human arrangements, and with the particular *historical character* of institutionalized practices (March & Olsen, 1989; Meyer & Scott, 1983; Powell & DiMaggio, 1991).

However, as we will explain below, the neo-institutionalist approach is not the only possible or only fruitful perspective. An extension and qualification of neo-institutionalist ideas may be created by drawing on Giddens's structuration theory (Giddens, 1976, 1979, 1984).

Giddens's structuration theory is an attempt to synthesize the diverse strands of social theory into a whole account of social conduct. Although it can be criticized on several accounts, it can extend and qualify some aspects of neo-institutional analysis. According to Giddens, institutional analysis is concerned with mechanisms behind *durable* patterns of social conduct (Giddens, 1984, p. 17). It is concerned with the properties that facilitate the reproduction of fairly similar social practices across relatively large spans of time and space. This view emphasizes institutions as historical phenomena related in important ways to temporality.

Neo-institutional analysis is often also concerned with temporality, typically as change over time. Through time, institutional forms emerge and develop. In a structurationist account, however, temporality is not understood only, or primarily, as change. Rather, temporality is a feature of the constitution of social conduct, executed in the tension between forms of social relations lasting only for a passing moment and deeply sedimented forms of social relations:

> An understanding of institutional forms can only be achieved in as far as it is shown how, as regularized social practices, institutions are constituted and reconstituted in the tie between the *durée* of the passing moment, and the *longue durée* of deeply sedimented time-space relations. (Giddens, 1979, p. 110)

According to this statement, institutional analysis is inherently temporal. Its temporality, however, should not be equated solely with the possible changes of social practices across calendar time. Rather, the *durée* of the passing time (calendar time) is meant to point out the fact that social action has to take place in time and space. Although in the *durée* of the passing time, interactions are produced and relations between people are executed, these relations do not necessarily produce change. Unlike most neo-institutionalist analysis, a structurationist account of the temporality of institutions would emphasize those features of social relations that are largely reproduced through daily interaction (see Giddens, 1984, pp. 35-36). The *longue durée* is a repetition that goes beyond the single individual. The repetition and reversibility of institutions both form and are formed through day-to-day experience via routinely executed practices.

This raises an important question concerning the relationship between the individual—who is presented as knowledgeable, intelligent, and resourceful in Giddens's theory—and institutionalized patterns of social conduct (Jepperson, 1991). Institutional conduct is largely unintended. In their daily lives, people interact (speak, exercise power, and sanction) with a view to upholding or transforming their relationships with others. The day-to-day interaction is motivated by personal desires. However, day-to-day interaction is not without preconditions. Day-to-day interaction is often serial and thus based on routine conduct, which forms and is formed through the pattern of relations of autonomy and dependence between agents.

The seriality of routine conduct not only produces a certain predictability of the behavior of social systems, it also presupposes a set of "good arguments" to which one can refer automatically without having to justify them discursively. These good arguments, although they can be challenged, reveal an underlying basic set of rules and resources that may have little explicit presence in the concrete activities produced in day-to-day life. They are "methodic" rules and resources needed to produce interaction, inasmuch as they exist only in their instantiation (Giddens, 1984).

The relationship between the agency of the individual and the continuity of institutional arrangements is, in Giddens's theory, largely a methodological one. Institutional analysis involves a methodological bracketing of the deliberate and knowledgeable conduct of individuals. In contrast, the analysis of strategic conduct focuses on the way agents draw explicitly on structural properties (Giddens, 1984). In neo-institutional analysis, the institutional perspective is a paradigm or a theory (Powell & DiMaggio, 1991); in structuration theory, institutional analysis is a particular methodological device or perspective on social conduct.

In most neo-institutional analyses, time is often, although not always (Krasner, 1988), understood as involving change and the emergence of new social practices (Baron, Dobbin, & Jennings, 1986; March & Olsen, 1989; Mezias, 1990; Tolbert & Zucker, 1983; Zucker, 1983). At least in much neo-institutional research, the point is to demonstrate how particular organizational forms or procedures become sedimented in a series of organizations. A structurationist analysis would, in addition to this, emphasize those social features—or structural properties—that govern the *continuity* of institutional arrangements.

In a structurationist analysis, institutional form both upholds and is upheld by three structural properties: signification, domination, and legitimation. Signification is concerned with language and communication. Domination concerns power. Legitimation is about the sanctions that come into play in social relations. These structural properties account for the mechanisms (the generic rules and resources) that underwrite a particular social system. The three properties are interdependent. All interaction is produced through language, power, and sanction.

One of these structural properties is explicitly echoed in neo-institutional analysis: legitimation. However, legitimation, in most neo-institutional analyses, concerns the mechanisms that to a certain degree separate a phenomenon from its image (Elsbach & Sutton, 1992; March & Olsen, 1989; Meyer & Rowan, 1977), or at least condition its image (Baum & Oliver, 1991). Neo-institutional analysis focuses on the window-dressing-activities of organizations—when organizations pay more attention to the appearance of what they do than to the actions themselves (Mouritsen, 1994).

In a structurationist analysis, however, legitimation is bound up with the rights and obligations of those who participate in the reproduction of an institutionalized social system. In such an analysis, legitimation directs attention to the sanctions that qualify a virtually existing arrangement, rather than emphasizing the way people distort their real doings. Legitimation is not separated from reality. Rather, we must look to reality to understand the sources of legitimation.

In keeping with neo-institutional analysis, analysis from a structurationist point of view pays attention to the social character of institutionalized conduct. However, sometimes—if not always—the social is referred to as the extra-organizational (e.g., the micro/macro split), and thus social factors are treated as being located outside the focal enterprise (Baum & Oliver, 1991; D'Aunno, Sutton, & Price, 1991; Meyer & Scott, 1983; Oliver, 1991). In a structurationist account, extra-organizational phenomena refer to phenomena that are larger than the focal enterprise but reproduced through the actions of the focal enterprise. In institutional analysis, the focal enterprise is a locale within which interaction draws upon the properties of institutions present in that locale. These properties exist outside any particular set of interactions (and thus outside the particular focal enterprise), but the locale acts as a forum for the articulation in concrete contexts of broad institutional properties. The translation between particular sets of interactions and general institutional principles is facilitated by the context of the locale.

In this sense, the extra-organizational aspect of institutions is not by definition outside the formal locale. Rather, the extra-organizational character of institutions refers to the point that institutional properties are reproduced in social interaction, even as they are the rules and resources drawn upon to produce this interaction. The institutional properties are in turn reproduced (unintentionally) by this procedure, because they exist in their instantiation as methodic procedures in practice.

To sum up, as has been suggested above, the institutional analysis offered here, with its reference to a structurationist account of social conduct, is in some respects a challenge to neo-institutional theory. Although both approaches share a concern with legitimation, the structurationist approach refers to this as the rights and obligations of agents, whereas in neo-institutionalist analysis, legitimation is often only window dressing. Both approaches are also concerned with history, but, whereas the neo-institutionalist approach emphasizes change and emergence, the structurationist approach looks at the mechanisms of reproduction. Last, both approaches are concerned with the social. The neo-institutionalist approach theorizes this as something outside the focal locale/enterprise. The structurationist approach, however, sees the social as consisting of properties that can be drawn upon in taking action in a locale/enterprise.

The Case of the Royal Theater

In the present paper, institutional analysis informs the discussion of the constitution of two institutions, art and accounting, in the Royal Theater in Copenhagen, Denmark. Established in 1772, the theater is not only the oldest theater in Denmark, it is also a powerful symbol of Danish culture. The analysis presented here will focus on the way art and accounting relate to each other. It traces art and accounting as two distinct, although related, aspects of the organization of the Royal Theater.

In a broad sense, accounting appeals to rationality and carefully considered choice, and it often works to organize the activities of organizations and societies toward collective ends (Mouritsen, 1994). Accounting may be considered as a mode of thought and a set of technologies through which resources are defined, surveyed, aligned, and distributed in order to control organizational and social activities (Miller & Rose, 1990). Such control typically, if not always, is justified by references to ideas like productivity, rationality, consistency, and managerial decision making (Meyer & Rowan, 1977).

Art, in a broad sense, appeals to the image of the educated person. It appeals to the image of sophisticated individuals familiar with the heritage of Greek drama, German and Italian opera, and French ballet. In various European cultures, art forms such as these are thought of as a sort of cradle of civilization.

The theater came to Denmark by the end of the seventeenth century, when Copenhagen was visited by theater groups, typically from Germany and France. Dissatisfaction with productions only in foreign languages led to the establishment of several theaters in Copenhagen in the period up to 1747, but with only little success. In 1747 a new theater was opened by the king; it was at this time a private theater. In 1770 the responsibility for running it was given (though not without resistance) to the municipality of Copenhagen, because of the theater's many financial problems. It was then named the Royal Theater. In 1772 it became a national theater.

In the period before 1772, the theater was primarily a theater for plays and recitals by opera singers. After 1772 the theater expanded its repertoire to include ballets and an increasing number of operas. A tradition of plays, opera, and ballet at the Royal Theater was established by the end of eighteenth century.

Today, this theater is organized into seven departments: *The Ballet* consists of a ballet school, a corps of dancers, and a number of solo dancers. *The Opera* encompasses an opera academy for training opera singers, several soloists, an opera chorus, and the Royal Orchestra. *The Play* includes dramaturgy and a number of actors. *The Production department* includes a group that provides props, a painting group, a tailor shop, and a sound shop. *The Stage technicians' department* is experienced in the handling of stage technical conditions, such as wings, props, stage carpets, stage machinery, and lightning. (There are three main stages: the Old stage which is primarily used by opera and ballet; the New stage, which is primarily used for plays; and a small Experimental stage for all three art forms.) *The Marketing department* provides press and information services, the audience consultant, a box office and a subscriptions office, an inspector office, a library, and an office for special arrangements. Last, there is an *Administration department*, which comprises an accounting office, an office of financial planning, and the office of building maintenance. As to staff, the Royal Theater employed 737 persons at the beginning of April 1990. Of these, the Ballet employed 132; the Opera/orchestra, 232; the Play, 52; Production, 96; Stage technicians, 146; Marketing, 26; and Administration, 53.

The productions of the theater during the 1989–1990 theater season included 709 performances, 78 tours in the province, 4 chapel concerts, 8 chamber concerts, 108 special events (e.g., specially requested performances) in the foyer and rehearsal rooms, and 26 Sunday events. Altogether, the Royal Theater has had an audience of 400,000 people.

Net expenses for 1992 total 331.9 million Danish Kroner (DKr.). Wages amount to 65% of total expenses. Box office earnings account for 86.9 million DKr., and state grants supply 236.6 million DKr. (About 85% of the theater's expenses are covered by government grants.)

The focus of this chapter is the relationship between two institutional forms present in the Royal Theater, art and accounting. The empirical context of the paper is the attempt by the state to align organizational praxis in the Royal Theater with broader changes in the management of the public sector in Denmark (Jørgensen & Melander, 1992; Skærbæk, 1992). These changes are often interpreted as a gradual implementation of bureaucratic systems, in the form of management accounting and a gradual redefinition of "responsibility" to include being concerned with budgets, rather than solely with art.

The dialectic between art and accounting is not new (as will be demonstrated below); it has been important throughout the history of the Royal Theater. This dialectic between art and accounting dramatizes the contradictory nature of modern civilization. The Royal Theater is a symbol that has additionally come to signify the formation of a civilized nation—in support of the sovereign state and its citizens and in rejection of the absolute monarchy with its subjects (Krasner, 1988).

To explore and illustrate this thesis, the remainder of the chapter is organized into two major sections. First, a brief account of the last 200 years of the Royal Theater is provided. The emphasis is on the discursive relationships between management control, state intervention, and national culture. Second, a discussion is provided concerning the content of the institutional properties that underwrite civilization. Art and accounting are discussed as reflections of a dialectical interplay between reflexivity and accountability, which are important dimensions of modern, civilized culture.

Some Empirical Observations on the Debates in and Around the Royal Theater Over a 200-Year Period

In 1772 the Danish king decided to hand his private theater over to the public. This is where our story of the Royal Theater starts.

Table 5.1 summarizes a set of issues in the history of the Royal Theater over a period of a little more than 200 years.[1] Our identification of focal issues for this chapter, as they are a subset of debates appearing over this period, is guided by our interest in the constitution of management as an institutional phenomenon. In particular, the themes of accounting, management, investments, and culture are important for constructing the dis-

TABLE 5.1 Topics in the History of the Royal Theater

1772–1849	1849–1852	1853–1858	1864–1870	1870–1899	1899–1905
Management control Running negotiations between the board and artists, and often the king himself, about spending at the theater. The question of earnings is irrelevant because of its status as primarily a theater for the court. No public accounting was practiced during the absolute monarchy. Lacking such accounting, the absolute monarchy was accused of being wasteful.	**Management control** Annual Treasury negotiations. 14% retrenchment in 1852 in spite of a commission report. Discussion in Parliament of levels of wages in order to reduce public spending. Wednesday subscription arrangement was implemented to increase income. **Privatization** Discussions of privatization as a means to decrease public spending. **Top management** The manager did not make a business plan as demanded. "It is meaningless." He was indifferent to the politicians. **Culture** 1851 commission report over "The Future of the Theater." Against privatization. Some decisions about wage and pension increases were decided. The importance of the theater to nation formation and culture was stressed.	**Management control** Annual discussions about retrenchments. Increased ticket prices as a reaction to deficits. **Privatization** On the agenda in Parliament. **Top management** The theater ran a deficit and neglected instructions from the Auditor General. **Investments** 1855—a commission looked into rebuilding the theater. The rebuilding was financed by loan from Sorø Akademi. Decided in 1857. **Culture** The importance of the theater to nation formation and culture was repeated in the annual Treasury debates in Parliament.	**Management control** In 1864 heavy retrenchments possibly as a reaction to national symbols because of Denmark's losing a war to Germany. In 1865 reductions in wages. 1868 —minor retrenchments. **Privatization** In 1870 privatization was suggested. **Top management** The theater ran a large deficit, and calculations at the theater were criticized as being improperly superficial. Because of retrenchments in 1865, the top manager resigned. **Investments** 1867—commission about the "future of the theater" and a new building. Decision about a new building, financed by loan from Sorø Akademi. It was stressed that a new building was necessary because the old one was "too disgraceful to the Capital and the Parliament."	**Management control** Heavy retrenchments as a punishment because of the budget overrun of the rebuilding project, 1870–1874. 1879–1903, the Auditor General forced the annual financial report to show deficits, which were then covered with state funds. This gave the theater a bad image and maintained a will in Parliament to make retrenchments. Extra performances in order to earn more money were implemented. 1893–1897 commission about possibilities for extra box office earnings, and retrenchment possibilities. **Top management** The top manager was discharged because of budget overruns in relation to the rebuilding project. **Culture/Investment** In 1874 the new building was opened and was thought of as a national symbol of recovery after the defeat by Germany in 1864.	**Management control** Debt to Sorø Akademi was released. The debt was structured as accumulated deficits over 45 years. No important cost saving initiatives. **Top management** The top manager, Colonel Fallesen, holds that position for the longest time, 19 years (1875–1894), partly because the debt was released. (See Culture for the second reason.) **Culture** Fallesen formulated the role of the theater, on which basis he became top manager: "For a country like ours whose power position has decreased, whose total area and population is small, it is the greatest challenge to support the intellectual spirit and thereby to win honor as it cannot be won in other ways." (He refers to the defeat by the British in 1802 and by Germany in 1864.) In his later years, he was accused of being too extravagant.

1905–1929	continued	1934–1954	1972–1974	1974–1980	1985–1987
Management control Proposals from committee of 1922 to increase income by playing in the month of June and to increase the number of performances outside the theater itself. And furthermore, to decrease wages and the number of administrative staff. **Privatization** Privatization was discussed in Parliament and, as a liberal said, "the state does not possess the competence to run a theater, but should leave it to a private business that could receive state subsidies." And in 1908, it was stressed by a top manager that the international opera was destroying the national playhouse, the core activity of the theater. The ballet and opera should be left for private business. **Investment** In relation to the discussion of building an extra stage, it is underlined that it is important to have the three art forms under the same roof because of a synergistic effect.	Again in 1923, the liberals wanted to separate the art forms. But it was rejected because the staff have pension rights for many years. **Culture** In relation to an attempt to merge the Royal Theater with a private theater in 1912, the artists of the theater protested by saying that "It would be improper for the national stage to reside in a rented hotel as it has its strength in the three art forms staying together."	**Management control** In a commission report in 1934, there was satisfaction with the fact that no significant budget overruns had taken place within the last couple of years and that self-induced retrenchments had taken place. But, it was decided to implement stronger administrative measures and increase financial influence (via a board) on the theater. **Privatization** In a commission report, it was discussed to separate the three art forms. But there was (as the report concluded) no financial argument for such an separation, and further, that privatization would require strong controls regarding the repertoire and artistic quality "unless the state wants to close down the national stage." **Top management** In the 1934 report, the manager was criticized as being too involved with artistic interests. Again, the focus was turned toward finding the right person. **Culture** The theater is a light that shines in the dark years of the occupation.	**Management control** A proposal to change repertoire planning in order to increase efficiency was not implemented. Retrenchments were discussed, and it was concluded that they were possible only with regard to support and administrative departments "because of general technical improvements." And it was concluded that it is not possible to increase box office earnings. **Investments** Report on rebuilding project finds a big need for major improvements because of many technical problems in the production of theater. Later, the Parliament decided on a reduced building project.	**Management control** Report from Auditor General criticizing budget overruns and extravagant spending. Critique of accounting practice because of wage payments for performances not involving the theater. The budget overruns reckoned to a lack of activity budgeting. Such an accounting system was ordered. A private consultant company designs a system, but the recommendations were never implemented, even though the theater reported to the ministry that the system's development was still going on. **Top management** Criticized as not having financial competence. **Investment** At the same time that the private consulting company works on its report, the large rebuilding is going on.	**Management control** Report from the Auditor General criticizing the spending at the theater, as a result of budget overruns. Examples of extravagant spending are given and criticized. For example, What does a financial controller do in Japan with the ballet? Is it necessary to spend much money in training a dog that only participates in a single play for a few seconds? And so on. **Top management** The management of the theater has not implemented the ordered activity-budgeting system. Another demand for an accounting system is made. **Top management** Heavily criticized as being administratively incompetent.

(continued)

TABLE 5.1 (Continued)

1987–1988	1989–1991	continued
Management control As a result of the report from the Auditor General, the theater is now the object of public criticism, and the Parliament demands certain consequences. In order to save the ministry, three committees with short timetables were set up. One of them, the accounting committee, worked on arguing the need for a new accounting system. **Top management** As a consequence of the dissatisfaction with the management of the theater, and the external will to make retrenchments, the top manager and the manager for plays resign. One of the three committees then attempts to demand a new top manager with an administrative background. **Privatization** In the public debate some liberals demanded that the theater be privatized, but the question was never seriously discussed in Parliament.	**Management control** The new top manager and the ministry set up two new committees (an accounting committee and an organizational committee) that were to operationalize and implement the recommendations from the three committees. A political process was then started up, and a lot of discussion and apathy appeared. The top manager almost closed down the accounting committee (whose proposal was too unrealistic) and moved the work to the organizational committee, where the top manager herself was chairman (as she was not in the accounting committee). A heavily reduced accounting system was then decided upon and technically implemented. Hourly budgeting in the production and art departments was never implemented. **Culture** The topic of culture was not addressed explicitly during the discussions about the management of the theater.	**Top management** Under the new top manager, new financial problems arise. The liberal government wanted to make further retrenchments as they were doing in general in the public sector. The top manager was networking with the arts majority in the Parliament, and in order to harass the government, they decided to spend 120 million Kr. over 3 years. Instead, for revenge, the government decided to establish a board that then discharged the top manager as "administratively incompetent." **Culture** As the artists reacted to the implementation attempts, it was stated that the theater is no sausage factory, but a high culture institution. Here our story ends.

cursive field that relates the management of the theater to the management of the state. Table 5.1 illustrates some of the debates that appear in commission reports and parliamentary discussions over this period.[2] The table is thus composed of a set of public debates, and though the impact of these debates on the practices of the Royal Theater cannot be assessed directly, such debates are probably most important in shaping overall support for, as well as concerns regarding, the Royal Theater.[3] The ideas about the Royal Theater expressed in these debates form some of the conditions of its existence.

Table 5.1 depicts a set of interrelated issues concerning the management of the Royal Theater: management control, intervention by the state, the role of the theater in society, and so on. These issues link two aspects of the Royal Theater: the organizational aspect involving its management as an enterprise through various forms of administration and accounting, and the artistic aspect involving contributions to the arts and national culture. In the second aspect, the Royal Theater stood as a symbol of a newly civilized Denmark.[4]

In the period 1772–1849, although the king had supposedly given the Royal Theater to the public, the public had no clear status; there was still no formal democracy (the first Danish constitution was created in 1849), and the king attempted to maintain his power over the theater in spite of the theater's transfer to the public. During this period, there was ample discussion of the theater's spending patterns, but effective discussions and actions were not viable because the theater's very accounting was said to be miserable. The administration of the theater was said to be wasteful, and it was under no obligation to provide the public with an account of its spending. The theater during this period was accused of being a good example of the wastefulness of an absolute monarchy. Jensen (1931, p. 16) comments on these debates: "Methods of Financial Control during the absolute monarchy could be criticized simply because it took place in closed offices without any accountability towards the public. The taxpayers could be nothing but suspicious when their money was spent 'in the dark.' " The preconstitutional debates introduced a new form of debate about accountability: Even the king should be accountable to the public for his spending.

In a sense, not until 1849 (when the first Danish constitution was passed) did the Royal Theater become a public enterprise. From that time until 1875, the Royal Theater was constantly exposed to talk of retrenchment and cuts, and simultaneously exposed to demands that it should raise its own revenues through box office sales. Such stringent managerial controls were inherently part of the discipline imposed by a changing society, which wanted to clearly differentiate itself from the way things had been under the absolute monarchy—it would allow no waste reminiscent of that period. One mechanism for distancing itself from that period was the construction of financial accountability.

A second was the attempt to use "rational management" to decide what art in the Royal Theater should be like. For example, a privatization program was proposed: Each art form should become financially self-sufficient. "[The main task was] from an economic point of view to investigate carefully and consider seriously whether anything of importance would be gained by giving up any one of the three art forms" (Ministry of Cultural Affairs, 1978, p. 10). In 1867 a commission evaluated the possibility of abandoning one of the three art forms—the ballet. The commission undertook a "marginal analysis" of the ballet. Although the commission in the end advised against excluding the ballet, the very fact of this form of analysis was intriguing. Such an approach allows art to be analyzed as a set of independent activities, the worth of each analyzed based on financial considerations, somewhat regardless of considerations of artistic merit. The gaze of accountants unimpeded by artistic considerations was thought to make possible the "rational" administration of the theater, which (in the accountants' view) had tried unfairly to portray itself as composed of an essential and indivisible trinity (the opera, the play, and the ballet). The form of analysis used by accountants is not just a technical matter—behind it is a mentality that art must be justified by proving itself to be clearly serving government purposes (Miller & Rose, 1990).

In the same period, however, the importance of the role that had been and could be played by the Royal Theater in forming a national culture was stressed again and again. In the annual treasury debates in Parliament, this point was raised year after year. For example:

I believe that the Royal Theater is of great importance for the education of the population and for its openmindedness. If Holberg, through his (satirical) comedies, had not created a Danish theatrical tradition, he would not have come to be for us what he is; and, Oehlenschläger's[5] dramatic works, particularly his tragedies, would not have been brought forth without the theater. (Nielsen, MP, quote from Parliamentary discussions, 1864, in Neiiendam, 1953, p. 602)

The Theater could and should, like universities and schools, function as the people's educational institution, a place where a knowledge of the world and better behavior are automatically contagious to the audience. . . . To an educated form of life belongs also an educated language . . . and particularly the Royal Theater could and should save the Danish language from decay. (Ministry of Cultural Affairs, 1872, in Rask, 1980, p. 20)

The Royal Theater thus was part of an ongoing attempt to educate the farmer, to turn the peasant into a person comfortable with the duties and privileges of a democracy[6]—to create citizens who would come to desire and appreciate the taste of civilization and who would save the Danish language and culture from decay.

In the years from 1864 to 1875, the Royal Theater gradually built up a gigantic deficit, primarily as a result of heavy investments in a new building. The budget overruns made the government act fiercely: In 1875, it forced the theater into agreeing to heavy retrenchment, an obligation to increase box office revenues, and a new accounting format. Although at first glance the change in the accounting system may seem trivial (the "new" financial report merely regrouped the line items of the accounts such that the grant was excluded from the revenues and reintroduced as a coverage for losses), when compared with the requirement to increase revenues (and cope with the accompanying decrease in grant support), the change in the accounting system created an image of the theater as having become more wasteful than previously, even though there was no change in the theater's cash flow. In consequence, the theater's top manager was discharged.

Although the financial matters of the theater continued to be discussed, the consequences of these discussions were no longer as dramatic as in the previous period. Instead, because all debts had been written off in 1875, from that point on, the theater was primarily thought of as a medium to instill pride and values in the population, rather than as an ordinary enterprise to be governed by administrative measures:

> Throughout the 80 years that the Parliament discussed the affairs of the
> Theater, the theater was immensely important for bolstering our sense of our
> own nationality—particularly in times in which the whole of our Royal Court,
> and the whole of our traditions, were influenced by German language and
> traditions. (H. Frisch, Socialdemocratic MP, 1894, in Neiiendam, 1953, p. 679)

One could thus say that the Royal Theater was thought of as an enterprise involved in the "production" of Danes—in constructing a Danish nationality, one that would clearly differentiate Denmark from other nations—especially Germany. The role of the theater in developing and creating a Danish nationality was strongly underlined.

In this period, the relationship between art and accounting was often portrayed as a duality, with weight given to the criteria of art as well as those of accounting—the Royal Theater "cannot and should not apply distinctly commercial criteria for its doings," although it must "solve its special tasks under strict financial considerations" (Retrenchment Committee of 1922). The 1933 report of the theater commission underscores this point:

> The financial aspect of the management of the theater has been placed in a too-inferior position vis-à-vis the artistic aspect. Obviously, purely business points of view cannot and should not govern the affairs of the theater because of the theater's special obligations (e.g., to our classical repertoire)—although these obligations have to be met with careful consideration of what is financially warrantable. (Theater Commission of 1933, p. 28)

This period, however, was followed by a period (1934–1954) in which additional attempts were made to explore the possibility of managerial control. These attempts to privatize some art forms were resisted on the grounds that private enterprises would not be sensitive to the need to support a "national stage." This metaphorical allusion to a national stage had behind it a second debate concerning ways in which the Royal Theater could take measures to expand its audience, allowing more people to come in contact with high Danish performance art:

> During the discussion in the committee of the educational importance for the general public of the Royal Theater, it was mentioned that it would be appreciated if the theater, as it did some years ago, could sell its performances to the workers' organizations. Since such performances may be seen as part of the efforts . . . to bring the theater's art to the whole of the population, the commission endorses the considerations that lie behind the wish that conditions be created to facilitate the resumption of these performances. (Theater Commission of 1933, p. 23)

Again we see that the role of the theater in educating the public is stressed. Although financial considerations may have played a role in this, accounting issues are clearly not dramatically stressed. Rather, art is being mobilized to educate workers to develop an appreciation consistent with finer tastes.

The symbolism of a national stage came to be very important during World War II: The Royal Theater, as a key part of Danish heritage, was a type of opposition to the German occupation. A historian, Neiiendam (1953, p. 689), describes this situation very poetically: "During the dark years of the occupation, the nation's big 'picture book' was a source of light, and what shone from that led through the nation's resurrection into all its future." The comparison of the Royal Theater to a national picture book that shows the highlights of Danish tradition suggests that the theater has a role not only in retelling history but also in helping the nation to orient itself toward its future.

Although in this period as well, commissions looked into the spending of the theater, their recommendations were rather soft.[7] The 1950s and 1960s witnessed a large increase in government grants as a percentage of total expenses—rising to a level of about 85% from about 50% before the war.

During the 1970s several attempts were made to put the brakes on the increasing expenditures of the theater. The Auditor General intervened with heavy criticism of the theater's administration, accounting, and budget procedures. Top members of management were criticized for not having adequate backgrounds in financial matters, and the Auditor General focused on the theater's extravagance, using it as a metaphor for the lack of management control. For example, the Auditor General in 1986 commented on a case in which it was arranged to have a poodle walk across the stage once—a 5-second appearance for which it had to be trained. The Auditor General criticized this use of funds as extravagant, arguing that the artistic benefit was not commensurate with the extremely high cost of arranging it.

The artists, however, attempted to say that art is simply not able to exist under strict financial constraints. A stage manager commented that "art will have difficulty breathing when it is locked up in too strict of limits and under demands for maximal financial returns."

Nevertheless, the recent history of the Royal Theater makes it clear that accounting issues continue to be important. The concepts of accounting systems, budgetary control, professional management, and privatization are used to define problems and solutions. Interestingly, however, in this period of pressure for retrenchment in general in the public sector (and therefore also in the Royal Theater), the building has been renovated yet again, at a cost of billions of kroner.

This set of stories that compose our history of the Royal Theater is quite brief (perhaps so brief that it hides rather than reveals the institutional nature of the theater). These stories suggest that the theater may be seen as an enterprise that is involved in the production of civilization. Taken as a whole, Table 5.1 suggests that (a) accounting and art are both institutional aspects of a theater company that cannot be wisely dispensed with, (b) the relative importance of art and accounting in guiding decisions may change over time, and (c) art and accounting are institutions that in this context struggle against each other without either being able to colonize the other.

Institutional Properties of the Royal Theater

The account presented above suggests that the Royal Theater is an enterprise that hinges on two different institutions, art and accounting, which have their roots in contradictory aspects of civilization and of modernity. The contradiction involved in this drama, however, has not resulted in the systematic conquering of one institution by the other. Rather, the relationship between art and accounting is a dialectical one that underscores the importance of modern civilization.

The remainder of this section analyzes aspects of the institutions involved in the production of the history presented above. On the basis of an analysis of the institutional properties of art and accounting, we specify a set of highly interrelated issues: institutional reflexivity, contradiction and crisis, accountability, and the nature of the dialectic between art and accounting.

THE INSTITUTIONAL PROPERTIES OF ART AND ACCOUNTING

Institutional analysis concerns the practices that exist across large distances of time and space (Giddens, 1984). In looking at art and accounting as institutions, we are referring to their potential for organizing and legitimating social arrangements across time and space. Art and accounting exist outside the Royal Theater, but in the locale of the Royal Theater, art and accounting embody forms of language, power, and legitimation that may act to support or undermine the Royal Theater.

Table 5.2 uses Giddens's (1984) analytical framework, which suggests that the mechanisms of institutional reproduction can be analyzed using the concepts of signification, domination, and legitimation. The table illustrates the nature of these two institutions in the context of the theater.

Table 5.2 is an idealized picture of these two institutions. We suggest that the mechanisms that facilitate the reproduction of bourgeois culture and liberal democracy are supported both by art, through contributing to the enlightenment of the population, and by accounting, through increasing accountability and rationality. As discussed above, the history of the Royal Theater is one of constantly alternating arguments stemming from these two perspectives or institutions embedded in the organization.

As described above, several investigations into the financial and administrative affairs of the Royal Theater have been conducted over the years. Because of these investigations, the Royal Theater has at times been compelled to take on administrative reforms designed to improve administrative efficiency and to increase box office revenues. However, the institution of art has been tremendously strong—it has figured prominently in the parliamentary debates concerning the Royal Theater. Even the Ministry of Finance has had to accept a certain level of freedom (independence from financial or accounting considerations) for art: "The artistic

TABLE 5.2 Institutional Properties of Art and Accounting in the Royal Theater

	ART	ACCOUNTING
Signification	Unity of art forms in the maintenance of high culture	Segmentation of art forms into discrete units so that each is amenable to intervention
Domination	Guarantor of the bourgeois state	Commodification of art
	Ideological basis for liberal democracy	Art as product whose value can be adequately calculated
Legitimation	Coherent, enlightened nation	A visible nation
	Production of civilized persons	Financial accountability
	Creation of a nation of citizens	Rationality in the utilization of resources

production has its own socially protected norms. We from the administrative side have to respect these norms—as long as they comply with the financial appropriation" (Interview with the financial controller, 1989). This statement illustrates the tension in the relationship between art and accounting. Likewise:

It is necessary to go on maintaining that a performance is not the same thing as the production of cars. A performance is a process that continuously changes and develops. That is the essence of art, and that is the real conflict, which is insoluble. (Interview with a member of the opera staff, 1990)

These quotations illustrate that there are important daily confrontations about the degree to which art can be rationalized for administrative purposes.

This analysis suggests that the contradictions between art and accounting within the Royal Theater are visible to all—they are part of the daily routine of the theater. However, these struggles are not merely the result of opposition between occupational groups occurring locally within the theater. They are also bound up with debates and struggles that are part of much larger historical events, suggesting that a deeper understanding of these social relations can be obtained through extracting these social relations from their contemporary presence. These social relations, as the institutional properties of art and accounting, are about 200 years old.

CRISIS AND THE REPRODUCTION OF CIVILIZATION

The confrontations described above between art and accounting are institutional—they have been recurring for about 200 years. Together they reproduce part of a particular version of civilization. We have seen how the nature of the roles art and accounting play in the life of the Royal Theater is often molded in debates taking place with an air of crisis. That is, in these debates, art and accounting seem mobilized against each other—we see attempts to shift the balance between the two in favor of one at the expense of another.

All the crises described in Table 5.1 illustrate that art and accounting are linked. Their relative positions are affected by these battles, but they are never secured because the war is never won. True, directors may be fired; they may choose to resign in protest; there may be retrenchments; and it may be that occasional victories are scored (for example, in the form of large grants given to improve the building). But in no situation has there been a clear colonization of one by the other. It may be that in some periods of time one of the institutions may seem to gain the stage for itself. In a certain sense, of course, this study covers a very limited area of time. Debates about accounting are invariably linked to debates about the role of art in society, just as debates about art are linked to debates about the provision of sound financial management.

In this sense, the crises between art and accounting are related to broad institutional characteristics in a paradoxical way: It is through such recurring crises that the institution of civilization becomes reproduced. The very fact that the same type of crisis recurs regularly draws attention to the point that it is actually through these crises that the broader idea of civilization is reinforced. Although art and accounting are in contradiction with each other, this contradiction seems to be a condition for the continuance of civilization. These outbursts constantly reconfirm the relevance of the properties of civilization.

Civilization is thus reproduced through the recurring confrontations between art and accounting. The precise relationship between art and accounting does change over time: In some situations, the relationship focuses on retrenchment and privatization; in other situations, it focuses on rebuilding the theater; and in yet other situations, art and accounting work together to facilitate more performances. The concrete content of the art/accounting relationship may change, constituting at the level of interaction a durée of the passing moment. However, the background of civilization against which the relationship between art and accounting is played out reconfirms both art and accounting as basic institutions of modern life.

INSTITUTIONAL REFLEXIVITY, ART, AND ACCOUNTING

An important part of modern civilization is institutional reflexivity (Giddens, 1990). Institutional reflexivity refers to a situation in which insights from the past are stored in the institution and used in constructing the future. Similarly, historicity refers to the reflexive making of history through history (Giddens, 1984, 1990).

Reflexivity is an important tool in accounting. Through segmenting the production of art into its components, accountants can calculate whether to support decisions about privatization, evaluate whether to drop an art form, and make decisions concerning the use of capacity, notably the stage facilities. Scheduling of theater activities and aligning the theater's resources with the plays, operas, and ballets to be performed requires a sense of the resources available (performers, workers, playwrights, directors, buildings) and the organization of these resources to produce a set of performances.

But it is not only accounting that is reflexive and makes the theater open to scrutiny—art is as well (Becker, 1982). Since almost the very first day of the theater's activities in the 1771–1772 theater season, a journal (*The Dramatic Journal*) sprang up to provide criticism of the theater's artistic performance. Today, this type of critique is an obligatory part of any newspaper.

As a result of such a systematic critique, the theater's activities were announced to and evaluated for the general public—even for individuals not able to attend performances.[8] This helped to create a sort of public awareness of the theater, bringing at least a sense of the theater's productions to those who would otherwise know nothing of it. This heightened public access helped to portray the theater as more a part of the daily lives of the population, making it possible for the theater to argue that it serves all Danes (a resource in its battles with the state for funding).

Thus, we can see that art is both discursive and reflexive: Art is continually evaluated in public—it does not take place in the dark, but indeed is daily confronted by its critics. In a sense, the critics help in the production of art in that they help to portray it as subjected to evaluation and debate.

Critiques facilitate reflexivity. Through criticism, the pieces of a particular performance are evaluated, fostering a discussion about what is "good" art and what is "bad" art (Becker, 1982). Such evaluations may be contested and disagreed with, but the fact remains that critics turn "nondiscursive" sentiments into discursive ones. For example, the importance placed on performing the classics indicates the institutional nature of art—the importance placed upon (re)producing a particular aesthetic. As Becker (1982, p. 133) comments:

A well-argued and successfully defended aesthetic guides working participants in the production of specific art work. Among the things they keep in
mind in making the innumerable small decisions that cumulatively shape the
work is whether and how those decisions may be defended.

Such a defense may be found in the comments of a 1979 committee on the
objectives of the Royal Theater:

> The committee on the theater's objectives has realized that there for society
> is both a historic and an actual obligation to ensure a theater which will be
> able to look after classical and contemporary theatrical tradition at the same
> time as Danish theatrical culture is supplied with new inspiration and initia-
> tives through experimentation. (Ministry of Cultural Affairs, 1978, p. 69)

It appears that the obligations of the Royal Theater to look after—and
define, it may be added—the classics is an important aspect of its funding.
These obligations of the Royal Theater to define and sustain the classics
and to cultivate new contributions to the tradition are the basis for its
continued relevance as a national stage.

Conclusion

In the Royal Theater, the interplay between the institutions of art and
accounting is manifest and has characterized an important set of issues
since the mid-1700s. Accounting concerns the construction of the type of
visibility that makes organizational activities amenable to calculation and
intervention. Accounting reconstructs the Royal Theater in such a way as
to see a series of separate activities, the cost of which can be calculated.
This is important both for the management of the enterprise and for demonstrating financial accountability, as the Royal Theater has been required
to do since the advent of modern society.

Art concerns the education of the Danish population in one type of
bourgeois aesthetic. Art is oriented toward giving the population access to
higher forms of art and making them able to participate in the liberal democracy characteristic of the post-18th-century Danish nation.

The argument of the chapter is institutional. In other words, it is concerned with the way in which *historical experience* is incorporated in the
theater. The chapter explores 200 years of debates over the art and accounting of the Royal Theater. The analysis portrays art and accounting as
dialectically related in the production of civilization. Both art and accounting, it is argued, are integral to civilization inasmuch as they legitimate

two different spheres of modern life: Accounting is concerned with the intelligent administration of social resources, and art is concerned with the finer aspects of modern existence.

Institutional analysis is also bound up with an emphasis on *extraorganizational phenomena*. The Royal Theater is a locale that has embedded within it two institutions, art and accounting, that link activities within the theater to wider social concerns, such as the values of the population in a liberal democracy and the rationality of modern enterprises. One could say that social relations in the theater may be seen as present in the larger society as well.

Finally, institutional analysis is concerned with *legitimation*. In this chapter, legitimation concerns the mechanisms that justify a particular social arrangement. In the Royal Theater, legitimation is bound up simultaneously with the concern that people be educated in such a way as to be sophisticated and fit to live in a bourgeois democracy, and the concerns for rationality and consistency in managing the affairs of the theater organization.

Civilization is bound up with reflexivity. Accounting's reflexivity concerns the construction of visibility that makes organizational activities amenable to intervention. Accounting reconstructs the Royal Theater in separated activities, allowing the worth of each activity to be better calculated. This is important both for the management of the enterprise and for the financial accountability to which the Royal Theater is subjected in a civilized country.

Art's reflexivity is somewhat different inasmuch as it is more concerned with the constitution of aesthetics. Through critics, the theater's activities are scrutinized publicly. The activities of the theater act to reflexively mobilize art as beauty in the form of classical plays, operas, and ballets.

Art and accounting may in some sense be contradictory. However, in order to understand the stable recurrence of the crises between them, it is important to understand that art and accounting are to be understood not only as mutually contradicting institutions but also as institutions dialectically involved in the production of civilization, and indeed democracy as we know it: Together they combat forces leading away from civilization or toward an old or new form of absolute monarchy.

Notes

1. This period of time is too long for a very detailed review of the conduct of the Royal Theater. However, in contrast to histories of organizations that concentrate on the period after World War II (e.g., DiMaggio, 1986a), this present study is able to do more than merely

identify change and the emergence of new practices; it is able to integrate ideas about change with ideas about continuity.

2. The data for this chapter are largely a set of commission reports (see References), a set of accounts by historians, and a set of interviews with people presently employed in the Royal Theater.

3. The relationship between talk and action, however, is not simple and linear (Brunsson, 1985). For talk to become action, talk may need to be repeated several times (March & Olsen, 1989).

4. The history of the theater in Europe and the history of theater in the United States are quite different. Montias (1986) shows that in Europe theaters were much more in the public eye than in the United States, because in Europe they were seen as a medium for educating and civilizing the population. For example, in 1774, the national theater of Austria was founded in order to develop "good taste and the improvement of morals"; in Germany in 1808, the Prussian theater was seen as an "educational establishment." Likewise, in most other European countries, art was heavily supported by the state. In the United States—where royal patronage was nonexistent and patronage of any kind was weak—there was largely no public support for theaters.

5. Ludvig Holberg and Adam Oehlenschläger are two of the most famous Danish authors. They are an essential part of the Danish classical theatrical repertoire.

6. Observe the comments of the historian Neiiendam (1953, p. 603): "Unlike the universities, the theater does not only relate to the few, no it relates to everybody, to the immediate feeling; you do not need to be refined to be able to like beautiful plays; you only need an open mind for beauty and the good. Therefore, it was democratic in its act."

7. For example, in one instance, a group concluded after about a half year of study that six janitors might be unnecessary (interview with an opera singer, 1990s).

8. Since the mid-1830s, when the king's accounts became available to the public during the preconstitutional period, there has been a struggle over the financing of the Royal Theater because of differential access to its performances: Citizens who live far from the theater, the argument goes, should not contribute to it financially because they tend not to use it very much. A dramatic account of this is provided by a comment made (in reference to a parliamentary debate) by the Director of the Ballet, August Bournonville, in 1859: "[Some] regarded arts and poetry as a luxury, unbecoming of a nation of farmers and cattle people. Envy of the capital's luxuries and the intellectuals' finer treats also played a part, and finally the old song about the poor, little country was repeated over and over again" (Ministry of Cultural Affairs, 1978).

6

The Incorporation of Multiple Institutional Models

Organizational Field Multiplicity and the Role of Actors

FINN BORUM

ANN WESTENHOLZ

Introduction

THE CASE

In 1917 a Danish businessmen's society launched efforts to create a business school on a par with other institutions of higher education. The entrepreneurs succeeded, and the final product of their efforts is today known as the Copenhagen Business School (CBS). However, this story of building an institution and obtaining its incorporation into an exclusive organizational field also harbors a concealed story about the organization's incorporation of different institutional models. The CBS of today is endowed with elements of five institutional models: private organization, public organization, university, political organization, and international business school.

AUTHORS' NOTE: We would like to thank the other contributors to this book for their helpful collaboration and their verbal and written constructive comments, which have greatly facilitated the production of this chapter. Special thanks go to W. Richard Scott, Theresa Lant, Dennis Gioia, Søren Christensen, Finn Junge-Jensen, and Kristian Kreiner.

We contend that the incorporation of several institutional models in the CBS of today can be explained in terms of two factors that mutually affect each other. First, the historical development of the CBS and of the field of higher education has, over time, introduced different institutional models into the composition of our focal organization. Second, various types of socially constructed actors within the organizational field have, through their actions, promoted or contested the various institutional models. Thus, our analysis of the case of the CBS develops two aspects of institutional theory: (a) the organizational field as a provider of multiple institutional models and (b) the role of actors within the organizational field.

ORGANIZATIONAL FIELDS AS PROVIDERS
OF MULTIPLE INSTITUTIONAL MODELS

New institutional theory argues that, by belonging to or entering into an organizational field, an organization becomes exposed to pressures to adopt certain patterns of behavior in order to achieve legitimacy and obtain resources (DiMaggio & Powell, 1983). Valued institutional components or "building blocks" (Meyer & Rowan, 1977, p. 345) may include social constructs like rules, procedures, roles, management systems, and structural blueprints, or more elaborated macro-constructions, such as university systems. An institution is "a human mental construct for a coherent system of shared (enforced) norms that regulate individual interactions in recurrent situations" (Sjöstrand, 1992, p. 1011) and may take many forms.

Institutional theorists vary with regard to their emphasis on the multiplicity of belief and rule systems (Scott, 1994b, p. 75). The case study that follows demonstrates that the institutional models provided by the organizational field and supported by various subcultures may be multiple and contradictory. The more dynamic and multiplex the organizational field is, the greater is the probability that a focal organization will reveal multiplicity—the result of processes through which institutional components are incorporated, through coercion, professionalization, or imitation, and "bricolaged" by constituents (DiMaggio, 1988, pp. 11-13).

These processes can partly be understood in terms of coercive, mimetic, or normative isomorphic processes (DiMaggio & Powell, 1983, pp. 150-154). *Coercive isomorphism* results from common formal and informal pressures exerted on the organization by other organizations and by cultural expectations within the organizational field. *Mimetic isomorphism* occurs when an organization, often as a response to uncertainty, models itself after similar organizations in its field that it perceives to be more legitimate or successful. *Normative isomorphism* stems primarily from professionalization resting on formal education and the elaboration of professional networks. As a result, an organization may incorporate multiple institutional models.

However, in order to emphasize the entrepreneurial aspect of organizational change and institution building, we will regard the incorporation of institutional models not only from a field and dissemination perspective but also from the perspective of the focal organization and its related actors as instituters of the institutional models.

These may differ across different groups of actors, but organizational actors may also institute many of the multiple institutional models to which they have been exposed during the organization's history. Not all of these are equally important or manifest at a given point in time, but models that play a modest role or are latent may be evoked by actors and events and thus lead to organizational change. Furthermore, over time an actor may adhere to different institutional models, adding to institutional complexity.

THE ROLE OF ACTORS WITHIN
THE ORGANIZATIONAL FIELD

Actors are brought into our analysis not in the sense of isolated rational-choice individuals but as social constructions (Scott, 1994b). As actors, and by their effort to reproduce their role, they are both using and reproducing organizational structures that make use of broader institutional models (Brint & Karabel, 1991, p. 345; DiMaggio, 1988, pp. 13-14; Oliver, 1991, pp. 151-159; Powell, 1991, p. 194; Scott, 1994a, p. 77, Sjöstrand, 1992, p. 1014). Such actors may engage in both anticipatory and obligatory action (March & Olsen, 1989, pp. 21-29).

Actors are perceived as being "equipped" with socially constructed goals/interests and cognitive schemata, which include general and specific knowledge about the organization, specifications of its attributes, and their interrelationship (Bartunek, 1988, p. 138).

Assuming that actors act anticipatorily, their behavior is strategic and consequential. In pursing their interests, they select and promote organizational forms, rules, and procedures, marshaling them to their support. To promote their own interests, such organizational actors may fight for change by linking up with specific segments of the given field, or they may fight for stability by linking up with other segments of the field. Our analysis will focus on the actors' interests in organizational control, legitimation, and acquisition of resources.

The actors' options include a menu of institutional models and components from which they can choose. Furthermore, actors may feel compelled to choose, because they experience the menu of structural components and the underlying institutional models as inconsistent.

Assuming that actors act obligatorily, they follow a logic of appropriateness. They act according to an institutional model (schema) and related structural components; these are often taken for granted. In their effort to reproduce their role as actors, they also reproduce or attempt to reproduce the conceded structural components. This may be an unobtrusive process rooted in daily routines and practices. But, within a dynamic and multiplex organizational field, conflicting assumptions may be sustained by various actors. In such situations, actors may have to fight for their own taken-for-granted assumptions in their attempts to reproduce themselves.

We thus argue that the organization is a social construction created by socially constructed organizational actors: institutional entrepreneurs— reproducers or destroyers—who through their actions strive to control certain interests and preserve specific frames of reference. This happens within opportunity fields (Brint & Karabel, 1991) that offer possibilities for obtaining resources and legitimacy by pursuing particular strategies. The actors may be more or less active, as will be indicated by referring to the passive/active scale of acquiescence, compromise, avoidance, defiance, and manipulation, formulated by Oliver (1991).

IMPLICATIONS

We argue that the CBS of today is endowed with five institutional models: private organization, public organization, university, political organization, and international business school. These models reflect both the specific genesis of the CBS and the general history of the field of higher education in Denmark.

The coexistence of several institutional models within the CBS reflects both organizational schizophrenia and a potential for redirecting the organization according to changes in the organizational field and in its institutional environments. Beneath the institutional surface, contradictory orientations substantiate an interpretation of the CBS that focuses on ongoing and future institutional change and transformation. Thus, our case study contributes by strengthening the institutional perspective's treatment of organizational change processes.

A Historical Analysis of the Shaping of the CBS: Seven Phases[1]

THE PRIVATE BUSINESS SCHOOL (1917–1951)

In the last half of the nineteenth century, agricultural, industrial, and artisan education were well established, and industry and agriculture had established institutions of higher education: the Technical University, founded in 1828, and the Royal Veterinary and Agricultural University, founded in 1858. The business sector had no comparable educational institution—only a few, small, private commercial schools.

In 1880 the Danish Society for the Advancement of Business Education (SABE) was established by a group of businessmen in Copenhagen, with the purpose of "offering to the young ones a cheap education supervised by excellent teachers . . . " (Vibæk & Kobbernagel, 1980, p. 7). Funds were raised through a private subscription, and evening courses for commercial apprentices, primarily within retail trade, were launched in January 1881. At the beginning of the 20th century, these activities had expanded considerably, and, combined under the name of Copenhagen Business College, the institution moved into its own, new building and offered evening courses in modern languages, bookkeeping, commercial law, correspondence, typing, and stenography (pp. 150-151).

Parallel to establishing a school for apprentices, thought was given—both within and outside the circles of the Copenhagen Business College and SABE—to the possibility of launching more advanced studies. After a couple of unsuccessful attempts by the head of the Copenhagen Business College to offer advanced courses in the form of a series of lectures, the chairman of SABE proposed launching a new program in 1917 with the aim of "providing younger businessmen with the possibility of gaining a thorough theoretical knowledge of the various fields of modern commercial life, involving insights into subjects such as economics, commercial law, etc., which in many cases constitute the background for a genuine understanding of specific commercial transactions" (Vibæk & Kobbernagel, 1980, p. 180).

To distinguish this education from the apprentice-like education provided by the Business College, the new teaching activities were located in a separate section of the Business College's building under the name of Business School Department and defined as an open study, implying no compulsory attendance (pp. 179-180). Thus, the strategy of the institutional entrepreneur (SABE) was to isolate its new school from the existing SABE-controlled organization (the Business College) with which it might be confused.

In 1922, when the first 2-year evening course concluded, SABE's board seized the opportunity to further demonstrate that the teaching of the Business School Department differed from that of the Business College, by changing the department's name to Business School.

Another element of the entrepreneurial strategy was to link the new organization to the field of higher education by incorporating elements from it. These comprised day courses, a dissertation as a prerequisite for obtaining a diploma, giving the teacher in accounting the title "docent" in

1922 (the university title for associate professors at that time), and introduction of a "Diploma Examination" to indicate a higher level of education (p. 181).

In 1924 a 2-year day course in economics was established. SABE's board found that the school's educational level was now on a par with the education provided by the Danish Technical University and the Royal Veterinary and Agricultural University, as well as with foreign universities (pp. 181-182).

The Business School was, however, very demanding of resources, requiring extensive negotiations in order to secure external financial support for its activities. In 1925-1926, the Merchants' Guild contributed DKK 2,500, and the state granted DKK 9,000 (raised 2 years later to DKK 32,000). The student tuition fee amounted to DKK 50,000, but SABE contributed only DKK 5,000, though SABE also assumed the liability for an accumulated deficit of DKK 65,000 (p. 185).

However, in return for financial support, the state (the Ministry of Commerce) demanded the establishment of a supervisory committee, headed by a senior civil officer from the Ministry of Commerce, who would be authorized to certify curricula and exams. This was a two-edged sword: On the one hand, the Business School achieved a larger degree of public recognition and funding; on the other, from 1925, SABE, which in principle owned the CBS until 1965, had to face a restricted, less autonomous position. In spite of this, SABE still felt itself in full control and, during the 1930s, it focused its efforts on the further development of the Copenhagen Business School (p. 101).

The school continued to accumulate a growing deficit, resulting in subsequent crises—the first one in 1943-1944. However, in spite of this, SABE declined offers from the State during the 1950s to increase public support. SABE wanted to keep public support just below 50% of the annual budget, to be able to claim to be "a majority shareholder" (p. 188).

Until 1951 no state acts were passed concerning the Business School. Its activities were regulated by a charter issued by SABE and supplemented by rules issued by either SABE or the Ministry of Commerce. In 1951 the first Act on Business Schools reserved to the Ministry of Commerce the right to yield accreditation to privately owned business schools and confirmed the supervisory committee's role as the responsible authority. Furthermore, the law protected the name "Business School" and the titles of the graduates. Several acts have subsequently been passed that regulate the specific activities of the CBS.

CONVERSION INTO A PUBLIC ORGANIZATION (1951–1965)

During the 1950s, SABE and the Business School faced increasing problems caused by a combination of the Business School's operating deficit, growing dependence on state subsidies, and expanding activities: "The Business School showed a continually increasing deficit. Even though tuition fees were raised a couple of times, the problems were insoluble by this means since students at other institutions of higher education were not required to pay tuition" (p. 99).

The financial problems were partly solved by the state's increasing its reimbursement (from the 1948–1949 school year to the 1961–1962 school year, there was an increase from 21% to 48% in total operating costs), and partly by SABE covering the annual deficit through earned interest. Still, SABE did not wish the state support to be increased beyond 48%—SABE wanted to remain the majority contributor and thus in control of its own activities (p. 99).

Parallel to SABE's becoming increasingly dependent on the state, the relations between SABE and the Business School became more conflictual. This should be seen in relation to the expansion and changing composition of the CBS faculty. Whereas the first CBS teachers recruited in the 1920s were nonacademics, university graduates made their entry during the 1930s and the 1940s. Of the first six full professors, five had a university education.

This recruitment facilitated the imitation of structural components from the university model, and with it came a network orientation and a mind-set different from that of the business sector. Thus, the professional quest for autonomy and control of their methods of work was articulated (Mintzberg, 1979).

In 1953–1954, the status of the CBS in relation to SABE became a topic of discussion. Should the Business School and the Business College be perceived as separate institutions from a legal perspective (p. 103)? SABE's board wanted to maintain control of "its" commercial school's curricula. The directors of the schools, on the other hand, resisted this influence, stressing that the two schools were subject to different statutes (p. 104). In 1954 the relationship among the three parties was settled by a "constitution," which by and large confirmed the status quo but strengthened the directors' authority relative to SABE, as well as their control of the school's budget and curricula.

In December 1956 the two schools' directors asked the Ministry of Commerce to confirm that SABE's administrator was not their superior—

which the ministry did (p. 106). In 1957, at the commemoration of the founding of the school, the new director of the CBS, Poul Winding, referred to himself as "rector"—the traditional title of university heads— and the SABE board of directors tacitly consented.

The situation of SABE became even more complicated because of developments within the field of higher education. By 1960 the Ministry of Education had abolished the remaining student fees at all educational institutions under its auspices, as part of the ongoing democratization of access to the educational system. This made it increasingly difficult to justify why, for instance, the Technical University collected no tuition fees from its students, but the Business School did.

The Ministry of Commerce, which had several educational institutions under its auspices, in an internal note raised the issue of the state's taking over tuition fees for students of the CBS for social reasons and calculated the costs involved. In 1961 the note was circulated among the institutions for comments.

SABE protested strongly against the plans and, at a meeting in May 1961, it argued that:

> [A]bolishing tuition fees would separate the schools and the business sector from one another and have a demoralizing effect on the students. The result of abolishing tuition fees might be less committed students. In addition to this, SABE feared that abolishing tuition fees would result in the State gaining more influence over the administration of the schools. (p. 113)

In order to gain legitimacy and resources, SABE had let the CBS enter the field of higher educational institutions. However, this implied both an increasing resource dependency on the state and pressure from the state on the CBS to become more like the other institutions of that field. This left the initial entrepreneur (SABE) in a dilemma, and, wanting to maintain control of its institution, until 1961 it defied the ministry.

It was still unclear how to recoup the annual deficit in this situation, but the government was in favor of financial support. In December 1961 the state took over the responsibility of paying students' tuition fees. Prior to this measure, the business schools were transferred from the domain of the Ministry of Commerce to that of the Ministry of Education. In spite of the previous conflict with the Ministry of Commerce, SABE was not pleased with the transfer because it regarded the Ministry of Commerce as its natural counterpart.

These decisions being implemented, SABE ceased to cover the annual deficit accumulated by the Business School. Nor did the state cover the deficit, but it allowed the CBS to transfer the deficit to the following year

(p. 114). As a result, the Business School accumulated a growing deficit—entered in the accounts as "expected to be covered by the State" (p. 114).

From 1962 to 1964 a Business School Commission worked on introducing a new bill that would regulate business schools and colleges. During this period, nothing was done to solve the problems of the Business School's growing deficit.

The bill distinguished between schools owned by associations and by foundations. Operating costs of the former would only be subsidized 84% by the state, but the latter type would be covered 100% by the state. On May 26, 1965, the new Act on Business Schools was passed, forcing the associations to turn themselves into foundations (p. 115).

ACHIEVING UNIVERSITY STATURE (1961–1975)

Right from the CBS's early years, SABE introduced elements from the university model through mimetic mechanisms as a means to achieve status as an institution of higher education. The first examples from the early 1920s have been mentioned; later important examples were:

1929: Institution of a gold medal thesis award;

1935: The two first full professorships.

Later on, the CBS faculty engaged in attempts to achieve professional status. Through normative and mimetic processes, the faculty gradually incorporated new institutional elements in order to obtain university stature. Important examples of such components were:

1959: Introduction of the Ph.D. degree;

1963: Introduction of the Master of Science degree;

1965: Introduction of the doctor's degree.

The 1965 Business School Act established the CBS as belonging to the field of higher educational institutions, changed its status to a foundation, and imposed a new structure that decoupled SABE from the CBS's main activities: teaching and research.

This was done through distinguishing among three governing bodies: the supervisory board, the presidency, and the faculty council. The faculty council was controlled by professors and directors of studies and was assigned primary responsibility for all academic issues. The act clearly confirmed the professionals' (faculty's) autonomy from SABE in academic questions; the supervisory board, which was controlled by SABE, was still in principle responsible for economic and administrative issues.

This structure was the outcome of two pressures put on SABE: pressure by the state to become a public institution, and pressure by faculty to achieve their independence relative to SABE and its Business College (p. 200).

The structural solution was not as radical as turning the CBS into a state institution. At that time, however, neither business sector interests nor the government was in favor of "socializing" business education (p. 198). In the same vein, neither faculty was interested in breaking completely away from SABE. During prolonged and tough negotiations, from 1962 to 1965, the faculty's attitude, represented by the faculty council, was that " . . . this council should hold sovereign power in issues concerning teaching and research in order to furnish CBS with the same status as other institutions of higher education . . . and the only reason for letting SABE keep some influence on teaching and research was a wish to maintain good relations with the association and the business sector" (p. 199).

Thus, the state and the faculty appeared to be defying SABE. The latter subsequently had to face the fact that the CBS had been converted into a foundation on which SABE had only limited formal influence, via its representation on the supervisory board. In their efforts, faculty referred to the tradition of professional autonomy within institutions of higher education and exploited the possibilities offered by the new legislation.

The CBS's status within the realm of higher educational institutions was confirmed in 1967, when it was accepted as a member of the newly established Council of Presidents. The CBS's formal statute and structure were altered twice during the following decade (in 1970 and in 1975), reflecting a continued approximation toward a standard model for organizations of higher education.

A final important isomorphic process was the CBS's adoption of the university job classification system in 1973. The implications were that teaching ceased to be a separately paid activity, and research became an obligation for all faculty members.

FORMALIZING THE POLITICAL ORGANIZATION (1970–1974)

Achieving status as a public institution made the CBS more exposed to the general political influences of society than had been the case during its era as a business sector school. Two important examples, which occurred even before the CBS had been fully transformed into an institution of higher education, were the democratization movement during the 1960s and the student revolt in 1968.

The president and the faculty council did not wait for legislative changes to be imposed upon the field by the state but entered into negotiations in order to cope with the growing pressure for participation in decision processes from students, faculty, and administrative staff. As a result, the CBS implemented a new statute, in February 1970, which not only represented an adaptation to democratization pressures but also, to a large extent, anticipated the contents of the University Law of 1973.

The composition of the supervisory board was changed to include the president and the vice president. The Faculty Council was replaced by an Academic Council and two School Councils (for the Faculty of Economics and the Faculty of Modern Languages). The "professorial power" was broken as *all* faculty members—including nontenured—obtained voting rights and eligibility to participate in the governing bodies. Students were ensured representation and parity in newly established Study Committees. Each department established its own council composed of faculty and students (p. 205).

In June 1973 a law applying to all universities and institutions of higher education further enforced the political model. All governing bodies were now to be composed of elected representatives of faculty, students, and technical-administrative staff. The latter group was not, however, represented in the parity student-faculty Study Committees that were in charge of educational issues.

In its Statute of 1970, the CBS had allowed for this development, which made it very simple to implement the necessary modifications and the new statute when it became effective in February 1975. The supervisory board's influence was further reduced. At the same time, the board was enlarged with two student representatives and one technical-administrative representative. This meant that SABE now held only 6 of the 11 seats—a situation that strongly reduced its possibilities for exerting influence on the CBS. Its remaining influence was primarily obtained through subsidizing activities that could not be covered by the state's budget for operating costs.

The Academic Council and the two School Councils (with 21 members each) now became the central governing bodies, in control of the most important decisions regarding resource allocation and staffing. The seats on these three governing bodies were occupied by faculty, students, and technical-administrative staff, in the proportion of 4:2:1. Members of the decision-making bodies were appointed through periodic elections, inspired by the elective system of local governments.

According to the statute, each of the central governing bodies was obliged to appoint an executive committee responsible for the budget. Over time, these committees were supplemented with multiple permanent or ad hoc committees, and the decision-making process often entailed issues circulating for lengthy periods among various committees and governing bodies.

Thus, rather than the former emphasis on expeditious action, a political model emphasizing multiple constituencies and process aspects—election to governing bodies and positions, interest group formation, students' participation in decision processes, and organizational politics—was introduced into the CBS.

REINFORCING THE PUBLIC ORGANIZATION (1974–1985)

At the time when the CBS achieved university status, the public control of these institutions changed dramatically: The Ministry of Education replaced the previous high degree of autonomy with central control.

This was a response to the uncontrolled growth in expenditures caused by unrestricted access to higher education. Ministerial officials lost faith in supply and demand as self-regulating forces. At the same time, the government was determined to stop the growth in public spending. Furthermore, the Ministry became increasingly suspicious of the ability of the previously installed political organization to handle retrenchment and reallocation.

In response, the Ministry implemented a system of central planning and resource allocation. Students' access to higher educational institutions, annual budgets calculated according to the intake of students, student graduation ratios, and student-teacher ratios were all regulated. In addition, efforts were made centrally to restructure programs of study in order to create a more standardized and flexible educational system (Christensen, 1986).

The CBS was, however, regarded as a growth area; education aiming at the business sector was given priority. From 1981 to 1989, the CBS's grants were tripled. The influx of students and faculty doubled. Consequently, the CBS was not subjected to budget cuts similar to those imposed on other institutions of higher education.

However, growth and the new systems of regulation increased the need for administrative staff (Lange, 1992, pp. 55-62). This was satisfied by almost doubling the administrative expenditures during the 1980s. In 1992 the CBS had an administrative staff of 322 persons (part-time), and faculty comprised 304 persons (full-time). The expansion of the administrative staff implied both external recruitment of persons with a public administration orientation and a strengthening of the CBS's central administration.

REVIVAL OF THE PRIVATE ORGANIZATION (1985–PRESENT)

During the 1980s the political organizational model institutionalized in the 1970s became subject to increasing criticism. This was part of a general political preoccupation with modernizing the public sector, which included substituting bureaucratic control and participatory decision systems with management systems inspired by private sector organizations.

At the CBS, this was reflected in much energy being allocated to internal discussions about organizational restructuring (1989–1991), strategy formulation (1989–1991), and revision of the CBS's statute (1990–1992). These discussions involved the CBS's governing bodies, including department councils, study committees, task forces, unions, rank-and-file faculty, technical-administrative staff, and students. These discussions were mainly initiated by members of the decision-making bodies who experienced outside pressures from the Ministry and the business community—and who perhaps also felt these pressures were in keeping with their own institutional schemata.

The CBS may have been particularly receptive to this type of pressure for two reasons. First, the CBS had tripled its population of students from 1970 to 1992, and it had become the second-largest institution of higher education in Denmark. This growth reflected, in part, the general growth in the number of students; the CBS was compelled to increase its intake of students because the CBS candidates were considered to encounter favorable employment opportunities. However, in line with the general pressure for cuts in public spending, the increase in allocated resources did not counterbalance the expanding intake of students (Junge-Jensen, 1992, p. 80). This expansion created a multitude of problems, resulting in recurrent attacks on the contents and quality of the CBS's curricula, research activities, and administrative systems.

Second, throughout its historical development, the CBS has been exposed to and embraced by the managerialism of the private business sector. This was the first institutional model to be incorporated, of which the supervisory council represents a formal, structural reminiscence. Faculty members are exposed to this model via their research projects and the content of their courses, oriented toward the private sector. Thus, the CBS may be open to a revitalization of the private model. The internal debate reflects the conflicting institutional models at work among the CBS's faculty: the CBS as a private organization versus a university versus a political organization.

A wide range of strategies—defiance, avoidance, and compromise— were employed by internal and external constituents in their efforts to contest, modify, or defend the "political regime." These efforts did not lead to a change of the formal, imposed structure, but the process built up tension and contributed to conflictual relations among faculty, the former "owner" (SABE), and business-sector interests in search of control.

This placed the president in the difficult position of an intermediary, as revealed in connection with criticism concerning the CBS statute formulated in 1990–1991 by SABE's then-chairman of the supervisory board. His proposals for a modification of the statute were inspired by well-known organizational structures from the business community: a board of directors, a more distinct definition of management responsibilities, and less participation. He argued that the supervisory board's role should be more like that of a board of directors; in other words, a return to the situation before 1961.

The proposal was presented at an open meeting, called by the CBS president, for faculty, staff, and students. It revealed a distinct difference between the supervisory council and faculty in terms of their rhetoric and managerial thinking. The conclusion was that the idea launched earlier by the president, that the CBS modify its management structure ahead of the other institutions of higher education, was not feasible. Being part of a wider organizational field makes difficult local changes of a general, codified, formal structure.

The discussions in and around the CBS were put to an end by the introduction of a new University Statute in April 1993, which imposed a new formal structure on institutions of higher education. At the CBS, this meant that the powers of the supervisory council, the president, and the academic council were strengthened. External representatives were nominated to the Academic Council and the School Councils, which were reduced in size.

The department councils were replaced by department boards, and the positions of department managers and directors of studies were strengthened. In keeping with the principles underlying the general legislation on cooperation—a widely accepted institutional form—the composition of the governing bodies henceforth reflects a distinction between management and employee representatives. In principle, the elective procedures for faculty, technical-administrative, and student representatives to boards and committees remain the same; however, the role of participation and the utilization of committees have been reduced.

ELEMENTS OF AN INTERNATIONAL
BUSINESS SCHOOL (1985–PRESENT)

The CBS has always been characterized by an international orientation by virtue of some of the subject matter taught (foreign languages and international trade). The same applies to SABE, which early on established schools abroad that it still operates. Internationalization is also mentioned as one of its present four strategic orientations (Junge-Jensen, 1992, p. 82). The growth in the number of the CBS students studying abroad, foreign students studying at the CBS, foreign visiting professors at the CBS, and the CBS staffs' publications in foreign languages indicates a strengthening during the 1980s of its international orientation (Vestergård, pp. 164-186, in Lange, 1992).

In the late 1980s, the president took the initiative as an institutional entrepreneur, acting in relation to both internal segments—the supervisory board and the faculty—and external segments—the ministry and the business sector. The strategy involved efforts to compromise by balancing expectations, to avoid institutional pressures by changing activities and domains, and to shape expectations via importing constituents, shaping values, and focusing attention.

Furthermore, imitating the activities and approaches of foreign business schools became an element of the overall strategy. This internationalization introduced a new institutional environment and a new basis for legitimation, most visible in the Community of the European Management Schools (CEMS) comprising selected European business schools and organizations. Associated with internationalization, new ideas have found their way into the CBS: the MBA (Master of Business Administration) degree, APIM (Advanced Program in International Marketing and Management, a semester course based on international student exchange), and SCANCOR (Scandinavian Consortium for Organizational Research, an international faculty exchange network of collaboration between Scandinavian institutions of higher education and Stanford University). Furthermore, new funding possibilities, via student fees, sponsoring, and participation in European programs, make it possible to a limited degree to offer faculty special remuneration for some activities.

One of the president's responses to outside skepticism and criticism has been to keep the CBS's constituents better informed about ongoing activities. The format chosen since 1991 is an annual report, equivalent to those of private enterprises, with a Danish and an English version. In the annual report, a selection of ongoing innovative activities is highlighted, and the special character of research and education at an international business school is emphasized.

Several constituents—internal as well as external—may be attracted by an international orientation. At the same time, the orientation toward an international network of related institutions may contribute in the long run to easing the resource dependency on the Ministry of Education.

Conclusion

ORGANIZATIONAL FIELDS AS PROVIDERS
OF MULTIPLE INSTITUTIONAL MODELS

During its history, elements of five different institutional models have been introduced or reinforced at the CBS:

1. The private firm (instituted in phase 1, reinforced in phase 6)
2. The public institution (instituted in phase 2, reinforced in phase 5)
3. The university (instituted in phases 1, 2, and 3)
4. The political organization (instituted during phase 4)
5. The international business school (elements assembled and added during phase 7)

Our analysis has focused upon three important organizational aspects of these institutional models: organizational control, organizational products and processes yielding legitimacy, and the main resource provider. On these dimensions, the five institutional models can roughly be described as depicted in Table 6.1.

The institutional model of the private firm was introduced by SABE in the first phase of the CBS's development. In their efforts to gain resources and legitimacy, entrepreneurs led the CBS into the field of higher education—an anticipatory action of imitative elements that had unintended consequences. First, the Ministry had to be given some control of the organization, which led to further coercive isomorphic pressures. Deficient resource provisions from both private business and students caused the CBS to became increasingly dependent on the state for resources. Consequently, the entrepreneurs lost control of their organization, and another institutional model—the public organization—became dominant.

With its incorporation into the field of higher education, the CBS was exposed to obligatory actions from the Ministry of Education, which, essentially through coercive processes, worked to make the CBS resemble the other institutions in the field. Furthermore, the CBS was exposed to the anticipatory and obligatory actions of its faculty, which, through normative and mimetic processes, installed the university institution. Some elements of this model were introduced by SABE from the very beginning, in the quest to acquire the status of a higher educational institution. Additional components were imported via the professional orientation of a large part of the faculty members. These were supported by the Ministry of Education, which was inclined to further the CBS's

TABLE 6.1 Institutional Models and Dimensions

	Organizational Control	*Legitimating Product or Process*	*Main Resource Provider*
1. The private firm	Management	Business-relevant studies	Business sector and students
2. The public institution	Ministry, administrators	Standard outputs and procedures	Public sector
3. The university	Faculty	Knowledge production	Public sector
4. The political organization	Multiple constituencies	Participative processes	Public sector
5. The international business school	Management	International standards	Public sector, business sector, international students and funds

isomorphism with universities and other higher educational institutions before resources became an issue.

Normative and coercive field processes led to the incorporation of the next institutional model, the political organization, which left the responsibility of organizational control to boards, councils, and committees composed of faculty, technical-administrative staff, and students. This was a response to the anticipatory actions of students demanding influence in educational institutions. As with the public institution and the university model, the public sector remained the main resource provider for the CBS.

The unmanageable resource demand from institutions of higher education forced the Ministry of Education to take anticipatory action. Accordingly, the Ministry reinforced and strengthened the public institutions within the field through the 1970s and 1980s. The process was mainly coercive and emphasized centralization and tighter control, through standards for resource allocation. It furthermore led to a strengthening of the local administration at the CBS.

However, reinforcing the public institution model did not solve the fundamental resource problem, and, in the 1980s, the private firm model gained strength as the social-political climate changed toward liberalization and managerialism. Several actors—the Ministry of Education, SABE, and parts of the CBS's faculty—were active in reinforcing this dormant model at the CBS through both anticipatory and obligatory mechanisms. Some components were imposed by the Ministry: students' tuition fee programs under the Open University Act, increased emphasis on business-sector relevance, and support to strengthen local management.

In this process, SABE, which under a liberal government had experienced a revival, played an active role by publicly criticizing the prevailing political organization and arguing for components corresponding to those of the private firm. As a result, SABE has regained some of its lost influence on the CBS.

As a supplement to these four institutional models, the international business school is currently emerging as a fifth model at the CBS. This social construction may distinguish itself profoundly from the four previous ones in that it changes the focus of comparison from local, national standards to international standards. In many cases, the faculty members at the CBS will collaborate more closely with colleagues at foreign universities than with colleagues at the CBS, and they will become more internationally mobile.

The CBS is growing increasingly dependent on adhering to this model. The business community, the Ministry, the politicians, and the faculty agree that, in order to guarantee high quality, institutions of higher education have to meet international standards. Via professional networks, faculty members are increasingly identifying themselves with foreign colleagues rather than with their local peers. Concurrently with the reduction in public subsidies allocated to the CBS, the management and the faculty have been looking for additional economic resources in some of the international programs administered by Nordic and European agencies. However, obtaining resources from these requires legitimation in terms of products, structural forms, and processes that often differ from those required by prevailing national standards.

This recent institutional model at the CBS may have a considerable impact, in that it may both further revive the earliest model—the private organization—and yet be compatible with the character of a university. On the other hand, the model of an international business school conflicts with that of a political organization, and so it will require some entrepreneurial work in order to be reconciled with the public institution model.

THE ROLE OF ACTORS WITHIN THE ORGANIZATIONAL FIELD

The historical analysis of the CBS has not produced a portrait of an organization that merely submits to field forces passively. As a supplement to exogenously generated change, a picture has emerged of several socially constructed internal and external actors who, through their interaction, contribute actively to shaping the institution. In a multiplex organizational field, where several institutional models are present, actors do this by using and fighting for particular structural components in order to support their own (socially constructed) interests, or by fighting for the structural components that they assume to be most appropriate. Control has shifted between the founders (SABE), the professionals (faculty members), and the state (the Ministry of Education). Aside from these actors, students and administrative staff have also been active in the struggle for control. No single constituency is in complete control today: Within the organizational field of higher education, the CBS both relates to different institutional environments and internally carries their schemata.

The five institutional models identified correspond to different rationalized myths about the CBS's control structure, raison d'être and core processes, and relations with its environment. These myths express not only values but also beliefs about the relationship between various organizational parts, and between the CBS and its environment. As such, these five models are frames or schemas, "best understood as a generalized cognitive structure, framework, or template people use to impose structure on, and impart meaning to, some particular domain. . . . Although schemata do not include affective and behavioral components, they cue and are cued by affect and behavior" (Bartunek, 1988, p. 138).

An institutional model introduced in one phase is not erased by those of the following phases. Organizational actors and segments of the environment continue to carry the old models, and so old models may coexist with the new ones; old models may survive in subcultures, or by being related to specific spheres of activity—or they may withdraw into latency from where they may later be evoked. This was the case with the institutions of university and political organization during the revival of the private firm.

Thus, the CBS of today is imprinted with several, and often conflicting, socially constructed institutional models, which represent both possibilities and constraints to entrepreneurial efforts toward organizational change. As none of the internal and external actors is in full control of the CBS, different trajectories seem possible, so much more so as the organizational field to which the CBS belongs is itself subject to transformation.

Note

1. Unless otherwise specified, all references in this chapter are to Vibæk and Kobbernagel (1980).

III. INSTITUTIONAL EFFECTS ON FIRMS AND FIELDS

7

The Competence View of the Firm

What Can Modern Economists Learn From Philip Selznick's Sociological Theory of Leadership?

CHRISTIAN KNUDSEN

1. Neo-Institutionalism and the Convergence Between Economics and Sociology

The intellectual fields of sociology and economics have traditionally been separated by a deep gulf. This gulf is due to the fundamental incompatibility of the different models of human behavior employed in the two disciplines. For decades, economics has been regarded as almost synonymous with the maximization principle (i.e., individuals will act to maximize their own utility), emphasizing the free choices of agents. The opposite, however, is said to be true in sociology; in sociology, social structures determine to a large extent the behavior of individuals and limit their freedom of action. Whereas economists have utilized an extremely voluntaristic view of the individual, sociology has, on the other hand, tended to work with what Dennis H. Wrong (1961) has labeled an "oversocialized" model of human behavior. Consequently, economic models study *agents,* that is, individuals whose main characteristic is their ability

AUTHOR'S NOTE: I wish to thank W. R. Scott, Stanford University; Philip Selznick, University of California, Berkeley; and Peter Abell, LSE, for comments on an earlier draft of this chapter.

to take independent action. Sociological models, on the other hand, study *actors,* that is, individuals who—like stage actors—are assumed to play certain roles in accordance with the expectations of others in their environment. According to J. Duesenberry (1960, p. 233), "economics is all about how people make choices," but "sociology is all about why they don't have any choices to make."

In the mid-1960s changes occurred at the border between economics and sociology; the exchange between researchers in both disciplines intensified. This was largely due to the influence of the Chicago school of economics, especially that of the 1992 Nobel prize winner Gary Becker, who sought to cross the traditional bounds of his discipline, not only in relation to sociology, but also in relation to other social sciences such as law, political science, anthropology, and economic history. The method and approach of the Chicago school were decidedly imperialistic; Becker and others sought to export the maximization model more or less intact into sociology and to use it to solve problems within the sociological domain. The negative attitudes of sociologists toward economists were reinforced rather than improved as a result of the imperialistic nature of these models (for example, Becker's and Stigler's maxim, *De gustibus non est disputandum,* with its insistence that all changes in social behavior should be explained by reference to relative prices or other changes in external constraints, rather than by changes in the values or preferences of the actors).

It was not until the mid-1970s and the early 1980s that the relationship between sociology and economics began to slowly improve. The reason for this improvement was a number of important changes within both economics and sociology. In economics (which has been almost synonymous with the maximization principle) a neo-institutionalist trend developed, identifiable by a desire to broaden the behavioral foundations of economics and by the introduction of a functionalist type of explanation. Developments within sociology went in the opposite but mutually supportive direction: The institutionalist perspective had always held a strong position in sociology, and in the late 1970s the rational choice perspective began to attract more attention. Interdisciplinary relations have improved ever since. The previous economic imperialism has given way to a more mutual exchange in which economists have not only been "exporters," but also "importers" from sociology and other disciplines. One of the best-known representatives within economics of this modified standpoint is George Akerlof, who described his multidisciplinary contributions in the following way:

> As you see I have gone the opposite way of Gary Becker: I have been trying to bring other things into economics; the other people have been trying to

bring economics into the other social sciences. . . . I guess that what I want to do is the opposite of what Becker does. I want to explain why the economy is not working; what interesting thing you need to bring in, so you do *not* get market clearing . . . and so on. (Akerlof, 1990, pp. 72-73)

In this chapter, a case from the modern theory of the firm will be presented in an attempt to illustrate how researchers in economics and sociology can learn more from each other. Today the theory of the firm is one of the most progressive areas within economics and is probably one of the areas in which interdisciplinary relations are most profound. The reason for this is that the neo-institutionalist tradition (and especially transaction cost economics) has greatly influenced the development of the theory of the firm since the mid-1970s. Neo-institutionalism has played a leading role in introducing a broader behavioral foundation to economics, even as the tendency to employ functional and more change-oriented explanatory models has been most pronounced.

The next section (Section 2) sketches current research within the theory of the firm. This will include some of the central themes behind the theory's development and a description of a number of newly emerging heterodox lines of research. With this background on the theory of the firm, we can move to discuss the future development of the theory. For example, Sidney Winter (1988) argues that a new competence-based or resource-based theory is presently being developed that is a synthesis of transaction cost theory and the evolutionary theory of the firm. Section 3 focuses on the problems associated with the construction of such a synthesis. I argue that there are currently a number of unclear points in this synthesis: what the behavioral foundations of this new theory are; what type of conception of the firm is assumed; and, consequently, what "conception of strategy" it involves. In Section 4, I argue that Philip Selznick anticipated some of the latest developments in the theory of the firm in his book *Leadership in Administration: A Sociological Interpretation* (Selznick, 1957). In this book, he presented an institutionalist theory of organizations, which, it can be argued, may today be used to help clarify some of the conceptual problems remaining in a competence view of the firm. In Section 5, I illustrate what can be learned from such a perspective.

2. Contemporary Research Programs Within the Theory of the Firm

Neo-institutionalism as a research program within economics can be identified by three central research themes, according to Richard Langlois (1986). First, it has tried to broaden the behavioral foundations of orthodox

TABLE 7.1 Four Contemporary Paradigms in Theories of the Firm

		FOCAL CONCERN	
		Production	*Exchange*
	Unbounded	Textbook orthodoxy	Working paper orthodoxy
RATIONALITY VIEWED AS			
	Bounded	Evolutionary economics	Transaction cost economics

economics. That is, it has attempted to replace the orthodox principle of maximization with a bounded and extended view of rationality. Second, instead of the previous preoccupation with the study of equilibria, priority has been given to the study of processes. Third, there has been a shift away from a one-sided focus on the institution of the market to include the study of other coordination mechanisms. These three themes are closely inter-related (cf. Knudsen, 1993b); that is, if we study the *processes* that have produced the equilibria that are studied in orthodox economics, this will create pressure to replace the traditional economic model of perfect ratio-nality with the concept of *imperfect* or *bounded* rationality. Because utility maximization can only be a well-defined concept in states of equilibrium, the study of disequilibrium processes per se will require an acceptance of the possibility of imperfect rationality. If we want to study not only perfectly operating markets but also systems with "market failures," it would then seem natural to inquire as to what alternative institutions can then support or replace the market as coordination mechanisms.

These three research themes have been particularly pronounced in the way that the theory of the firm has developed over the past two decades. The most important contemporary research programs in this area are summarized in Table 7.1 (Winter, 1988, p. 173, Figure 1).

The two dimensions that Winter uses to classify and compare different theories of the firm are (a) whether the firm is seen from a "production perspective" or from an "exchange perspective" and (b) the concept of rationality (bounded or unbounded) that is used. Winter thus argues that within the theory of the firm there are four major paradigms: textbook orthodoxy, working paper orthodoxy, transaction cost economics, and evolutionary economics.

2.1 TEXTBOOK ORTHODOXY: THE FIRM AS A
PRODUCTION FUNCTION AND UNITARY DECISION MAKER

Textbook orthodoxy (or standard microeconomics) has regarded the firm as if it were a unitary decision maker to which a certain objective or set of preferences can be attributed. It is normally assumed that the firm maximizes its present value or its profits. The firm has therefore, as David Kreps (1990) puts it, been perceived as if it were an individual. This is because this tradition has not sought to explain the firm itself, but rather has used the firm as a "logical atom" in explaining how prices are determined in different types of markets. The firm therefore constitutes the unit of analysis in microeconomics, but the level of analysis has typically been the industry.

Another important characteristic of textbook orthodoxy is that it emphasizes a typological form of analysis rather than a population perspective. That is, an industry is conceptualized as an aggregation of identical firms rather than as a distribution of heterogenous firms. In the typological perspective, heterogeneity or variation among firms is treated in such a way that all the unique qualities of a firm are stripped away, leaving an ideal type. Firms within the same industry are therefore regarded as essentially identical; they are described as having the same demand curves, cost curves, and the like. However, with the increasing tendency to open up the "black box" of the firm, the typological perspective has been gradually abandoned in favor of the population perspective.

Another central feature of standard microeconomics is that the firm is conceptualized as a "production function." That is, the firm is described as a unit that efficiently transforms a number of production factors or inputs into outputs. Therefore, the firm has been viewed primarily as a production unit rather than, for example, a contractual arrangement, a political institution, or an internal organization.

If this conception of the firm as a production unit is combined with a typological perspective of industries, a blueprint analogy of technology emerges (R. R. Nelson, 1992). In neoclassical theory, firms in the same industry are assumed to have equal access to the most efficient techniques; they can therefore immediately switch to new and more efficient techniques as changes occur in relative prices. New production techniques will therefore immediately be available to all firms in the industry, and firms are assumed to be able to absorb these into their existing and identical funds of knowledge (Cohen & Levinthal, 1990).

2.2 WORKING PAPER ORTHODOXY: THE FIRM
AS AN OPTIMAL CONTRACTUAL ARRANGEMENT

The conception of the firm in textbook orthodoxy has been exposed to various criticisms since the 1930s. Empirical studies by Hall and Hitch (1939) and Berle and Means (1932) were of particular importance, because they resulted in the emergence of two new heterodox lines of research in the 1960s: managerialism and behavioralism. These research traditions, managerialism and behavioralism, were involved in undermining the profit and the maximization aspects, respectively, of the profit maximization hypothesis. They were also both important precursors to the "exchange perspective." It was from within the exchange perspective that principal agent theory emerged in the 1970s, leading many orthodox economists to see it as legitimate to open up the black box view of the firm in their own working papers.

However, in contrast to textbook orthodoxy, the firm was no longer the basic unit of analysis it had been in the economists' traditional studies of different market structures, but was now perceived as it had been in the working paper version of orthodoxy. This is seen most clearly in agency theory, which, according to Jensen and Meckling (1976, p. 310), perceives the firm as a "nexus for a set of contracting relationships among individuals." The firm is seen as a fictitious "legal personage" who, as a central agent, enters into a number of bilateral contractual relations with the firm's different interest groups. The advantage of this view was that it avoided "a personalization of the firm": The firm was no longer seen as if it were an individual, a single decision maker, to whom a definite "objective function" could be attributed (p. 311). Rather, the firm was now analyzed as a complex set of relations, in that its behavior was now regarded as a system phenomenon, that is, the outcome of a complex equilibrium process. The firm was therefore no longer merely a unitary rational decision maker but a complex equilibrium structure of bilateral and optimal contracts that the firm entered into with its various interest groups.

Although, in comparison to textbook orthodoxy, working paper orthodoxy no longer viewed the firm as a unitary decision maker but rather as an equilibrium system, there was no fundamental shift in the basic behavioral assumptions. Maximization and perfect rationality formed the hard core of both the textbook and the working paper version of orthodox theory. It was not until the emergence of neo-institutionalism—and, in the context of the theory of the firm, of transaction cost theory—that some economists began to argue that the standard rationality concept constituted too narrow a conception of human reason to help us understand why institutions exist in the first place. The existence and emergence of institutional arrangements, they claimed, were inseparable from the existence of genuine uncertainty. Institutions therefore only existed in decision situations in which unforeseen contingencies could take place and which economic agents could not handle in a perfectly rational way by merely formulating "state-contingent contracts." The firm, therefore, had to be explained as an institutional response to such "open" decision-making situations—orthodox equilibrium models and the concept of perfect rationality were replaced with a functionalist or adaptive explanatory model and the concept of *bounded* rationality.

2.3 TRANSACTION COST THEORY: THE FIRM AS AN INSTITUTIONAL ADAPTATION TO MARKET FAILURES

Transaction cost theory can be traced back to Ronald Coase's classic article of 1937, "The Nature of the Firm." It was this article which, in the 1970s and 1980s, formed the starting point of Oliver Williamson's transaction cost paradigm. The central thesis of this paradigm was that there are different ways of organizing transactions, and that these different ways are associated with different costs. In Williamson's words, "transactions are assigned to and organized within governance structures in a discriminating (transaction-cost economizing) way" (Williamson, 1981, p. 1564). This implies that Williamson does *not* explain different governance structures as resulting from a rational plan, intention, or design, but rather that they have "beneficial consequences," economizing with respect to the costs of transactions. Thus, the standard equilibrium explanation has been replaced by a functionalist explanation.

To Williamson, the firm is an example of such a "governance structure," emerging as a response to the fact that economic agents are "boundedly rational" and opportunistic, yet at the same time are required to complete transactions with high degrees of uncertainty and asset specificity. In such situations, it would be either impossible or at least very costly to formulate a "state contingent contract" that specified what the partners should do in any conceivable situation in the future. An efficient adaptation to a situation in which genuine surprises could occur would consist of formulating a governance structure ex ante, which would indicate the methods to be used by the parties to the transaction to solve any conflicts that might arise between them. An example of such an "incomplete contract" is the employment relation between a firm and an employee. Such a contract is relatively more efficient than a state contingent contract, as it enables the firm to adapt to unforeseen contingencies.

It is a characteristic feature of both equilibrium explanations and the functional/adaptive explanations of transaction cost theory that they attach priority to the study of relatively stable conditions and social patterns at the expense of those processes that are assumed to have brought these about. The behavior of the firm and its organizational structure are merely seen as the final outcome of a process that cannot be studied explicitly and that is tacked onto the model as an ad hoc hypothesis. Only more genuinely change-oriented analyses attempt to change this situation. Such change-oriented analyses see the firm as an entity that exists in historical time. Nelson and Winter's (1982) evolutionary theory of the firm is one of several theories based upon such a change-oriented explanatory model.

2.4 EVOLUTIONARY THEORY: THE FIRM AS A REPOSITORY OF KNOWLEDGE

As in textbook orthodoxy, evolutionary theory focuses on the firm as a production unit and takes a technological rather than a contractual perspective. Evolutionary theorists argue that the firm should be seen as an adaptive unit with limited economic decision-making competences. However, they abandon the sharp distinction (characteristic of textbook orthodoxy) between a firm's technical capabilities and economic decision-making capabilities. The reason why evolutionary theorists do not uphold this distinction is that they conceptualize the firm as having not only limited technical capabilities but also—in accordance with the assumption of bounded rationality—limited economic capabilities or competences; that is, they are unable to consistently make optimal choices. The firm is thus seen as a bundle of technical, organizational, and economic routines that act as a repository for the experience and knowledge that the firm has been able to accumulate during its lifetime. Thus, in the terminology of evolutionary theory, the firm is said to be a hereditary mechanism that passes on accumulated knowledge—understood as its "capabilities" or its ability to perform certain tasks—from one period to the next. In this sense, it can be said that evolutionary theory breaks with the purely adaptive or functional model upon which transaction cost theory is based, by explicitly modeling the firm as an entity that exists in historical time and not merely as the efficient outcome of such a process.

To evolutionary theorists, the amount of "rationality" that can be attributed to a single firm is greatly restricted. In agreement with Alchian's classic article, "Uncertainty, Evolution, and Economic Theory" (1950), the focus has been placed on the ability of the environment to shape the behavior of a surviving firm, although the ability of the firm to purposely adjust to changing environments is not completely excluded. Nevertheless, the amount of rationality that can be ascribed to a single firm in evolutionary theory is more limited than is the case in transaction cost theory.

Within the evolutionary research program a distinction can be made between two main types of theory, ontogenetic and phylogenetic (see, e.g., Hodgson, 1993). *Ontogenetic theories* are concerned with studying how a single organism (in economics, a single organization) develops during the course of its existence. An example of this type of theory is Edith Penrose's (1959) *The Theory of the Growth of the Firm*. On the other hand, *phylogenetic theories* are concerned with the historical development of a whole species, illustrated by Alfred Chandler's (1990) study of the development of new organizational forms, from simple structures to conglomerate firms, during the past 150 years of economic development. Although Nelson and Winter's evolutionary research program contains both of these theoretical elements, even within their program the relation between these elements is quite undeveloped. A clarification of the relationship between ontogenetics and phylogenetics is therefore an important task in creating an improved evolutionary theory of the firm.

3. A Competence-Based View of the Firm: Toward a Synthesis of Transaction Cost Theory and Evolutionary Theory

If we are to attempt to sum up developments in the theory of the firm over the past few decades, two underlying and mutually reinforcing tendencies clearly emerge. On one hand, economists have proven increasingly willing to revise textbook orthodoxy by opening up the black box view of the firm. It has become apparent that the firm is a complex institution that should not only be seen as a production unit but also be analyzed from organizational, contractual, political, and knowledge perspectives. Economics has therefore been considerably extended to include law, political science, organizational sociology, and so on. The other main factor affecting developments in the theory of the firm is the gradual broadening of the orthodox concept of rationality. Maximization is no longer the sole behavioral concept of rationality within economics. Economists appear to have realized the necessity of introducing different kinds of imperfect rationality. It seems that many economists have recognized that optimal solutions to complex and uncertain decision-making situations do not always exist. As economists have become more and more willing to study the realistic and complex decision situations faced by firms, they have been under pressure to extend the behavioral foundations of their theories. From having been a relatively monoparadigmatic field in the early postwar years, the theory of the firm has become a more pluralistic area of research with many heterodox research traditions, coming to resemble organizational sociology as a result. Much recent theory building has therefore been concerned with constructing syntheses based on already existing theories, rather than with creating completely new theories.

One of the theories that has preoccupied some economists and strategy researchers is the recently developed knowledge-based, resource-based, or competence-based theory of the firm. This theory—which can be traced back to Alfred Marshall (1920) and, more recently, Edith Penrose's theory, "Limits to the Growth and Size of Firms" (1955)[1]—can best be understood as an attempt to create a synthesis of transaction cost theory and the evolutionary theory of the firm. Sidney Winter (1988) and Dosi, Teece, Winter (1992) use the term *organizational economics* to refer to such a theory and characterize it as an attempt to integrate the exchange perspective of transaction cost theory on one hand with the production perspective of evolutionary theory on the other. At the same time, they argue that the concept of bounded rationality has been maintained as the behavioral foundation of this new theory.

The attempt to integrate these two perspectives into one coherent theory was a natural outgrowth of their complementary nature. The idea was to discover whether the weaknesses of one theory could be overcome by the other, and vice versa. It was hoped that integrating the two perspectives would then resolve some of the problems encountered by each of these theories separately. Let me illustrate this, as follows.

Transaction cost theory can be characterized as a basically functional or adaptive explanatory model. In other words, one can study, when various processes of selection have been completed, the way in which a firm organizes its economic activities. That is, the different organizational patterns are seen as the end result of processes that are not studied per se, but that are only assumed to be active. As Williamson puts it, the study of different governance structures implicitly " . . . relies in a general background way on the efficacy of competition to perform a sort between more and less efficient modes and to shift resources in favor of the former" (Williamson, 1985, p. 22). However, as Williamson himself indicates, such intuition (an ad hoc treatment of social processes) will "nevertheless benefit from a more fully developed theory of the selection process" (p. 23).

If we are not satisfied with the functional or adaptive explanatory model of transaction cost theory, but require an explicit and other than ad hoc introduction of *processes* into the model, this necessitates a number of far-reaching changes in the theory. In the first place, we must, as in evolutionary theory, model the firm as a "hereditary mechanism" that accumulates more and more complex behavioral patterns over a period of time. The organizational structure of a firm can therefore no longer be regarded as determined by its transaction costs, but rather by its accumulated competences or capabilities (which cannot be assumed to be exogenously given). The knowledge or competences of the firm are accumulated during its lifetime, either through its individual trial-and-error learning or through social learning (learning by imitating older and more experienced organizations). Such learning processes will also typically be assumed to be path-dependent.

Nelson and Winter's evolutionary theory can be said to supplement the adaptationist model used in transaction cost theory with a more genuine change-oriented form of analysis. However, Nelson and Winter's evolutionary analysis, in which the firm is perceived as a hereditary mechanism that transmits its routines and therefore its accumulated knowledge, may also be criticized on several points. It can be argued that Nelson and Winter's theory was primarily developed as a phylogenetic, not ontogenetic, theory. Their theory is—like Darwin's theory of the origins of species—primarily a theory of the creation and evolution of new routines, but it lacks the morphological aspect of the evolutionary process: It does not include an ontogenetic aspect that would attempt to explain the development of the single firm and its manifestation in specific organizational forms; it is only a theory of underlying mechanisms; it is the development of the competences that affect the manifest forms. In a more complete theory, both ontogenetic and phylogenetic aspects, as well as their interrelationship, should be incorporated; this necessitates a two-tier language[2] in which the *underlying mechanisms* that lead to the accumulation of knowledge are analyzed as interrelated with *the more manifest structure and forms of organization*, which are the expression of this accumulated knowledge. It is exactly at this point that the more latent production or knowledge perspective of evolutionary theory therefore needs to be supplemented with the more manifest exchange perspective of the transaction cost theory.

A rudimentary way to view the firm from a combined phylogenetic and ontogenetic perspective was proposed in Edith Penrose's "Limits to the Growth and Size of Firms." To Penrose, it is the knowledge and experience accumulated by a firm that determines its subsequent growth. She emphasizes, however, that a firm or organization—unlike an organism—will never be *exclusively* determined by the information that is coded into its genes or its routines. The social sphere will therefore be characterized by far more feedback between the underlying genetic or competence level on one hand, and the phenomenal or morphological level on the other, as a result of human consciousness and intentionality. The inertia that can be seen in connection with the development and adaptation of an organization to a changing environment therefore not only will be determined by its latent competences or capabilities but also is likely to result from self-imposed developmental constraints and commitments built into its structure in the past.

At any rate, neither the work of Penrose nor the subsequent competence-based theory explicitly dealt with two important questions. The first of these questions concerns how the development of an organization can be modeled as a continuous exchange between the latent competence level and the morphological or manifest organizational level. That is, how can the production or knowledge perspective and the exchange perspective be united in one and the same model if the interplay is to be modeled as a cumulative process of growth? Second, what are the actual behavioral foundations of modern competence or resource-based theory? It does not appear to be sufficient here to assume, as do Winter (1988) and Dosi, Teece, and Winter (1992), that the behavioral foundation of the competence theory of the firm is based on the conception of bounded rationality. The reason is that such a concept of rationality seems inadequate for a theory focusing on cumulative processes. Nor does such a concept appear sufficient as a foundation for a theory of firm strategy. Instead, in the rest of this chapter, it will be argued that a reexamination of Philip Selznick's classic *Leadership in Administration: A Sociological Interpretation* (1957) can be of great assistance in helping us answer these and other questions regarding the modern competence-based theory of the firm.[3]

4. What Can Modern Economists Learn From Philip Selznick's Sociological Theory of Leadership?

4.1 INTRODUCTION

In the 1980s there was among sociologists a growing interest in Philip Selznick's contribution to organizational theory, especially with regard to his proposal for an institutionalist theory of organizations. This interest can be seen as a consequence of the fact that organizational theory has not merely focused on the single organization but has also introduced a number of new and higher levels of analysis, such as the organizational field. Developments within the sociology of organizations have therefore paradoxically gone in the opposite direction of the theory of the firm. Much of what has happened in the theory of the firm may be described as opening the black box that the firm constituted in textbook orthodoxy. The purpose of this research has been to replace theories that analyzed the firm from the industry level, which focused primarily on the market behavior of the firm, with theories whose focus of explanation was the individual firm itself, focusing on its internal organization. Thus, both the sociology of organizations and the theory of the firm have developed into complex fields of research, with a multitude of different perspectives, levels of analysis, and explanatory models. There are a number of similarities in these two research traditions that would enable their cross-fertilization. The relationship between the competence view of the firm and Selznick's institutionalist theory of organizations is only one example of this. Another example is the relationship between evolutionary economics and organizational ecology.[4]

The following sections will profile three themes of Selznick's institutionalist theory of organizations that seem to be directly relevant to the development of a competence-based theory of the firm. First, it will be shown how Selznick, through his critique of the adaptationist paradigm within organizational sociology, indicated the necessity of developing a more change-oriented model in which static efficiency is replaced by a concept of dynamic efficiency. This involves the replacement of a view of organizations as passive role adaptors with a view of organizations as actively role creating. The second theme considered below also shows the relevance of Selznick's work for the development of a competence view of the firm. When organizations are no longer seen as the outcome of a process of selection, and when we wish to model organizations as entities existing in historical time, processes can no longer be handled in loose ad hoc hypotheses, but need to be integrated into the model itself. This implies the need for an extension of the behavioral foundations of economics; this is true of both the concept of perfect rationality used in equilibrium models and the bounded rationality concept associated with the adaptive paradigm. We need to avoid portraying organizations both as hyper-rational decision makers, as in the orthodox paradigm, and as efficient organizations formed by their environments via a selection process, as in transaction cost economics. Selznick succeeds in avoiding both of these alternatives. His institutional theory of organizations is based on a concept of *extended* rationality, in which organizations are said to consciously shape their own identity by voluntarily giving up their freedom of action, thereby binding their future behavior to certain precommitments. This discussion of the behavioral foundation of economics will then lead us to the third theme of Selznick's theory that is important to the development of a competence-based theory of the firm. Transaction cost theory, with its focus on bilateral contracts, does not adequately portray the nature of the firm. It will therefore be argued that the competence-based or knowledge-based theory of the firm must extend its contractual metaphor and, like Selznick (1957, 1969), analyze organizations as if they were political constitutions. That is, organizations should be seen as if they were political institutions that, by establishing a procedural base for future decision making, are able to set up a credible organization. This is done through signaling to the various owners of resources that it is safe to invest resources in the firm in question and to develop firm-specific human capital.

4.2 SELZNICK'S CRITICISM OF THE ADAPTATIONIST PARADIGM IN ORGANIZATIONAL THEORY

Selznick's institutionalist perspective of organizations can be seen as an implicit critique of the adaptationist explanatory model, a model that for many years has been central to organizational sociology and one that still maintains a dominant position in the contingency school and elsewhere. In other words, Selznick's theory stands in confrontation with the adaptionist explanatory strategy, which attempts to treat organizations as if they were organisms that achieve a fit between their environments and their organizational structure, either via a selection process or via more conscious adaptation.

The adaptationist explanatory model has several special features. First, organizations are viewed from a purely "synchronous" perspective.[5] That is, organizations are analyzed at a given point in time as if they were the efficient end result of a process of adaptation. No attempt is made to incorporate this process into the model; it is rather tacked onto the model as a loose ad hoc hypothesis. Second, the adaptationist paradigm tends to analyze organizations from an atomistic point of view. That is, organizations are treated as if there were a bundle of independent and autonomous traits, and each trait is thought to be acquired via the process of selection. The bundle therefore converges into an efficient organizational form over the long run.

In contrast to this adaptationist view of organizations with its emphasis on a concept of static efficiency, Selznick (1957) claims that an *adequate* study of organizations "requires a genetic and developmental approach, an emphasis on historical origins and growth stages. There is a need to see the enterprise as a whole and to see how it is transformed as new ways of dealing with a changing environment evolve" (p. 141).

As we shall see below, there is a close connection between viewing organizations from a diachronous rather than a synchronous perspective, and employing a holistic rather than an atomistic method of analysis. Both points are also of central importance in creating a sound competence- or resource-based theory of the firm.

Selznick's (1957) emphasis on the need to understand organizations in the light of a diachronous perspective is most apparent from his rather critical attitude toward Herbert Simon's understanding of organizations and its subsequent development within the framework of the behavioralist research tradition. Like Simon (1962), the behavioralists basically build their understanding of organizations around Chester Barnard's inducements-contributions schema. Just as in working paper orthodoxy, they tend to see organizations as "the outcome of a complex equilibrium process" (Douglas, 1990, p. 100). In this view, the leader of a firm is primarily perceived as an "interpersonal agent," an agent whose primary task is to secure a truce among the different interest groups within an organization. To Selznick, this is far too narrow a view of leadership, because it does not allow for the possibility of analyzing how the basic values of an organization or its distinct competences are formed. In Selznick's diachronous perspective, the picture of the leader of the firm as an "interpersonal agent," whose primary task is to act as a mediator between divergent and conflicting interests, is therefore replaced with a picture of the leader as an "institutionalization agent," who plays a more fundamental role in creating and shaping the character and identity of the organization. This implies replacing the synchronous perspective with a diachronous perspective, which enables researchers to analyze how the mission and identity of an organization emerge over the long term through a process of institutionalization. This comes very close to evolutionary theory's analysis of the organization as a "hereditary mechanism" or "cultural transmission mechanism." At the same time, Herbert Simon's "consequentialist" and "imperfect" rationality assumption is replaced with a concept of rationality in which the rationality of fundamental values and norms becomes the object of analysis, and they are not merely regarded as exogenous variables.

Another consequence of a transition from a synchronous to a diachronous form of analysis is that an atomistic understanding of organizations is replaced with a more holistic understanding. Although the adaptationist model has tended to analyze organizations as collections of independent parts, each of which can be regarded as if it were the result of an efficient adaptation to its environments, the position in a diachronous type of analysis is that organizations must be studied as relatively integrated units, and that the selection mechanism has relatively few opportunities to directly shape the individual components of an organization. For the very same reason, adherents of such a diachronous type of analysis within the modern theory of the firm have adopted a very critical position on the heuristic of transaction cost analysis. Transaction cost analysis takes individual transactions as the unit of analysis and examines to which governance structures they should be assigned in order to minimize or economize on transaction costs (cf. Chandler, 1992a). For example, adherents of a knowledge-based theory of the firm argue, in keeping with critics of the adaptionist paradigm, that the early differentiation of an organization into a number of functional areas, fields of specialization, roles, and the like, and their subsequent integration into coordinated units, is such a vulnerable process that disturbances during the first phases will have great and accumulated effects, making it rather unlikely that new and viable structures will develop. Rather, most sizable organizations seem to have been through a phase of differentiation and integration, what Mintzberg (1983) describes as a process in which an initial simple structure comes to constitute a core building block for a subsequently created U-form, which in turn becomes the subsequent M-form. In other words, if an organization develops by transforming such integrated modules, and the individual parts of the organization are consequently not subject to separate selection pressures, this suggests that the traditional adaptationist paradigm will have little explanatory content.[6] Rather, the burden of explanation must lie with the "developmental constraints."[7] Or, as Gould and Lewontin (1979, p. 269) put it, "Too, often the adaptionist program gave us an evolutionary biology of parts and genes, but not of organism. It assumed that all transitions could occur step by step and underrated the importance of integrated development blocks and pervasive constraints of history and architecture."

An attempt to overcome the same type of weaknesses in the adaptationist paradigm seems to have provided the motivation behind Philip Selznick's institutional theory of organizations. The main purpose of his theory was to explain how an organization develops over time through the interchange between consciously or rationally designed coordination mechanisms on one hand and organic or spontaneous mechanisms on the other. Selznick's theory can therefore be regarded as a dual theory that simultaneously examines how formal organizations are designed to solve specific coordination problems and how institutionalization in an organization produces spontaneous and informal solutions to new social problems. It also examines how these solutions are in turn incorporated into the formal structure of the organization.

Therefore, to Selznick, an organization has to be understood in the context of its history and the problems it faced; with its development, solutions are infused into the formal structure of the organization itself. Solutions to new problems often arise through unconscious reinforcement mechanisms having the character of "emergent strategies." Meanwhile, the maintenance and diffusion of these solutions takes place through a mechanism in which human consciousness takes a far more prominent position than in Skinner's original reinforcement mechanism (Skinner, 1953). Infusion will typically consist of different norms and conventions, which can either be built into the functional and role divisions of the formal organization or can be found as internalized values within the participants in the organization and therefore be included as an element of the culture of the organization. Because the norms are perceived as obvious routines or behavioral patterns by the organization's members, they do not need to be monitored, just as it is unnecessary to design incentive structures in order to secure compliance. The institutionalization process means that these norms form what James Coleman (1988) described as the "social capital" of the organization.

Finally, Selznick's more-than-35-year-old sketch of how "unconscious" or "spontaneous" adaptation can be integrated with a "pragmatic" or formal organization concept appears to be increasingly relevant today. Williamson argues, for instance, that a future organizational science and theory of the firm must try to integrate von Hayek's (1948) study of the market as a spontaneous institution with Chester Barnard's (1938) study of organizations as pragmatic or designed adaptations:

> I submit that adaptability is the central problem of organization and that both Hayek and Barnard are correct. That both are correct is because they are referring to adaptions of different kinds, both of which are needed in a high-performance system. The adaptions to which Hayek referred could be implemented autonomously: each part examined prices in relation to his own opportunities and responded autonomously. . . . By contrast, the adaptions with which Barnard was concerned involved that kind of cooperation among men that is conscious, deliberate, purposeful. (Williamson, 1991b, pp. 163-164)

Conflicting with transaction cost theory—but in keeping with institutional organizational theory—the modeling of how the process of institutionalization leaves its mark on the formal and designed structure of an organization should not be based on an adaptationist model, but on what Selznick called a "genetic and developmental model." Only this type of analysis clearly pictures the "epigenetic," "path-dependent," or "cumulative causation" nature of the process. That is, each step in such a process forms the initial conditions for the subsequent process. This point of view also complies with the critique of the atomistic research strategy of the adaptationist paradigm, a strategy that often neglects the fact that selection mechanisms are not creating structures de novo, but rather start from existing structures and make them fit new functions. A possible point of departure for building such models of cumulative causation processes would be Herbert Simon's (1962) theory of complex phenomena.

4.3 THE BEHAVIORAL FOUNDATION OF SELZNICK'S INSTITUTIONAL THEORY OF ORGANIZATIONS

The introduction of a diachronous perspective on organizations implies that Selznick, in giving priority to the study of processes per se, attempted to incorporate the study of processes directly into his basic understanding of organizations, rather than merely treating such processes in separate ad hoc constructions, as in equilibrium explanations and adaptationist explanations. Selznick therefore proposed that the behavioral foundation of his theory should be extended both in relation to the maximization assumption of economics, and to the adaptationist paradigm of organizational theory and its tendency to see organizations as primarily shaped by their environments. Where equilibrium explanations and the use of a consequentialist concept of rationality are concerned, Selznick (1957, p. 74) argues that such explanations are expressions of an "excessive or premature technological orientation." The reason for this is that the means of achieving exogenously given objectives are focused upon, but there is less attention to ascertaining how the goals of an organization are formed: "The ends of action are taken for granted, viewed as essentially unproblematic 'givens' in organization-building and decision-making. The enterprise is conceived of as a tool whose goals are set externally" (Selznick, 1957, p. 74).

It is specifically when a diachronous and more long-term analysis is applied that this conception of rationality proves too narrow. Frank Knight explains this as follows:

> Wants are usually treated as the fundamental data, the ultimate driving force in economic activity, and in a short-run view of problems this is scientifically legitimate. But in the long-run it is just as clear that wants are dependent variables, that they are largely caused and formed by economic activity. The case is somewhat like that of a river and its channel; for the time being the channel locates the river, but in the long-run it is the other way around. (Knight, 1956)

Nevertheless, Selznick is just as critical toward the adaptationist paradigm, with its focus on static efficiency (that is, the assumption that the structure of an organization achieves a fit with its environment after a process of adaptation). The structure is argued to be formed by the environment via a selection mechanism. According to Selznick, from such a starting point, one would tend to emphasize the short-term and opportunistic interests of the organization, with adaptation to the environment occurring on a purely case-by-case basis; one would fail to emphasize as well behavior that is bound by general principles and more long-term interests. To Selznick, this is unsatisfactory, because it portrays organizations as being controlled by their environments and without any autonomy, identity, or distinct competences.

However, Selznick claims that there is a third alternative to the utopianism of economists and the opportunism of adaptationists. There is a wide no-man's land between the traditional subject areas of economists and sociologists. According to Selznick (1957, p. 149), responsible leadership of an organization consists of finding "a course between utopianism and opportunism." Leadership responsibility consists of

> accepting the obligation of giving direction instead of merely ministering to
> organizational equilibrium; in adapting aspiration to the character of
> organization, bearing in mind that what the organization has been will affect
> what it can be and do; and in transcending bare organizational survival by
> seeing that specialized decisions do not weaken or confuse the distinctive
> identity of the enterprise. (Selznick, 1957, p. 149)

Selznick compares his "institutional" view of organizations with the study of personal identity in clinical psychology. This involves analyzing how an organization limits its own future freedom of choice by making "character-defining commitments" in order to create or develop its own identity. Paradoxically, it is by renouncing their freedom of action (understood as the ability to make decisions on a case-by-case basis, and thereby achieve static efficiency) and by committing their future behavioral patterns to some specified principles that individuals and organizations can develop their own unique identity. They cannot, therefore, be considered to be mere organisms without the ability to work for self-preservation. It is thus through the institutionalization process that formal organizations are infused with value, and thus acquire a certain character or role. It is in this sense that organizations are not seen as passive role adaptors, but rather viewed as active in creating their own future role.

4.4 CAN SELZNICK'S CLINICAL PSYCHOLOGICAL ANALYSIS OF ORGANIZATIONS BE ILLUSTRATED IN TERMS OF A MODEL OF EXTENDED RATIONALITY?

Many economists will no doubt perceive Selznick's clinical, psychological analysis of how individuals and organizations attempt to define their own character, role, and distinct competence as being outside the scope of the domain of economics, which they see as confined to the study of logical or rational behavior. The economist would merely conceive identity, personality, or the character of a decision maker as superfluous details belonging to the domain of psychology, psychoanalysis, and possibly sociology. But, like Harry Frankfurt (1971), Amartya Sen (1977), and others, one may ask whether the existence of these subjective phenomena suggests that the behavioral foundation of economics is too "narrow" or "thin." Sen (1977) argues, for instance, that the structure of the standard rational choice model in economics is inadequate as it only ascribes one set of preferences to an agent, and lets this set of preferences represent such different things as the agent's interests, well-being, values, choices, and behavior. To Sen there is no doubt that the concept of preference cannot represent all these things simultaneously, which is why one should look to a more elaborate conceptual structure. Several economists have therefore argued for replacing the maximization model with a so-called multiple-self model.[8]

This model portrays the decision maker as representing a set of successive "subagents" or "selves," trying to solve a dynamic, intertemporal decision-making problem. Assume that an agent must choose an action plan for a series of future periods and that he or she wants to maximize the utility of the overall plan. Strotz (1956) was the first to point out that agents with normal time preferences will be facing a problem of dynamic inconsistency. During each of the future periods, the individual is likely to choose a behavior that is inconsistent with his original optimal plan. When I, for instance, set the alarm for 6 o'clock in the morning, I certainly intend to get up at that hour. However, when the alarm goes off at 6 o'clock, I sometimes turn it off and go back to sleep. This example illustrates how problems of intertemporal inconsistency may suggest a multiple-self model in which there is intrapersonal conflict between the individual's long-run and short-run interests. Thus, in a dynamic decision-making situation, the individual will be facing what Thomas Schelling (1984) calls a "self-command" problem and Jon Elster (1985) calls a problem of "weakness of the will," where the long-run interests, personified by Thaler and Shefrin (1981) as "the planner," must attempt to dominate or control the short-run interests, personified by Thaler and Shefrin (1981) as "the doer." This "self-control problem" is modeled by Jon Elster (1985) as an *intrapersonal* prisoner's dilemma between the individual's long-run interests—"the controller"—and the short-run interests—"the doer"—leading to a suboptimal outcome if nothing is done by the controller to constrain the doer.

It is evident that a "multiple-self" model is a much better basis for reconstructing the behavioral foundation of Selznick's theory than the standard rational choice model. Thus, Selznick's interest in adapting clinical psychology studies of personal identity to the study of organizational phenomena cannot be accomplished within standard rational choice theory. However, a multiple-self model focusing on self-command problems would be a good starting point. In fact, Selznick implicitly refers to the problem of dynamic inconsistency when he warns against organizations adopting a technical rather than an institutional form of leadership. According to Selznick (1957, p. 143), technical leadership, which consists of establishing a truce between the organization's interested parties, is exactly "the pursuit of immediate short-run advantages in a way inadequately controlled by considerations of principle and ultimate consequences." In other words, some organizations are controlled by a series of short-run interests, adapting to different internal and external problems without being subjected to long-run planning. To Selznick this kind of case-by-case adaptation represents an "irresponsible form of leadership," as it does not leave the organization with autonomy in relation to its environment, and hence signifies the lack of "willpower" in many organizations. In order to solve self-command problems, Selznick recommends *institutional* leadership in order to " . . . look to the long-run effect of present advantage . . . and how changes effect personal or institutional identity" (Selznick, 1957, p. 143).

To overcome self-command problems, a decision maker can use a number of different precommitment strategies. An important group of such strategies, according to Jon Elster (1979), consists precisely of attempts to manipulate one's character or personal identity. The paradigmatic example of this type of precommitment strategy is Aristotle's conception of moral education: "the more good deeds you do, the better a person you become." Preferences are usually assumed to be the cause of behavior, but in this case it is the behavior that causes the preferences. To act according to a rule (e.g., a moral principle) may initially be very demanding and require great personal sacrifices; however, when the decision maker repeats the action, he or she develops a disposition or a preference for a particular type of behavior. By repeating the behavior, a "habit" may be formed (Aristotle uses the term *hexis*), which more or less automatically generates the proper behavior. In other words, a process of self-socialization makes it unnecessary for the individual to convince himself or herself every time of the long-run interests associated with complying with a particular rule. This type of precommitment strategy rests on the actor's exploiting his knowledge of the psychological mechanisms behind the emergence and change of habits with the deliberate purpose of manipulating his own character or identity. The type of precommitment strategies involving manipulation of one's identity essentially has as its most significant characteristic a conception of the individual as being able to gradually transform or change his or her own identity. Thus, in line with Elster, one could say that the model is one of "cumulative character formation."

Turning again to Selznick's theory, the responsible leader must resort to exactly such precommitment strategies of shaping character, identity, or distinct competence when trying to solve the self-management problems of the organization. Furthermore, by identifying institutional leadership with the model of cumulative character formation, Selznick's commitment to a "developmental and genetic type of analysis" is emphasized,[9] in that the previously accumulated fund of social or organizational capital constitutes the initial condition for accumulation in the subsequent period. But, what are the concrete mechanisms that make it possible for the institutionalization process in Selznick's theory to be characterized by a cumulative growth process—what economists refer to as "increasing return to scale"? In order to answer this question, we can create theory that runs parallel to Edith Penrose's theory of the limits of firm growth. Penrose's theory assumes a kind of permanent variation mechanism in the routinization of managerial problems, thereby releasing new resources that make further organizational growth possible. However, in Selznick's theory, it is not the routinization of managerial tasks, but rather the internalization and institutionalization of new norms for collaboration and coordination, that releases additional resources. That is, in Selznick's theory the institutionalization process plays a role similar to the routinization of managerial tasks in Penrose's theory, because both facilitate a gradual accumulation of organizational or social capital in the organization.

Working from these more general perspectives on leadership, Selznick reaches a number of conclusions concerning strategic issues which are in agreement with the results of the modern competence- or resource-based theory. When, for instance, unrelated diversification has been perceived as problematic from the point of view of a competence-based view of the firm,[10] this is because the "core competences" of the firm are passed over too quickly, leading to possible fragmentation and incoherence within the firm's organization, and possibly to the loss of leadership control. In accordance with this, Selznick argues, "A decision to produce a new product or enter a new market, though it may set goals, is nevertheless irresponsible if it is not based on an understanding of the firm's past and potential character" (Selznick, 1957, p. 144).

In Selznick's view, a strategy that is not in harmony with or does not extend the historical development of the "distinct competences" of the firm in question is an expression of "irresponsible leadership." This compels a static rather than a dynamic approach to efficiency. The fact is that a static view of efficiency will be closely tied to a purely adaptationist view of organizations, merely juxtaposing strategy with the ability to obtain a fit between the organization structure and its environment. In such an instance the nature of leadership becomes opportunistic and short-sighted, carrying with it the risk that in the long term the distinct competences of the organization may be eroded and undermined, hindering as well any chance of further developing these competences and capabilities. A dynamic approach to efficiency, on the other hand, implies that the organization must attempt to secure a more coherent and coordinated pattern of action, trying to maximize organizational learning capacities over time. Concretely, this means that the organization will avoid problems of dynamic inconsistency by coordinating its temporally separated selves, thus ensuring the development of a coherent and cumulative competence that will facilitate the gradual accumulation of social capital.[11]

4.5 FIRMS AND ORGANIZATIONS AS CONSTITUTIONAL SYSTEMS

Thus far we have focused on Selznick's analysis of organizations from the perspective of the clinical psychologist. From this perspective, organizations are—like in textbook orthodoxy—viewed as individuals who are capable of setting goals, appraising alternatives, making decisions, and so on. However, contrary to textbook orthodoxy, Selznick applies a diachronic organizational perspective: He does not take the firm's objectives for granted, but focuses on the process shaping the organization's objectives and hence its mission and/or role over the long term.

However, being a sociologist, Selznick knows the limitations of viewing organizations from the perspective of a clinical psychologist—organizations constitute collective entities and so cannot automatically be ascribed preferences, the ability to make decisions, and so on. Therefore, Selznick prefers to view organizations as institutional arrangements established as a response to multipersonal problems of coordination and collaboration. This does not imply, however, that Selznick would subscribe to the working-paper version of orthodox theory and its conception of the firm as an optimal contractual relationship. By applying a contractual or an exchange perspective of the firm, "personalization of the firm," one of the weaknesses of textbook orthodoxy (Jensen & Meckling, 1976) is avoided. Furthermore, Selznick would also likely view the contractual metaphor of working-paper orthodoxy as being too narrow and replace it with a metaphor viewing organizations as political constitutions. The advantage in doing so would be that the firm will not be viewed merely as an institutional solution to a multipersonal problem, but also as a solution to an intertemporal decision-making problem. This conception of organizations would better comply with the behavioral assumptions of Selznick's theory and would transcend some limitations of the contractual metaphor.[12] Let us briefly examine the background for Selznick's introduction of the constitutional metaphor (Selznick, 1957), and his subsequent elaboration on this in *Law, Society and Industrial Justice* (Selznick, 1969).

As was pointed out in Section 4.2 above, Selznick was highly critical of the behavioralists, and in particular of the fact that they based their theory on Chester Barnard's "inducements-contributions" schema. That is because this model started out with a synchronous view of organizations and was thereby implicitly based on a concept of "technical leadership," in which securing a truce among the various interest groups within an organization was of primary importance. The behavioralists therefore came to focus almost exclusively on the short-run or opportunistic interests of an organization, whereby they overlooked the process of institutionalization, and therefore the process whereby both the distinct competences of the organization as well as its more long-term goals were developed:

> [T]he important point is that *decision-making in the light of long-run benefits presumes a concept of the institution.* The enterprise as a going concern, as a relational entity, becomes the focus of policy and strategy. This has nothing to do with formal incorporation. It has to do with all the empirical requirements of organizational survival, including survival as a certain *kind* of organization. (Selznick, 1969, p. 47)

However, Selznick's criticism of behavioralism (and implicitly of Chester Barnard's inducement-contribution schema) also seems to apply to much of contemporary literature on contractual economics, especially to the theory of transaction costs. The latter explains the firm as an institutional solution to market failures occurring when boundedly rational and opportunistic agents attempt to implement transactions of a high degree of asset specificity. As mentioned earlier, one of the problems of transaction cost theory is that it primarily studies given institutional arrangements, merely suggesting, at a very informal and ad hoc level, the processes that have produced these institutions. This is especially apparent from the fact that transaction cost theory specifies its central assumption of opportunism as "self-interest with guile," whereas Selznick's theory interprets opportunism as myopic or short-sighted behavior. In his conception of the organization as a "going concern," Selznick more clearly suggests the significance of the time dimension. Although Williamson, in his more formal analysis, tends to view the firm as an institutional solution to a relatively static problem of market failure, the constitutional understanding views the firm rather as a solution to an intertemporal decision-making problem in which a team of resource owners subject themselves to a series of procedures for making collective decisions and dividing the joint outcome of their collaboration.

Thus, a firm is not merely a series of bilateral contracts (as the "nexus-of-contract" theory implies), but is rather a multilateral system of contracts characterized by an exchange of commitments between individual resource owners, with the purpose of accepting certain constraints on their future options. The purpose of such an institutional arrangement is to protect the property rights of the individual organizational member against other members' potential rent seeking. Only if the firm is able to solve this appropriability problem will individuals feel an incentive to cede control of some of their resources and agree to subject these resources to the constitutional decision-making basis of the firm. According to this constitutional conception of the firm, leadership will thus consist of creating a basis that establishes conditions for accumulating resources and knowledge within the framework of the firm.

By introducing the constitutional metaphor, Selznick not only introduces a new perspective on the management-controlled firm that conflicts with the nexus-of-contract theory, but also a perspective that turns upside-down the latter's rationale for why firms exist. Managerialism and agency theory, which originated as a result of the introduction of limited companies and the consequent separation between ownership and management, are characterized by the problem of "discretionary" and "opportunistic" managerial behavior. Agency theory viewed the firm as a solution to the incentive problems that had emerged between owner and management or, more generally, between principal and agent. However, if one views the firm from a constitutional perspective, the modern firm must be seen as an institutional arrangement that has emerged in order to protect the owners/shareholders/principals as a group against the interests of individual members of this group, and to protect its long-term interests against its more short-term interests. That is, exactly by delegating its power to an independent class of managers and binding the firm's future decision-making to a certain procedural basis, shareholders were able to protect themselves against being dominated by "short-term" shareholders and against the risk of the firm's being unraveled as "a going concern." In other words, the introduction of a class of professional managers was the "master" whom the shareholders as a class needed to protect themselves against one another.[13]

> With the decline of family management in industry, for example, the justification for authority is more and more referred to claims of competence, service, and rational principles of administration. The historic significance of this transition is the rise of self-restraint as a hallmark of enterprise

management. Pre-bureaucratic management was typically one-man rule. . . .
The relation between the "big boss" and his staff was personal and he
expected unreserved loyalty and obedience. In the bureaucratic setting
authority is more impersonal, more systematic, more limited, and more
effectively delegated. . . . And all officials, including top management, accept
a framework of established rules. In this sense, bureaucratic authority is
constitutional. (Selznick, 1969, p. 82)

As a constitutional arrangement, the firm was a solution to the problem of "dynamic inconsistency" faced as a group by the shareholders
and which, in the long run, threatened to undermine the firm as a going
concern. However, by committing the firm's future decision making to a
certain procedural foundation and simultaneously delegating their decision-
making rights to a class of professional managers, the shareholders protected themselves against case-by-case behavior by creating incentives for
cumulative character development, fostering improved intertemporal coordination of decisions made in individual subperiods.

But, as pointed out by Viktor Vanberg (1992), another advantage of
the constitutional view of organizations is that it demonstrates how it is
possible, from an individualistic point of view, to treat organizations as
decision-making units, in spite of the fact that we know that the behavior
of a firm results from the complex interaction of several individuals. When
compared with several other paradigms within the theory of the firm, this
is clearly an improvement. Textbook orthodoxy, for example, perceives the
firm as a unitary decision maker that can be ascribed preferences, goals,
and the ability to make decisions. The problem is, however, that this
perspective is quite illegitimate from an individualistic point of view,
because no single objective exists when the firm is a collective institution.
Only individuals can properly be described as having an objective. On the
other hand, working-paper orthodoxy can be said to have emerged as an
attempt to comply with the principle of methodological individualism.
However, it is difficult to explain why organizations have the ability to act
as relatively well-organized and well-coordinated units at all. This theory
treats the organization as merely a fictitious unit, which only exists in a
legal sense and only has the power to do that which it is conceded by law.
The constitutional view of organizations surmounts these difficulties of
textbook and working-paper orthodoxy. It does so by explaining how an
organization can act as a coordinated and well-organized unit by committing itself to a procedural foundation, and simultaneously comply with the
principle of methodological individualism, without having to assume that
there exists some organizational goal derived from the preferences of the
individual organizational members.

5. Conclusion

The introduction of a more long-run and change-oriented perspective within organizational theory required, according to Selznick, settling scores with both the sociologists' oversocialized models of human behavior and the economists' voluntaristic model of rational individuals. Sociologists had been too inclined to perceive organizations as plastic, viewing their structure as shaped by environments through some unspecified selection process. Economists, on the other hand, tended to view organizations and their behavior as designed by a perfectly rational decision maker, striving to discover the most efficient means by which to reach a set of exogenous goals. Common to the two models was the fact that they study organizations as the outcome of a process that was not made subject to any kind of in-depth analysis, but merely tacked onto the original model in an ad hoc way.

Like much modern institutional economics, Selznick's introduction of an institutional analysis of organizations can therefore be understood as an attempt to introduce a process perspective within organizational theory that would make the processes per se (not just their outcome) the object of analysis. With respect to both *homo oeconomicus* and *homo sociologicus*, Selznick had to expand the behavioral foundation of organizational theory. This way he was able to dissolve one of the most tenacious and persistent contrasts—rational choice versus rule following—that had contributed to the freezing of the border between the two disciplines. To Selznick—like to modern institutional economists—this was a false dichotomy. Nothing prevented an agent from both acting rationally and being a rule follower. Only by introducing a genuine process perspective would this false dichotomy between economics and sociology vanish. In the extended process perspective, rational behavior lies in choosing the constraints of one's future behavior. In this model rational action consists in choosing a series of precommitments through which one, by voluntarily binding oneself to various rules, attempts to escape inconsistent dynamic behavior and hence shapes one's own character or role.

Finally, let us compare the economic interpretation presented here with a corresponding sociological interpretation of Selznick's theory. W. R. Scott (1992) put forth such an interpretation, classifying all organization theories according to three basic categories: he refers to them as (a) rational, (b) natural, and (c) open systems models.[14] Scott argues that Selznick's theory basically utilizes a natural systems model but has been combined with an open systems model. Such an interpretation is very much in line with the interpretation, presented in Section 4.2 of this chapter, that Selznick's work is a critique of a functionalist or adaptationist model and advocates the use of a more genetic and developmental model. However, Scott's sociological interpretation neglects the extended behavioral foundation of Selznick's model, which I have tried to bring to light. No doubt my inclination to stress this rational element of the theory, and Scott's corresponding inclination to diminish this element, are brought about by the fact that we each base our interpretations on the "path-dependencies" of our disciplines. Although it is evident that Selznick's work should be interpreted as an early "transgression" of the disciplinary boundaries between economics and sociology, it still remains to be seen whether the contemporary institutional theorists within these disciplines will be able to collaborate and progress beyond Selznick's original analysis.[15]

Notes

1. Recent contributions include those by Jay Barney (1986), B. Wernerfeldt (1984), Richard Rumelt (1984), and David Teece (1980, 1982).

2. The existence of a two-tier language within evolutionary economics has been demonstrated by P. P. Saviotti and J. S. Metcalfe (1991): "The units of observation that we choose (e.g., organisms, species, organizations, industries, technologies, etc.) have a physical outer appearance . . . and a more fundamental part which is less easily visible and more difficult to modify" (pp. 13-14). Oliver Rieppel (1990, p. 297) particularly emphasizes that "ontogenetic development . . . is the only (biological) process of transformation of form directly amenable to observations," whereas phylogenetic development is at a latent, unobservable level.

3. For an updated view, see Philip Selznick (1992, Part 3).

4. Compare J. V. Singh (1990).

5. The distinction between a synchronous and a diachronous perspective on organizations corresponds within organizational theory to Lawrence B. Mohr's (1982) distinction between "variance theory" and "process theory."

6. Milgrom and Roberts (1992, p. 30) have suggested (probably in an attempt to counter similar criticism) that we introduce, apart from dimensions such as frequency, uncertainty, and asset specificity, an additional dimension—degree of connectedness—when analyzing how transactions are organized most efficiently. However, this way of countering the criticism of the underlying atomistic research strategy of the functionalist or adaptationist type of analysis must be characterized as rather arbitrary and ad hoc. A similar criticism can be raised against Williamson's (1991b) discussion of the specific "systems effects" that are supposed to characterize Japanese firms. As is clear above, a more adequate and direct way of handling such problems would be to replace the static analysis of the adaptationist paradigm with a more change-oriented analysis focusing on the organization's growth process and the "developmental constraints" it faces.

7. This point of view seems to be well in keeping with Herbert Simon's (1962) thesis that complex systems will develop much more rapidly if stable, intermediate systems emerge early in the evolutionary process, thereby constituting the building blocks for constructing even more complex systems. According to this thesis. it is to be expected that the structure of complex phenomena will be hierarchical.

8. Compare Geoffrey Brennan and James Buchanan (1985), Robert Frank (1988), Albert Hirschman (1984), Thomas Schelling (1984), R. H. Thaler and H. M. Shefrin (1981), Jon Elster (1979), Edward McClelland (1990), George Ainslie (1982), and Drazen Prelec and R. J. Herrnstein (1991).

9. Under the heading "identity matters," Williamson (1993) argues that it is not only the "competence perspective" but also transaction cost theory that ascribes importance to the identity of a firm. His argument is that the "asset specificity" assumption of transaction cost economics plays the same role as the identity concept of the competence perspective. The difference between transaction cost theory and the competence perspective is, however, that Williamson (contrary to authors like Selznick and Penrose) applies an adaptationist explanatory model. Williamson has not been explicitly interested in modeling the cumulative or path-dependent process during which the firm creates and shapes its identity, but only in the outcome of this process.

10. For example, Cynthia Montgomery and Birger Wernerfeldt (1988) found that more focused, less diversified firms performed better in terms of "Tobin's q" (a measure of the value being created in a firm) than more diversified firms.

11. Dosi, Teece, and Winter's (1992) coherence concept plays almost the same role as they particularly focus on an organization's ability to coordinate its behavior over time, avoiding an ad hoc and case-by-case pattern of behavior.

12. R. Nelson and S. Winter have presented an almost identical argumentation. They claim that "the imputation of . . . an objective function to the firm is not a *sine qua non* of effective theory construction" (1982, p. 57). Consequently, Nelson and Winter suggest that we view firms as "a treaty among the participants, according to which they will jointly seek to deal with their common environment." Oliver Williamson (1990) has put forward a similar suggestion to view organizations as if they were treaties between sovereign nations. This implies, however, that we not only view firms from a contractual or legal perspective but, to a larger extent, also emphasize the firm as a political institution and hence include results and theories from political science. Finally, A. Gifford, Jr. (1991) and Vanberg (1992) have, in keeping with Selznick (1957, 1969), suggested that we specifically view organizations as political constitutions.

13. See, for example, Schumpeter's (1942) very similar analysis of how the bourgeoisie benefited from aristocratic governance as it needed a "master" to protect it against itself.

14. Scott's classification of organizational theory is largely comparable to mine. Scott's "rational" models correspond to my "equilibrium and rational choice" models, his "natural" models correspond to my "adaptationist" explanations, and his "open system" models to my "change-oriented" models. For a discussion of my classification system, see Christian Knudsen (1993b).

15. For some progress in this direction, see Scott (1994b) and D. C. North (1990).

8

Using Institutional Theory
to Understand For-Profit Sectors

The Case of
Financial Reporting Standards

STEPHEN J. MEZIAS

THE INSTITUTIONAL APPROACH TO THE STUDY OF ORGANIZATIONS has
produced a tremendous amount of interest and research in recent years
(DiMaggio, 1988; DiMaggio & Powell, 1983; Meyer & Rowan, 1977;
Meyer & Scott, 1983; Powell & DiMaggio, 1991; Scott, 1987). At the same
time, interest in financial reporting practices has increased among organization theorists; this is manifested in a stream of literature that has addressed accounting practices from both a general sociological perspective
(Perrow, 1986, p. 272; Zald, 1986) and the institutional perspective
(Boland, 1982; Covaleski & Dirsmith, 1988; Meyer, 1986). Scott (1987)
has declared the institutional paradigm to be in a contemplative phase of

AUTHOR'S NOTE: This chapter is based in part on work from my dissertation; special
thanks to chairman J. March and reading committee members J. Pfeffer and D. Palmer. An
earlier version of this chapter was presented at the Complex Organizations Seminar,
sponsored by the Institute for Social and Policy Studies at Yale University; I owe many thanks
to the participants at these workshops. This version was presented at the Institutional Theory
Workshop on Møn Island, Denmark. The helpful comments of the various participants at that
conference were instrumental in improving the paper. Finally, I want to thank T. Lant, W. R.
Scott, and F. Milliken for comments on earlier versions. The helpful stewardship of Paul
DiMaggio is acknowledged gratefully. As is customary, I take full responsibility for
remaining errors, ambiguities, and problems.

more deliberate development, a time of consolidation and careful assessment. One of the central features of his assessment of the institutional perspective was a review of how the theory has been used in empirical work. This study is intended to pursue an agenda urging the more deliberate development of empirical applications of the institutional perspective. I examine directly the multiple forms of institutional explanation described by Scott (1987, pp. 501-507). More specifically, the research setting will be that sector of the American polity where financial reporting rules are determined. This setting allows me to contribute to the development of institutional theory by demonstrating its applicability in a setting that has been dominated by other perspectives. In this study, these multiple forms of institutional theory are used to develop a model of the determination of financial reporting practices at the Fortune 200.

I believe that such an investigation has the potential to make several theoretical contributions. First, it addresses one of the directions for expanding the scope of institutional theory discussed by Powell (1991, p. 183), who objected to the partitioning of environments into "market-driven sectors and institutionalized sectors." Second, it demonstrates the applicability of the sociology of organizations generally (Zald, 1986), and institutional theory more specifically, to understanding issues previously relegated to rational models and related perspectives. Third, this use of institutional theory to understand for-profit organizations could illuminate the extent to which the institutional and rational perspectives complement or contradict one another. Thus, success in addressing institutional theory to for-profit sectors would address the need to further develop the relation between the institutional and rational perspectives. Fourth, a further contribution of the chapter will be empirical: I propose a series of measures that will operationalize the multiple institutional sources of financial reporting practices. In a reanalysis of data presented by Mezias (1990), I reinforce the theme that firm-level accounting choices are strongly tied to actions by entities at the environmental level of analysis. A fifth contribution is developed by examining the important effects of legitimacy as a conferred status, largely controlled by entities at the interorganizational level (Mezias, 1990). This finding can be contrasted with existing rational choice models of these practices (Dhaliwal, Salamon, & Smith, 1982; Hagerman & Zmijewski, 1979; Salamon & Smith, 1979; Watts & Zimmerman, 1986; Zmijewski & Hagerman, 1981), which have tended to deemphasize embeddedness in institutional environments (Granovetter, 1985). Further, institutional theory locates the determinants of firm-level characteristics in the institutional environment. Such an analysis emphasizes that many of the constructs to test firm-level arguments are representations of preferences or interests that "are institutionally defined and shaped" (Scott, 1987, p. 508).

In addition to developing empirical predictions based on the multiple forms of institutional explanation, I hope to contribute to the development of institutional theory by exploring the integration of the institutional model with previous theories. An important corollary to this is the development of institutional theory by clarifying how it can be distinguished from previous theories. These goals are accomplished in a discussion of hypotheses based on a multidimensional model of institutional sources of financial reporting practice. Distinctive contributions of the institutional approach are highlighted in a discussion of the linkages of these hypotheses with previous research, especially work based on the rational choice and resource dependence perspectives. By highlighting underlying differences in the theories of action, this discussion presents a challenging research agenda to those interested in pursuing institutional theory. This contribution is reinforced by a discussion of how the results of an empirical exploration of this model refine the suggestions for further research discussed in developing the theoretical argument. Before the broad version of institutional theory developed here can gain wide acceptance as a worldview, either in the narrow domain of financial reporting standards or in the wider domain of organization theory, careful testing of the differing mechanisms discussed here must occur.

INSTITUTIONAL THEORY AND FINANCIAL STATEMENTS

Mezias (1990, pp. 434-435) has suggested several reasons why institutional theory may be useful as a lens to study the interorganizational field where American financial reporting procedures are determined. First, the development of complex relational networks over the past century has accelerated in response to the explosive growth of companies with securities that are traded publicly. Second, the degree of collective organization of the environment has increased steadily in the 50 years since the federal government first regulated securities markets. Third, the certified public accounting profession, represented by both the leading accounting firms and its powerful professional associations, has grown in importance. Finally, the leadership efforts of individual organizations in establishing prevailing accounting practice and affecting its codification in generally accepted accounting principles has also become increasingly important. In addition to these reasons for believing that institutional theory should be applicable, Mezias (1990, pp. 437-438) also argued that there was a variety of methodological reasons why financial reporting practice is a good choice for studying institutional processes. First, the study of financial reporting practice represents an opportunity to study how routine behavior corresponds with the dictates of institutional environments, including regulatory pressures, norms of good practice, and professionalization. Second, important actors in determining financial reporting include the accounting profession, individual organizations, and regulatory agencies, covering phenomena at both the organizational and the interorganizational levels. Third, because of the routineness of the choice and its importance to different organizational constituencies, the data are fairly reliable and readily available. For all of these reasons, this study will focus on the spread of a financial reporting practice among the Fortune 200 from 1962 to 1984. The particular practice examined is the recording on the income statement for financial reporting purposes of the *investment tax credit* (ITC).

THE INVESTMENT TAX CREDIT

Contained in the Revenue Act of 1962 was a provision to grant companies making qualified capital investments a credit that reduced income taxes. A percentage of qualified investments, initially 7%, was to be credited toward payments of income taxes in the fiscal year in which those investments were made. For example, a company making a $1,000,000 investment in equipment covered by the law could deduct $70,000 from taxes payable in the year in which the investment was made. Companies losing money in the year of eligible capital investments were allowed to bank the credit until a year when income was earned and there were taxes payable. Eventually, companies were even allowed to sell the credits they could not use immediately. However, this study concerns only those fiscal years in which a company was eligible to take some portion of their investment tax credit to reduce taxes payable. If XYZ Co. had received a $70,000 credit in 1964 and had an income tax bill of $800,000, then taxes payable would be reduced to $730,000 by the credit. Typical entries for such a transaction as they would be made on the financial statements for tax purposes[1] are depicted in Table 8.1, upper panel.

Based on prevailing accounting practice, two generic alternatives for reporting the credit in the income statement for financial reporting purposes existed. The credit could be *amortized*, or the credit could be *expensed*. In either case, the amount of the credit still reduces taxes payable in the year it is obtained; the two methods differ, however, in how the tax credit is presented on the income statements for financial reporting purposes. If amortized, the company is said to have used the *deferral method* (DM). This is illustrated on the middle panel of Table 8.1. Normally, some portion of the tax credit is used to reduce income tax expense in the current

TABLE 8.1 Income Statement for Tax and Financial Purposes

INCOME STATEMENT FOR TAX PURPOSES

Income Taxes Due $800,000
Investment Tax Credit   70,000
Taxes Paid $730,000

INCOME STATEMENT FOR FINANCIAL REPORTING PURPOSES

DEFERRAL METHOD

Income Statement Entry		Balance Sheet Entry
Income Taxes Expenses	$800,000	Reserve for Investment Tax Credit Deferred $63,000
Less Tax Credit Amortized	7,000	
Total Tax Expense	$793,000	

FLOW THROUGH METHOD

Income Statement Entry		No Balance Sheet Entry
Taxes on Current Income	$800,000	The ITC is "flowed through" the income statement
Less Tax Credit	70,000	
Total Tax Expense	$730,000	

year; in the illustration, 10% of the credit, or $7,000, is reported this way. The result is an increase in net income on the financial statements for financial reporting purposes. The remainder of the credit, $63,000 in the illustration, is put into a special reserve on the balance sheet, called Investment Tax Credit Deferred. Some portion of that reserve will be used to reduce income tax expense in future fiscal years; as a result, the net income number on the financial statements for financial reporting purposes will increase. Net income is increased gradually rather than all at once; the boost to net income from receiving the tax credit accrues to the company over several fiscal years. If expensed, the full amount of the credit against income taxes payable enters the income statement in the year of the investment; the company is said to have used the *flow-through method* (FTM). As a result, net income is increased by the full amount of the credit in the fiscal year during which taxes payable are reduced. Financial statement entries for this reporting method are presented in Table 8.1, lower panel.

These alternatives represent an organizational choice in which the institutional environment intervened: How should a tax decrease, which was given in the current year to encourage the purchase of long-lived investments, be recorded on the financial statements? Companies had to choose whether to expense the credit, reflecting the benefit of the credit in current income, or to amortize, reflecting the credit in current income over a number of years as the equipment for which it was obtained was actually used. Mezias (1990, pp. 433-434) offered several reasons why the ITC was a particularly good choice for a study of the impact of institutional pressures on financial reporting practices. First, the timing was right: The recent founding of the Accounting Principles Board (APB) had created high expectations that major progress would be made in resolving financial reporting questions; accounting for the investment tax credit became an important issue when the APB attempted to decree how it should appear on financial statements. Second, the controversy over the proposed decree was well documented. Third, in response to this controversy, individual companies kept good records of how they accounted for the credit. Fourth, options for recording the investment tax credit on financial statements were limited to two: expensing or amortizing. Finally, the study is simplified because the vast majority of firms started by amortizing and eventually changed to expensing. Not one firm in the sample resumed use of the DM after adoption of the FTM.[2]

Research Hypotheses

Scott (1987, pp. 501-507) describes several variants of institutional explanation, distinguished by underlying causal arguments. The theme of this section is that these forms of institutional explanation can be applied to detail the adoption of the FTM by the majority of the Fortune 200.[3] The constellation of forces suggested by Scott is combined in an institutional model of sources of financial reporting practices at for-profit organizations. Sections below elaborate each of these variants of institutional explanation. The application of each to the ITC is explained, and hypotheses are derived. The final section outlines the chief differences between the proposed institutional model and existing models, especially rational choice and resource dependence.

THE IMPOSITION OF FINANCIAL REPORTING PRACTICE

The imposition of organizational practices is argued to occur when institutional fields or sectors contain environmental agents that are powerful enough to impose practices on organizations (Scott, 1987, p. 501). In the case of financial reporting practice, the designated standard setting agency, with the backing of the Securities and Exchange Commission, can impose financial reporting practices. In addition, there are several regulatory agencies that impose accounting standards on firms under their jurisdiction. Thus, the first hypothesis is that regulatory pronouncements will affect the probability of adoption of the FTM.

Hypothesis 1: Regulatory pronouncements will affect the probability of adoption of the FTM.

The first variation on this hypothesis is that the policies of the standard setting agency, in this case the Accounting Principles Board, will affect the likelihood of adoption of the FTM. The Accounting Principles Board had been created in the late 1950s as a new agency to oversee accounting standards. A large part of the motivation for its creation involved the widespread belief that the Committee on Accounting Procedure, the predecessor agency, had been allowing too much discretion in the preparation of financial statements. The first mission that the Board adopted was the development of a theoretical basis for the resolution of accounting controversies; its attempts failed. High expectations that the Board would move to reduce multiple, conflicting accounting practices were dashed. In 1962 the investment tax credit became the foil on which it first attempted to limit discretion by requiring firms to use the DM. Much controversy ensued, with some accounting firms refusing to enforce the prohibition, and both firms and certified public accountants lobbying the Securities and Exchange Commission against the Accounting Principles Board ruling. The Board refused to change its ruling but was backed only partially by the Securities and Exchange Commission, which allowed for use of the FTM for no more than 48% of the ITC received. Thus, during fiscal years ending in 1962 or 1963, a prohibition against use of the FTM for the full amount of the credit was in effect. In 1964, however, the Securities and Exchange Commission, ostensibly in response to changes in the legislation governing the credit, decided to allow for full use of the FTM. The Accounting Principles Board reversed itself and allowed firms to use either the FTM or the DM to record the full amount of the ITC on financial statements. The effect of this change in the regulatory environment was to increase the probability of adopting the FTM.

Hypothesis 1a: The probability of adopting the FTM is increased by the end of the prohibition against that method by the Accounting Principles Board in 1964.

The Interstate Commerce Commission and the Federal Power Commission regulated the rates charged in two monopolistic industries. The normal formulae to determine rates were based on net reported income. Because the DM tended to lower that income relative to the FTM, these agencies required companies subject to their regulation to use the FTM on financial statements. This leads to two hypotheses:

Hypothesis 1b: The probability of adopting the FTM is increased among companies subject to regulation by the Interstate Commerce Commission.

Hypothesis 1c: The probability of adopting the FTM is increased among companies subject to regulation by the Federal Power Commission.

It is important to integrate the notion of imposition into existing literature, especially because the hypothesis regarding the imposition of organizational practice is that regulatory pronouncements will affect financial reporting practice. This is hardly the first study of the effect of regulation on organizational behavior; however, as Scott (1987, p. 502) has pointed out, the institutional perspective "gives special emphasis to authority relations: the ability of organizations, especially public organizations, to rely on legitimate coercion." A brief review of some of the previous literature on regulation can help to explicate further some of the points of similarity and difference between the institutional model and other models.

A first important literature to address questions about American political institutions has been the positive theory of institutions (DiMaggio & Powell, 1991, pp. 8-11), which represents an attempt to provide a general rational choice theory of social institutions. The key similarity is that both the positive theory of institutions and the institutional model seek to explain the imposition of organizational practices by centralized, usually state, actors. A review of the two literatures suggests, however, that there are also important differences. First, the two theories offer divergent characterizations of the centralized actors. The regulatory agencies of the positive theory of institutions tend to be unitary actors with well-defined interests (Niskanen, 1971; Shepsle, 1986; Shepsle & Weingast, 1987). In institutional theory, the agents of the collectivity may be loosely coupled, more akin to organized anarchies (Cohen, March, & Olsen, 1972; March & Olsen, 1976) than unitary actors (cf. Moe, 1990). Second, in institutional theory, regulation is embedded (Granovetter, 1985) in the context of an American state characterized by fragmented centralization (Abzug & Mezias, 1993; DiMaggio, 1988; Meyer & Scott, 1983). Organizations and agencies may operate in multiple sectors, each of which may display different types and levels of regulation. This is illustrated in the present case by the different practices sanctioned by the Accounting Principles

Board, the Securities and Exchange Commission, the Interstate Commerce Commission, and the Federal Power Commission. Third, and partially because of the second and first reasons, isomorphism with institutional environments (DiMaggio & Powell, 1983; Meyer & Rowan, 1983), even compliance with regulatory pronouncements (Mezias, 1987), is variable in institutional theory and becomes a specific object of research attention (Tolbert & Zucker, 1983; Zucker, 1983).

A second important literature that has addressed the question of the regulation of organizations is resource dependence (Pfeffer & Salancik, 1978, pp. 188-222). Both perspectives share a view of legitimacy as socially constructed and stress that the management of social legitimacy is important in organizations. In addition, the fragmented centralization of institutional theory is analogous to the degree of dependence dimension in resource dependence. The chief point of difference between these perspectives is in topics of explicit attention in the analysis. Resource dependence tends to stress the benefits of regulation that accrue to those organizations or groups of organizations that recognize their self-interest and are powerful enough to affect regulation. Conversely, institutional theory has tended to emphasize the cognitive dimension (Zucker, 1977, 1983, 1988) of imposition and the emergent nature of its process (DiMaggio & Powell, 1983; March & Olsen, 1984, 1989; Meyer & Rowan, 1977). Further, as pointed out by Powell (1988, p. 133), resource dependence has tended to emphasize focal organizations and examine the effect of environments on individual organizations, "essentially ignoring the wider system of relations in which the focal organization is a participant." It is exactly this wider system of relations that is an explicit focus of an institutional analysis.

THE AUTHORIZATION OF FINANCIAL REPORTING PRACTICE

The difference between authorization and imposition according to Scott (1987, p. 502) revolves around the fact that "the subordinate unit is not compelled to conform but voluntarily seeks out the attention and approval of the authorizing agency." As DiMaggio and Powell (1983) argue in their discussion of normative isomorphism, such authorization is likely to take place in highly professionalized sectors. For this reason, the relationship between firms and the certified public accountants who serve as external auditors of financial statements is examined. The structure of authority in the institutional environment is such that external auditors cannot impose financial reporting practices on management. They may note an exception to generally accepted accounting principles, which may render the financial statements unacceptable to the Securities and Exchange Commission;

however, unless the practice that engendered the exception is forbidden under generally accepted accounting principles, rejection by the Securities and Exchange Commission is not a certainty. In addition, a decision by one external auditor to note an exception may trigger a search by management for an external auditor who is more sympathetic to the financial reporting practice in question. This auditing firm may very well not note an exception. Thus, external auditors may advise firms of their opinions regarding financial reporting practice, lending such practices legitimation and expert authorization; however, they usually do not impose preferred practices on their client firms (Boland, 1982).

Hypothesis 2: Authorization of the FTM by the firm's external auditor will increase the likelihood of adoption.

When the Accounting Principles Board voted on its Pronouncement #2, forbidding the use of the FTM, four of the Big Eight firms voted against this rule. Representatives of these firms announced publicly that they might not note an exception to generally accepted accounting principles for firms using the FTM, even though the pronouncement mandated this. Conversely, four of the Big Eight firms voted for the rule. It is hypothesized that firms using one of the Big Eight firms that voted to prohibit the FTM would be less likely to adopt the FTM.

Hypothesis 2a: Having as the firm's external auditor one of the four Big Eight firms that voted for the requirement that the FTM be prohibited will decrease the likelihood of adoption.

Integration with previous theories is important for understanding the authorization of financial reporting practices as well. Hypothesis 2 predicted that authorization of the FTM by the firm's external auditor will increase the likelihood of adoption. Among organizational theories, institutional theory has had the clearest focus on the role of professionals in and the effects of professionalization on organizations (DiMaggio & Powell, 1983; Meyer & Scott, 1983). Other theories have not focused simultaneously on professionals in organizations and the relationship of this to the effect of professionalization on organizations. For example, resource dependence goes into some detail on the conditions under which certain participants, for example, professionals, will have power in organizations (Crozier, 1964; Hickson, Pugh, & Pheysey, 1971; Pfeffer & Salancik, 1978, p. 48). In addition, the theory addresses the question of the benefits of professionalization for members of the profession (Pfeffer & Salancik, pp. 208-210). The main difference between institutional theory and resource dependence is that the former has focused on professional-ization as an interorganizational phenomenon of distinctive importance. Understanding the convergence of institutional and professional control has received research attention (Scott, 1983) as part of an attempt to give simultaneous consideration to the level of professionalization, the effect of this on the institutional environment, and the effects of this combination on organizations (DiMaggio & Powell, 1983; Meyer & Scott, 1983; Powell & DiMaggio, 1991; Zucker, 1988).

THE INDUCEMENT OF FINANCIAL REPORTING PRACTICE

As Scott (1987, pp. 503-504) describes the process of inducement of organizational practices, it involves those agents that possess the ability to provide "strong inducements to organizations that conform to their wishes." With respect to financial reporting practices, the complexity of the institutional environment suggests two observations that expand this argument. First, institutional conventions are such that several parties may possess inducements of value to organizations; there is no guarantee that these inducements will converge to encourage only a single practice. Second, these various inducements may have different effects on different firms or on different participants in the same firm.

Hypothesis 3: Inducement of the FTM by powerful firm constituencies will increase the likelihood of adoption.

The first variant of this hypothesis is a negative inducement story. Institutional conventions are such that firms with relatively less powerful owners, so-called managerial controlled firms, behave differently from so-called owner-controlled firms (Salamon & Smith, 1979; Williamson, 1964, 1967). One result of this tendency might be that managers at firms where stockholders are relatively less influential, so-called managerially controlled firms, will tend to use income-increasing accounting methods. In this context, adoption of the FTM, which increases net income in the year of adoption, would be predicted.

Hypothesis 3a: Manager-controlled firms will be more likely to adopt the FTM.

In their discussion of political visibility, Holthausen and Leftwich (1983) cite criticism by unions, employees, consumers, politicians, and bureaucrats as the main cost to firms. Consequences of criticism by these social actors include antitrust actions, imposition of taxes such as the windfall profits tax, boycotts, demands for wage increases, and so on. As a result of these institutional pressures, Watts and Zimmerman (1978, 1986) argue that large firms, being more visible, tend to adopt standards that lower reported earnings to try to reduce these costs. In this context, the argument would be that large firms would be less likely to adopt the FTM.[4]

Hypothesis 3b: Large firms are less likely to adopt the FTM.

DiMaggio and Powell (1983) suggest that pressures to conform to norms of usage might come from the sources of firm capital, principally insurance companies and commercial and investment banks. The argument is that these sources of firm capital have neither the legitimate authority to impose nor the normative power to authorize use of particular financial reporting practices. Nonetheless, by controlling critical firm resources (Pfeffer & Salancik, 1978), they can create powerful and coercive (DiMaggio & Powell, 1983) incentives to adopt the reporting methods that they prefer.

Hypothesis 3c: Financially controlled firms will adopt the FTM at a different rate from other types of firms.

Inducement arguments can be contrasted with existing theories in the literature. Hypothesis 3 suggested that inducements from powerful firm constituencies will increase the likelihood of adoption of the FTM. The idea that certain firm constituencies possess the ability to offer material awards or other incentives to organizations that conform to their wishes is not new. Scott (1987, p. 504) argues that "(i)nstitutional theorists differ primarily in stressing the somewhat unexpected importance of these mechanisms for public organizations." The sample used in this study contains no public organizations; however, a brief review of previous inducement theories illuminates some other points of similarity and difference between institutional and other theories of inducement. The chief theories that have been used to make inducement arguments are rational choice theories of financial reporting practice and resource dependence.

A first contrast between institutional theory and rational choice theory in the form of the accounting literature occurs in the models of what guides the inducement behavior of firms. The latter theory is one of organization-level rationality (Pfeffer, 1982), based on theories of managerial economics (Dhaliwal et al., 1982; Hagerman & Zmijewski, 1979; Monsen & Downs, 1965; Salamon & Smith, 1979; Williamson, 1964, 1967; Zmijewski & Hagerman, 1981). Institutional theory begins with the prediction that firms will comply with the requirements of the institutional environment as articulated in generally accepted accounting principles, regulatory requirements, and professional norms. Clearly, there will be situations in which these two sets of predictions will converge. For example, once the Accounting Principles Board reversed the requirement that firms use the DM, both theories would predict increased adoption of the FTM. However, the basic models that form the bases of the two theories are quite different; the contrast is between a model of rational choice and a model of obligatory action. The former involves the rational calculus of economic man, and the latter implies the matching of behavior repertoires to situations by the criteria of appropriateness (March, 1981b).

A second contrast between the two theories is the difference in emphasis on social context (Granovetter, 1985; March & Olsen, 1984, 1989). Rational choice theories posit organization-level rationality and concentrate on the characteristics of firms that affect financial reporting practice. Studies based on these explanations have tended to ignore the effects of the social context, even regulatory pronouncements (Dhaliwal et al., 1982; Hagerman & Zmijewski, 1979; Salamon & Smith, 1979; Zmijewski & Hagerman, 1981). Conversely, an institutional perspective stresses that the interpretation of firm-level variables must be placed in social contexts that define what are appropriate ends to be pursued as well as the legitimate means for pursuing them (Scott, 1987, p. 508). Thus, an institutional analysis does not end with the explanation that firms adopted or did not adopt the FTM because certain of their characteristics made increasing reported net income desirable or undesirable to their dominant coalitions. An institutional analysis of the effect of these variables on the adoption of the FTM looks to the forces in the organizational field that influence the dominant coalition, stressing the inducement of organizational practice. In such an explanation, the constraints on rational choice, the externalities of economic analysis, become a central concern. One of the key concepts in such an analysis is the increasing structuration of organizational fields (DiMaggio & Powell, 1983). Consistent with this vision, an institutional interpretation of the effects of managerial or financial control looks to the forces in the environment, especially the content, enforcement, and interpretation of legal rules and regulations governing exchanges that make organizations more responsive to some constituencies (Abzug & Mezias, 1993; Edelman, 1990, 1992; Scott, 1987). Similarly, an institutional interpretation of the effect of political costs imposed on large firms is that they result from the increasing organization of ordinary citizens and the creation of networks of collective interests that need not always advocate similar outcomes (DiMaggio, 1988).

Inducement from the institutional perspective must be interpreted in the light of the external control of organizations (Pfeffer, 1982; Pfeffer &

Salancik, 1978). This is a chief point of similarity between the institutional and resource dependence versions of the ability of external constituencies to induce certain organizational practices. The two theories also share the view that legitimacy is a conferred status that enhances the survival value of organizations that receive it. The theories differ somewhat in the focus on resources as the inducements offered to organizations. Institutional theory would tend to emphasize, somewhat more than resource dependence, that legitimacy will be among the inducements offered to organizations in return for adopting certain practices. A second difference is the emphasis in the resource dependence literature on the distribution of resources as a characteristic of the environment, for example, continuums from munificence to scarcity, or concentrated to dispersed. The institutional perspective places more explicit emphasis on the rationalization of society, the endogenous process by which certain social actors are granted legitimate authority over resources, which can be used to induce particular practices (Meyer & Scott, 1983). As in the discussion of imposition, the chief point of difference between the resource dependence and institutional perspectives is in topics of explicit attention in the analysis. Resource dependence tends to stress the resource benefit of accepting the inducements that powerful organizations or groups of organizations offer. Conversely, institutional theory has tended to emphasize the cognitive dimension (Zucker, 1977, 1983, 1988) of inducement and emergent nature of the rationalization process (DiMaggio & Powell, 1983; March & Olsen, 1984, 1989; Meyer & Rowan, 1977; Powell & DiMaggio, 1991).

THE ACQUISITION OF FINANCIAL REPORTING PRACTICE

The acquisition of organizational structure involves an attempt by actors at the organization to "model their own structures on patterns thought to be, variously, more modern, appropriate, or professional" (Scott, 1987, p. 504).[5] The primary source of such legitimate methods for use on financial statements is prevailing practice in the organizational field. In this way, the collection of choices made by all firms functions as a compelling model to firms in the field. The notion of acquisition is especially applicable in this case for at least three reasons: First, during the 1962 to 1964 period, there was considerable controversy regarding what was the appropriate method for reporting the investment tax credit. The Accounting Principles Board and other regulatory agencies disagreed, and the Securities and Exchange Commission even refused to enforce the prohibition against the FTM that the Accounting Principles Board attempted to impose. Second, after 1964 generally accepted accounting principles as defined by the Accounting Principles Board, and subsequently by the

Financial Accounting Standards Board, allowed for either the FTM or the DM. Third, at the same time that this controversy (and then vagueness) dominated the regulatory pronouncements, there was a clear trend in prevailing practice. During the fiscal years of 1964 and earlier, prevailing practice was to use the DM. Beginning in 1965 prevailing practice changed, and the FTM became the dominant method for reporting the investment tax credit on financial statements.

Hypothesis 4: Pressures favoring the acquisition of the FTM will increase as the use of this reporting method becomes more widespread.

As indicated by Scott (1987, p. 504) the acquisition of an organizational practice will be related to mimetic pressures bearing on the firm. As argued by DiMaggio and Powell (1983), these mimetic pressures to adopt the normatively sanctioned practice would be greatest for those firms facing the most uncertainty. The hypothesis about the acquisition of the FTM derived from this argument is based on the assumption that firms facing the largest variance in the amount of investment tax credit may face significant uncertainty. As a result, they are more likely to conform to prevailing practice. During the early years, when the DM was the prevailing practice, these firms would be most likely to follow the Accounting Principles Board directive and not adopt the FTM. However, once the FTM became the prevailing practice, these same firms become more likely to adopt it. Thus, these firms will display decreased likelihood to adopt the FTM up to 1964, before it became widespread, and increased likelihood from 1965 to 1984, after it became widespread.

Hypothesis 4a: Firms with high variance in the amount of investment tax credit on their financial statements are more likely to conform to prevailing practice.

The acquisition of organizational practices also may be affected by turnover in personnel, which is a source of the diffusion of normative models and prevailing practices (DiMaggio & Powell, 1983). The focal point of the hypothesis based on this argument is the top management team. The argument is structured similarly, with the effect of turnover depending on which method is the prevailing practice; firms with high management turnover will display decreased likelihood to adopt the FTM up to 1964 and increased likelihood from 1965 to 1984.

Hypothesis 4b: Firms experiencing high turnover among the top management team are more likely to conform to prevailing practice.

THE INCORPORATION OF FINANCIAL REPORTING PRACTICE

In the incorporation of practices by organizations, the key distinction is that not all that happens is intended (March & Olsen, 1984, 1989). Organizational routines of first-order sensibility may not be coordinated well; apparent rationality in the short run may conflict with either long-run rationality or definitions of rationality at some time in the future. An argument stressing the incorporation of organizational practices envisions a world of organizations where financial reporting practices evolve "over time through an adaptive, largely unplanned, historically dependent process" (Scott, 1987, p. 506). Attempts to coordinate the organization with its environments, both technical and institutional, at one point in time increase the complexity of the organization and constrain what it may do in the future (Selznick, 1949, 1957). With respect to financial reporting practices, incorporation suggests that adoption of the FTM will be affected by how such a choice fits into current attempts to manage environments and by how past efforts to do the same have constrained financial reporting practice. All of the hypotheses discussed in this section represent attempts to assess efforts by the firm to use financial statement numbers as a buffer against the environment. Two assumptions about underlying behavior of organizational decision makers form the basis of further hypotheses. The first is that management acts within the bounds of conventional accounting wisdom. Examination of the institutional environment reveals knowledge of current accounting practice that can be used to make predictions about the adaptive, relatively unplanned, history-dependent financial reporting choices made by firms. The second assumption is that the management of firms attempts to smooth income, especially in response to performance below some target level of performance (Cyert & March, 1963; Payne, Laughhunn, & Crumm, 1981).

> **Hypothesis 5:** The past history of financial reporting practices at the organization interacts with current perception of a need to change to affect the likelihood that the FTM will be adopted.

The first hypothesis about the incorporation of financial reporting practice emphasizes the effect of the past history (Levitt & March, 1988) of financial reporting practices on the decision of how to account for the ITC. In particular, I draw a sharp distinction between the choice to adopt a new financial reporting practice and the maintenance of an existing practice. As summarized by Hypothesis 1a, the change in regulatory pronouncements in 1964, allowing firms to use the FTM, would be predicted by an imposition perspective to have a profound impact on whether firms would adopt that practice. Thus, I have predicted that there will be a great increase in the propensity of firms to adopt the FTM in that year. Further, I would argue that firms that do not adopt in response to this proximate change to what regulatory authorities permit have demonstrated a commitment to retain the DM and forgo use of the FTM. I interpret incorporation arguments to suggest that this failure to act, when regulations change, engenders commitment to maintain the DM despite the regulatory change. Thus, I predict that a history of failing to adopt the FTM in 1964 will reduce the likelihood that a firm will adopt that method at a later date.

Hypothesis 5a: Firms that did not adopt the FTM in 1964 are less likely to adopt the practice in subsequent years.

The second hypothesis about the incorporation of financial reporting practice is based on differences in firms in the amount of investment tax credit they receive. When the exigencies of short-run adaptation to the perceived environment point to the need to have higher reported income, switching to the FTM is one way to accomplish this. One simple prediction is that those firms for which this accounting manipulation is most effective are most likely to use it. Firms for which the investment tax credit is most significant relative to earnings—in "accountingese," most material—will be most likely to adopt the FTM.

Hypothesis 5b: Firms with the largest amounts of investment tax credit will be most likely to adopt the FTM.

The perceived necessity of actions to smooth reported income at an organization are quite history-dependent. The argument is made frequently that previous years' reported income becomes an expectation for performance by a firm. Managers as well as other organizational constituencies focus attention on this target level of performance (Cyert & March, 1963). More specifically, managers are assumed to want to avoid variation about some trend of reported income considered normal for their firm (Ronen & Sadan, 1981). Therefore, if income is highly variable and tends to decrease, then the FTM is more likely to be adopted; it dampens deviations from target by providing an upward boost to the otherwise downward trend.

Hypothesis 5c: Firms that have highly variable incomes with a downward trend are most likely to adopt the FTM.

The arguments about incorporation of organizational practices as an institutional source of financial reporting practices at organizations can be contrasted with the previous literature. Hypothesis 5 implied that the past history of the incorporation of financial reporting practices at the organization, as well as a current perception of a need to change those practices, will affect the likelihood that the FTM will be adopted. The argument revolves around attempts to manage the environment of the organization. This summary of the argument highlights its similarity both to certain economic arguments and to resource dependence. The principal difference between incorporation as an institutional source of organizational practice and the predictions of resource dependence lies in the close attention to the institutional environment as an endogenous and important influence on the process. This is epitomized by the assumption that management acts within the bounds of conventional accounting wisdom as encoded in generally accepted accounting principles. Examination of the institutional environment reveals knowledge of prevailing practices; I argue that these will be perceived as largely beyond the purview of the individual firm (Meyer & Rowan, 1977). The principal difference between incorporation of practice as an institutional source of organizational practice and an economic model that would predict income-smoothing is in the assumptions about behavior. In the income-smoothing literature, managers are assumed to want to minimize variation about some trend of reported income considered normal for their firm (Ronen & Sadan, 1981). In the institutional model, the process by which managers make decisions about financial reporting practice is coarsely adaptive, relatively unplanned, and history-dependent (Levitt & March, 1988; March & Olsen, 1984, 1989; Scott, 1987); at the level of the individual manager, the institutional model of behavior is that of obligatory action rather than consequential choice (March, 1981b).

REVIEWING THE INSTITUTIONAL MODEL AND OTHER MODELS

The discussion of the previous sections is summarized in Table 8.2, which highlights perspectives that have made some of the same predictions as the model of institutional sources of organizational practice. For each of these theories, the numbers of the hypotheses that they might predict are listed in the table. The distinctive contributions of institutional theory with respect to each of these theories, discussed after each of the hypotheses, are highlighted in the table as well. It is also interesting to note that the institutional perspective offers a broad sweep of phenomena at several levels of analysis, resulting in a multidimensional model. The breadth of the theory in encompassing these many effects from multiple literatures

TABLE 8.2 Comparison of the Institutional Model With Other Theories

Theory	Hypotheses Predicted	Distinctive Contribution of Institutional Theory
Resource Dependence	1, 2, 3, 6	(1) Cognitive dimension (2) Emergent process (3) Focus on rationalization of society (4) Legitimacy as a resource (5) Focus on professionalization (6) Endogenous environments
Rational Choice	1, 3, 6	(1) Organized anarchies (2) Organizational rationality constrained by institutional environments (3) Fragmented centralization (4) Obligatory action (5) Structuration of organizational fields

highlights the need to outline how it is different from other theories and what its distinctive contributions are (DiMaggio, 1988).

Results

THE SAMPLE

Data for firm years from 1962 through 1977 were constrained by the availability of empirical measures for such constructs as financial and owner control. Because of this missing data problem, the sample mimics that of Kotz (1978). That is, it consists of the 200 largest nonfinancial corporations in the United States in 1969. Because the Fortune 200 for 1969 was the sampling criterion, but the sample began in 1962, the number of different companies actually in the sample is 207. The experience of companies in the sample, according to their adoption of the FTM, is as follows. Of the 207 companies, 10 had no annual reports available covering the period when the FTM was adopted. Thus, missing data made it impossible to determine when adoption occurred. Of the remaining 197, 46 did not report the year of adoption of the FTM, though annual reports were available. Both of these types of companies, 56 in total, were excluded from the sample. Of the remaining 151 companies, one was excluded because the majority of its income was subject to Canadian tax laws even though it was nominally an American company. The remaining 150 companies are diversified by industry, including utilities, transportation, merchandising, and manufacturing companies. The majority of the companies had adopted by 1965; 15 companies were right censored and had not adopted the FTM by 1984 when the study ended.[6] Dependent and independent variable data came from annual reports of this sample of companies, from 1962 to 1984. Some data for independent variables for years after 1972 was obtained using COMPUSTAT and proxy statements.

DEPENDENT VARIABLE MEASUREMENT

The unit of analysis is the firm fiscal year. Each row of the data matrix represents observations on all variables for a single fiscal year. The dependent variable is coded to provide a contrast between maintenance of the DM and adoption of the FTM; the data to code it came from the annual reports of the firms in the sample. It is coded 0 if the firm maintained the DM during the fiscal year; it is coded 1 if the firm adopted the FTM during the year in question. Firms that adopt the FTM are included up to and including the year of adoption; after that, they are removed from the sample. This approach does not mix years in which the use of the FTM was maintained with years in which it was adopted; the result is a more powerful test of the factors associated with the decision to adopt the FTM. The removal of firms is not problematic because no firm resumed the use of the DM after switching to the FTM.

INDEPENDENT VARIABLE MEASUREMENT

Empirical proxies for the underlying theoretical constructs of the research hypotheses are discussed briefly with the number of the associated hypothesis. The hypothesis number, variable names, and the null and alternative hypotheses are summarized in Table 8.3. The first set of hypotheses concerns the effect of regulatory pronouncements on adoption of the FTM. All of these are measured using dummy variables. Hypothesis 1a concerned the effect of the end of the Accounting Principles Board's prohibition against the FTM. Because this occurred in 1964, it is measured by a dummy variable indicating whether the observation represents a firm fiscal year ending in calendar year 1964; it is called FY64. Hypothesis 1b is measured using dummy variables that indicate whether the firm was under the jurisdiction of the agency in the fiscal year represented by the observation. These variables are called ICC and FPC, acronyms for the regulatory agencies in question. The second set of hypotheses, measuring the effect of the authorization of financial reporting practice, concerns the use of one of the Big Eight accounting firms that supported the prohibition

TABLE 8.3 List of Variable Names, Null and Alternative Hypotheses

Number of Hypothesis	Name of Variable	Null Hypothesis	Alternative Hypothesis
1A	FY64	$b = 0$	$b > 0$
1B	ICC	$b = 0$	$b > 0$
1C	FPC	$b = 0$	$b > 0$
2A	ADTR	$b = 0$	$b < 0$
3A	MC	$b = 0$	$b > 0$
3B	SIZE	$b = 0$	$b < 0$
3C	FC	$b = 0$	$b \neq 0$
4A	EVCE	$b = 0$	$b < 0$
4A	LVCE	$b = 0$	$b > 0$
4B	ECHMT	$b = 0$	$b < 0$
4B	LCHMT	$b = 0$	$b > 0$
6A	LATE	$b = 0$	$b < 0$
6B	MTLTY	$b = 0$	$b > 0$
6C	ASPR	$b = 0$	$b < 0$

against the FTM. This also is measured by a dummy variable. It is coded 1 if the firm's auditor in the fiscal year represented by the observation was one of the Big Eight that supported the prohibition. Otherwise the value is 0; the variable is called ADTR.

The third set of variables represents measures of the effects of the inducement of particular financial reporting practices. The measurement of these is derived from the literature of managerial economics that has explored firm-level determinants of the adoption of financial reporting standards (Dhaliwal et al., 1982; Hagerman & Zmijewski, 1979; Salamon & Smith, 1979; Zmijewski & Hagerman, 1981). Hypothesis 3a concerns managerially controlled firms. This effect is measured by a dummy variable, coded 1 if the firm is categorized as managerially controlled in the fiscal year in question, and 0 otherwise; it is called MC. For fiscal years 1962–1972, the measurement is based on Kotz's (1978) classification. It is coded 1 if a firm was not under at least partial owner control. For fiscal years from 1972–1977, the classification is based on Herman's (1981) classification. For years after 1977, a firm is coded as under management control if no individual owned 5% or more of the voting stock of a firm according to the 10k report. From these classifications, a dummy variable called MC was created to measure the effect. Hypothesis 3b concerned the effects of size on the propensity to adopt the FTM. To create a measure of this construct that would be comparable both cross-sectionally and longitudinally, the following procedure was used: For all firm fiscal years that ended within a particular calendar year, the median total assets was determined. This was subtracted from the total assets of each firm in that year; the difference then was divided by the median total assets. The result is a measure of size equal to each firm's position above or below the median total assets of all firms in the sample that year, stated as a percentage of that median. A negative value means that the firm was smaller than the median firm in that year; a positive value implies the opposite. The variable is called SIZE. Hypothesis 3c concerned the effects of financial control. For fiscal years 1962–1972, the measurement is based on Kotz's (1978) classification of a firm as being under at least partial financial control. For fiscal years 1972–1977, the classification is based on Herman's (1981) classification. For years after 1977, a firm is coded as financially controlled if a financial institution owned 5% or more of the voting stock of a firm according to the 10k report. From these classifications, a dummy variable called FC was created to measure the effect.

The fourth set of hypotheses concerned the deliberate acquisition of financial reporting practices by firms. Hypothesis 4a concerned firms with high variance in the amount of investment tax credit. The proxy for this will be the absolute value of the coefficient of variation of capital expenditures over the five periods up to and including the current fiscal year.[7] I used absolute value of the coefficient of variation, rather than the variance, in order to correct for the fact that larger firms would have greater capital expenditures and hence greater variance in those expenditures. I believed that a relative measure, deflating variance in capital expenditures by the absolute value of the mean expenditure, was a better measure of the uncertainty facing each firm with respect to the amount of its tax credits. I predict that the greater this measure of uncertainty, the more likely the managers at a firm are to conform to prevailing practice. This variable is called VCE. The hypothesis predicts that this variable will have a negative effect from 1962 to 1964 and a positive effect from 1965 to 1984; two variables are created. The first is equal to VCE from 1962 to 1964 and is 0 if the year is later than 1964; it is called EVCE. The second is equal to VCE from 1965 to 1984 and is 0 if the year is earlier than 1965; it is called LVCE. Hypothesis 4b concerned the influence of changing personnel among the top management team as a source of normative pressures to conformity with prevailing practices. The top management team is operationalized as the Officers of the Corporation listed in the annual report. Turnover is measured as the percentage of the current year's top management team who were not members of the top management team in the previous year. The hypothesis predicts that this variable will have a negative effect from 1962 to 1964 and a positive effect from 1965 to 1984; as above, two variables are created. The first represents management turnover from 1962 to 1964 and is 0 if the year is later than 1964; it is

TABLE 8.4 Descriptive Statistics for All Variables

Variable	Mean	S.D.	Minimum	Maximum
METHOD	.14	.34	0	1
FY64	.14	.35	.00	1.00
ICC	.03	.18	.00	1.00
FPC	.10	.30	.00	1.00
ADTR	.41	.49	0	1
MC	.21	.40	0	1
SIZE	1.31	4.95	−.96	47.57
FC	.30	.46	0	1
EVCE	.16	.22	.00	1.35
LVCE	.18	.22	.00	1.25
ECHMT	.05	.09	.00	.58
LCHMT	.07	.10	.00	.92
LATE	.53	.50	.00	1.00
MTLTY	.07	.15	.00	2.00
ASPR	.00	.28	−2.15	3.56

NOTE: Number of observations is 934 for all variables.

called ECHMT. The second represents management turnover from 1965 to 1984 and is 0 if the year is earlier than 1965; it is called LCHMT.

The final set of hypotheses is derived from arguments concerning the incorporation of financial reporting practice. Hypothesis 5 summarized the argument that firms that did not adopt the FTM in 1964 were less likely to adopt the FTM in subsequent years. This effect is measured by a dummy variable for fiscal years ending during calendar years between 1965 and 1984; it is called LATE. Hypothesis 5b involved the prediction that firms with the largest amounts of investment tax credit will be most likely to adopt the FTM. The proxy for this will be amount of investment tax credit included in the current year's calculation of net income on the financial statements; it is stated as a percentage of total net income in the current year and is called MTLTY.[8] Hypothesis 5c concerned the effect of high variance in net income with a downward trend. This is measured using percentage changes in the earnings per share of the firm over the 5 fiscal years up to and including the current fiscal year. The mean percentage change in this series is multiplied by the variance; thus, a large negative number implies that the firm had a mean change that was negative as well as a large variance in those changes. This variable is called ASPR and is expected to have a negative effect. Descriptive statistics for the independent variables are reported in Table 8.4.

ESTIMATION PROCEDURES

The time series data used in this study represented cross-sectional observations over a finite and relatively small number of periods. For this reason, the assumption of continuous time estimation, necessary for many longitudinal estimation techniques, was not appropriate. A maximum likelihood LOGIT estimation (Allison, 1984; Flath & Leonard, 1979) is an efficient estimation technique for a categorical dependent variable. The assumption implicit in using such a technique for time series observations is that, except for variation in the independent variables, the probability of an event, in this case adoption of the FTM, is time invariant. The validity of this assumption is supported for these data as discussed by Mezias (1990).

MAXIMUM LIKELIHOOD LOGIT ESTIMATES

Given the adequacy of the assumption of constant hazards within periods distinguished in the model, a model including all of the independent variables was estimated; results are presented in Table 8.5. The model as a whole is a very significant predictor of the adoption of the FTM. The chi-square statistic, 301.57, allows rejection of the null hypothesis of no effect from the independent variables, $p = .001$. Hypothesis 1, concerning the imposition of financial reporting practices is supported strongly. Hypothesis 1a is accepted against the null of no effect, $p = .001$. Hypothesis 1b is accepted as well, $p = .01$; the mandate to use the FTM issued by the Interstate Commerce Commission had the expected effect of increasing the probability of adoption. However, Hypothesis 1c is rejected; a similar mandate by the Federal Power Commission did not affect significantly the probability of adoption of the FTM among firms subject to its regulation. Hypothesis 2 is rejected; the authorization of financial reporting practices as measured by the ADTR variable does not seem to have a significant effect on the probability of adopting the FTM. Hypothesis 3, concerning the inducement of financial reporting practices, is supported partially. Specifically, Hypothesis 3b is accepted, $p = .01$. The results are consistent with the argument that the political costs imposed on large firms, as measured by the variable SIZE, induce these firms to avoid adoption of the FTM. However, Hypotheses 3a and 3c are rejected; the null hypotheses of no effect are accepted for both MC and FC. Managerially controlled firms were no more likely to adopt the FTM than owner-controlled firms. Similarly, being under financial control seems to have had no systematic effect on the adoption of the FTM.

Hypothesis 4, concerning the acquisition of financial reporting practices, is supported partially as well. Hypothesis 4a is rejected; thus,

TABLE 8.5 Results of Maximum Likelihood Logistic Regression

Explanatory Variable	Estimated Coefficient	Standard Error	T Variable
Constant	−2.211	0.419	−5.273*
FY64	3.394	0.323	10.516*
ICC	1.864	0.498	3.747*
FPC	0.379	0.529	0.717
ADTR	−0.300	0.277	−1.087
MC	0.335	0.309	1.086
SIZE	−0.258	0.094	−2.610*
FC	−0.024	0.279	−0.084
EVCE	−0.837	0.750	−1.117
LVCE	0.653	1.224	0.534
ECHMT	−2.946	1.503	−1.961*
LCHMT	3.737	1.586	2.358*
LATE	−1.992	0.719	−2.772*
MTLTY	2.028	0.587	3.454*
ASPR	−0.132	0.385	−0.343

*$p < .05$ for rejection of null hypothesis. $R^2 = 0.5032$. $N = 934$.

uncertainty, as measured by the variance in the amount of capital expenditures that are the basis for the investment tax credit, was not a significant predictor of conformity to prevailing practice. The null hypothesis of no effect is accepted for both EVCE and LVCE. However, Hypothesis 4b, concerning the diffusion of personnel and the adoption of prevailing financial reporting practices, is accepted. During the years 1962 to 1964, when the majority of firms still used the DM, change in the top management was associated with a lower probability of adopting the FTM. However, beginning in 1965 and through to the end of the study in 1984, the majority of firms used the FTM by the beginning of the fiscal year. In these years, turnover in the top management at firms that had not yet adopted the FTM was associated with an increased probability of adopting it. The evidence is consistent with the argument that prevailing accounting practices are acquired by firms when they bring new personnel into the top management team. Finally, Hypothesis 5, concerning the incorporation of financial reporting practices, is supported for two of the three derived predictions. Hypothesis 5a posited that a history of having maintained the DM in 1964 would make it less likely that a firm would adopt the FTM in subsequent years. This tendency was measured by the dummy variable LATE; the prediction is supported, $p = .01$. Firms that did not adopt the FTM when first allowed to in 1964 were significantly less likely to adopt the FTM in subsequent years. Hypothesis 5b posited that management is more likely to incorporate a practice when it serves the short-term goal of increasing net income. This idea, as measured by the effect of the variable MTLTY, is supported, $p = .01$. The very-short-term nature of the history dependence posited by the incorporation of organizational practice is emphasized in the rejection of hypothesis 5c. Here, a more long-term measure of the use of a switch to the FTM as a means of smoothing the net income stream of the firm was posited. This more long-term, strategic manipulation of the income number, as measured by the variable ASPR, is rejected. It should be noted that these significant results were obtained despite some modest to high correlations among the independent variables; these are reported in Table 8.6.

Discussion and Conclusions

The discussion of the results will focus on what can be learned about institutional sources of financial reporting practice and how this fits with other theories. To do this, I will discuss how the results might be used to illuminate the relationship between institutional theory and other theories that have made the same or similar predictions (cf. Table 8.2). Hypothesis 1a is supported in that the mandates of the APB were followed; prior to 1964, when an APB prohibition of the FTM was in place, firms were less likely to use it. Perhaps more interesting than support for this hypothesis is the fact that some firms adopted the FTM even during the period when it was prohibited. The institutional reasons for this are two. First, Scott (1987, p. 501) explicitly argued for the relevance of the distinction between "imposition by means of authority vs. imposition by means of coercive authority." The relevance of the distinction is that imposition by coercion is more likely to be met by resistance. The split in the Big Eight accounting firms and lukewarm support of the APB prohibition by the Securities and Exchange Commission denied it the aura of authority; instead, the prohibition was widely perceived as imposition by coercion (Mezias, 1990). Thus, although the institutional perspective would expect the APB prohibition to inhibit firms from using the FTM, it would also anticipate that this prohibition would be resisted. Second, the fragmented centralization that has been a central focus of institutional theory (Meyer & Scott, 1983) undermined the APB position against the FTM: The Securities and Exchange Commission failed to back the prohibition, and prominent regulatory agencies with rule-making authority over financial statements, such as the ICC and the FPC, advocated the FTM despite the APB prohibition.

TABLE 8.6 Correlations Among Independent Variables

	FY64	ICC	FPC	ADTR	MC	SIZE	FC	EVCE	LVCE	ECHMT	LCHMT	LATE	MTLTY
ICC	0.044												
FPC	-0.072	0.000											
ADTR	-0.061	-0.081	0.156										
MC	0.029	-0.049	-0.137	-0.099									
SIZE	-0.037	-0.029	-0.021	0.136	-0.092								
FC	0.054	0.036	-0.157	-0.094	-0.170	-0.103							
EVCE	0.375	0.147	-0.166	-0.147	0.061	-0.130	0.112						
LVCE	-0.342	-0.155	0.013	0.145	-0.124	-0.038	-0.029	-0.618					
ECHMT	0.254	0.137	-0.106	-0.044	0.022	-0.023	0.065	0.461	-0.456				
LCHMT	-0.269	-0.122	0.037	0.014	-0.024	0.050	-0.082	-0.486	0.504	-0.359			
LATE	-0.438	-0.198	0.145	0.161	-0.069	0.093	-0.119	-0.791	0.780	-0.584	0.615		
MTLTY	-0.035	-0.043	-0.049	0.048	-0.025	-0.033	0.000	-0.185	0.232	-0.142	0.157	0.242	
ASPR	0.009	-0.025	0.001	0.018	0.068	-0.016	0.004	-0.085	0.002	-0.027	0.043	0.032	0.053

The other two perspectives that would predict results similar to the imposition of organizational practice are resource dependence and rational choice theory. From a resource dependence point of view, the fact that some firms did use the method despite the prohibition may be harder to understand. It would seem that some additional analysis suggesting why certain members of the Fortune 200 were less dependent on the government might be necessary. Generally, I would suggest that one way to distinguish the institutional and resource dependence perspectives in future work would be to study noncompliance with institutional mandates and see whether explanations based on resource flows compare with explanations for noncompliance from an institutional perspective (Oliver, 1991). For a rational choice approach, the additional analysis would have to focus on why some firms decided it was in their self-interest to disobey the APB prohibition and use the FTM. Mezias (1990) found no evidence that any of a myriad of variables based on rational theories could explain why some firms never adopted the FTM. The challenge for future research would be to compare institutional and rational explanations for noncompliance directly.

The split support for attempted imposition by the Interstate Commerce Commission, which did affect use of the FTM, and imposition by the Federal Power Commission, which did not affect use of the FTM, is problematic for all three theories. From an institutional perspective, the main question has to be why one regulatory agency succeeded in exercising coercive pressures for conformity with its mandates, but the other did not. I have no evidence to suggest, for example, that the Interstate Commerce Commission exercised imposition by authority and the Federal Power Commission exercised imposition by coercion. Similarly, I have no evidence to suggest that the patterns of resource dependence of firms subject to regulation by the one agency would be systematically different from the patterns among firms subject to regulation by the other agency. Finally, I have no a priori explanation of why the self-interest of firms subject to regulation by one agency would lead to compliance but the self-interest of firms subject to regulation by the other would not. I interpret the results for Hypotheses 1b and 1c to suggest that a comparative study of differential compliance in varied organizational fields might be a useful way to begin to distinguish institutional, resource dependence, and rational choice predictions.

The professional authorization of particular financial reporting practices is not supported by the results of this study. This presents a dilemma for both the institutional prediction that professionals are important actors in institutional environments and the resource dependence argument that they control legitimacy, which is an important resource. One obvious explanation would be that the sanctioning of accounting practices by the certified public accounting profession does not matter. Given the strong evidence that the professions do influence organizational practices (Baron et al., 1986; Edelman, 1990, 1992; Scott & Meyer, 1983), I believe that accepting such an explanation would require a further explanation for why professionals are unimportant in this field. Mezias and Chung (1989) have provided strong evidence that the accounting profession is the single most important actor in affecting the content of the institutional rules embedded in accounting principles. As a result, I do not believe that it is correct to conclude that professionals are not important actors. Instead, I believe the explanation lies in the particular choice examined here. Of particular importance are the facts that both the FTM and the DM had received some support from members of the Big Eight, and that the Securities and Exchange Commission had issued a rule that allowed for either method. The result was a set of conflicting signals from the institutional environment (D'Aunno, Sutton, & Price, 1991).

Given this, auditing firms that favored the DM may have been unwilling to risk a relationship (Levinthal & Fichman, 1988) with a client to back the APB. Other prestigious members of the profession had not voted to pass the rule, and the Securities and Exchange Commission had declined to back the APB. As a result, it was more likely that clients could argue that they had legitimate reasons for not choosing the DM. Thus, even focusing exclusively on the institutional concepts of rationalization and legitimacy, there is reason to expect that the accounting firms that had voted in favor of the APB prohibition of the FTM would not refuse to authorize its use by their clients. A resource dependence perspective suggests an additional reason why the accounting profession may have failed to influence firms to choose the DM: If any auditing firm insisted on rejecting the FTM in the face of a client's claims that it was allowed under officially sanctioned rules, the client firm would have no trouble finding an audit firm that was not so insistent. All large companies knew that four of the Big Eight firms had not supported the APB in the first place. Both of these explanations for the null finding suggest some implications for future research. The split in the profession and the multiplicity of contradictory institutional rules suggest the need for a more complete articulation of professions within institutional theory. In particular, we need a theory to explain those instances in which professions are successful in defining their practice as objective, exterior truth (Boland, 1982), as opposed to acting as if solutions to problems addressed by the profession are political. Merging institutional theory and resource dependence would suggest research that would begin to address the success of professions in defining themselves and the question of relative power of a profession versus its clients (Meyer & Scott, 1983).

The results for Hypothesis 3 are a good illustration of how rational choice arguments can be contextualized by institutional arguments. As Scott (1987, p. 508) has argued, institutional environments can be seen as shaping what ends are seen as legitimate and what appropriate means for pursuing those ends might be. The acceptance of Hypothesis 3b, regarding size, shows that large firms seemed to want to avoid boosting their income. Scott's (1987) argument would seem to suggest that as various stakeholders other than owners have organized themselves, large, visible firms have seen that there is an advantage in decreasing reported earnings. Examination of the interaction of institutional mechanisms and the resulting changes to firm-level rationality both over time, that is, in response to changing organization of stakeholders, and as firms grow larger would be a fascinating area of investigation concerning the interaction of the rational and the institutional. Similarly, the effect of size would suggest that the resource dependencies of firms change as they grow. In particular, it would seem that large firms can best deal with significant interdependencies by adopting financial reporting practices that reduce reported income. Documenting these interdependencies and demonstrating how they develop into changing sets of legitimate financial reporting practices for small and large firms would do much to explore how the resource dependence and institutional perspectives might interact.

The rejection of Hypotheses 3a and 3c regarding owner and financial control are similarly interesting. Closer examination of how accounting and control at owner-controlled firms differ from those at firms that do not have such concentrated ownership would be interesting. It could begin to shed light on the institutional mechanisms that owners attempt to use to control firms, and that firms use to manage the differential interdependencies created by more-widely versus less-widely dispersed ownership. Looking to examples more contemporary than the ITC, one could examine how the accounting practices to compute the earnings to be put into the incentive compensation scheme for executives are determined (Healy, 1985). From the perspective of institutional theory, an argument based on isomorphic pressures could be made. From the perspective of rational choice, an argument could be made in terms of its incentive alignment properties. Finally, from a resource dependence perspective, an argument could be made regarding which constituencies of the firm are represented and how this representation helps the firm manage important interdependencies. The rejection of Hypothesis 3c could be investigated with similar questions. In fact, the starting point of this investigation could focus on an issue suggested by existing literature: Financial institutions able to specify the accounting practices used in measuring compliance with debt contracts, which usually are not identical with the accounting methods used to prepare financial statements for financial reporting purposes. Thus, the leading organized suppliers of capital have been able to force borrowing organizations to engage in the effort of preparing special financial statements (Fogelson, 1978; Leftwich, 1981). A comparison of institutional, resource dependence, and rational choice explanations for the ability of these firms to specify their terms could be tremendously interesting.

The support for Hypothesis 4, regarding the acquisition of organizational structure, presents an interesting paradox. The source of uncertainty closest to the actual practice in question, varying amounts of capital expenditures leading to varying amounts of tax credit, had no effect on the decision. However, uncertainty at a broader level, deviation from prevailing practice, coupled with turnover in top management, did tend to increase the likelihood that firms would conform with prevailing practice. Thus, in years prior to 1965, the first year in which FTM was the prevailing practice for firms at the beginning of the year, firms with high turnover were *less likely* to adopt the FTM. However, in years subsequent to 1965, firms with high top management team turnover were more likely to adopt the FTM.

There is support for the incorporation of practices by organizations: A history of having maintained the DM in 1964 was associated with a subsequent reduction in the likelihood of adopting the FTM. In addition, firms tended to use the FTM to boost reported net income. In terms of rational choice theory, this result presents a dilemma: Why should firms take a short-run gain in net income at the expense of the long run? Similarly, why should firms be so opposed to the DM, given that in the long run it will yield the same results as the FTM and there are no effects on real economic income? A sophisticated model of multiperiod rationality requires an articulated theory of why firms appear to focus so much on the short term. This is made more problematic by the rejection of the more sophisticated model of income manipulation with the insignificance of the income-smoothing variable, ASPR. From the point of view of resource dependence, the interesting aspect of the findings about income manipulation is a determination of which constituencies controlling which resource contingencies are mollified by boosting net income. Together with an institutional focus on cognition, professionals, and the endogeneity of environments, an investigation of how the firm decides to respond to which constituencies might be an interesting approach to the integration of resource dependence and institutional theory. For both theories, adding an institutional perspective serves as a reminder that managing the coordination of organizations with their environments is complex at any given point in time and becomes rapidly more complex as various processes of organizational and environmental change unfold over time. Using institutional arguments to justify the assumption that management acts within the bounds of conventional accounting wisdom may be a good simplifying assumption for moving forward with either perspective.

The object of this chapter has been to move forward the important research agenda of using institutional theory to study for-profit sectors. I believe that the strong results are suggestive of the utility of moving away from a partition of environments into market-driven and institutionalized sectors (Powell, 1991, p. 183). In addition, I interpret the findings as a further demonstration of the applicability of organization theory and institutional theory more specifically to understanding financial reporting practices. Most past models of these practices have relied chiefly on applied theories of rational choice. Also, I believe that I have helped to refine our understanding of the extent to which the institutional and rational perspectives complement or contradict one another. In particular, I have suggested some very specific questions that might be investigated, with the goal of further development of the relation between the institutional and rational perspectives. To help the investigation of these questions, I have proposed and demonstrated the empirical utility of a variety of measures to operationalize the multiple institutional sources of financial reporting practices. In closing, I would emphasize that addressing the key theoretical issues facing the institutional perspective suggests that research in this perspective must increasingly address its applicability to the study of for-profit organizations.

Notes

1. For those not familiar with financial reporting, a bit of explanation might clarify some issues. The critical distinction is between the income statements for tax purposes and the income statements for financial reporting purposes. Income statements for tax purposes are those prepared for authorities charged with collecting taxes. Income statements for financial reporting purposes are sent to outside parties in forms like the 10k and annual reports. These two types of financial statements are distinct, and the net income numbers on them need not agree. The focus of this study is on how the tax credit taken on the income statement for tax purposes is entered on the income statement for financial reporting purposes.

2. It should be noted as well that there are no direct effects on the cash flow to firms; this simplifies measurement tremendously. The only cash flows that accrue to firms as a result of the credit are from reductions in income taxes. These are reflected in full on the income

statements for tax purposes (cf. Table 8.1), regardless of whether firms use the FTM or DM to report the ITC on income statements for financial reporting purposes.

3. Two forms of institutional explanation listed by Scott (1987, pp. 506-507), the bypassing of organizational structure and the imprinting of organizational structure, are not discussed here. Imprinting arguments apply at firm birth; all of the firms studied here are large existing firms. Bypassing is not studied because it addresses phenomena internal to firms. Financial reporting is external reporting; thus, internal bypassing of firm structures or practices is not relevant.

4. An argument could also be made that large firms are more inert, and hence, that size is really a variable more related to incorporation than inducement. Given the predominance of the size variable in existing rational choice models of financial reporting practices, I record it here with those interpretations while noting that an argument stating that large firms were more inert would make the same prediction.

5. From our perspective, acquisition is a purely institutional phenomenon, not predicted by either resource dependence or rational choice; thus, no integration with these theories will be discussed for these hypotheses.

6. The discussion of this data by Mezias (1990), from which this paragraph is drawn, provides more detail on this sample for the interested reader.

7. Capital expenditures are used because for early adopters there is no series with which to estimate the variance in the actual amount of ITC.

8. As Mezias (1990, p. 444) notes, this measure may be biased in favor of rejecting the null hypothesis. However, supplementary analysis reveals that correcting for this bias, possible only for later years, does not change the fact that the effect is significant, although it is reduced somewhat.

IV. INSTITUTIONAL EFFECTS ON INDUSTRIES

9

Accounting for Acquisition Waves

Evidence From the
U.S. College Publishing Industry

PATRICIA H. THORNTON

ECONOMIC AND BUSINESS HISTORIANS (Chandler, 1990; Nelson, 1959) have documented that acquisition activity occurs in waves and it galvanizes significant change in the organization of firms and industries. Chandler (1990, p. 79) has described merger waves as the single most important factor in the restructuring of industrial enterprise in the United States. The period from 1890 to 1904 saw created corporate monopolies; the 1920s, oligopolies; and the mid-1960s to the mid-1970s, conglomerate forms. The merger wave of the 1980s has yet to be categorized, but nascent views see it as changing the mode of corporate governance to a market for corporate control (Davis & Stout, 1992; Lazonick, 1992).

Given that acquisition activity occurs in waves and that it has important implications for organizational and industrial change, why then has acquisition activity as collective action remained unexplored? Why have modern accounts of acquisition activity remained at the level of the individual firm when it is the case that many firms within and across industries make similar strategy decisions to engage in acquisition activity at approximately the same time? Moreover, when more aggregate approaches are employed, why are these investigations conducted on firms across industry

AUTHOR'S NOTE: I wish to thank Dick Scott and the conference participants for their helpful comments on the presentation of this research.

boundaries in a fashion oblivious to social system dynamics? Such approaches ignore the social and cultural forces that motivate acquisition activity.

The majority of research on acquisition activity has been driven by financial and managerial economists and has emphasized the role of economic efficiency (Benston, 1980; Ravenscraft & Scherer, 1987; Williamson, 1988) and managerial agency (Marris, 1964). A few organization theorists have investigated the role of resource dependence (Pfeffer, 1972; Pfeffer & Salancik, 1978; Thornton, 1993), organizational learning, (Amburgey & Miner, 1992), and social networks (Fligstein and Brantley, 1992; Fligstein & Markowitz, 1993; Haunschild, 1994).[1] Although these micro-level approaches make important contributions to understanding acquisition activity, they cannot account for the observed waves of mergers and acquisitions. Without detracting from these earlier arguments, this investigation suggests that current accounts of acquisition activity may be incomplete.

To account for the collective nature of acquisition activity, this study investigates the institutional forces operating at the wider social system and organizational field levels. I draw upon the work of institutional theorists (DiMaggio & Powell, 1983; Meyer, 1994; Scott, 1994b, 1994c; Scott & Meyer, 1983, 1991a; Strang & Meyer, 1993) to develop a model using two levels of analysis: the global business culture and the organizational field. In my characterization of global business culture, I rely on historical accounts of the evolution of management ideologies during eras of acquisition waves (Chandler, 1962, 1990, 1992b; Lazonick, 1992). To portray the life cycle of organizational fields, I use a longitudinal case study of the U.S. college publishing industry. To motivate specific arguments on the social and collective nature of acquisition waves, I present data on the frequency of mergers and acquisitions of five industries across two acquisition waves, in the late 1960s and the late 1980s. Two characteristics of acquisition waves are illustrated by these data: (a) that they occur at relatively the same time across diverse industries and (b) that there are some notable differences in the timing of waves at the industry level. To explicate these outcomes, I present industry-level data using both an economic perspective (which looks at the performance of capital markets) and a social perspective (which looks at the formation of an organizational field).

The central premise of this model is that acquisition activity occurs in waves across diverse firms and industries, because firms are responsive to trends in the global business culture. Moreover, I argue that differences in the timing of waves across industries can be accounted for by the stage of development of local organizational fields. Figure 9.1 and subsequent sections of this chapter elaborate key examples of this model. Research propositions are formulated to guide further investigation.

A Collective
Action Model of Acquisition Activity

MANAGEMENT STRATEGY FROM
ORGANIZATIONAL FIELD AND GLOBAL CULTURE:
THE RATIONALIZATION OF MANAGEMENT IDEOLOGIES

Barley and Kunda (1992) and Meyer (1994) argue that an important source of influence on the behavior of firms and the performance of organizational fields is derived from the rationalization of management ideologies at the global cultural level. Meyer (1994) contends that local firms and organizational fields derive models of appropriate strategy from general ideologies rationalized in larger environments. Over time, cultural environments have become increasingly rationalized by the processes of exchange and domination among elite organizations, nation-states, and the sciences and professions. The outcome of these "rationalizing agents" is the development of isomorphic models of strategy. Meyer, for example, describes management, accounting, consulting, and personnel administration as not limited to specific types of organizations, but as general models that surface almost everywhere in trends or waves (Meyer, 1994, p. 31).

Other organization theorists and economic historians have described the rationalization of management ideologies in respect to specific business challenges during different historical eras (Chandler, 1962, 1992b; Davis, Diekmann, & Tinsley, 1994; Davis & Stout, 1992; Fligstein, 1990; Lazonick, 1992). Chandler (1992b), Lazonick (1992), and Davis and Stout (1992) have described the coevolution of eras of management strategy in relation to waves of acquisition activity. For example, at the turn of the century, entrepreneurs sought to collectively solve the problems of over-capacity and fierce competition by practicing horizontal integration, resulting in the first merger wave. In a subsequent era, the strategy of vertical integration to manage the uncertainty of relationships with scarce suppliers led to the second merger wave of the 1920s. During the 1960s maturing American industry sought to bolster diminishing returns by diversifying into higher growth industries. The popularization of this strategy was a key factor in the unprecedented number of acquisitions in the 1960s (Chandler, 1992b). In the 1980s, the market for corporate control became the dominant strategy, encouraging a wave of acquisitions that repositioned corporate assets through public securities markets to enable the highest returns to "brokers" and shareholders (Chandler, 1992b, pp. 275-281; Davis & Stout, 1992; Jensen & Ruback, 1983; Lazonick, 1992).[2]

The central argument in this historical analysis is that eras of global business culture coevolve in a nonrecursive fashion with corporate strategies and waves of acquisition activity. This raises the question: Which mechanisms link and diffuse global-level ideologies that encourage acquisition activity with local industry strategies?

ORGANIZATIONAL FIELDS

To theorize this relationship, I draw upon the concept of an organizational field because it defines how organizations engaged in constructing, competing, supplying, distributing, supporting, and regulating one another are linked to each other and the wider societal culture (DiMaggio & Powell, 1983, p. 142; Hirsch, 1972, 1985; Scott, 1994c; Scott & Meyer, 1983, 1991a). Organizational fields take into account culture and nonrational influences, such as the construction of belief systems and symbolic frameworks governing logics of action in firms and in the field. Organizational field boundaries are distinct from conventional boundaries because they do not assume similar products and services, but include dissimilar organizations that influence performance such as suppliers, customers, and regulators. Economists (Chandler, 1962, 1990; Rumelt, 1974; Williamson, 1975) have described how firms and industries grow across industry boundaries through diversification, vertical integration, and strategic alliances; therefore, an organizational field, as distinct from an industry, is a useful concept for analyzing and for establishing boundaries.

Organizational fields, through the process of structuration, are powerful vehicles of social order. DiMaggio and Powell (1983) contend that an organizational field in the emergent stage is composed of isolated and specialized organizations. Over time, however, as organizations become aware of one another and increase their level of interaction, status hierarchy and strategy isomorphism arise from cooperative and competitive interorganizational and interfield relations.

THE EVOLUTION OF ORGANIZATIONAL FIELDS:
CONNECTING FIELDS AND GLOBAL CULTURE

Organizational fields have been theorized as an intermediate unit of analysis linking individual organizational strategy and structure to the wider societal culture (DiMaggio, 1986b, p. 337; Scott, 1994c). Moreover, organizational fields can be categorized on the basis of the level of isolation from or connection to trans-field belief systems (Scott, 1994c).

Thus, an organizational field is constituted by interfirm relationships and structures within the field, as well as by events, relationships, and structures that connect firms, fields, and wider institutional environments. This assumes that the origin of business practices sometimes comes from the structural and symbolic links between the organizational field and broader societal systems and ideologies (Meyer, 1994; Scott, 1994c).

More specifically, Strang and Meyer (1993) theorize that the diffusion of ideas between organizational fields and global culture occurs through the development of "theorists" and organizations with world stature[3] that interpret and define the institutional environment around abstract cultural constructs.[4] Individuals and organizations within organizational fields symbolically identify with these cultural constructs and adapt them to their local situation.[5]

I argue that the potential for symbolic identification with global culture is determined by the degree to which institutions and organizational structures develop at the organizational field and wider society levels. For example, the spread of the M-form organization and the concomitant use of management consulting firms in a field signal the advent of formalized training based on general models (Meyer, 1994; Scott & Meyer, 1991b).[6] The rationalization of business programs in elite universities[7] leads to the popularization of business strategies (Abrahamson & Fombrun, 1992). These are examples of forces that serve as conduits and homogenizing influences to diffuse business practices.[8] The penetration of these institutions into organizational fields signals the strength of the field's connection to standardized management trends and ideologies originating in the wider institutional environment (e.g., the diversification movement and acquisition waves).

I present supportive evidence for this model from a longitudinal case study of the college publishing industry. With the coevolution of global business culture and the local organizational field, management practices and organizational structures developed and served as conduits through which general financial ideologies were imported into the specialized industry of publishing. At the global level, this was fostered by M-form organizations diversifying into publishing and exposing the field to management practices and organizational structures predicated on growth by acquisition. At the local field level, the diffusion of acquisition strategies crystallized from several organizing processes. Over time, dominant firms emerged and set models of practice within the context of increasing status competition. Interfirm exchange practices increased as markets proliferated, the company size mix changed, and large corporate publishers sought economies of scale, handling distribution for small publishers. Moreover, corporate publishers created in-house acquisitions departments, and boutique "deal-makers" emerged to "shop" acquisitions within the industry. The description provided below will help to elaborate these arguments.

ASSUMPTIONS ABOUT CULTURE
PRODUCTION, DIFFUSION, AND ISOMORPHISM

Certain assumptions about culture production, diffusion, and isomorphism in relation to management strategy warrant discussion. Meyer's (1994) general thesis assumes that distant information in the form of cultural constructs is an important means of diffusion.[9] This is consistent with recent findings in network analysis indicating that isomorphism can occur without direct network ties under conditions of structural equivalence (Burt, 1987; Galaskiewicz & Burt, 1991). There are, however, other views of the determinants of culture, diffusion, and isomorphism. Theorists have emphasized concrete, bottom-up, and meso-level influences, such as interlocking directorates (Fligstein & Brantley, 1992; Fligstein & Markowitz, 1993; Haunschild, 1994), the state (DiMaggio & Powell, 1983; Fligstein, 1990), and the coercive role of powerful actors (DiMaggio, 1988).[10] These approaches leave unanswered questions about how bandwagon effects and isomorphism occur among dissimilar firms and industries, even without the presence of direct ties or influence from the state (DiMaggio, 1992; Meyer, 1994; Meyer et al., 1987). Moreover, they engender sticky arguments about rational choice versus the adoption of inefficient forms.

Research Methods and Data Sources

CHOICE OF INDUSTRIES AND OBSERVATION PERIOD

Institutional theorists have called for research in the context of private profit-making firms with minimal impact from the state and the professions (Powell & DiMaggio, 1991, pp. 27-29). Industries in this analysis were selected to represent entrepreneurial firms in labor- and capital-intensive industries. Following SIC codes and Chandler's (1986) system of classification, textiles and publishing were chosen as labor-intensive industries; oil and gas, chemicals, and mining and minerals were selected as capital-intensive industries.

According to Chandler (1986), differences in potential economies of scale in the production technologies that are used suggest the rationale for the creation of large hierarchical firms. Capital-intensive industries have potential economies of scale, creating a close relationship between large

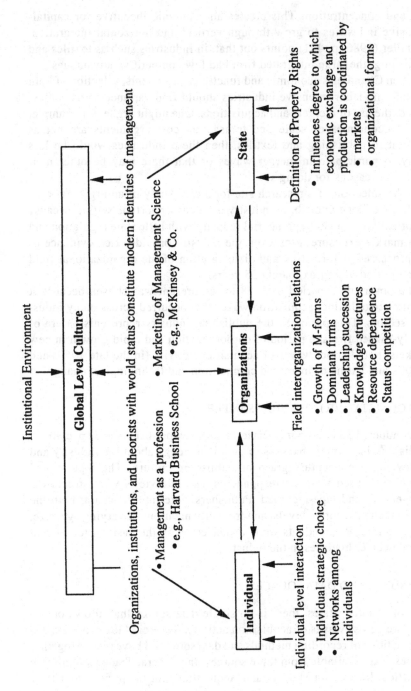

Figure 9.1. Factors Shaping Organizational Fields

Institutional Environment

Global Level Culture

Organizations, institutions, and theorists with world status constitute modern identities of management

- Management as a profession
  - e.g., Harvard Business School
- Marketing of Management Science
  - e.g., McKinsey & Co.

State

Definition of Property Rights

- Influences degree to which economic exchange and production is coordinated by
  - markets
  - organizational forms

Organizations

Field interorganization relations

- Growth of M-forms
- Dominant firms
- Leadership succession
- Knowledge structures
- Resource dependence
- Status competition

Individual

Individual level interaction

- Individual strategic choice
- Networks among individuals

size and concentration. This creates an economic incentive for capital-intensive industries to grow through vertical and horizontal integration. Chandler (1986, p. 421) points out that, in industries such as textiles and publishing, the large integrated firm had few competitive advantages.

Given Chandler's economic and functional arguments, selection of both capital- and labor-intensive industries should find variance across industries in the use of mergers and acquisitions. One might argue, for example, that if economies of scale and transaction cost arguments are not as relevant to publishing and textiles, then these industries would be less likely to participate in merger waves or that there may be other non-economic reasons for doing so.

In the selection of a research site for a case study of an organizational field, the college publishing industry offers an opportune setting because historically it is an entrepreneurial industry with little state regulation and high market exposure. Moreover, the industry provides rich evidence of the processes of formation and disintegration of the organizational field over a period of approximately 35 years.

The observation period of 1958 to the present was chosen because it captures two distinct acquisition waves that occurred across many industrial sectors. This period in the publishing industry represents an era of family-owned firms, a period of corporatization and rapid growth in new markets, two distinct waves of acquisition activity (in the late 1960s and 1980s), and a time of increased competition and technological change.

THE QUALITATIVE INTERVIEW SAMPLE

I conducted 30 one-hour interviews with key publishers and specialized publishing investment bankers to gain knowledge about the industry and to develop a conceptual grasp of publishing culture. The reputational method was used to select respondents, and interviews were structured, open-ended, and tape-recorded. Publishers were interviewed at both the editorial and executive levels, and from organizations of varying age, size, and structure. Respondents were also selected on the basis of tenure and notable career histories in the industry.

MEASURES AND DATA SOURCES

In the United States, there is no single data source that allows one to compare across waves of acquisition activity. See Reid (1968, pp. 20, 32) for a critique of recording methods and data sources. I have pieced together the best data available from three sources: the Federal Trade Commission Statistical Reports on Mergers and Acquisitions for the period from 1961 to 1979, *Mergerstat Review* for the period 1981 to 1991, and the *Literary Market Place* for the period 1958 to 1990. Acquisition activity is measured by a count of the number of merger and acquisition transactions on a yearly basis.

Industry-specific stock indices are used in this analysis as a proxy for the speculative opportunities offered by the market and as a measure of changes in the economic value of firms in a particular industry. Economists argue that stock price data are the most objective measure both of the performance of the capital market and for determining whether acquisition activity is motivated by concerns for efficiency (Jarrell, 1988; Manne, 1965; Nelson, 1959, p. 116). These data are obtained from Standard and Poor's Security Price Index Record Statistical Service.

Evidence Related to
Global Cultural Influences

Figure 9.2 presents a comparison of the time trends of acquisition activity for the oil and gas, chemicals, mining and minerals, textiles, and publishing industries for two merger and acquisition waves in the late 1960s and the mid- to late 1980s. These data indicate that, across diverse industries, merger and acquisition activity tends to occur in waves at approximately the same time.[11] Graph analysis in Figure 9.3 compares the publishing industry with all other industries and indicates a similar result. In general, these data provide evidence of collective action across diverse industries.

CAPITAL MARKETS AS
INCENTIVE FOR ACQUISITION WAVES

Several economists (Beckenstein, 1979; Golbe & White, 1988; Melicher, Ledolter, & D'Antonio, 1983; Nelson, 1959, p. 7; Steiner, 1975) have found positive, though not decisive, support for the development of capital markets as a motive for acquisition waves.[12] This line of work argues that the condition of the capital market, as reflected in stock price changes, is a more important influence on merger waves than are other industrial conditions. Essentially, the argument is that acquisition waves rise and fall with the rise and fall of the stock market.

The underlying microtheories in this line of research offering specific predictions have evolved over time with trends in management discourse. Particularly prominent during the era of diversification and conglomerate building, price/earnings theory argued that acquisitive companies search

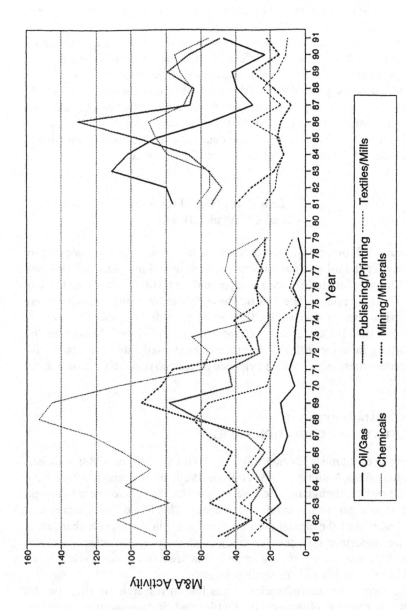

Figure 9.2. Merger and Acquisition Activity in Five Industries: 1961–1991

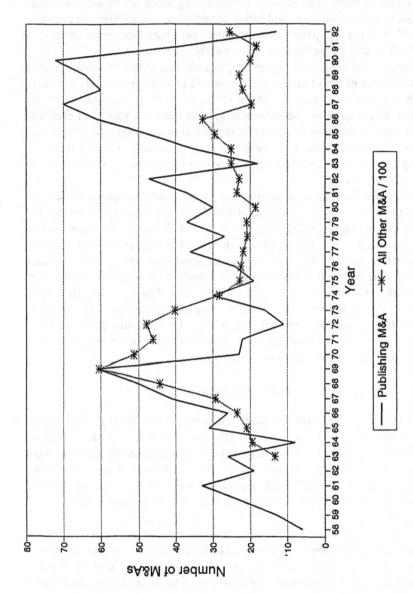

Figure 9.3. M&A Activity: 1958–1992 Publishing Versus All Other Industries

for targets with rising stock prices as a means to improve their own profitability by the transfer of earnings between acquired and acquiring companies (*Mergerstat Review*, 1990). Rising stock prices are good indicators of present earnings and future expectations concerning the corporation.[13] A target company whose earnings per share have been rising is a more desirable target than one whose earnings have not.[14]

Given these efficiency arguments, price/earnings theory would predict that the peak of the acquisition wave should precede or correlate perfectly with the peak of the stock market (Nelson, 1966, p. 63; Steiner, 1975, p. 98). The acquisition wave lasts as long as there is a supply of earnings enriching targets and decreases with declining corporate price earnings ratios. Economists have suggested a way of testing this argument by comparing changes in acquisition activity with changes in stock prices at the industry level.

The graph in Figure 9.4 compares the time trend of acquisition activity with the time trend of the Standard and Poor's stock market index for the book publishing industry during two waves.[15] Figure 9.4 shows some association between the performance of capital markets and merger and acquisition activity, but, contrary to price/earnings theory, it also reveals an unpredicted result.[16] The timing of the peak of the acquisition wave lags the peak of the stock market wave in both waves. The lag for the first wave is approximately 1 year and for the second wave approximately 2 years.[17] These lag periods are noted in black on Figure 9.4. In subsequent sections, I draw on an institutional account of the evolution of an organizational field to explicate this economic anomaly.

EVIDENCE RELATED TO INDUSTRY DIFFERENCES

In returning to Figures 9.2 and 9.3, it is noteworthy that there are slight, but clearly observable, differences in the timing of the beginning, duration, and end of acquisition waves across the five industries. Specifically with respect to publishing, Figure 9.3 shows that in the first merger wave, the industry began and ended the acquisition wave sooner than many other industries. Moreover, the second wave suggests evidence of a "bandwagon effect."[18]

Early work by Nelson (1959, pp. 38, 43) identified temporal differences in merger waves across industries. He identified that certain industries appear to have "spearheading effects" on the acquisition activity of other industries. This observation continues to be made in the business press as well (Pethokoukis, 1994). This phenomenon led Nelson to fruitlessly investigate potential economic explanations for these differences in timing at the industry level. He found that growth retardation, cost-price relation-

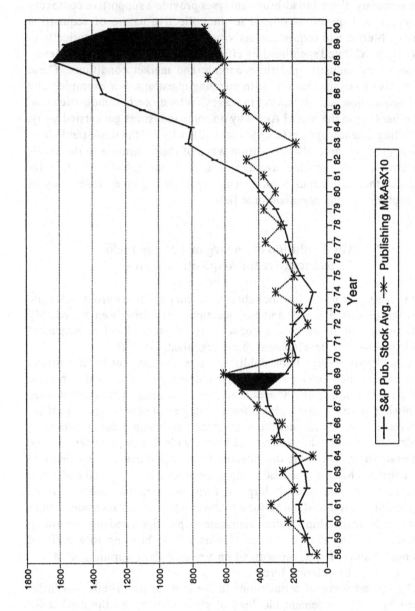

Figure 9.4. Stock Market and M&A Activity Publishing 1958–1990

ships in firms, and transportation costs, however, bore no relationship to the observed spearheading effects.

In summary, these broad-brush analyses provide a supportive context to pursue critical questions related to the collective nature of acquisition activity. Merger and acquisition activity has been presented historically in waves that exhibited spearheading effects and that could not be completely explained by industry-specific economic and market conditions. These descriptive analyses leave us with puzzling questions. For example, why does acquisition activity occurs in waves? Why do certain industries lead and others lag in the wave? And why do some industries get carried away, exhibiting a bandwagon effect? Specifically, why did the book-publishing industry exhibit an early acquisition wave of short duration in the 1960s and a wave of longer-than-average duration in the 1980s? We glean insights to these questions from a richer, more fine-grained case study of the evolution of the organizational field.

The Evolution of an Organizational Field as Incentive for Acquisition Waves

It is useful to foreshadow the substantive story about to unfold and relate it to the proposed model and the questions that have been raised. My description will focus on the coevolution of global-level management ideologies and the development of the organizational field.

In the 1960s college book publishing was an emergent organizational field. Formal networks were not highly developed. The field consisted primarily of publishing "houses," unitary form organizations, that were "publisher driven"[19] and isolated from strategies of how to "grow profits" by acquisitions. The acquisition wave in the publishing industry in the late 1960s was driven by the evolution of business ideologies practiced in large corporate firms external to the industry. Fortune 500 firms diversified into the industry, changing the leadership of estate-model firms and reshaping them into divisions of their large M-form organizations. This wave of acquisitions introduced the M-form to the industry on a mass scale, setting in place new leadership, modern management practices, and organizational structures linking the once-sleepy industry of publishing to a national business culture. It was an acquisition wave of short duration, as it was largely driven by external forces.

The second wave of acquisitions in the mid- to late 1980s was influenced by the management ideology of globalization and the market for corporate control. Foreign firms were key players in this wave of acquisitions and served to link book publishing to an international business sector. The acquisition wave exhibited a bandwagon effect, resulting from the penetration of global financial strategies and the structuration of the local organizational field (Thornton, 1994). Local organizing occurred through the development of dominant firms, interfirm resource dependencies, the emergence of status competition, and locally developed investment bankers. Subsequent sections describe in detail how national and global management strategies encouraged acquisition activity and how these strategies were introduced into the organizational field and spread by local organizing processes.

Global Business Culture and Industry Environment During Acquisition Wave Eras in the Late 1960s and 1980s

WAVE ONE

The first acquisition wave in the publishing industry, from 1967 to 1970, was propelled by two main factors: the exogenously driven diversification movement and the field life cycle of family-owned companies seeking capital, corporate status, and management expertise to expand into growing markets. During this period, publishing companies were the darlings of Wall Street and viewed as profitable targets by financially sophisticated corporations and acquisitive conglomerates. Most of the "hunters" were outsiders to publishing. They were large corporations such as IBM, ITT, Litton, Raytheon, Xerox, CBS, and RCA that, armed with the latest theories of management, sought to reduce the uncertainty of business cycles and bolster profits by transferring assets to high-growth industries. During this era, the environment was munificent. College enrollments were burgeoning and there were substantial increases in state and federal funding for education, libraries, and scientific research (Coser, Powell, & Kadushin, 1982).[20] Acquired firms in the 1960s framed acquisition positively as an opportunity to not only learn modern management practices but also obtain corporate resources to expand into new and growing markets.

This first wave of acquisitions linked the once-specialized character of the craft of publishing with general management strategies in Fortune 500 firms operating in a national business environment. Consistent with secular trends evidenced earlier in other industries (Chandler, 1962; Fligstein, 1985), this signaled the beginning of the shift from a family-estate model to a modern corporate enterprise.

WAVE TWO

The second acquisition wave, in the late 1980s, took place mostly within a broadened industry involving large multidivisional publishers and communications firms.[21] The hunters of this wave were publishers or captains of the communications industry. They were dominant individuals and major corporations such as Maxwell, Murdoch, Paramount, Pearson, Thomson, and Times Mirror. The ideological forces driving this wave were globalization and the market for corporate control. Compared to other business sectors, this wave exhibited a bandwagon effect. I argue it was fostered by local consolidating forces and the penetration of financially driven strategies introduced in the first wave that were subsequently spread by field-organizing processes and structures.

The second wave is further characterized by industry maturity and overcapacity, by the development of fierce competition and a decline of resources. The rate of growth of new markets was leveling off with the flattening of college enrollments and the declining growth rate of colleges and universities. Competition and uncertainty intensified with the development of the high-speed, high-resolution copy machine, the computerized distribution of used books, and an increasing density of publishing companies.

Moreover, foreign publishers who had unsuccessfully tried to found American divisions in the 1970s were favorably poised to acquire American publishers and gain access to American mass markets. Eight of the 11 major acquirers of U.S. educational publishing companies in the 1980s were foreign firms.[22] Thus, this wave of acquisitions linked U.S. publishing to the larger international business sector. Consistent with the global ideology of the market for corporate control, the cultural meaning of acquisition for target firms in the 1980s was quite different from the 1960s (Hirsch, 1986). There was concern with issues of control, survival, and preservation of identity.[23] For example, with respect to the 1980s, a prominent publisher stated:

So you lost those great publishing imprints. It took 50 to 75 years to get the market identification, and the acquiring company is like Attila the Hun. They have won and so their attitudes on a personal level are, we're okay and you're not. By and large the acquiring company treats it like a land grab. . . . For example, Harper ended up with 10 introductory psychology books to add to their own. So they now have psych to burn because they could only publish one or two revisions and new books a year.

In summary, economic motives only partially explain participation in the acquisition waves of the 1960s and the 1980s. It is also important to emphasize the role of organizational fields in institutionalizing management strategies that encourage acquisition activity. This suggests the following relationships between the evolution of management ideologies, organizational fields, and acquisition waves.

Proposition 1: Acquisition waves coevolve with the rationalization of management ideologies that encourage acquisition activity.

Proposition 2: Acquisition waves vary by industry in relation to the evolution of organizational fields.

Proposition 2a: Industries with highly elaborated organizational fields are more likely to lead and exhibit bandwagon effects in acquisition waves.

Proposition 2b: Industries in emerging organizational fields are less likely to participate in acquisition waves or at least will do so minimally.

Changes in the Nature of Governance: From Craft House to Corporate Enterprise

By the late 1980s the U.S. college publishing industry had evolved from a number of independent, family-owned companies by the absorption of many of the small and most of the medium-sized firms under several multidivisional publishing giants. In 1990 one ex-publisher turned investment deal-maker stated it this way:

> Today, the smaller companies are gobbled up faster by people doing acquisitions than they were 30 years ago. You look at today's roster at the Association of American Publishers meetings and there are about 3 privately owned companies out of the 140 that are here. I think if you went back 10 years ago, there were probably 12 or 15 privately owned companies, and . . . if you went back 30 years you might find that 80% of them were privately owned.

In the period 1958 to 1969, 17% of the firms in the industry had a multidivisional structure. By the 1980s, 40% had become multidivisional forms (Thornton, 1993).

Along with these changes in organizational form and size came changes in organizational and interfirm relations. I will describe the forces that structured the organizational field in the 1980s and how these conditions fostered homogeneous strategies that explain the occurrence of acquisition activity such as waves and bandwagons.

LOCAL CONDITIONS IN THE ORGANIZATIONAL FIELD
LEADING TO ISOMORPHIC GROWTH OF DOMINANT FIRMS

There is ample evidence concerning the growth of a few dominant firms in the industry that had the impact of creating strategy isomorphism. Beginning in the 1960s and 1970s, companies such as Prentice-Hall performed a significant "filtering" function (DiMaggio & Powell, 1983), with its unusually routinized business practices, monolithic sales training program, and early strategy to acquire and spin-off subsidiary companies. The initial training for many people who entered the business in the 1950s and 1960s was with Prentice-Hall and the few large counterpart firms. Indeed, because of characteristically high employee turnover in the industry, it is not uncommon to find senior-level executive publishers in competing publishing houses who were initially trained by the "P-H method." Prentice-Hall developed a "mothership" business strategy to acquire, clone, and spin-off subsidiary companies like Allyn & Bacon, Wadsworth, Dickenson, Merrill, Goodyear, and others. This had the effect of spreading variants of what was known in the business as the "P-H model." Consistent with emerging industries, other competing companies in the 1970s began to follow acquisition and spin-off strategies as well (Porter, 1980). In the 1980s, for example, with respect to imitation of acquisition activity, one executive stated:

> Certain individuals and actions drove it. . . . The publishing industry is a tiny neighborhood where everyone knows each other and everyone watches everybody. . . . We had a discussion about how we were noticing that a few big firms were making all these acquisitions, and we decided to be proactive about it, and that's when we started drawing up a hit list of acquisitions.

This suggests:

Proposition 3: Organizational fields with dominant firms are more likely to collectively engage in strategies.

INTERFIRM EXCHANGE DEPENDENCE

One way interfirm interaction increased was through the development of distribution contracts among publishers. Typically, for many book publishers, a major obstacle in founding and growing a successful com-pany is the cost of marketing and distribution. In the start-up years of a small independent company, it is not uncommon for these publishers to make arrangements with larger established publishers for the sale and distribution of their books. This is a form of resource dependence among small and large companies that easily diffuses information about competi-tors' products, strategy, markets, and potential acquisition candidates (Pfeffer & Salancik, 1978). Organization researchers contend that inter-firm exchange dependencies foster isomorphism (DiMaggio & Powell, 1983) and encourage growth by acquisition (Pfeffer, 1972; Thornton, 1993). For example, one publisher, speaking in reference to scouting acquisition targets, stated: "Sometimes you try distribution deals and other kinds of venture to get started and get to know these people. . . . With respect to Times Mirror acquiring Wolf Medical Publishers, Yearbook, a Times Mirror Company, had been Wolf's major distributor."

As the organizational field evolved, and growth by acquisitions became an accepted practice (Thornton, 1993), many mid-sized firms with their own distribution channels disappeared as a result of being acquired. At the same time, the continued entry of small firms into the field had the effect of increasing the overall level of resource exchange in the industry and thus the conditions that foster isomorphism and acquisition growth. For example, prior to the first acquisition wave, only 17% of the firms in the field had interfirm distribution contracts; in later periods, 45% engaged in such exchanges.

Thus one might expect that:

Proposition 4: Fields characterized by interfirm exchange depen-dencies, such as contractual distribution agreements, are more likely to collectively engage in strategies.

Proposition 4a: Fields characterized by interfirm exchange depen-dencies are more likely to participate in waves of acquisition activity.

Local Conditions in the Organizational Field
Leading to Acquisition Strategy Isomorphism

There were four changes in the publishing organizational field that set the stage for the "acquisition mania" of the 1980s. The first was marked by the spread of the multidivisional form corporations. The second was the development of specialized investment bankers. The third was a change in the mobility patterns of chief executive officers (CEOs). The fourth was the development of status competition among the dominant firms.

DEVELOPMENT OF MULTIDIVISIONAL
ORGANIZATIONS IN THE FIELD

The conglomerate acquisition wave in the 1960s was an exogenous catalyst that introduced the M-form into the organizational field. As the M-form diffused within the field, it had the effect of centralizing capital and setting standardized practices for accounting and strategic planning (Chandler, 1962). Parent companies act as banking facilities and formally train their executives in modern management techniques. As publishing companies divisionalized over time, they became internal labor markets that shifted executives horizontally across operating companies, with the effect of standardizing cultures and practices (DiMaggio & Powell, 1983). Through formalized training and the common practice of using outside consultants, M-form organizations provide a conduit for management discourse from the larger business environment. Thus, M-form organizations function to import cosmopolitan business strategies into previously parochial environments. The development of the M-form facilitated the integration of acquired businesses and enabled rapid growth through acquisition (Chandler, 1962; Davis, Diekmann, & Tinsley, 1994; Williamson, 1975).

SHOPPING ACQUISITIONS WITHIN THE INDUSTRY

In the 1980s changes were occurring in the general investment banking business that were modeled in the local organizational field (Thornton, 1994). As the practice of bankers, who finance new investment, shifted to brokers of companies, general investment banking houses developed specialized acquisition departments (Chandler, 1992b). Similarly, in publishing, M-form publishing firms created in-house administrative positions charged with the mission of growth by acquisitions. Positions such as director of due diligence and strategic planning became commonplace in larger firms. These positions were nearly nonexistent in publishing companies in the 1960s and early 1970s. Moreover, investment bankers specializing in the publishing industry developed within the organizational field. Many of these deal-makers are former publishers with extensive networks among publishing executives. They relate only peripherally as consultants to the large Wall Street investment houses.

The development of the M-form, as well as the formal organization of specialty investment banking organizations within an organizational field, creates the conditions for isomorphism and greater use of acquisition strategies, hence the ingredients for acquisition waves.[24]

Thus, one might expect that:

Proposition 5: Organizational fields with organizational structures that serve as conduits to the wider business cultural environment, such as M-form organizations, are more likely to collectively engage in acquisition strategies.

Proposition 6: Organizational fields with specialty investment banking organizations and firms with acquisition departments and strategic planners are more likely to exhibit a bandwagon effect in an acquisition wave.

CAREER PATTERNS OF CEOS

The training and background of the CEO is important to the development of corporate strategy. Organization theorists (Fligstein, 1987, 1990; Pfeffer & Salancik, 1978, p. 242) have argued that across eras, cohorts of CEOs reflecting different trends in corporate strategy have come to power and have offered differing solutions to corporate problems. In many of the large corporations in the 1960s, CEOs with financial backgrounds became empowered by the shift from U-form to M-form organization, and they attempted to solve the problems of risk and growth by strategies of acquisition. For example, a CEO with a publishing background will define and pursue organizational goals differently from a CEO with a financial background. In the publishing industry in the 1960s, CEOs were primarily publishers, trained and socialized by upward mobility through the ranks of publishing sales and editorial experience. The cognitive mind-set of the publisher CEO emphasizes organic strategies that focus on long-term internal development and sales growth, such as founding a new imprint or adding editors to develop new authors and subject areas. Compared to acquisition growth strategies, the rate of return on organic investment is much slower and the risk of failure is higher.

By the mid-1980s, with the increasing embeddedness of publishers under large parent companies, the managerial orientation in college publishing began to change from a publisher to a finance conception (Fligstein, 1987, 1990; Jensen & Meckling 1976; Lazonick, 1992). During this period, publisher CEOs were replaced by financially oriented publishers and industry outsiders with accounting and finance backgrounds. CEOs trained in ideologies of finance were essentially dropped in place from parent firms operating outside the culture of book publishing. This change in the functional backgrounds of leadership redirected publishing strategies to focus on rapid size and short-term profit increases, thus setting the stage for the acquisition wave in the later 1980s. This is exemplified by the following comment by an ex-president of Macmillan: "I think that among New York houses now, the control of the houses shifted from editorial to sales and marketing, to financial." Another publisher stated:

> Thirty years ago having anybody knowing anything about accounting or finance within an operating position of a publishing company was unheard of. But . . . over time publishing has moved from being a small business of privately held family companies, to a business financed by public stock ownership. This has introduced a new set of requirements with regard to earnings and a focus on profitability which caused publishers, particularly during the '80s to have to look for year-to-year revenue and profit growth. That was different from the orientations in the '40s and '50s and to a declining degree in the '60s and '70s. . . . Over the last 30 years there has been consolidation in publishing, moving from lots of small independent publishers, to publishers nested into very large organizations under a single owner.

Not knowing much about how to grow organically, and being pressured by the parent company for yearly increases in profits, financial managers embraced acquisition strategies. Here is how one investment deal-maker described the shift toward acquisition growth in the 1980s:

> Instead of being able to manage your business for the value of future cash flow, you had to manage it for yearly profits transferred to the parent company. It tended to drive publishers to the notion that every year had to be better than the previous year. The bigger the elephant got, the bigger you had to make the circus. The only way to get bigger if you can't reinvest and grow internally is to go outside and buy some more. Then you set up a new kind of industry competitiveness, which is, I want to buy this other company because if I don't our competitors will get it. So the attention shifts from publishing to what it is we can buy. (paraphrased)

There are two central arguments with respect to CEO succession. First, the background of corporate leaders affects firm strategies. Second, merger waves represent large-scale institutional change and have a concomitant effect on CEOs as well. Financial CEOs were born of exogenous culture; they were not a product of local publishing culture but were first introduced by large corporations that diversified into the industry in the merger wave of the late 1960s. In the second acquisition wave of the 1980s, the strategies of financial CEOs had become well entrenched in the industry and acted to accelerate the rate of acquisition growth (Thornton, 1993). This suggests:

Proposition 7: Organizational fields with predominantly financially trained CEOs are more likely to collectively engage in acquisition strategies.

STATUS COMPETITION

The fourth force in the local organizational field that fostered acquisition strategies was the development of status competition (DiMaggio & Powell, 1983). In the late 1970s and early 1980s, trade newsletters, such as the *Educational Marketeer* and *BP Report*, were founded. They focused on competitive discourse among dominant players in the field. These publications were distinct from established trade magazines that featured books and publishing houses. Instead, these newsletters emphasized industry financial information on mergers and acquisitions and focused on competition and dominance among firms by ranking companies by size and market share. I argue that the emergence of these newsletters is an example of new forces in the organizational field similar to what Abrahamson and Fombrun (1992, p. 176) describe as mass media production of macro-culture governing entire industries. These newsletters acted to acquaint the specialized publisher with general financial strategies and engender competitive discourse among dominant publishers in the organizational field, further fueling the competition to acquire.[25] For example, one executive in charge of strategic planning for a large New York publisher talked about status competition with respect to acquisitions:

> There is a certain public posturing and a psychological macho and competitiveness that drives acquisition activity. . . . To grow by acquisitions is faster, easier, it's more sexy, it's bigger. . . . There are a few big companies that make things happen. We can't ignore the effects of Murdoch, Maxwell, and Thomson on acquisition activity in the '80s.

Another publisher stated: "The larger the unit you command, the higher your compensation and the more stars on your epaulets."

Thus, one might expect that:

Proposition 8: During acquisition waves, evidence of status competition in an organizational field increases the likelihood of a bandwagon effect.

Conclusion

Prevailing arguments from economic and organization theory do not address why acquisition activity occurs in waves. Graph analysis shows that acquisition activity does indeed occur in waves, and that some industries lead and others lag in the wave. One economic approach advocating acquisition waves as a corollary of the performance of capital markets has been illustrated. Longitudinal graph analysis of the rise and fall of share price indices at the industry level does not, however, consistently support capital market explanations.

These theoretical anomalies and empirical observations motivate an alternative set of institutional arguments to explain acquisition waves as collective action. This chapter proposes that acquisition waves are contingent on the coevolution of global-level business culture and local organizational fields. I argue that differences in why some industries collectively embrace acquisition strategies and others do not, or do so with bandwagon effects, is related to the nature of the conduits between local organizational fields and global business culture. Some organizational fields are collections of disparate organizations where collective diffusion of models of strategy is less likely. Other organizational fields exhibit structuration and are tightly coupled to global business environments that make them subject to collective diffusion of management trends such as acquisition waves.

Conditions illustrated in this case study of the college book publishing industry describe some of the forces that fostered collective strategies. The development of M-form organizations and patterns of CEO succession were largely driven by global influences. The formation of dominant firms, interfirm resource exchanges, localized investment banking, and status competition were primarily the product of local field organizing processes.

The exercise of proposition generation from the case of the college book publishing industry is meant to encourage further research. Aspects of the relationship between acquisition waves and the coevolution of global management ideologies and organizational fields may be generalizable. Thus, I state these relationships as general mechanisms in proposition form. The question of whether these relationships are both correct and generalizable clearly awaits more rigorous investigation within various industrial and temporal contexts.

The intent of this chapter is to begin a discourse and to develop research propositions that view corporate strategy and acquisition waves as constituted from the external social context at two levels: (a) the global cultural environment and (b) the organizational field. Firms are embedded in organizational fields that are embedded in larger cultural systems. Industries have been viewed as social systems that have unique histories, yet they also have common cultural identities that homogenize managerial actors into collective action.

Notes

1. Haunschild (1994) argues that social networks, operationalized as board ties, are the genesis of acquisition activity. She demonstrates that, through interorganizational imitation, firms with director ties to other firms are more likely to engage in acquisition activity. Amburgey and Miner (1992) present evidence that organizational competencies such as how to grow by acquisition become institutionalized and thus act as propellers for further acquisitions. These approaches, however, do not explain acquisition activity in waves.

2. The point is well stated by Davis and Stout (1992, p. 608) in their discussion of the crucial role of the rise of financial economics in bringing about the 1980s takeover wave through a quasi-scientific justification for an unrestricted takeover market. "Takeovers had played a prominent role in finance-based theories of the firm, in particular, agency theory, well before they played much role in reality."

3. For example, on the theorist level, Peters and Waterman (the corporate culture movement) and Michael Porter (competitive strategy); on the organizational level, McKinsey and Co. and the Harvard Business School.

4. Strang and Meyer (1993) claim that diffusion of cultural models is most effective when "cultural categories are informed by theories operating with high levels of complexity and abstraction," and individuals (Mead, 1934) may take on abstracted models of the theorized actor (symbolic interactionism). The important conduit is awareness of theorists that construct cultural abstractions.

5. The concept of corporate strategy is viewed as the articulation of the firm's self-identification (Burgelman, 1983, p. 66).

6. For example, McKinsey and Co. alone has an army of 3,100 consultants and 58 offices worldwide (Huey, 1993).

7. Barley and Kunda (1992) for example, describe how the Harvard Business School acted to legitimate and diffuse Taylorism during the scientific management movement.

8. Chandler (1992b, pp. 275, 277) offers a specific example by describing how the growing flood of business school graduates has been trained in abstract cost accounting methods divorced from the complexities of specific industries, with the idea that what was learned for one set of industries could be easily transferred to another.

9. Strang and Meyer (1993) argue that connectedness is not a necessary condition for diffusing practices if adopter identities are rich in social and cultural meaning and are manifested through culturally analyzed similarities and theorized accounts of actors and practices.

10. The argument is that merger waves are caused by enactment, interpretation, and enforcement of antitrust legislation (Davis et al., 1994; Fligstein, 1990). The Sherman Antitrust Act of 1890 outlawed collusion and precipitated the first merger wave; the Federal Trade Commission and Clayton Acts of 1914 occurred before the second wave; and the Celler-Kefauver Act of 1950 restricted horizontal and vertical mergers, therefore precipitating diversified mergers in the last two merger waves. I argue these changes need more than legal impetus; they require a theory of business.

11. The focus of this chapter is not to distinguish the terms *merger* (the integration of two or more firms) and *acquisition* (the purchase of a firm by another); therefore, they are used interchangeably.

12. It is unclear from this approach if market performance is a cause or consequence of acquisition waves.

13. According to the efficient capital market hypothesis, share prices reflect, in an unbiased manner, the economic effect of all publicly available information at or very shortly after the time information becomes available regarding the future stream of income to the security owner (Jarrell, 1988). In financial economics, there is a large literature that uses stock market prices as a proxy for efficiency measures of acquisition activity. The share price is viewed as an objective sign of management performance, and it equates the behavior of the firm with the performance of the market (Jensen & Meckling, 1976). For this reason, many researchers have attempted to measure the effect of acquisitions by examining changes in share prices of affected companies (event studies). Changes in share prices before and after an acquisition announcement provide a valid measure of the benefits or costs of an acquisition as valued by investors (Benston, 1980, pp. 37-38).

14. This is in contradiction to Manne's (1965) theory of the market for corporate control, in which attractive targets are firms with falling share prices. According to this theory, acquiring firms have the incentive to bid on discounted firms, take control, and infuse new management to drive the target firm's value back up and therefore realize a gain. This theory gained renewed popularity in the merger wave of the 1980s as issues of corporate control and bust-up value became dominant. There are several problems with this logic. Empirical evidence from the acquisition wave in the 1960s indicates that target firms were more profitable than acquiring firms and were used to boost overall profits of acquiring firms (Melicher & Rush, 1974; Mueller, 1977, p. 327). Moreover, recent empirical studies of the 1980s merger wave show that both well-managed and poorly managed firms are acquired (Davis & Stout, 1992).

15. Comparative measures of volume on the vertical axis are not analytically important here; it is the slopes of the time trend on the horizontal axis that are of interest.

16. Index values represent the aggregate market values of the common stocks of representative publishing companies. Market price movements of representative stocks must in general be responsive to changes in industry affairs. Care is taken to avoid construction of a group index in which the movements of a single, dominant stock would effectively determine the movements of the group index.

17. In a parallel analysis of the other industry sectors, the predicted association between capital markets and merger and acquisition waves show mixed results. The oil and gas and textile industries showed the economically predicted order: Acquisition waves precede or match the rise and peak of the stock market. The relationship between acquisition waves and the capital market for the chemical and mining and mineral industries was opposite to economic predictions: The market lagged the merger wave.

18. A bandwagon effect is when organizations adopt a practice not because of an individual assessment of efficient returns, but because large numbers of other important organizations have adopted the practice (Abrahamson & Rosenkopf, 1993; Tolbert & Zucker, 1983).

19. Publisher-driven strategies focus on how to increase sales by publishing new books and related products.

20. Sales of college-level books in 1956 were approximately $67,000,000, and in 1990 sales had grown to $1,991,300,000. College enrollments during the same period went from 3,095,000 to 14,105,000. The double-digit percentage increases occurred in the 1960s and 1970s.

21. Standard and Poor's no longer lists financial data under the separate category of the book publishing industry. These data are now aggregated with the communications industry.

22. The major foreign acquirers of U.S. publishers were Bertelsman, Hachette, Holtzbrinck, Maxwell Communications, News Corp., Pearson Longman, Thomson, and Wolters Kluwer.

23. Hirsch (1986) has described how the cultural framing of takeovers has changed over time. In the 1960s, it was considered a "deviant practice" and only in the 1980s did it become institutionalized as an accepted practice, complete with its own specialized language. As evidence, Hirsch notes that the category of hostile takeover did not exist in W. T. Grimm's reported data until 1976.

24. Clearly, merger waves existed before the innovation of M-form organizations. I am arguing that M-forms are the modern conduit for diffusion of management discourse from the larger business cultural environment, rather than entrepreneurial personalities of prior eras.

25. The reporting of market share estimates among the major publishers is an analogy from the general business culture and is somewhat of a misnomer in the publishing business where the average life of an edition in college publishing is about 3 years. Application of "market share" to the publishing industry is a global strategy without a good local fit, but it constructs an organizing myth to foster competition.

10

Coupling the Technical and Institutional Faces of Janus in Network Industries

RAGHU GARUD

ARUN KUMARASWAMY

TECHNOLOGY PERVADES ALMOST EVERY FACET of our daily lives, yet we seldom pause to reflect upon how a technology works, our cognitive abilities and interests circumscribing the complexity that we can or want to confront. Seldom, too, do we pause to inquire into the origins of a technology, its roots and subsequent evolution becoming opaque to scrutiny with the passage of time. As these facets become taken for granted, the entire technology becomes a black box (Rosenberg, 1982).

Occasionally we, as regulators, policymakers, and technology users, attempt to pry open the black box and ask: *How do technologies evolve?* At first, we might be inclined to adopt a functional perspective, assuming naively that the most efficient technology will prevail. However, even as we use our QWERTY keyboards, we realize that inefficient technologies persist despite our knowledge of more efficient alternatives (David, 1985).

The keyboard illustration underscores the taken-for-granted nature of technologies where institutionalized rules, social customs, and powerful elites shape their evolution (Powell, 1991). A similar realization of the

AUTHORS' NOTE: We thank Dick Scott, Søren Christensen, Jan Molin, Bhatt Vadlamani, members at the Møn Conference on Institutional Analysis, and participants at the Academy of Management Review Theory Development Workshop for their comments. We thank Sue Frost for her help in gathering data on the workstation market of the computer industry.

taken-for-granted facets of organizational life led to the enunciation of institutional theories in organization studies (DiMaggio & Powell, 1983; Meyer & Rowan, 1977; Scott & Meyer, 1983; Zucker, 1977). These theories noted that organizations confront either technical or institutional environments, each exerting different types of pressures.

Upon reflection, institutional theorists realized that viewing organizations as confronting either a technical or an institutional environment at any given time creates a false dichotomy. Instead, by cross-classifying these two dimensions, they offered a typology in which certain organizations may be subject simultaneously to strong technical and institutional pressures. In particular, Scott and Meyer (1983) proposed that contradictory demands placed by these environments on organizations would lead to higher levels of internal conflict. They also proposed that organizations dealt with this dialectic tension by adopting more complex administrative systems, such as the matrix organizational form.

This dialectic view, however, falls short of an appreciation of the dualistic relationship between the technical and institutional environments confronted by organizations. For instance, Orrù, Biggart, and Hamilton (1991) challenge Scott and Meyer's (1983) argument that simultaneous technical and institutional demands promote internal conflict. Instead, they suggest that institutional pressures themselves are essential for the emergence of market order. Indeed, Powell (1991) and Dobbin (this volume) argue that institutional environments set the very criteria against which technical efficiency is judged (also see Barley, 1986, and Orlikowski, 1992, for related discussions).

It is this dualistic relationship between the technical and institutional environments that we explore in this chapter. Specifically, we focus on the evolution of unbounded technological systems[1]—multicomponent systems that can be linked together in network industries (Garud & Kumaraswamy, 1993a). *Our core proposition is that we can understand and better shape the evolution of technological systems by coupling their institutional and technical environments (which we liken to the two faces of Janus).* This dualistic relationship between the institutional and technical environments creates a dynamic setting in which it is difficult for a dominant design to emerge. Therefore, we offer the notion of transient designs—designs that serve as stepping-stones for future product offerings.

Our chapter is organized as follows: In the next section, we provide an introduction to the technical and institutional environments of technological systems. Scott and Meyer (1983) define technical environments as those in which a product or service is produced and exchanged in a market such that organizations are rewarded for effective and efficient control of their production system. Institutional environments are those characterized by the elaboration of rules and requirements to which individual organizations must conform if they are to receive support and legitimacy. In a similar manner, we suggest that the technical environment of a technological system consists of innovations and performance enhancements at the product level. The institutional environment of a technological system consists of a mosaic of interface and performance standards that together constitute the architecture of the technological system. These architectural standards prescribe the rules of engagement between system components and the criteria by which functional efficiency of the technological system is interpreted (Powell, 1991, p. 186). In this way, architectural standards are to technological systems what institutional environments are to organizations. We argue that there is a dualistic interaction between activities in these technical and institutional environments in several network industries. To illustrate this interaction, we explore dynamics associated with the evolution of Reduced Instruction Set Computing (RISC) systems in the workstation market of the computer industry. In the discussion and conclusion section, we explore the implications of these dynamics for theory and practice.

Conceptual Framework

Technological systems consist of a set of components that together provide utility to customers. System performance is dependent not only upon the performance of constituent components but also upon the extent to which they are compatible with one another (Gabel, 1987, p. 93; Henderson & Clark, 1990; Tushman & Rosenkopf, 1992). Compatibility between system components may be achieved by designing to a common set of standards. Standards are codified specifications that prescribe rules of engagement among components. Together, specifications about the form and function of components and the rules determining interaction among them define a system's architecture.[2]

TECHNOLOGICAL DICHOTOMY AND DOMINANT DESIGNS

The evolution of a system's components and its overall architecture is best captured by the notion of technological trajectories (Dosi, 1982). Technological trajectories represent progression paths of technological systems in directions determined by previous choices (Powell, 1991). Trajectories also are determined by current perspectives of what is possible and feasible with a particular approach (Nelson & Winter, 1982).

During early stages of a system's evolution, several technological trajectories might exist, each with its own system architecture. Components that perform well together as a system under one architecture might be incompatible with those that perform well under another architecture. To this extent, each architecture represents a unique configuration of components. As each architecture's overall performance is determined cumulatively by the dimensions of merit of individual components comprising it (Tushman & Rosenkopf, 1992), different architectures will have different dimensions of merit.

During this "era of ferment" (Tushman & Anderson, 1986), there is little agreement on the rules of engagement and criteria on which performance should be measured. Therefore, each technological trajectory requires the creation of a distinct institutional environment that includes both the rules of engagement and the measurement criteria (Constant, 1980). Once created, each institutional environment forms the basis for stable expectations among mutually interdependent firms, thereby fostering complementary innovations and product refinement.

However, these very institutional environments constrain the development of each trajectory. Garud and Rappa (1994) illustrate how these institutional environments prescribe boundaries for future exploration, rendering researchers blind to the virtues of alternative trajectories as they ignore, deny, or distort performance reports that are not consistent with their own testing routines. Moreover, as these trajectories progress over time, researchers and firms develop idiosyncratic competencies that lock them into particular trajectories (Arthur, 1988; Cohen & Levinthal, 1990; David, 1985). Unable to redirect efforts toward pursuing alternate trajectories, rivals compete to shape emerging architectural standards that eventually congeal into a dominant design (Anderson & Tushman, 1990; Utterback & Abernathy, 1975).

Over time, architectural standards defining the dominant design become taken for granted as we use them routinely to prescribe which components (and consequently which firms) can interact, and which criteria should be used to evaluate system performance. Representing very high degrees of social order and cognitive construction (Jepperson, 1991) and prescribing the very basis for technological reality, this dominant architecture is to technological systems what institutions are to organizations. Gradually, an "inversion" occurs (Latour & Woolgar, 1979, p. 240), wherein rules of engagement and evaluation routines themselves become the basis for technological reality and competition during the era of incremental change. In this manner, the locus of interfirm competition shifts from the institutional to the technical environment after the emergence of the dominant design.

TECHNOLOGICAL DUALITY AND TRANSIENT DESIGNS

Though this two-stage model has served us well, its applicability in contemporary markets characterized by continual technological change must be reconsidered. In these continually changing markets, it is not possible to wait for a dominant design to emerge before proceeding to compete on technical merits. Nor is there any cessation of changes in the institutional environment of architectural standards. Instead of evolving through two distinct stages—one characterized by competition to shape institutional environment and the other by competition in the technical environment—these markets are characterized by simultaneous competition in both environments, one shaping the other in a reciprocal manner (see Van de Ven & Garud, 1994). In other words, these markets are characterized by dualism instead of a dichotomy.

We explore this dualistic process of technology evolution in network industries. Network industries consist of interrelated markets, each producing components of a larger technological system (Garud & Kumaraswamy, 1993a; Langlois & Robertson, 1992). These industries are also characterized by network externalities—situations in which the benefits a user derives from a product increase as others also use compatible products (Farrell & Saloner, 1986; Katz & Shapiro, 1985). For instance, the benefits derived by an individual subscribing to a data-sharing network increase with the number of other individuals subscribing to that network. Similarly, a complementary product, such as computer software, becomes cheaper (or more readily available) as the size of the network increases. Besides these direct benefits, indirect benefits of belonging to a large network include improved quality and lower price of after-sales service.

Several forces have led to a confluence of the institutional and technical environments in such industries. For instance, in the workstation market of the computer industry, advances in microprocessor technology and digital switching have led to connectivity between systems manufactured by different firms, thereby creating unbounded systems. Benefiting from the widening of their network boundaries, customers are demanding that firms offer systems that conform to industry-wide standards. In response to customer demands, manufacturers have begun offering systems that conform to industry-wide standards that no one firm controls. In such a setting, firms compete to shape the emerging institutional environment of architectural standards. One approach is to sponsor their technologies by licensing them freely to others, thereby creating an "open" architecture.[3] Customers are attracted to networks built around these open architectures because open architectures promote compatibility among systems manufactured by different firms. As the size of the open network increases, so do benefits to customers and the viability of systems belonging to that network.

Open architectures that emerge through the sponsorship of standards foster competition in the technical environment as rivals offer alternative systems employing the same architectural standards. Therefore, even as firms shape architectural environments by sponsoring their technologies, they have to compete in their technical environments by innovating continually (see also Meyer & Rowan, 1977). Innovation in the product market, however, has to occur within the architectural umbrella that has been established so far. Otherwise, new product offerings will destroy earlier designs—a cannibalization process that is difficult to sustain indefinitely for both customers and manufacturers. At the same time, these product innovations extend and modify the very institutional environment that constrained and shaped them.

This interaction between the technical and the institutional environments represents a process of dualistic change wherein firms' activities can be likened to rebuilding a ship (the architecture) plank by plank (through product innovations and enhancements) even as it sails. In such a setting, we suggest that products must be designed for transience, wherein any product is but a stepping-stone for future products. Such transient designs (Garud & Kumaraswamy, 1993b) lie at the nexus of the interactions between the technical and institutional environments. Because they conform to architectural standards, transient designs can be upgraded easily to offer new performance dimensions by rendering some facets obsolete, retaining some, and extending yet others. At the same time, innovations at the product level extend and reshape architectural standards.

In the next section, we illustrate this dualistic process of technology evolution and change in the workstation market of the computer industry. The computer industry was not always characterized by dualistic change. In the 1950s, during early stages of its evolution,[4] the computer industry was characterized by product competition with an absence of architectural competition (Quadrant 1 of Figure 10.1). Several rival firms such as IBM, Control Data, Sperry, and Philco were active in the mainframe market, offering stand-alone systems that were comparable in functionality (Flamm, 1988, pp. 102-105). Firms could not shape industry-wide standards because networking capabilities were neither well developed nor considered important.

In the 1960s, when IBM's System 360 architecture became dominant, the industry evolved to Quadrant 2, with an absence of both product and architectural competition. Product competition was weak because IBM's large installed base created "transient incompatibility" costs (besides switching costs) for customers if they migrated to a system with a different

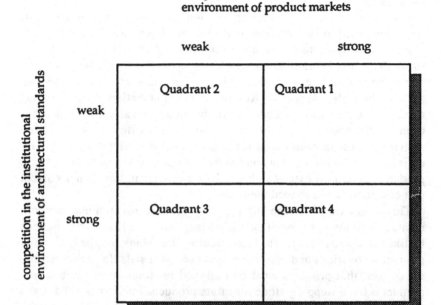

Figure 10.1. Architectural and Product Competition in Network Industries

architecture. Architectural competition was weak because IBM, the dominant firm, could control system specifications through "undisclosed interface manipulations," thereby rendering the rivals' components "allergic"
to its systems (Adams & Brock, 1982, p. 36).[5]

A shift to Quadrant 3 began in the 1960s and 1970s when architectural
competition occurred between systems conforming to different concepts
of computing (distributed computing vs. time-sharing). Several firms (e.g.,
DEC) had begun developing systems initially targeted toward segments
not serviced by IBM. Over time, these segments began encroaching on the
mainframe market. Rather than compete on dimensions of merit specific
to mainframes, these systems—minicomputers—began redefining the
very nature of computing. In particular, minicomputers decentralized data
storage and processing by offering customers the flexibility to install
systems wherever required in the organization. Additionally, for control
purposes, these minicomputers could be networked. Thus, minicomputers
offered an alternative architectural solution to the monolithic mainframe
computer.

By the early 1980s advances in microprocessor technology and digital switching facilitated networking among computer systems, thereby paving the way for the introduction of workstations and the realization of Quadrant 4 dynamics (Figure 10.1). We explore these dynamics by examining events in the workstation market. To simplify our illustration, we focus on the effect of technological changes in one of the many components that constitute the workstation's overall architecture: its microprocessor.[6]

Evolution of RISC Microprocessor Systems in the Workstation Market

At the broadest level, the functionality of a microprocessor can be improved by increasing its speed or modifying its architecture. Since 1978 computer engineers have increased microprocessor speeds by a factor of eight, these advances coming from improvements in semiconductor materials and IC fabrication technologies (Touma, 1993). However, there are limits to increasing speed by these methods. Aware of these limits, engineers have attempted to improve functionality by modifying microprocessor architecture.

A microprocessor's architecture depends on the instruction set that it uses. Traditionally, microprocessors have been designed using Complex Instruction Set Computing (CISC). CISC uses a comprehensive and lengthy set of instructions that requires greater microprocessor execution time. CISC chips have to be designed with duplicate circuitry to compensate for slower execution times, thereby increasing their size and complexity. An alternative to CISC is to employ a smaller instruction set that contains only those instructions that are used frequently. This approach is called Reduced Instruction Set Computing (RISC). RISC chips are faster because they have to execute a smaller instruction set ("A Risky New Architecture," 1985).

Despite its apparent superiority, RISC encountered resistance from proponents of CISC. Citing trade-offs between the two architectures, proponents of CISC questioned the very basis for RISC's superiority. They pointed out that performance measures employed to promote RISC, such as millions of instructions executed per second (MIPS) and millions of floating point operations completed per second (MFLOPS), were misleading. Specifically, CISC proponents argued that it was meaningless to compare the MIPS rating of systems with different instruction sets because the metric itself depended on the instruction set used (Hennessy & Patterson, 1989).

Of greater importance than the number of instructions processed per second, according to proponents of CISC, was the time taken by the system to execute typical programs. By this measure, CISC could perform as well as RISC. Because the CISC instruction set is elaborate, a CISC instruction can perform the task of several RISC instructions. Therefore, a typical software program written for CISC has fewer instructions to execute than one written for RISC and can run as rapidly (Touma, 1993). Thus, as with any new technology, there was an extended debate over the relative merits and performance measurement criteria of RISC and CISC.[7] These debates led industry analysts to conclude that RISC would not become a commercial threat to CISC in the foreseeable future ("A Simpler Path," 1986; "Gambling on RISC," 1986; "High RISC Factors," 1986).

Established computer manufacturers were reluctant to use RISC for fear of cannibalizing their traditional markets built around CISC systems. For instance, despite pioneering research on RISC in the mid-1970s ("Towards Faster," 1985), IBM was reluctant to use RISC architecture in its computers for fear of cannibalizing its CISC-based mainframe products (Ferguson & Morris, 1993; "Gerstner's New Vision," 1993). Intel and Motorola, both dominant CISC microprocessor manufacturers, refused to initiate research on RISC, pointing to the adequacy of CISC architecture for commercial applications ("How Intel," 1987). Of the established computer manufacturers, only Hewlett Packard (HP) pursued the RISC architecture and, of the established microprocessor manufacturers, only National Semiconductor began experimenting with RISC ("Gambling on RISC," 1986). As is the case with the introduction of many new technologies, it was left to peripheral actors within the computer industry to commercialize the new RISC architecture.

RISC IN THE WORKSTATION MARKET

As in the wider computer industry, CISC microprocessor architecture was well established in the workstation market. Apollo pioneered the workstation market in 1981, with its proprietary CISC-based systems. Sun Microsystems also entered this market, in 1982, with workstations based on CISC microprocessors, but followed an unconventional open systems philosophy. In essence, this philosophy was to develop systems using standard, off-the-shelf components, and to license proprietary innovations to all firms without restriction (see Garud & Kumaraswamy, 1993a).

In 1985 William Joy of Sun Microsystems concluded that only RISC-based systems could meet customers' demand for more power and functionality. Intel and Motorola, the dominant microprocessor manufacturers, spurned his suggestion that they develop RISC microprocessors. Subsequently, Sun Microsystems began efforts to develop its own RISC microprocessor in collaboration with Fujitsu. By 1987 Sun completed development of Scalable Processor ARChitecture (SPARC), its own RISC architecture. Sun also announced the Sun-4 line of workstations based on its powerful SPARC architecture.

Consistent with its open systems philosophy, Sun announced its intentions to license SPARC to microprocessor manufacturers and rival computer manufacturers without restriction. In response to concerns about its continued intention to maintain SPARC as an open architecture, Sun, in 1989, created SPARC International, a trade group to promote SPARC. The mandate for SPARC International was to both ensure unrestricted licensing of SPARC technology and develop standards to ensure compatibility among different SPARC implementations.

Sun's actions can be understood only in the context of important changes occurring in the workstation market and the computer industry at large. Advances in networking technologies allowed computer systems to be linked, thereby paving the way for distributed computation. Clearly this required that computer systems be built keeping multivendor compatibility issues in mind. Moreover, with the introduction of the IBM-PC in 1981, customers experienced the benefits of open systems built with standard, off-the-shelf components. Over time, they began demanding greater compatibility among systems offered by computer manufacturers throughout the computer industry—especially in the workstation market, where distributed computing and networking were important.

Opening up an architecture encourages decentralized innovation as licensee-firms innovate to a common architectural standard. Also, conformity to an open architecture increases compatibility among systems and components offered by licensee-firms. Eventually, an open architecture leads to unbundling of system components and the creation of a competitive market in complementary components. Instead of being locked into bounded networks of firms that restrict access to their proprietary technologies, customers enjoy the flexibility of mixing and matching compatible components to suit their specific needs. In addition, users find it easier to link disparate systems together in networks and enjoy the benefits of belonging to a growing, unbounded network. Thus, opening up an architecture makes it easier to mobilize widespread support among customers, potential rivals, and manufacturers of complementary components.

Though an open systems approach helps a firm mobilize support for its architecture, it also exposes the firm to competition in both the institutional and technical environments. In the institutional environment, the firm has to compete with rivals to establish its own system architecture as the architectural standard. At the same time, it has to compete in the technical environment with licensee-firms that offer compatible systems and components conforming to its architecture. Events subsequent to

Sun's introduction of SPARC architecture illustrate dynamics that result from simultaneous competition in institutional and technical environments.

ARCHITECTURAL COMPETITION
AMONG RISC-BASED WORKSTATIONS

Sun's strategy of licensing SPARC without restriction had the intended consequence of mobilizing support for SPARC architecture, and for RISC-based systems in general. Initially, other workstation manufacturers responded to Sun's SPARC systems by offering more powerful CISC-based workstations. As acceptance of SPARC architecture grew, rival workstation manufacturers became concerned that Sun would transform itself "into a shark trying to force its whole architecture down our throats" (MIPS's John Mashey, quoted in "The Revolutionary," 1988, p. 1).

Rival workstation manufacturers introduced their own RISC-based systems to prevent Sun's SPARC from becoming the standard architecture for RISC-based systems. HP introduced workstations based on its PA-RISC microprocessor architecture, and IBM introduced workstations based on its own POWER RISC architecture. Some firms that had waited too long to make the transition from CISC to RISC introduced workstations built around RISC microprocessors supplied by third-party vendors. For instance, Digital Equipment Corporation (DEC) introduced workstations based on MIPS's R2000 RISC architecture.

Dominant microprocessor manufacturers (Intel and Motorola) perceived these events as direct threats to their markets and initiated development of their own RISC architectures. Motorola introduced the 88000 RISC microprocessor. Intel, in a halfhearted attempt to enter the RISC microprocessor market, hurriedly repositioned 860, a RISC coprocessor design, as a full-fledged microprocessor ("The Microprocessor," 1989). Meanwhile, MIPS Computer Systems, one of RISC's pioneers, promoted its own Rx000 RISC architecture by forming alliances with workstation and component manufacturers like Silicon Graphics, DEC, LSI Logic, and Siemens.[8]

Appreciating the significant benefits of open architectures, these firms also initiated efforts to open their microprocessor architectures. Motorola established 88 Open Consortium Limited, a consortium to establish 88000 standards ("RISC Chip," 1988). DEC developed its 64-bit Alpha RISC microprocessor and offered to license it to all manufacturers without restriction ("Digital Unveils," 1992). Silicon Graphics, a niche player, acquired MIPS Computer Systems and undertook to keep MIPS's RISC architecture open ("SGI Vows," 1992). HP made a limited attempt to open up its PA-RISC architecture by forming Precision RISC Organization (PRO), a tightly knit nine-member association. However, HP decided not to license its RISC architecture broadly to prevent excessive competition from compatible systems ("HP Gathers," 1992).[9]

PRODUCT COMPETITION
WITHIN SPARC ARCHITECTURE

Every step to promote an architecture as the industry standard by making it open means a step toward more intense competition in product markets. In the market for SPARC-compatible workstations, Solbourne Computer introduced its Series4 line of SPARC-compatible workstations in 1988. Immediately thereafter, Solbourne announced the release of its next generation of workstations—the Series5—based on Cypress's speedier SPARC microprocessor ("Series 5 Caches," 1989). Elsewhere, Sony and several firms from the Far East entered the workstation market with SPARC-compatible systems ("Taiwan's PC Makers," 1991). In 1991 alone, more than six different manufacturers introduced SPARC-compatible systems ("Six SPARC-Based," 1991). These SPARC-compatible systems typically offered better performance at prices comparable to (or lower than) Sun's own systems ("A Raft of Sun Clones," 1991). For instance, Solbourne offered multiprocessing capabilities in its systems—features not offered by Sun—and cut prices by as much as 50% to make these the lowest priced workstations in the market ("Solbourne Targets," 1991).

As Ferguson and Morris point out (1993, p. 143), opening up a *static* architecture is "merely giving the business away to clones."[10] Firms that open up their architectures can survive only by innovating continually. Indeed, Sun stayed one step ahead of rivals such as Solbourne only by "being nimbler than its competitors in bringing out an endless succession of software and hardware products." Sun introduced new families of SPARC systems with improved performance-to-price capabilities—SPARCstation1, SPARCstation2, and the easily upgradable SPARCstation10. Further, Sun initiated development efforts with Texas Instruments (TI) and Fujitsu to create future-generation SPARC chips. Sun also introduced several software products that improved compatibility of its SPARC systems with rival workstation manufacturers and made it easier for users to network disparate systems.

Competition among SPARC-compatible systems demonstrates the dualistic interaction between the technical and institutional environments. In the case of an open architecture like SPARC, standardized specifications are transparent to all licensee-firms, so licensees can innovate within the umbrella of the open architecture. As licensee-firms innovate, they have to integrate these innovations into the architecture to maintain compatibility. Over time, the architecture itself changes as these innovations become assimilated.

Sun and licensee-firms created the SPARC International consortium, keeping these very dynamics in mind. As Sun and SPARC licensees introduced innovations to the original SPARC architecture, SPARC International developed standards to ensure compatibility among different implementations of SPARC. Slowly, as the original SPARC architecture changed, SPARC International developed V9, a 64-bit architecture extension to SPARC. Immediately, new entrants like Hal Computer Systems adopted the V9 architecture and enhanced it further as they attempted to build systems with greater functionality and enter new markets ("Developers Race," 1992).

DUALISTIC CHANGE AND TRANSIENT
DESIGNS IN THE WORKSTATION MARKET

The above description is illustrative of dynamics in the workstation market, where innovations create changes in both the institutional and technical environments. Continual changes in both environments make it difficult for a dominant design to emerge. Consequently, it is difficult to distinguish between eras of ferment and incremental change. Both eras are compressed in time, resulting in a continual process of structuration (Giddens, 1979).

In such an environment, firms have to work with transient designs that evolve constantly. The SPARC architecture well illustrates the notion of transient designs. According to analysts, SPARC is the only practical implementation of RISC among many available in the industry that is flexible enough to be implemented on a variety of substrate materials, including silicon and gallium arsenide ("AT&T," 1988, p. 17). This implies that the SPARC chip can be enhanced as advances in substrate materials occur. Moreover, the SPARC architecture is scalable and can be used in a variety of systems ranging from personal computers to supercomputers.

There is an additional layer of complexity that makes it difficult for a dominant design to emerge. As different markets and their corresponding architectures converge, "technology transmutation" occurs (Davidow & Malone, 1992), creating new dimensions of merit. As transmutation occurs, the very basis for architectural competition itself may change. For instance, as the workstation and PC markets converged, competition between RISC and CISC systems spilled over to the PC market.[11] Meanwhile, Microsoft created Windows NT, an operating system that had networking and multitasking capabilities. Microsoft decided to port Windows NT to several microprocessor architectures, to make it a viable alternative to UNIX. Realizing the threat that Microsoft's action posed to their competitive positions, several workstation manufacturers, including Sun and HP, agreed to develop a common interface to their diverse UNIX versions so that applications software written for the common interface could run on any workstation, irrespective of microprocessor architecture or UNIX version ("Computer Firms," 1993). Gradually, the locus of architectural competition is shifting from microprocessor architectures to operating systems.

This shift in the locus of architectural competition is an inherent consequence of the characteristics of multicomponent systems with open architectures. In a multicomponent system with several core components, the overall system architecture is determined by respective architectures of core components. Innovations occur in several core components simultaneously, and innovating manufacturers compete under several technical and institutional environments at the same time. Depending on the intensity of competition within different sets of environments, one set or the other gains salience. For instance, once workstation manufacturers create a common UNIX environment, the underlying RISC architecture will become irrelevant. So will the difference between PCs with RISC processors (Motorola-Apple-IBM's PowerPC and DEC's Alpha) and those with CISC processors (Intel's Pentium or 80486) once Windows NT becomes a viable operating system. Different criteria and rules of engagement might become salient, redefining the very institutional and technical environments in which firms compete. Thus, as technological systems become more complex, more unbounded, and more open, traditional concepts about technology evolution and competitive strategies may have to be rethought.

Discussion and Conclusion

We began this chapter by asking: *How do technologies evolve?* Our description of the evolution of RISC microprocessor suggests that the widely accepted two-stage, dominant-design model needs to be recast for technological systems within network industries. Instead of the dichotomy between technical and institutional environments implicit in the two-stage model, we suggested a dualistic process wherein the technical environment continually shapes, and is shaped by, the larger institutional environment of architectural standards.

An explanation for this dualistic process lies in the network characteristics of technological systems. With advances in networking technologies, once-bounded technologies are becoming increasingly unbounded, thereby benefiting customers. In such an unbounded environment, "linking mechanisms" (Garud & Kumaraswamy, 1993a) are more important than "isolating mechanisms" (Rumelt, 1984), thereby placing a premium on the extent to which a technology is open to scrutiny and connection. Opening a technology allows others to build complementary technologies to a common standard, thereby ensuring rapid technological advances (Langlois & Robertson, 1992). Thus, linking mechanisms benefit firms and users by enhancing their ability to reap network externality benefits and external economies (Langlois, 1992).

In these unbounded and unbundled networks, standards are determined jointly by component manufacturers and system manufacturers (Langlois & Robertson, 1992). No single member of the network has control over the architecture, and any firm that tries to dictate standards in a decentralized network risks being isolated if users and other producers do not follow. Even products that are demonstrably superior in a technical sense may be disregarded if there are transient incompatibility costs (David & Bunn, 1990).

Opening an architecture to create industry-wide standards that facilitate networking and compatibility represents the creation of a "plastic cage." We propose the metaphor of the plastic cage in contrast to the metaphor of the "iron cage" initially proposed by Weber (1952) and revisited by DiMaggio and Powell (1983). The iron cage evokes an image of rigidity and permanence that is characteristic of institutions once they become taken for granted. In contrast, the plastic cage evokes an image of malleability and change, even as it channels innovations in certain directions. This is because the plastic cage is open to scrutiny, enabling network members to innovate to a common architectural standard without the need for explicit coordination.

The linking mechanisms that constitute the plastic cage preclude sustained monopoly profits. Therefore, there are pressures on individual firms to innovate and build their innovations into emerging or existing standards. Over time, these innovations are assimilated, resulting in a new version of architectural standards. This recast plastic cage sets the stage for subsequent technological change.

Thus, in network industries, we have contradictory forces for conformance and divergence shaping the evolution of technological systems. Agreeing to common standards and building on them represent forces of convergence that enable coordination among firms in their efforts to offer compatible systems. Without these industry-wide standards, continual innovation in the technical environment of product markets would be detrimental to its diffusion, because potential customers would wait for innovation to subside (Rosenberg, 1982). Without innovation in the technical environment, agreement on industry-wide standards would lead to stagnation. Indeed, innovations are necessary for the creation of transient monopoly positions for firms.

These innovations occur within the confines of existing architectural standards that enable networking and compatibility. Working within architectural boundaries to exploit untapped technological degrees of freedom results in competency-enhancing improvements (Tushman & Anderson, 1986) that allow firms to offer products with higher performance by leveraging off past efforts. In turn, these competency-enhancing improvements at the technical level unleash a fresh round of negotiations among firms on specific extensions to existing architectural standards.

Thus, the interaction between the technical and institutional environments in the computer industry creates a dynamic process in which firms work with transient designs. Such transient designs can only be accomplished by creating products that conform to architectural standards, thereby promoting modular upgradability. Modularity provides system designers with the flexibility to substitute only certain system components while retaining others. Upgradability provides designers with the opportunity to work on an already-established technological platform, thereby preserving their core knowledge base. In this way, modular upgradability leads to the preservation of knowledge across generations and simplifies the task of coping with very short product life cycles.

Not so long ago, frustrated with the persistence of a dominant design, we used to ask: *Why don't technologies change more rapidly?* Now, we wonder at the rapidity of technological change, sometimes wishing that a dominant design would emerge. It is as if opening the technology black box has unleashed continual change. Noting this fact, Bill Joy of Sun Microsystems stated:

> We have something that economists find truly amazing which I certainly didn't appreciate. We all know that committees take a long time to make standards, and it also appeared, say ten years ago, that the marketplace took a long time, because everybody just sort of dug in their heels. What we have now is this kind of funny interplay between committees (*institutional environment*) and the marketplace (*technical environment*), each trying to outdo the other to set standards, thereby driving the industry forward far more quickly than the other would have done by itself. This is a truly amazing phenomenon. (Joy, 1990)

Based on these observations, we conclude the chapter with two suggestions. First, it is important to consider both the technical and institutional environments in our efforts to appreciate the evolution of technological systems. Second, we must appreciate the dualistic nature of interaction between these two environments. Failure to do so will lead to an incomplete understanding of the evolution of technological systems in network industries.

Notes

1. Tushman and Rosenkopf (1992) label these as "open systems," a term that we reserve to denote systems that are built using standard, off-the-shelf components and, therefore, have open architectures.

2. In the case of computers, standards would have to specify "how programs and commands will work and data will move around the system—the communication protocols that hardware components must follow, the rules for exchanging data between application software packages and the operating system, the allowable font descriptions that can be communicated to a printer, and so forth" (Ferguson & Morris, 1993, p. 120).

3. Other complementary approaches to shape architectures include (a) co-optation of institutional bodies (Hirsch, 1975), (b) lobbying to shape emerging regulation (Leone, 1986), and (c) the propagation of a standard through committees (Farrell & Saloner, 1988).

4. The computer industry traces its origins to military applications, with the government as its main sponsor. By the late 1940s (the point of entry for us in this chapter), computer applications had diffused into the commercial sector.

5. It is important to distinguish between our classification and the one offered by Scott (1992, p. 133). Scott demarcated four different contexts based on the strength (or weakness) of the technical and institutional environments that organizations confront. In this chapter, we are operating in a context where *both technical and institutional environments are strong.* Given the presence of strong technical and institutional environments, our focus is on *whether there is competition within each of these two environments.*

6. Other core components that determine a workstation's architecture include its operating system, memory, systems bus, and networking hardware.

7. After RISC became a commercially viable alternative to CISC, several benchmark measures came into vogue to make valid performance comparisons between CISC-based and RISC-based systems. Over time, SPEC (Systems Performance Evaluation Cooperative) gained wide acceptance as the leading benchmark to measure system performance (Weicker, 1990).

8. By the end of 1990, Sun's SPARC architecture commanded a 35% share of the workstation market, with MIPS (24%) and Motorola (12%) being the other major players ("RISCy Business," 1990).

9. In 1992 Sun's SPARC systems accounted for 38% of the workstation market, with HP (17%), DEC (12%), and IBM (7%) being the other major players. Still, no single architecture was dominant.

10. This observation is well illustrated by IBM's experience in the PC market, where IBM's inability to innovate continually and keep up with clone makers cost it market dominance.

11. A group of IBM-compatible PC manufacturers led by Compaq—the ACE Consortium—endorsed a partial shift from Intel's 80x86 CISC microprocessors to powerful RISC microprocessors designed by MIPS Computer. Intel quickened its product development efforts to create CISC microprocessors like 80486 and Pentium that were comparable to RISC's functionality. Citing its product development efforts, Intel persuaded Compaq to stay with its CISC microprocessors, and, to an extent, neutralized the threat of large-scale defection of PC manufacturers from its CISC microprocessors to RISC ("Compaq Emerges," 1992). Apple and IBM, two firms that had suffered loss in market position in the PC market, decided to collaborate with Motorola to develop a new RISC microprocessor called PowerPC. They also announced their intention to make the PowerPC microprocessor an alternative open standard to Intel's CISC microprocessors ("Apple/IBM Birthday," 1992).

11

Institutional Interpretations and Explanations of Differences in American and Danish Approaches to Innovation

PETER KARNØE

THIS CHAPTER ARGUES THAT THE SHARP DISTINCTION between institutional and technical environments embedded in the earlier versions of organizational institutionalism has detracted attention from the fact that even the social organization of technical practices is institutionally shaped. Technical practices are exposed to strong legitimate, coercive, and normative pressures, with social rules and norms strongly guiding acceptable and appropriate ways of organizing economic activities. In this sense, technical practices may be seen as institutionally constructed social practices.

I support this argument with empirical research on the different innovative practices associated with the communities of Danish and American entrepreneurs that created modern wind power as an energy technology. This study covers the emergence and early consolidation phase of modern wind turbine technology from 1974 to 1990. Actors in both countries were supported by government market subsidies to stimulate the installation of wind power and by a test and research center designed to support industrial technological development. I will attempt to demonstrate how the different

AUTHOR'S NOTE: The initial research for this chapter was made while the author was a visiting scholar at the Department of Economics, Stanford University. This stay was supported by the Danish Social Science Research Council and made possible by Professor Nathan Rosenberg. The author has in different phases benefited from comments by and encouragements from Frank Dobbin, Raghu Garud, Dennis Gioia, James Höpner, Kristian Kreiner, Peer H. Kristensen, James March, Nathan Rosenberg, Dick Scott, and Ed Steinmüeller.

approaches to innovation pursued by the social actors in the Danish and American "technical systems" were shaped and constrained by an institutional environment. Each group of entrepreneurs constituted its technological learning processes according to a set of social practices that were "logical" with respect to the social roles, skills, and attitudes of engineers and workers. This set of social practices affected (a) the forms of work organization, (b) the degree of technological novelty of the product design, (c) the perception of dominant problems and of adequate problem-solving methods and research strategies, and (d) the interaction between industrial R&D and external research with respect to the type of external research and support that was thought to be most supportive for the development of industrial technology.

In the case of wind turbines, the Danish approach to innovation was characterized by the pursuit of rather simple technological designs and a hands-on, practical, problem-solving approach. The first entrepreneurial efforts were conducted in small machine-shop-like firms, with a few practical engineers and a skilled workforce. The American entrepreneurial efforts were conducted either by aerospace companies or by start-ups with a strong engineering base. The "logic" of the American approach implied the pursuit of more advanced technological designs, and it relied on and sought to develop more formalized, theoretically based knowledge. The two approaches were not only different in character; they also differed in terms of productivity with respect to the functional performance of wind turbines. Despite intense competition from American and other European companies in the early 1980s, the Danish companies involved became world leaders in this technology and captured almost 50% of the American home market for wind power from 1980 to 1990.

The high degree of isomorphism (homogeneity in organizational forms and practices) within the technological communities in each country, and the sharp difference between the two nations' industries, call for a changed conception of how technical practices are affected by the nature of institutions. This chapter seeks to expand the new institutionalism in organizational theory with an understanding of the social embeddedness of technical practices, as well as an understanding of how processes of institutionalization can be nation-specific—both areas have only recently begun to be developed in institutional industrial sociology. Based on such new institutional conceptions, this chapter provides a framework for analyzing the institutional embeddedness of technical practices. The practices described herein resemble more widespread social practices, and, specifically, they can be seen as following the beliefs and norms that are institutionally embedded in educational systems, state agency practices, and engineering cultures. After a short introduction to the origins and status of modern wind power technology, the framework proposed in this chapter is used to comparatively describe Danish and American innovative practices.

Institutional Environments and Technical Practices

The basic proposition that formal organizational structures often conflict with efficiency criteria was forwarded by Meyer & Rowan (1977). The general idea was that "rational" organizational forms reflect not only technical rationalities but also ceremonial adoption of institutionalized myths or taken-for-granted rules about legitimate and appropriate organizational forms. The proposition was that organizations were trapped between conflicting demands from technical and institutional environments, and that organizations in response to this inner conflict try to buffer or decouple their technical activities from such institutionally imposed "irrationalities." Organizations such as banks, which are particularly required to meet both institutional and technical efficiency demands, were expected to have a high degree of internal conflict as a result of trying to match these very different environments (Scott & Meyer, 1983). DiMaggio and Powell (1983) continued this line of work by arguing that homogeneity in organizational forms and practices is driven by two different sources of isomorphism. One form is competitive isomorphism, which occurs "for those fields in which free and open competition exists," and the other form, institutional isomorphism, "is a useful tool for understanding the politics and ceremony that pervade much modern organizational life" (DiMaggio & Powell, 1983, p. 150).

This distinction between market-driven and institutionalized sectors may have been fueled by the implicit assumption of market efficiency in modernized economies (Granovetter, 1985) and by the empirical research focusing on nonprofit organizations and public agencies. One of the major problems with this "restricted" (Powell, 1991) institutionalism is that it leaves out the social construction of market-linked technical practices, seeing such practices as institutionally embedded or context specific. Even though there has been conceptual work clarifying the different organizational norms in technical and institutional environments, the basic idea that technical environments give rise to "a set of prescriptions for matching means and ends in ways that are efficacious in producing outcomes of predictable character" (Scott & Meyer, 1991a, p. 124) is not accurate. It implicitly presumes that there is a set of natural solutions to technical imperatives, thereby asserting too strongly the prevalence of market-generated isomorphism, where "rational" organizations are evaluated only by their outputs.

It is not my intention to deny that technical environments often, or to a certain extent, face competitive economic pressure. The price and performance of a product, among other things, may indeed exert pressures on organizations and certain select organizational practices, and thereby organizational forms and strategies, to survive. The question posed here is whether technical environments are so strong that they can neutralize or override all institutional effects. My intention is also to note that there may be several ways to achieve some "best practice[s]" and that there can be several opinions (ways of thinking) regarding what the most "efficient" ways of achieving some desired end might be.

In support of this perspective, a large amount of empirical and conceptual work in industrial sociology has focused on different ways of organizing in order to adapt to the technical environment. Some of this work has looked at such important issues as work organization, the nature of business groups and the way they are governed, and the market-hierarchy determination of subcontracting.

Maurice, Sorge, and Warner (1980) demonstrate how, in firms that are similar with respect to their sector, age, size, and so on, the micro-level organization of work processes (use of skill bases, task specialization, and roles and career options) seems to coexist with specific authority and control systems or regimes.[1] Also, many studies of differences between Japanese and American firms cause one to consider how the nature of the firm may differ in different contexts. The different types of logic behind American and Japanese portfolio strategies, financial versus technological objectives (Prahalad & Hamel, 1990), and mutual ownership means that East Asian enterprises are not short-term, episodic strategic business unit (SBU) combinations of convenience (Orrù, Biggart, & Hamilton, 1991; Whitley, 1992a). Further, while American manufacturers continued to integrate the value chain in the 1950s and 1960s, Japanese car manufacturers developed interdependent networks of suppliers, a market-hierarchy structure that evolved over time along with the social structure and techno-economic problems in internal production (Sabel, 1993).[2]

No universal economic logic explains these differences in organizational forms of economic activity. Instead, this chapter argues that they may be perceived as social constructions of economic activity. Whitley (1992b), in work similar to that of Granovetter (1985) and Granovetter and Swedberg (1992, p. 18), synthesized much of the empirical work on societal differences in his framework for a research program on the institutional embeddedness of national business systems. The idea is to understand how distinctive patterns of economic organization become established and institutionalized in different societies. "These patterns concern the nature of economic activities that are coordinated through managerial hierarchies and how these hierarchies organize their cooperative and competitive relations through markets" (Whitley, 1992b, p. 6). In his taxonomy, Whitley (1992b, p. 9) operates with three basic components of business systems: (a) the nature of the firm, (b) the market organization, and (c) the authority and control systems.

Whitley (1992b, p. 19) uses two types of institutions: (a) *macro- or society-level, proximate social institutions*, such as the state, financial systems, and educational systems that are more directly involved in the economic system, and (b) *background social institutions*, which shape the deepest values of the society, structuring trust, cooperation, and subordination. During the modern industrialization process, these background social institutions strongly influence dominant micro- and macro-organizational forms and institutions, thus creating a distinct business system. This path-dependent coevolution is socially constructed and creates a specific context of embeddedness against which acceptable and appropriate ways of organizing economic activities must be evaluated and legitimated.[3] Whitley's framework is especially aimed at explaining variation as well as homogeneity in organizational forms and practices. Across nations or other regional entities, there may be variation around some "mean" (Sorge, 1991), depending on the homogeneity of a culture and of the dominant institutions (Whitley, 1992b). There is no determinism implied, but instead the dominant business system creates limitations on the possible variation in organizing economic activities.

Whitley's framework is institutionalist by nature, and the argument is parallel to the structuration argument of Giddens (1984). However, Giddens does not specifically address how proximate social institutions, such as educational systems and state agency policies, materialize and reproduce some of the structural properties of social systems (1984, Ch. 6). Related to our view, the point is that the collective actions of (competing) social groups create a set of structural principles (meanings, identities, norms, etc.) that, embedded in proximate social institutions, serve to guide and constrain social practices. These structural principles also affect technical practices, because these in our view are inseparable from social practices. In another view of institutionalism, Berger and Luckmann (1967) see institutionalization as the typification of habitualized social action that "repeated frequently becomes cast into a pattern" (p. 53). This perspective comes from an understanding of the social construction of reality as it occurs in social groups. As for the structuralist view, Berger and Luckmann do not look at the process of institionalization at the societal level. Both Giddens and Berger and Luckmann could benefit from specifying how specific proximate social institutions constrain and guide what are to become social practices—in this case, what become "appropriate" and taken-for-granted ways of approaching innovation.

Combining aspects of organizational institutionalism with Whitley's institutional perspective will facilitate the institutional interpretation and explanation of differences in Danish and American approaches to innovation.

THE SPECIFIC ANALYTICAL FRAMEWORK

The proposed framework combines elements from the new organizational institutionalism and industrial sociological institutionalism. The general purpose of the framework is to explain the institutional shaping of social practices resulting in a specific set of technical practices with respect to innovation. I draw a distinction between institutional sources, institutional mechanisms, and institutional effects. The framework is shown in Figure 11.1. *Institutional sources* are the major proximate social institutions (educational systems and the state agency policies) that are seen by industrial sociologists (Kristensen, 1992; Lane, 1992; Whitley, 1992b) as important shapers of social and thereby technical practices. However, we include other industrial organizations as institutional sources for mimeticism. *Institutional mechanisms* (DiMaggio & Powell, 1983) are the coercive, normative, and mimetic forces, and each corresponds to an institutional source. *Institutional effects* are not related directly to technical practices, but to social practices.

It is mainly institutional mechanisms that account for nonfunctionalistic organizational forms driven by institutional isomorphism. Asking why these mechanisms should not be active with respect to isomorphism in technical practices seems obvious. In our view, these institutional mechanisms may affect ritual aspects of organizations as well as real aspects of technical practices: (a) seeking legitimacy from a government agency to get an R&D contract, (b) conforming to peers when confronted with uncertainty about the "right and best" technical solution or organizational structure, and (c) normatively induced isomorphism stemming from "professionalization as the collective struggle of members of an occupation to define their conditions and methods of their work . . . and to establish a cognitive base for their occupational autonomy" (DiMaggio & Powell, 1983, p. 152). These may all influence the technical performance of a given task.

The influence of *governmental agencies* includes effects on the degree of technological novelty and the type of learning process that are both encouraged and evaluated as legitimate, based on current policies regarding industrial R&D support. The *educational system* is an important

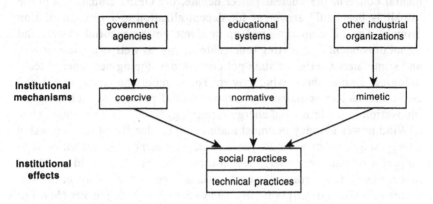

INSTITUTIONAL SOURCES

Figure 11.1. Analytical Framework for Understanding the Institutionalization of Technical Practices

generator of the portfolio of technological competencies, shaping the types of professionals available (engineers or skilled workers). Professionalization rests on formal education and anticipatory socialization; they provide social norms about personal behavior (one's role in a work organization) and a cognitive base for selecting and solving problems. Further, attitudes toward types of work methods, relevant problems, and roles may be institutionalized in terms of dominant worldviews, identities, or the cultures of particular social groups (such as workers or engineers) (Sabel, 1982). The mechanism for this particular influence is typically normative, operating either by explicit or implicit cultural standards.

This model provides a framework for exploring and demonstrating how the two different approaches to innovation were societally generated by institutions that reinforced and reproduced two different systems of meaning, or norms of appropriate, acceptable, and legitimate ways of innovating. In this sense, they may be perceived as distinct, implicit, socially embedded "logics" of innovation followed by the social actors involved.

Origins and Status of Modern Wind Power

During the 1970s and 1980s, a new industry and energy technology emerged, with markets and technological development primarily in the United States, Denmark, the Netherlands, Germany, and the United Kingdom. The development of modern wind power was triggered in the early

1970s by a complex societal situation, consisting of increased environmental concern, the nuclear power debate, the OPEC embargo, and the "small is beautiful" argument for decentralization and zero population growth. The oil embargo sped up concrete entrepreneurial efforts and social movements supporting renewable energy, as well as nuclear power, and stimulated a series of state policies for developing new energy technologies, among these wind power. Thus, important larger social and economic factors initiated the entrepreneurial process of technological innovation in modern wind energy technology.[4]

Wind power is today the most mature and productive of the renewable energy sources, but even 20 years of development does not allow it to outperform established energy technologies such as oil, gas, and coal-fired power plants. On average, the cost of state-of-the-art wind power is close to conventional power plants. By 1993 about 3,100 megawatts (MW) of wind power had been installed worldwide, of which 1,700 MW was in the United States, notably California, where 1.3% of the electricity consumed was produced by wind power. In Denmark in 1993, about 3% of the electricity consumed was supplied by wind power; the German and British markets, as well as other European and Third World markets, are also expanding.

CHARACTERIZING WIND TURBINE TECHNOLOGY

Modern wind technology is not based on dramatic new inventions or recent scientific discoveries. The designs of modern wind technology are the result of a cumulative synthesis of the inventive and innovative efforts of the 20th century (see Karnøe, 1993).[5] Wind turbines are electricity-producing machines that exploit solar energy by transforming the kinetic energy in wind to rotation energy in the rotor of the turbine. A wind turbine is a complex system technology (Rosenberg, 1982) of different components and materials, such as hot and cold mechanical components, electronics, software, hydraulics, and advanced materials (in fiberglass or wood epoxy blades). The basic design configuration can be done in a number of ways, depending on the intentions of the innovator with respect to the degree of novelty in the basic design: two or three blades, weight, materials, size, power control, and the like, all of which affect the design's potential as well as its realized performance and cost-effectiveness. A designer may try to build a Maserati or Ford Model T to go for a spin.

When wind technology reemerged in the early 1970s, the problem was not so much that designers did not know how a wind turbine looked. The problem was a low level of knowledge; wind turbines were rather poorly understood. In hindsight, we know that no well-developed body of technological or engineering knowledge existed that could be directly applied and thereby make life easier for the designers by reducing uncertainty or improving performance (Garrad, 1988; Stoddard, 1990; Thresher & Dodge, 1990). The dominant turbulence models were 40% wrong in predictions (Castello & Elliot, 1991). The technical problems in developing wind turbines can roughly be divided into categories with respect to how they are cognitively perceived and dealt with. First, in more abstract engineering terms, the general problems are related to the areas of aerodynamics and structural dynamics. Aerodynamics refers to the way the highly random and turbulent wind loads are absorbed in the rotor blades (transforming kinetic to rotational energy) and how these loads affect the derived structural dynamics in a given mechanical configuration of the wind turbine. Structural dynamics are the damaging vibrations that affect the required dimensions and lifetime of components, the use of materials, repairs, and thereby costs. Second, these same problems may be dealt with more concretely by referring to the real configuration of the wind machine; for example, how to design, construct, and assemble components exposed to severe loads (fixing blades to the hub) and working with the hot parts of the transmission system, such as the shaft, gear, generator, cooling, and brakes. High-quality products are essential, because a wind turbine has more than 45,000 hours of operation in a 15-year lifetime, hopefully with minimal maintenance cost. How the mixing of the more theoretical, engineering approach and the more practical, problem-solving orientation turned out was determined by the heuristic approach taken rather than by purely technical needs.

DEVELOPMENT STRATEGIES IN
MODERN WIND TURBINE TECHNOLOGY

To gain a clear picture of the achievements of Danish and American innovations, it is important to briefly survey significant development strategies.[6] Basically, a distinction is made between bottom-up, market-driven innovative activities and top-down, government-directed innovative activities (see Table 11.1). The United States' top-down strategy was initiated in 1973–1974. It was a government-sponsored R&D program with very limited exposure to real economic market criteria. It was primarily guided by design and performance criteria that were set by government agencies (Karnøe, 1993). Despite $330 million in public R&D funding, these large-scale, top-down activities—by NASA, Boeing Engineering, Westinghouse, and Lockheed—did not result in any commercial wind

TABLE 11.1 Characteristics of de Facto Innovation Strategies in Danish and American Wind Turbine Development, 1974–1992

	Top-Down		Bottom-Up		Top-Down
Characteristics	U.S. government-directed R&D		U.S. market-driven R&D	DK market-driven R&D	DK government R&D
Technology					
size of WT	large	small	small	small	large
sophistication	high	high	high/medium	low	low
R&D spending $mill. (1974–1992)	330	120	unknown share of	27	25
Market shares on American market (1980–1992 (comm.)[1]	0	0	40%	45%	0
World market share by 1993	0	0	25%[2]	53%[3]	
No. of major manufacturers left	0	0	1	4	

SOURCES: Karnøe (1993, Table 4); Gipe (1995); *Politiken* (a Danish newspaper), March 23, 1994, section 4, p. 8.
NOTES: 1. This is a measure of the share of the commercial market held and does not include prototype installations.
2. By the end of 1993, only very few American wind turbines had been exported, although US Windpower is working on international projects. Therefore, the 25% refers to the American manufacturers' share of their own home market, which consists of about 50% of the actual installed wind power capacity.
3. Danish manufacturers' own home market share is 100%, and the Danish home market made up about 15% of worldwide installed capacity in 1993. The Danish share of the European market was 66%.

turbine technology. By 1988 all of the large-scale "dinosaurs" had been dismantled; none of these contractors is currently active in wind power (Davidson, 1993; Stoddard, 1990). The other part of the U.S. top-down program involved the development of small-scale wind turbines; these were based on development contracts awarded by an agency of the Department of Energy (DOE). The firms awarded these development contracts included McDonnell Douglas, Alcoa, Kaman, and United Technologies, as well as a few start-up firms. Despite $120 million in public R&D funding, no commercial wind turbine has yet come out of this program, and none of the contractors is commercially active in wind power.

Today's modern commercial wind power emerged from pioneering activities in the United States and Denmark that were market driven. The only surviving American wind turbine manufacturer came from the market-driven type of innovation. Even though the American government program gave $120 million to the creation of small-scale wind turbines, this R&D

activity was not of much use to market-driven companies, as they did not meet the requirements for R&D contracts.

I have chosen to focus in this analysis on the nature of innovation within the market-driven areas of American and Danish wind turbine manufacture. The possibilities for comparison between Danish and American wind turbine entrepreneurs using a bottom-up strategy are unique: (a) Both Danish and American entrepreneurs started out at the same time (in the mid-1970s); (b) in both countries the new pioneers were inspired by and chose to build upon design traditions developed earlier in the century (a technological path dependency) (Karnøe, 1993); (c) further, in both countries, the already active entrepreneurs were stimulated by market incentives almost at the same time (1979–1980); and (d) finally, both the Danish and the American emerging industries were supported by newly established test and research centers focusing on small-scale wind turbines (1977–1978). With respect to the type of technology, the time in history, the presence of market stimulation, and the presence of R&D-supporting institutions, almost identical circumstances were created in both countries.

Despite these similarities, however, the approach taken and the outcomes that resulted—in terms of the level of performance that resulted from attempts at innovation—differed significantly in the two countries. In the years of rapid growth in the California market (1982–1986), the Danish market share increased from 0 to 68%; 45% of all wind turbines in California are Danish built. Today, the cumulative Danish world-market share is 53%, but the American share is only about 25%, and of the 13 major American bottom-up wind turbine manufacturers, only 1 was left in 1988—but 4 major Danish manufacturers remain. The decisive factor behind this high market share is the superior performance of the Danish-built turbines.[7] Capacity factors[8] show that from 1986 to 1989, Danish wind turbines on average produced 70% to 100% more energy than their American competition. In our view, during the initial and early consolidation phases of the development of modern wind power technology (1975–1990), the difference in the results of Danish and American bottom-up strategies stems from the different types of logic behind innovation in the two countries. These different beliefs and actions created different breeds of inner logic that drove the technical practices observed in each approach.

So, how did the Danish and American innovators proceed, and what types of heuristic frames, conceptions of appropriate overall design, and problem-addressing and problem-solving behavior are observed?[9] And how do these behaviors reflect socially possible, rather than technically efficient, approaches? The next section seeks to identify differences in the technical practices of each approach and to relate these differences to institutional sources.

The American Bottom-Up Approach

ORIGINS AND TYPE OF INNOVATORS

Entrepreneurial activities in the reinvention of small-scale wind energy technology had their origins in very different teams of innovators: grassroots or "hippie" innovators, university research teams, and market-driven innovators. It was these market-driven innovators who dominated the commercial market for wind power. The dominant innovators in the United States were all engineering-based companies. Notable innovators were Carter, Sr. and Carter, Jr., who had backgrounds as design engineers in helicopter design and had access to new materials from the Polaris project. Among the top seven manufacturers of the 1980s, Energy Sciences International (ESI) was established in November 1980 as a spin-off of the newly established U.S. test and research center, the Solar Energy Research Institute (SERI). The most commercially prominent (and only surviving company) of the U.S. manufacturers had its origins in some very important development work done at the University of Massachusetts. In 1972–1973 a group of researchers there won a grant from an environmental program to design a wind turbine. The young researcher who was assigned the task of designing this turbine had worked for a few years as part of a helicopter design team.[10] Over the next several years (1975–1981), he was in charge of development, and a lot of prototypes were tested with the assistance of aerodynamicists and experts on the blade material (steel, wood epoxy, fiberglass) at MIT. This was, in a sense, a high-tech start-up with many resources, including connections to research institutions. In 1981 the same researcher designed, as a consultant, a wind turbine for another company. That company became the fifth-most-successful (in terms of sales) wind turbine manufacturer of the 1980s, before poor product performance forced it out of business (Karnøe, 1993). What these companies have in common is that they were all driven by design-oriented engineers. In the following section, we will look more closely at the innovative practices of these companies, as well as how the governmental test and research center worked and interacted with the industry.

INTERNAL WORK ORGANIZATION:
THE DOMINANT ROLE OF DESIGN ENGINEERS

In the American companies, the design and production process was either divorced from or poorly integrated with practical experience. In two major manufacturers, the design and R&D functions were geographically separated from production functions. The primary activity in the company was clearly design. In one company, of the 15 engineers hired, all were design engineers—there was nobody to take care of production in the remote facility. Production was not something of great concern and it was not perceived to be something important from which engineers should learn. Also, skilled workers were not well represented in the workforce. In one company, production did attract more concern, mostly as a result of learning from failure. This company, by improving the stability and performance of one of its designs, achieved a degree of success. (Success in this case is defined as manufacturing a well-working wind turbine—the company never sold outside its vertically integrated income circle in which it installed its own wind turbines and sold electricity to utilities.) However, this company also had the reputation of having a good production-oriented engineer who acted to create the company's success. In this company, the focus on production was shaped by a strategy of driving the costs down and harvesting on a standardized design. The successful design was produced for about 10 years (1982–1992), product development stopped, and the original design engineers left. The new design was not initiated before 1986, and in 1992–1993 the new, larger (300 kW) design, which was thought to be ground-breaking (*EPRI Journal*, 1990, p. 20), was ready to take over.

In the early years, when the basic design was developed, the working climate among the engineers was one of self-motivation and dedication to the product. Although the engineers were not allowed to talk to others within or outside the company, they felt they had a productive learning circle. After production began, however, this feeling changed because of the installation of an organizational structure characterized by functional specialization and hierarchy.[11] The tough policy on secrecy and the organization's reluctance to include others besides top-level R&D managers in design reviews discouraged many engineers, and it probably also interfered with internal learning. In general, there seems to be little internal collaboration and communication between groups and functions regarding problems.

This pattern seems consistent with general observations about work organization and functional integration. After World War II, the linkage between the R&D and design functions changed "in thought and practice" and became more and more separated from "such essential downstream engineering functions as verification and testing of design, manufacturing, and product and process improvements" (Dertouzos, Lester, & Solow, 1989, p. 79; Hayes, Wheelwright, & Clark, 1988; Imai, Nonaka, & Takeuchi, 1985; Mowery & Rosenberg, 1989). Jobs in basic science and R&D became the most prestigious engineering jobs; the design of manufacturing processes, manufacturing technologies, and production operations acquired at the engineering schools a reputation for being lowbrow activities (Dertouzos et al., 1989). In this sense, engineering education was a primary source of organizational change, induced by normative forces. This process is likely also to be spurred by mimetic forces, because patterns of perceptions and practices concerning adequate organizational forms and behavior emerged in peer organizations and then diffused first as the "best," then as a taken-for-granted way of organizing.

The American educational system developed to meet the needs of employers in a mass-production economy. The wartime decline in apprenticeships that occurred within companies was continued, and the new managerial idea of efficient production and limiting the amount of skills needed by workers resulted in a shortage of skilled workers in the early 1950s (Noble, 1984). Even Taylor called for continuous training of workers (Wren, 1987, p. 126). The postwar American system of education is weak in its ability to educate workers. No governmental or industry-based technical schools for educating workers emerged—skilled workers and broad skills were not needed in industry. Also, the vocational high school education available in the United States is seen as a poor substitute for practical apprenticeships, and the two are not linked at all as they are in Germany and Denmark. The scarcity of the remaining apprenticeships outside construction (Piore & Sabel, 1984) combine with short in-plant training of workers in narrow skills, and with a management system that keeps workers out of workplace organization and production problems. Managers interviewed in about 1987, regarding worker skills and new technologies, stated that there was no problem (Dertouzos et al., 1989, pp. 82, 89). As a result, the bottom two thirds of the workforce in Japan and Germany are better skilled than their U.S. counterparts (Thurow, 1992, p. 53).

ATTITUDES REGARDING APPROPRIATE
DEGREES OF NOVELTY AND THE CHOICE OF A DESIGN

American engineers in wind technology typically went for the breakthrough innovation, or at least a design that had radically changed features compared to existing technology, in order to give them a technology-based competitive edge in the market. USW's recent groundbreaking 7-year development project, M-33; Carter's search for the ultimate design (extremely lightweight, with a teetered rotor, but still not successful commercially after 16 years of development and sales); ESI's innovative design; and numerous other American wind turbine designs were typically quite sophisticated. The Danish design was known from pictures, but it had no appeal in the United States. It was thought of as much too simple and old-fashioned, with no real engineering challenge. This tendency to go with radical changes can be clearly seen in strategies for upscaling the size of the wind turbine. One jumped from 25 kW to 300 kW, another from 100 kW to 300 kW, a third from 80 kW to 300 kW. As Woddy Stoddard put it: "(1) we [engineers] felt bright and able to solve anything, (2) we thought in a typical American fashion that there would be inevitable breakthroughs that would make the 'pedestrian' Danish approach obsolete overnight" (letter to the author, January 5, 1993).

The desire to come up with something radically new, to pursue breakthrough innovations, seems to be a deeply embedded and almost taken-for-granted American value. U.S. technoculture is built on more than a century of genius and technological enthusiasm (Hughes, 1989). However, lately this tendency has been referred to in many recent studies as a problem (Dertouzos et al., 1989, pp. 74-75; Florida & Kenney, 1990). One could ask, what are relevant technological ambitions? What degree of novelty in design characteristics, materials, and performance is perceived as appropriate, or how many fundamental changes in the modification of an existing design can be seen as being appropriate? Rosenberg and Steinmüeller (1988) show that, despite Japanese examples of the economic benefits of imitation, imitation has never been perceived as appropriate in American industry. One American engineer stated that during his education he was exposed to the "S-curve" of technological evolution and taught that the task of an excellent engineer was to change the curve by coming up with something new.

Breakthrough thinking was also the ruling logic in government technology policy. The system was very much mission oriented: Why spend government money on a wind turbine that already exists? As Woddy Stoddard put it, "the government program discouraged taking the Danish design" (letter to the author, January 5, 1993). This ambition or pressure to achieve breakthroughs was also strongly present in DOE and SERI, and it worked as a direct coercive force on those applying for a development contract (see below). From its start, SERI defined the standards or evaluation criteria that had to be met to get a contract. Lightweight, advanced designs, aerospace design codes, highly mathematical, sophisticated—this is what was needed to get the low cost of energy (COE) that was demanded (V. Nelson, 1984). Despite the success of the Danish design, there is still strong skepticism in the DOE and SERI (Davidson, 1993).[12] However, this did not prevent Mitsubishi from copying the Danish Gedser design as the basis for its entrance into the wind power market.[13]

Not just breakthrough thinking influenced the "choice" of the light, high-speed American design. Mimetic forces were at work, too. There was a widespread perception that to get costs down, wind turbines had to be

light and have high aerodynamic efficiency. This approach was constructed by engineers who either deliberately took over Hütter's design
principles (see Note 5) or themselves came from the aerospace and helicopter industry. Further, they believed that Boeing and NASA were not
wrong in using an aerospace design heuristic, even though the large design
was not seen as the right approach. Not until the mid-1980s was this design
criteria really questioned. "Helicopter design codes have been woefully
inadequate for designing wind turbines" (Stoddard, 1990). "We were
guilty of steady-flow aerospace-type thinking, and largely did not appreciate the range and difficulty of the wind environment" (Stoddard, 1986,
p. 85; see also DOE, 1984). In this sense, American designers were blinded
in their concern for structural dynamics in construction, resulting in too
much faith in lightness and high aerodynamic efficiency, and also resulting
in the low robustness and poor performance of many American turbines.

THEORETICAL DEPENDENCY AND
ORIENTATION IN PROBLEM SOLVING

To American design engineers, the problems of designing wind turbines
were mainly perceived in terms of engineering science; concepts such as
aerodynamic and structural forces had to be dealt with in detail and with
great accuracy in specifying the components. Technical problems were to
be solved by theory rather than by practical means, such as the construction
of prototypes and learning through trial and error. Learning and advances
in the design are mostly based on new and improved theoretical knowledge, used in advanced CAD/CAM equipment, that is tested on prototypes.
American engineers also, of course, learned from experience and from
failures—but not in the same ways as practical Danish engineers and
skilled workers. As Stoddard put it, "we trusted our engineering tools too
much, and felt they could solve the hard problems [with structural dynam-
ics] (which they couldn't), and we simply didn't believe that the engineering problems was as hard as it was (sic)" (letter to the author, January 5,
1993).

When the components for wind turbines were produced and assembled
in a function either geographically or mentally removed from the design
function, this set-up combined with the theoretical orientation of engineers
and the lack of skilled workers to constitute a problem for the technological learning process. Design engineers were not much connected to the
day-to-day, practical, hands-on problems, and they were weak on integrating the knowledge gained on the shop floor with their own stock of
knowledge. The engineers pursued, valued, and depended upon theoretical
knowledge.

Again, this is a widespread American practice (Aoki, 1986). Relating this observation to normative mechanisms, Seely (1993) states that after World War II, the traditional, practical engineering education finally gave way to the newer scientific engineering. Federal research and development favored fundamental research, and engineering education followed suit, thereby conforming to the long-held beliefs of the proponents of "basic" science. By the mid-1960s American engineering colleges and academic engineers embraced the methods and goals of "science." In the report of the MIT Commission of 1989 (Dertouzos et al., 1989), it is said that MIT and other elite universities played a major role in the change in engineering education toward "greater emphasis on the fundamental principles of engineering and less on familiarity with industrial technology. There was a pronounced trend away from industrial practice in the engineering curriculum" (Dertouzos et al., 1989, p. 78). Government funding practices encouraged this shift by assigning increasing importance to basic and applied scientific research. However, Hughes (1989, pp. 47-75) has shown that great inventors, such as Sperry and Edison, mix theory and practical experimentation in a productive manner. Despite the fact that many "true" scientists arrogantly ridiculed the empirical approach, the empirical approach was perceived to be appropriate by those inventors trained in formal engineering science who were working on the leading edge of technology. In our view, the productive integration of theory and practice, seen from the 1880s to the 1930s, weakened after World War II.

THE TEST AND RESEARCH CENTER
AND INDUSTRY SUPPORT: SERI/NREL

Governmental R&D support for small-scale wind turbines started in 1977 and was carried out by way of a test and research center. (Formerly called SERI, its name was later changed to National Renewable Energy Laboratory, or NREL.) Its aim was to support small-scale wind turbine research, but the program was a top-down program and did not provide support to the commercial, bottom-up activities. The first three researchers to be hired were (a) a professor in electrical engineering, (b) a person who had studied aerodynamic forces on buildings, and (c) another who was one of the first individuals to graduate from the University of Massachusetts wind-turbine design program. The managers came from the DOE. The basic purpose of this R&D program was to support the development of commercial wind turbines through awarding government-sponsored contracts to selected candidates, using the criteria mentioned above. In other words, the government agency decided which were promising designs and which were not. SERI never developed deep and continuing relationships with the commercial wind turbine industry. Except for an initial test of the first wind turbines, there was no systematic testing of commercial wind turbines. The organization did not participate in ad hoc troubleshooting when unexpected problems arose and thus missed the opportunity to have the industry participate in setting the agenda for research activities. Industrial distrust of SERI increased in 1981, after one of the test engineers left and formed his own company and test reports were not released until 2 years later. Apart from weakening the position of market-driven commercial products, the weak linkage between SERI and the commercial industry hampered research activities as well, because tests were conducted on old designs, with no follow-up using full-scale modern designs. In 1992 the largest wind turbine at the test site was a 12-year-old, very small wind turbine (10 rotor, 20 kW output) (Summers, 1992). However, this lack of real state-of-the-art wind turbines was not a concern to the center, because it did not feel it was supposed to solve practical problems. Rather, the research strategy and rationale behind supporting industry was to pursue fundamental engineering science research in order to establish the theoretical basis for the design of an "ideal" wind turbine. Fundamental engineering science research is more abstract and theoretical than practically oriented experimental engineering research (Vincenti, 1990, p. 231). It therefore does not "need" full-scale technology. Nevertheless, even theoretically oriented American designers claim that the form of knowledge gained from governmental research activities is too theoretical and abstract to be of use in practical design. The knowledge produced was more like formal modeling than insightful interpretations about the nature of wind turbine technology (see Karnøe, 1993, regarding the case of design codes for dealing with structural dynamics). Some very sophisticated and adequate design codes, however, have been developed (Thresher & Dodge, 1990) and have been purchased by the Danish research center.[14]

The emphasis seen in the United States on developing the basic science underlying wind turbines is consistent with the general characteristics of American engineering education as described above. The mission orientation exemplified by the search for the "best" or "ideal" wind turbine also reflects a normal practice in American military and aerospace R&D contracts, the types of research that dominated postwar governmental R&D. The main architect of the postwar governmental approach to technology and science policy in research and education was Vannevar Bush, the former director of the well-known, mission-oriented Manhattan Project (Layton, 1976; Noble, 1984). The spirit of the era in which science became institutionalized was that "what is good for the scientist is good for science and good for society." Basic science research was seen as extremely important for long-term technological and economic strength (Layton,

1976, p. 689). Three major characteristics of postwar federal funding have been that (a) Between 50% and 80% of government R&D funding over the past 30 years has gone to the military (if space research and atomic power are included, the total comes to almost 100%); (b) the Department of Defense (DOD), the DOE, and NASA were responsible for allocating 97% of the federal R&D monies to industrial firms; and (c) federal funding has mostly funded basic research (Mowery & Rosenberg, 1989; Noble, 1984). DOE's agency SERI followed this pattern.

The Danish Bottom-Up Approach

THE ORIGINS OF INNOVATORS

In 1978–1979 three small companies (employing staffs of 10, 30, and 120) that originally produced agricultural equipment diversified into wind turbines in response to stagnating agricultural markets. They were supplemented by about five to eight smaller entrepreneurs—do-it-yourself builders; together these formed the group of early entrepreneurs entering the field of wind turbine design. By 1981 the new organizations already dominated the Danish market; during the 1980s, they became in addition the world leaders, as measured in market shares and level of product performance (Karnøe, 1991, 1993). The technology bases of these small firms were very similar—each had between none and two hands-on engineers and a core of skilled workers. These small firms had no formal relations with research facilities and did not have any formal R&D or product development departments, although they did engage in both design and construction. Making customized and continuously updated versions of small tanks, electrical trucks, small hydraulic cranes, watering equipment, and the like was part of the normal business of these companies. Accordingly, products were produced in small batches or series. In 1982 a Danish firm was established that had the second-highest level of exports to California (1,400 wind turbines). It was started by a production engineer who left one of the established firms. He was a blacksmith with 3 years of practical engineering school. Until the late 1980s, the technology base of this firm was the owner who was also the production engineer, one hands-on design engineer, and a skilled workforce in a barnlike production facility.

ORGANIZATION OF WORK AND SOCIAL ROLES

Although of course there was some variation among the "big four," they all shared the same basic characteristics in their work organization. The early development work was organized by a small team of practical engineers, mechanics, fitters, and the like. Redesign, operational experience, and production went on hand in hand, in an organic, integrated process. A learning process of practical experimentation increased their technological understanding of how to make wind turbines work. Gradually, design engineers came to be responsible for heading the development process, but no ivory tower hierarchy or functional separation was developed. This was true even after 1983, when a more formalized design and development function became part of the organizational structure. Developing more sophisticated designs for new versions became more and more difficult, needing more and more engineering calculations (in part for the documentation purposes of the Danish Wind Turbine Test Station, to achieve legitimacy with American insurance companies, and later with certification companies, such as Germanisher Lloyd). In 1988 the four major firms employed between 7 and 15 engineers, a dramatic change since 1980. Out of 20 people in development, only 5 held academic degrees in engineering; 13 were "practical" engineers who often do an apprenticeship in preparation for another 3 years of study at an engineering school. The two dominant firms changed their heads of their development departments around 1987, but instead of hiring academic engineers in this "new, more professionalized era," both engaged R&D managers who had begun their hands-on experience in the late 1970s, whereas the biggest American manufacturer hired a university researcher with a Ph.D. as its R&D manager. The frequent traffic between the shop floor and R&D offices can be seen by the amount of oil on the carpet between the two. Although it has not yet been studied deeply, it seems that a flat and flexible, modernized, craftlike organization still works—that is, coordination, communication, and respect among the different groups and functions are highly productive. This improves information processing and learning capacities because many problems are dealt with instantly without too much paperwork and without needing to pass too many levels and departments.[15]

Even though the Danish companies were competitors, they formed in practice a community of practitioners, continuing from the formative years in which practitioners met several times a year. In a questionnaire in 1988, the engineers in the big four answered that they communicated informally, or "had a barter economy," about solutions for different problems. Further, they engaged in more formal cooperation (than was the case in the United States) with the Danish test and research center, helping to set the agenda for research projects. In other words, mimetic forces were at work, with the community of practitioners functioning as a cognitive community that developed a shared understanding of technological problems, solutions,

and research agendas (Constant, 1984; Laudan, 1984).[16] Danish wind turbine manufacturers also created with their Danish suppliers a strong industrial network, which further strengthened this community (Karnøe, 1990).

THE INSTITUTIONAL EMBEDDEDNESS OF THESE PATTERNS

When the observed patterns in the organization of work among Danish
wind turbine companies are compared to Danish industry in general, a high
degree of isomorphism emerges. The Danish wind turbine industry originated in a region of Denmark in which a particular type of firm and work
organization is extremely dominant (Kristensen, 1990, 1994). It is therefore understandable that they have in common distinct patterns of social
organization, skill bases, and problem-solving approaches. The dominant
type of work organization in this area was the small and medium-sized
craft shops or factories, and they are still are a major part of the Danish
manufacturing system. Many of these companies produced advanced products for export markets, and though many have been bought by large
corporations, they have been allowed to keep the style of work organization that attracts a core of skilled workers (Kristensen, 1988). As will be
shown later, this is not the only type of work organization in Danish
industry. However, in our view, these particular patterns of work organization and social roles are not only spread by mimetic forces but are instead
reproduced on a deeper level by normative mechanisms. The so-called
"craft-educational complex" (Kristensen, 1992) has been the most important institutional form engaged in and sustained by Danish skilled workers,
and it helps them to reproduce social roles maintaining high autonomy
within work organizations (Kristensen, 1990). From the 1870s onward
local craft associations established local technical schools educating apprentices in drawing, calculus, and other skills that were relevant for
specialized crafts. This process continued in the 20th century, and although
it was initially driven by the crafts and the supporting labor movement, it
became corporatized, developing into part of the official Danish labor
market policy designed to support technical schools and to encourage firms
to have a high retraining rate. In fact, technical training and retraining are
driven internally—by the members of work organizations—because following the newest courses and learning the newest technologies are part
of how prestige is allotted on the shop floor. Elaborate education has also
been offered for unskilled workers, allowing them to combine many
courses in their lifetime. In sum, this broad system for educating the
workforce is why the lowest two thirds of the Danish workforce is as highly
skilled as German and Japanese workers.

Concerning the role and skills of engineers, it is important to note that Denmark has two types of engineering education. The first, the Danish Technical University, was already established by 1829, and it aimed at letting academic scientific methods replace conservative craft methods. Academic engineers were mostly employed in research, governmental agencies, and large firms—but even the explosive number of academic engineers produced, beginning in 1965, did not change the practical logic of most Danish firms. The practical logic was protected by a special engineering education. Early in the 20th century came the other institution—the advanced technical schools (Teknikum) where a skilled worker could get a 3- to 4-year education and become a "technicum engineer." This allowed skilled workers to compete with the emerging academic engineers in obtaining managerial careers (Kristensen, 1992, 1994). This secured continuity in thinking and in understanding between the shop floor and managers. Even now, these practical engineers secure the majority of managerial positions in production and development in the machine industry. However, recent attempts by the Ministry of Education and the Danish Technical University to upgrade the teknikum engineers—to train these engineers further in engineering fundamentals—may tend to undermine the advanced technical schools, making it possible that they will be transformed.

At any rate, the institutional embeddedness of social roles, skills, and patterns of work organization created a different logic for approaching innovation; this will be evident in the choice of design and of problem-solving orientation, as shown below.

CHOOSING THE DANISH DESIGN

Despite many low-cost experiments with alternative designs, the reintroduced Juul/Gedser design was the one with the best performance record, as of 1977. The biggest firm, Vestas, after some failed experiments, bought a license from a blacksmith neighbor for his version of the Juul/Gedser design. Two other companies started from scratch; one entrepreneur began as a mechanic making agricultural watering equipment in his father's machine shop, and the other was a specialized supplier of water and oil tanks. All three copied the best design on the market, the Juul/Gedser design, but each firm has always added to the Danish design its own distinctive micro-configuration. In a sense, Juul's simplicity and robust construction matched the technological competencies of these entrepreneurs. Part of its appeal was probably because of the way it was described in rather simple terms in Juul's own technical papers, which had been found.

The degree of sophistication and novelty pursued by the Danish technological community was low compared to the United States. Why was this design acceptable to Danish designers and engineers? The simple answer is that it was proven the best in competition with other designs tested in the early years (from 1976 to 1979/1980). Furthermore, small companies learned from other small-scale innovators that it was possible to produce it, sell it, and make a profit (even without understanding the scientific processes behind it). Imitation was seen as a part of the learning process, so it did not bother them. Different variants of the dominant Danish design, however, resulted in differences in performance among Danish manufacturers.

DANISH PATTERNS OF INNOVATION

Incremental innovation seems to be a typical Danish pattern of innovation. There is not much research on these subjects in Denmark, but in 1985 a study was designed to identify and study small and medium-sized (6-500 employees) companies' strategies for innovation, with the ambition to identify more radical innovations (Christensen, Karnøe, Larsen, Lotz, & Valentin, 1990). The firms in the study were selected because they had high growth dynamics and high export shares. To the great surprise of the researchers, these companies were neither making nor pursuing radical new technological innovations. Instead, they were making advanced, but still bread-and-butter, incremental-type technological innovations (Ergas, 1986). This type of approach to innovation has been found to characterize an advanced, skilled workforce, which configures new product innovations and applies and incorporates new technologies in advanced, high-performance products and production processes in mechanical engineering, furniture (design and process technologies), and electronics/instruments. In this sense, the patterns of innovation observed in the Danish wind turbine industry resemble a more widespread Danish practice in innovation. Apart from the high R&D shares in the Danish high-tech sector, not much is in fact known about general Danish practices concerning innovation. The observed patterns of innovation are most likely linked to the absence of a high-tech, radicalism-for-the-sake-of-radicalism, American-type breakthrough orientation in Denmark. Therefore, such ideologies or technocultures of engineers, workers, and owners are not present, nor are they induced by the financial system and governmental institutions, as they are in the United States (Florida & Kenney, 1990). However, these issues do sometimes occur at a rhetorical level, when discussions regarding a technology gap take place in the ministries and the media;

however, to our knowledge (admittedly based on little research as of yet), they are not yet dominant in practice.

THE PROBLEM-SOLVING HEURISTIC

As the origins of these innovators indicate, they did not have any special previous knowledge about wind technology or aerodynamics. In this sense, the "natural" beliefs among the designers dominated. In the early years, the whole approach was not about getting the wind turbine light and elegant, but rather the dominant heuristic was that of a mechanical design and construction crew who struggled to get the turbine working reliably by designing and redesigning components that failed or could be improved. The intensive product development work of the first wind turbines was indeed characterized by practical, ad hoc engineering and construction. All kinds of problems with rotor speeds, broken yaw systems, blade-and-hub linkages, gear boxes, burned generators, twisted main shafts, and so on were handled. Design and construction were guided by trial and error, and by simple design rules of thumb. There are stories of simple drawings on paper towels. Gradually, there was an accumulation of practical, hands-on knowledge about the poorly defined and poorly understood technology involved; this knowledge improved the design rules, which changed from simple, hand-calculated parameters to rules that relied on more advanced empirical analysis. Today, CAD/CAM equipment is frequently in use as well.

The problems facing the Danish designers were not stated in formal, theoretical language. They were defined much more in terms of practical (mechanical or material) problems derived from failures or from hands-on construction and analytical reflection. These failures were often solved by "throwing metal on [the problem]," as one American observed, commenting on the heavyweight Danish designs. In fact, the "overweight" Danish approach lessened the negative effects of the severe structural dynamics (vibrations) that gave American designs a shorter or poorer life: "Low speed Danish-type turbines have reduced this design risk by: 1. Limiting exposure to aerodynamics loads, 2. letting internal (weight) forces overshadow the aerodynamic loads, 3. preventing dynamic motions" (Stoddard, 1986, p. 89).

The Danes had not even intended this for any theoretical reason. The strategy for improvement has been one of incremental innovation. In a rather slow, step-by-step upscaling, the size of Danish wind turbines grew from 20 kW to 45 kW and then to 55 kW during the period 1976–1980, and then gradually in the following steps: 75 kW, 100 kW, 120 kW, 150 kW, 180 kW, 200 kW, 250 kW, 400 kW, and finally, 500 kW in 1993.

Although not all companies have chosen exactly the same steps, all proceeded without jumps as large as those characterizing the American companies. Danish innovators built on existing knowledge and refrained from taking risks that might be too high. These innovators, not bothering to think of problems in terms of their formal aerodynamic and structural dynamic aspects, found this mechanical work, with the dimensions and fatigue properties of a mechanical architectural structure with hot and moving machine parts, to be familiar territory where their skill bases and work practices were easily applicable. Learning and advances in the product stemmed from an integrated design and practical construction process where hands-on experience combined to deepen understanding. New and improved ways of design emerged from real models, operational experience, and production. This pattern seems consistent with the lack of a breakthrough technoculture and the dominance of the craft ethos in the organization of work, in roles, and in the skills of workers and engineers, as mentioned above. In this sense, normative forces seem more influential than mimetic forces.

THE DANISH WIND TURBINE TEST STATION

The Danish Wind Turbine Test Station (DWTS) was established in 1978, specifically to support the emerging Danish wind turbine industry. DWTS was established on the initiative of a group of engineers committed to wind energy. They applied for a grant from the Danish Energy Agency, with the objective of supporting the emerging industry. The first 3-year grant was for about $1 million. DWTS was located at the Danish Nuclear Research Center, one of Denmark's "big science" institutions. The first engineers and, by institutional definition, would-be researchers knew each other from grassroots work with wind turbines or the governmental wind turbine measurement program on the old Danish "Gedser-mill" (1977–1978, in collaboration with U.S. Department of Energy).

A major challenge for the researchers and engineers at DWTS was to develop an adequate mode of interaction with the highly skeptical practical industry. This mode of interaction started with getting the confidence of the industry by awarding a prize for the two best designs. However, during the first year, 1978, the industry was not forced to interact with DWTS, but in late 1979, a Danish government act installed a coercive mechanism, a compulsory approval system for wind turbines. This approval system was set in place to ensure that a new Danish market subsidy (comprising 30% of total investment) paid to buyers of wind turbines would not be wasted on poor technological designs. This approval activity was the dominant factor that shaped DWTS research activity in terms of the type of problems addressed and the type of knowledge developed. It also was a means for forcing industry to interact with DWTS.[17] The Danish state *imposed* a change in practice on these Danish machine-shop-like firms, in the sense that the firms *had* to interact with a test and research center in order to get the technology they developed approved. The early skepticism stated in interviews suggests that if such interaction had been voluntary, these artisan machine shops would not likely have interacted as intensely with DWTS as they did.

The approval system forced DWTS to measure the whole system, not just one component. Emphasis was put on structural characteristics and safety in operation. Full-scale tests, measurements, and experiments with real wind turbines provided data for the first empirical parameter models and simple theory building.[18] Beginning in about 1982 with simple measurements (a method was developed to enable the meaningful interpretation of data), DWTS used simple or rough-hewn theory to calculate some minimum load factors for a formalized design rule for industry use, which was applied to evaluate each wind turbine. It was a conservative rule but it was safe, and the high minimum load factors supported overweight models. If a company wanted to go below this standard, it had to convince the engineers during the test that it could work (DOE, 1984). Instead of a process of filing formal papers, the personal contact created during the development and approval phases, and the visits to development and production facilities to do checking and to discuss problems in design after design, became a direct channel for the building of cumulative knowledge, sharing, and research agenda setting (Dannemand Andersen, 1993).

If one looks at the reports and the research output from the test station, not much engineering science appears to have been produced over the first several years—that is, at least not much in the way of advanced, abstract, complex, mathematical, theoretical models or codes for describing aerodynamics or structural dynamics in turbines was put forward. To the designer, however, the knowledge created from interpreting measurement data at DWTS was very important. For example, it gave one a basic understanding of the nature of the dynamic (not just static) forces, an understanding that could serve as a guideline for practical design work. One of the leading American pioneers in research and design[19] said that, out of the 25 most important papers from the 1980s written to guide the design process (i.e., to provide an understanding of the nature of wind turbines in terms of basic design problems and trade-offs in the design process), 12 would be Danish, and the authorship of the rest would be distributed among the United States, the United Kingdom, and the Netherlands.

The research activity was characterized by technological practice rather than theoretically oriented fundamental engineering science. At DWTS the research activity had a strong practical orientation with respect to problem definition and knowledge generation. It was very different from the U.S. theoretically oriented, fundamental engineering science research activity. Design engineers from industry determined the output orientation—they took primary responsibility for shaping research and output forms. No senior scientists were among the first group of engineers at DWTS, and all these engineers still identify themselves more as wind turbine engineers than as scientific researchers. They are more concerned with what the Danish industry thinks about the reports than what foreign researchers think (Dannemand Andersen, 1993, pp. 181-182).

INSTITUTIONAL INTERPRETATION OF DWTS

Obviously, DWTS has been extremely important in supporting and upgrading the technology base of the industry in the past 15 years. The formal and informal patterns of communication linked, in a very productive way (a) industry knowledge about practical solutions; (b) experiments that had a research-based, practical, problem-solving focus; (c) systematic research developing reliable, empirically based models; and (d) more formal engineering science, especially later on. If viewed from the perspectives of "good technology is applied science" and "governmental research should be mission-oriented," the DWTS has failed. It did not work according to these widespread beliefs. What made DWTS possible in Denmark may be best understood from an institutional perspective.

The craft-educational complex was supported by an important institution for advanced technology. In 1906 the Danish Technological Institute was established to support small and medium-sized craft firms with the diffusion of knowledge and methods. It was also established as an institution for testing and retraining in the newest technologies. Later a number of specialized Technical Institutes sprang up, with the specific purpose of supporting the small and medium-sized companies. With this historical perspective, we can see that the establishment of the DWTS followed a Danish tradition of industry support. Normally, these institutions do not conduct basic research, as the DWTS is doing today—normally, they provide testing and consulting.

The Framework and the Construction of Social and Technical Practices

This study has demonstrated how different technical practices resulted from a set of social practices that affected (a) the skill bases and forms of work organization, (b) the degree of technological novelty of the product design, and (c) the perception of not only dominant problems but also what constitutes adequate problem-solving methods and research strategies. These social practices also affected the construction of the interaction between industrial R&D and external research, especially with respect to the type of research and support thought to be the most supportive for industrial technology. Each approach activated a set of technological competencies and search-and-learning heuristics that were neither technically rational nor idiosyncratically random. It was rather the activation of a specific set of societally and institutionally embedded social practices. As a strategy, then, each approach was not an "open choice from the menu"—instead, each approach may be conceived of as activating a set of social practices, forming into a distinct pattern of activity (Mintzberg, 1987). Moreover, each approach or strategic pattern seems to have been fashioned according to a distinctive institutional environment, fashioning what was seen as rational and natural behavior after the image of its environment. Indeed, each approach was unlikely to "emerge and survive" in the institutional context of the other. In a sense, we have identified competing "rationalities" behind appropriate innovation practices. However, this rationality does not refer to any system or output rationality that would determine which approach will be the winner in the long run. The Danish approach turned out to be the most productive one for the first 15 years of modern wind turbine technology. Of course, major shifts in the assets needed for a competitive advantage, a shift from product technology to such assets as finance or turnkey sales, might in the future handicap the Danish companies.

The American approach emerged from the micro-level practices and the dominant managerial and engineering beliefs about production and innovation that have arisen with the American-style mass production and breakthrough-oriented, science-based innovation system. Despite Taylor's own intentions, his ideas were generally associated with efficiency gains and the technical elements of time and motion studies and the simplification of tasks (Wren, 1987, p. 126). Indeed, it seems important to distinguish between the "early Taylor," the "late Taylor," and Taylorism as practiced. From the 1920s until World War II, it seems that worker involvement in problem solving in production was more prominent than the spread of mass production led us to assume (Noble, 1984, p. 35;[20] Piore & Sabel, 1984, p. 46[21]). This situation changed, however, particularly in the 1950s. Production problems were increasingly handled as part of the abstract planning of operations research; they were to be dealt with optimally with given volumes, efficient operations, and production technology (Wren,

1987, pp. 397-398). The perception of production problems changed from a dynamic to a static optimization view, which came to be characteristic of American industry (Wheelwright, 1987).[22] The nature of concern over production problems changed and, as a result, concern for the education of skilled workers decreased (Dertouzos et al., 1989). As a proximate social institution, the educational system for workers was changed in such a way as to make it consistent with this type of thinking.

As far as the American approach to innovation goes, as measured in terms of values, skills, and organizational forms, it shifted from a practical orientation, around the turn of the 20th century, toward a too theoretical approach, from the 1950s to the 1970s. Also, the functional integration between R&D and production decreased. Further, some important changes in this century in the dominant value system of engineers (Kranakis, 1989; Layton, 1976) and in engineering education (Seely, 1993) have affected engineering practices. Spurred by a one-sided interpretation of the truly major accomplishments of integrating science and technology during World War II, the ideology of a productive, direct, linear linkage between fundamental basic science and technological innovations emerged and materialized in the actions of institutions and social actors. The postwar R&D approach was the outcome of a contest between the "losing" Truman faction, which wanted a democratically controlled science designed to serve society, and a faction of powerful scientists, large space and military contractors, and elite universities, headed by Vannevar Bush, the former director of wartime military research, and a Republican-controlled Congress (Noble, 1984). In weighing "sub-optimum," "theory-practice," and "science-technology," it seems fair to conclude that Americans have exaggerated the economic benefits that flowed from the truly unchallenged leadership at the scientific frontier (Rosenberg, 1992). The impact of this change from a practical to a theoretical orientation in the country's technological capabilities must of course be seen together with the changes in the organizational role of the new type of engineers, educated in design and R&D and divorced from production, leading to the deterioration of a complementary, higher-order, mechanical skill base on the shop floor (Dertouzos et al., 1989; Hayes et al. 1988), and to effective competition from Germany and Japan.[23]

What made the Danish approach possible? During the 1930s dominant intellectuals, academics, politicians, and industrialists attacked the large number of small Danish firms and demanded that efficient mass production be installed, as in the new Ford and General Motors firms in Copenhagen (Kristensen, 1988). In the 1950s American management thinking, emphasizing efficiency, deskilling, time studies, planning, and operational research, was widely diffused (Andersen, 1990). Great numbers of managers and engineers were educated according to these principles, and they dominated management thought until the early 1980s. In contrast to the American case, the skilled workers in Denmark won—or were never completely defeated by Ford-like thinking engineers and managers—as the social construction of industrialization proceeded. As mentioned above, the craft-educational complex *institutionalized* and *reproduced* (although modernized) the identities and roles of the skilled workers on the shop floor. The "teknikum engineer" education opened further management positions in production and product development, even in larger, modern organizations. This expanded the domain of the craft ethos to the broader organization (Kristensen, 1992, 1994). The recent seminal works of Kristensen (1990, 1992, 1994) present a reinterpretation of the social construction of the Danish process of industrialization. One of the most recent interpretations of the nature of the present Danish industry structure[24] and its inner organizational and behavioral characteristics point at the evolution of two competing models driven by very different rationales for growth and efficiency. One model is that of large companies, driven by Taylorism—mass-production principles and economies of scale. The other model is that of companies dominated by the skilled worker, driven by a craft ethos of variability of products, high shop-floor autonomy, and continuous learning, even in large organizations. Its socio-technical principles and proximate social institutions have been either almost invisible or poorly understood and recognized. In Kristensen's view, this reproduction is mainly carried out by the craft-educational complex, which has been built by the social forces of craft organizations and labor unions. It is not the best system in the world but was enough to institutionalize socio-technical practices that gave Danish industrialization a distinct path. It also gave the Danish wind turbine manufacturers their distinctive technical practices even in a modern world, practices that go beyond classic Taylorism and Ford-like production processes.

Thus, the framework proposed in this chapter has captured some essential aspects of the constitutive forces behind each approach. The institutional sources that were active included both proximate social institutions such as educational systems and state agencies, suggested in the new industrial sociology; and mimetic, coercive, and normative sources, suggested by the organizational institutionalist. Further, I illustrated a dynamic process of reciprocal contingency of these micro-level organizational characteristics with dominant belief systems and proximate social institutions (educational systems, workforce management systems, and state agencies).

Expanding the Framework on the
Institutionalization of Social Practices

This study intended to demonstrate that technical practices indeed may be understood as institutionalized social practices, and that the contemporary conception of organizational institutionalism does not capture this phenomenon adequately. Changing, in organizational institutionalism, the conception of the institutional embeddedness of technical practices does not lead to abandoning the important message in institutional theory that strong environmental forces account for isomorphism. Nor does it argue that decoupling may not occur. Still, organizations located in the same institutional environment are expected to develop similar structural forms and practices. Organizations embedded in different institutional contexts are not likely to respond in the same way to identical technical environments. In this sense, the term *logic* implies that, in their approach to innovation, the Danish and American innovators activated a kind of socio-institutionally embedded meta-routine that both created and constrained the road chosen. Contrasting the early versions of organizational institutionalism with the new industrial sociological institutionalism shifts our attention to the effects of the wider institutional environment, effects that reinforce and reproduce social and, thereby, technical practices.

Thus, our framework, combining Whitley and the new organizational institutionalism, is adequate for distilling more or less broad characteristics of dominant business systems in nations or regions. However, the framework still needs further development in terms of the variation and changes within business systems, for example, those discussed as occurring in the history of American mass production. This problem may be framed as a problem of structuration, which more explicitly addresses how social action is constituted. More work on the mutual reinforcement among social actors, institutional mechanisms, and institutional sources is needed.

Notes

1. Further, these differences in micro-level patterns of work organization are mirrored in the type of educational systems and managerial regimes that are seen. These differences have been documented as well in Lane's comparison of Britain and Germany (1992).

2. Ironically, Toyota's idea of just-in-time (JIT) production was based on the "no-stock-order and shelf-filling" norms of American supermarkets (Sabel, 1993).

3. An illustration of this is Dore's notion (1983) that relational contracting practices in Japan are widespread because such arrangements can be relied upon. As socioeconomic practices, they are further embedded in principles such as the importance of sustaining high

levels of trust in relations, honesty, and obligation toward other members of the community, rather than principles stressing individualism and taking advantage of "free rider" possibilities. These principles or basic cultural values pervade the economic life of Japan and have had a major impact on subcontracting practices in intermediate markets, on labor markets, and on relations between business groups.

4. For a historical account of the social construction of Danish wind technology, see Jørgensen & Karnøe (1994).

5. The most important inspirations came from a Dane, J. Juul, an American named Putnam, and a German, Hütter. From 1947 to 1958, Juul experimented and developed the "Danish design"—a three-blade, stall-controlled, low-speed, upwind, grid-connected turbine of heavy construction. Juul was a practical engineer, and his design philosophy was shaped by scarce resources and a preference for simplicity in mechanical design. This was in sharp contrast to the American Putnam's ambitious "high-tech" project (from 1937 to 1945), and to the resources and new materials available, during the Nazi regime, to the German Ph.D. in aerodynamics, Ulrich Hütter. Hütter continued experimenting with his extremely light, high-speed constructions in the 1950s and was Juul's main competitor (Golding, 1955; OEEC, 1953).

6. A more comprehensive analysis of the American government-directed strategy (also called a top-down strategy) is provided in Karnøe (1993).

7. The high-interest, anti-inflation policy of the early Reagan years led to an overvalued dollar, which made Danish turbines cheaper, strengthening the Danish position in the years 1983–1986. However, at that time, Danes could go as low as 5-7 DKr./$1, far from the 1985 rate of 10-12 DKr./$1.

8. See Karnøe (1993). A *capacity factor* is defined as the ratio of actual energy output to the amount of energy a turbine would produce if it operated at its full-rated power, 24 hours a day, over a given period (California Energy Commission, 1990, p. 6). Changes in capacity factors over time reflect improved technology as well as the development of better routines for operation and maintenance.

9. A process of continuous revision of the design is inseparable from the changes in the cognitive frame—technology as knowledge—(Layton, 1974) and in the heuristic frame, with its focus on certain problems, methods, and solutions (Dosi, 1982, 1988; Laudan, 1984). Despite this insight, it is highly uncertain which ways of combining practice and theory bring about the "best" recipe for advancing a particular technology.

10. The researcher developed a graduate mechanical engineering course specializing in wind turbine technology. About 30 engineers from this program went to work in the emerging wind industry.

11. As one former employee put it: "Suddenly you had to communicate and agree that this problem is a problem and has to be fixed. You have to go two layers up to be able to communicate with someone at your own level in another department or specialized group."

12. Because a wind turbine will normally never be airborne, there was no logical or compelling need for it to be lighter. More weight and solidity could have stabilized wind turbines' performance and income generation. Nevertheless, creating a lighter turbine was the only option perceived as rational by the dominant community of practitioners in U.S. research institutions and the American wind turbine industry.

13. *WindPower Monthly*, November 1986: "The Japanese wind turbine philosophy can be compared to that of the Danes. They prefer heavier turbines and insist on a high safety factor—preventing cost-effectiveness. But Dr. Ushiyama is confident ways can be found to build an economically viable turbine with a high safety factor."

14. At least in terms of programs, a new trend is emerging in the DOE wind power program (see Davidson, 1993; Gipe, 1994), The Valued Engineering Turbine (VET) and the Advanced Wind Turbine (AWT).

15. Danish practical engineers may tend to not master the kind of tools that allow for the transfer of more abstract or generalizable information concerning the nature of wind technology and abilities to other fields of technology. A large part of the practical knowledge gained is transferred in response to a specific problem, in a direct process of communication. Viewed from the perspective of analytically and theoretically oriented engineers, practitioners are often viewed as prisoners of tradition (Hayes et al., 1988, p. 29). However, it seems that both groups are prisoners of their own socialization or identity patterns, and of their views of what constitutes natural or superior engineering practice.

16. Several American engineers visiting Danish research centers or companies were surprised at the amount of shared knowledge in Denmark. When this is added to the secrecy demanded in one of the American companies, in our view this indicates that the American group of practitioners was characterized by a weaker shared understanding.

17. Contrary to what many Americans think, DWTS never picked which designs were to survive; it only determined some minimum standards needed for approval. Of course, as most Danish companies made use of the Danish design, some would read its role as one of "Communist state control," as has been stated.

18. All of the first engineers were out making measurements—they started with field measurements in order to not be identified solely with engineering—not until the mid-1980s did new engineers begin their work with PCs (Dannemand Andersen, 1993, p. 180).

19. This individual wrote the first book on the new engineering science for wind turbines, to bridge the gap between pure engineering science and technological design. However, some Danish designers found the book too mathematical, even though it was much less so than NASA and SERI reports. The book was Eggleston and Stoddard (1987).

20. In hindsight, the survival of these principles until World War II suggests a plausible hidden factor or partial explanation of the extreme rates of innovation, production volumes, and productivity in U.S. war production (see Hayes et al., 1988, pp. 44-51). In other words, within American-style mass production, behaviors characteristic of more dynamic mass-production systems (like those of postwar Japan and West Germany) were still in existence.

21. On this issue Wren (1987, Ch. 8, Ch. 9, p. 175, on work shop councils in the 1920s) refers to the work of D. Nelson (1980). This is compatible with Piore and Sabel: "Put in another way, the American Plan was compatible with craft systems of shop floor control in large firms in that it permitted workers to exercise autonomy without threatening the rights of workmates or undermining their collective position against management" (Piore & Sabel, 1984, p. 130).

22. The production problem was perceived as solved, as stated by the influential economist J. K. Galbraith in 1958 (from Hayes et al., 1988, p. 53).

23. This critique is not intended to say that fundamental research may not, with adequate precision and maturity, induce or speed up technological development. Nor do I intend to say that Americans were not world leaders in R&D, innovation, and basic research in the 1950s and 1970s. It is rather to address the problems related to understanding the complex nature of alternative balances of theory and practice that may exist in specific contexts and may have specific outcomes. Indeed, there is no clear recipe for what combination of practice and theory is best for advancing any particular technology. Although it is difficult to adequately capture conceptually, it is generally accepted that the American approach to technology in the past few decades has leaned too heavily toward science.

24. The Danish manufacturing industry has 17,000 firms: 10,000 firms have fewer than 10 employees, and there are 7,000 manufacturing firms with more than 6 employees. Only about 1.5% (or about 90 firms) employ more than 500 people (the largest employs some 12,000 people). In terms of fabrication or production units, the Danish industry structure is truly dominated by small and medium-sized companies. However, about one third of these companies are owned by larger corporations, which are responsible for about 40% of total industrial turnover.

12

The Origins of Economic Principles

Railway Entrepreneurs and Public Policy in 19th-Century America

FRANK DOBBIN

FROM THE PERSPECTIVE OF THE LATE 20TH CENTURY, American economic history appears to many as a monument to the principle of the free market. Yet the U.S. economy followed very different principles for most of the 18th and 19th centuries. Up to the time of the Civil War, regional governments played active roles in promoting development. Economic historians have dubbed this the period of "rivalistic state mercantilism." Between the end of the war and about 1900, economic life became less localized, governments eschewed participation in development, and price fixing became widespread. Industrial cooperation through business associations, cartels, and trusts characterized this period. Only at the end of the 19th century did Washington attempt to enforce price competition, and only then did the "free market" come to dominate economic practice and thought. In this chapter, I argue that these three patterns of economic organization were produced in large measure by industrial policies. Focusing on the rail industry, I show that each of three successive policy regimes produced distinct business strategies, and each led actors to infer a different set of "universal" economic principles.

AUTHOR'S NOTE: My thanks to the other contributors to this volume for helpful feedback, and especially to Søren Christensen, Peter Karnøe, and Jan Molin for detailed comments on an early draft.

The Institutional Construction of Efficiency

For much of the 20th century, neoclassical economists made teleological assumptions about American economic institutions. Macro and micro institutions were subjected to parallel assumptions. At the macro, institutional level, antitrust law was taken to exist because it was the optimal solution to problems posed by competition and collusion. At the micro, individual level, competitive pricing was taken to exist because it led to optimal prices and efficient production. The functionalist premise underlying economic theory led analysts to neglect questions of *why* these particular institutions had emerged and *whether* these institutions were optimal, and instead to deduce theories of *why they were* optimal. Economic historians were largely taken in by the functionalist premise, even the best of them (e.g., Chandler, 1977).

Three tendencies that emerged from these assumptions had unfortunate intellectual consequences. The first was that American economic institutions were presumed to have followed a single logical trajectory that led inevitably to the outcome we see today. Periods of government leadership and industrial cartelization were read, post hoc, as anomalies that proved the rule of market efficiency. Each new economic institution was taken to be a functional response to a potential problem, such that each was explained by its apparent consequences. Because the United States enjoyed unparalleled growth, it seemed plausible that America's economic customs were optimal.

Thus the second unfortunate tendency was that of treating institutional changes as driven by their putative effects rather than by social and historical factors. Antitrust law, which was adopted to protect economic liberties (Wilson, 1980), was interpreted after the fact as the only way to reinforce the natural selection mechanisms that were key to growth. Never mind that no other successful country adopted it. In the face of unprecedented economic growth, Americans concocted stories to explain why each and every one of their economic customs was optimal. At best, Americans derived unnecessarily narrow laws of causation from experience (e.g., antitrust alone can produce growth); at worst, they mistook coexistence for causation.

Third, the presumption that extrasocietal economic laws govern the universe led analysts to treat economic principles that were drawn from experience as *causes* of social institutions rather than *results* of them. For instance, when federal law encouraged price fixing, analysts had dubbed the rail industry "naturally cooperative." Yet after federal law outlawed cartels and enforced price competition, leading railroads to merge to escape rate wars, analysts dubbed the industry "naturally monopolistic" and predicted eventual consolidation. Instead of drawing the lesson that government anticartel law made merger a sensible business strategy, analysts drew the lesson that economic laws produced antitrust legislation and competitive pricing alike. In short, by beginning with the premise that policy choices are driven by extrasocietal economic laws, analysts naturalized policies and hence presumed that they did not need to be explained.

HISTORICAL INSTITUTIONALISM
VERSUS ECONOMIC FUNCTIONALISM

If social practices are not products of transcendental economic laws that are revealed to humanity through experience, a different epistemological approach to economic life is needed. We should be searching not for the regularities in economic behavior that reveal fundamental economic truths, but for the properly institutional origins of behavior patterns and the processes by which actors glean general laws from those practices. In short, if economic behavior is structured by social factors rather than by transcendental laws, then its explanation must lie in social life.

There is wide agreement in the social sciences that in rationalized societies, actors search for general economic laws with which to guide their behavior. At issue is whether the laws they identify represent ultimate truths or simply glosses on experience (Berger & Luckmann, 1967; Geertz, 1983; Weber, 1968). A growing number of social scientists have taken the second view. They have explored national industrial and economic policies at the macro level, and business strategies at the micro level.

Institutional students of comparative politics seek the origins of industrial and economic policies in history (Hall, 1993; Katzenstein, 1985; Zysman, 1983), countering the view that differences among nations can be put down to differing functional demands (Gerschenkron, 1962). The new institutionalists in politics take a view that is broadly consonant with the views of Alexis de Tocqueville (1945, 1955) and Andrew Shonfield (1965). They insist that institutional history explains much of the character of national policies even though policymakers may self-consciously try to orient policies to economic universals. These analysts take the view that public growth policies, like other social customs, can only be explained socially and historically.

Comparative studies of policy confirm that, far from conforming to narrow, universal precepts, economic practices and beliefs vary dramatically across developed nations. Analysts trace policy decisions in part to the structural and conceptual constraints imposed by prior policy and constitutional choices (Krasner, 1984; Scott, 1994b; Thelen & Steinmo, 1992). Thus, for instance, U.S. rail policy options in the 19th century were severely delimited by America's weak federal structure (Skowronek, 1982). In general, history explains growth policies better than economics. Once institutionalized, public policies tend to persist because they become integrated with wider economic institutions and ways of thinking (Dobbin, 1993; Hall, 1986; Krasner, 1984; Thelen, 1991; Zysman, 1983).

Neo-institutionalist organizational theorists (e.g., DiMaggio & Powell, 1991; Dobbin, 1994a; Meyer, 1994; Meyer & Rowan, 1977) operate at a lower level of analysis but subscribe to many of the same tenets. Ideas about efficiency are socially constructed from economic experience and thus will vary over time and space as wider institutions vary. The policies that political institutionalists study figure prominently as independent variables in these organizational studies. Neither public policy nor business practice is overdetermined by economic exigency. Policies shape business strategies and ultimately affect economic thought by structuring the economic environment. In one of the few such studies that extends far back into history, Neil Fligstein (1990) has shown that the Sherman Antitrust Act of 1890 made mergers the favored business strategy at the dawn of the 20th century and popularized a new theory of the firm that reinforced horizontal integration. Then after World War II, the Celler-Kefauver Act, amending Sherman, made diversification the favored American business strategy and helped to popularize finance management and portfolio theory.

Unlike Fligstein, most organizational institutionalists have sought to show that even *within* the antitrust policy regime, seemingly modest shifts in the policy environment can produce major changes in business strategy (Abzug & Mezias, 1993; Baron et al., 1986; Dobbin, Edelman, Meyer, Scott, & Swidler, 1988; Edelman, 1990; 1992; Mezias, 1990). In this chapter, I go back to before America's antitrust policy regime to explore three starkly different policy regimes and their effects on business strategy and economic thought. One goal is to highlight a point that economic historians have frequently made: Early U.S. industrialization occurred under policies antithetical to today's antitrust, procompetition, policies (Fallows, 1994). Another goal is to trace the origins and consequences of the antitrust policy regime, which Americans so often treat as neutral—noninterventionist—in the belief that it merely reinforces natural economic conditions. My broader goal is to show the striking effects of public policy on business strategy and economic ideas, even within a single country and industry.

In each of the three periods examined below, public policies generated business practices and attendant economic theories. To tap changes in business practice I use primary and secondary historical sources. To chart emergent changes in economic thought, I examine the writings of railroaders and industry observers, drawing on such sources as Thomas Cochran's

(1965) vast compendium of letters written by industry leaders: *Railroad Leaders 1845–1890: The Business Mind in Action*. For each period, I also sketch the contemporaneous experience of Britain to show that the policies adopted in the United States were by no means inevitable and to show that where different policies were pursued, entirely different kinds of business practices ensued.

WHERE DO BUSINESS STRATEGIES COME FROM?

My argument builds on historical studies that have shown two things. First, in the modern world, actors derive rationalized economic principles from experience and employ those principles to guide their own actions. The collective identification of such principles is termed "the social construction of reality" by Peter Berger and Thomas Luckmann (1967). As Andrew Shonfield has said of early British efforts to draw rules from experience: "Classical economics, which was largely a British invention, converted the British experience—or rather what the British hoped would eventually emerge from the trend which they had detected in their own story—into something very like the Platonic idea of capitalism" (1965, p. 71). Today actors constantly scan the environment for new empirical evidence and new theories of efficiency that might explain that evidence.

Second, the experiences actors glean economic principles from are very much shaped by public policy. Karl Polanyi (1944) argued that the idealized "free market" of modern economics was, in Britain, created quite deliberately through public policy during the 18th and 19th centuries. It was the outcome of the *presence* of a wide range of public policies rather than, as the rhetoric goes, the complete *absence* of public policy. Or, as Harry Scheiber (1981) describes America's early economy: "[T]he wonderful abstraction called the 'market' had structure and distribution of advantage defined in large part by conscious political decision-making" (p. 104). The contrary idea, that perfect markets exist in the complete absence of state institutions, shaped early British economic tracts as well as political rhetoric. From 1830 the rhetoric of laissez-faire reinforced the idea that economic institutions were given structure by transcendental laws rather than by human agents and governments. As Leon Lindberg and John Campbell (1991) put it, "The very notion of intervention perpetuates the imagery of a clear separation of state and economy where markets, for example, can, or at least did, once upon a time, exist in a truly laissez-faire condition, completely autonomous of the state's influence" (p. 356).

In this chapter I focus on the effects of policy changes on business strategy and economic thought. In each period, I explore the business practices generated by public policies and the economic principles railroaders derived from their experiences. For present purposes, I treat policy choices as exogenous. How did Americans arrive at the conclusion that rivalistic state mercantilism was the most effective means to growth? How did they come to believe that approach was wrong, and support cartels? How did they decide to crush cartels and enforce price competition? I address these questions in a book that explores the historical construction of industrial strategy in the United States, Britain, and France (Dobbin, 1994b). These questions are frequently asked by political historians, because powerful railroads often lost political battles they had invested heavily in. The short answer is that the American polity contained an exceptional, and highly institutionalized, antipathy toward the appearance of concentrated power. Policy shifts occurred when observers perceived illicit concentrations of power in the hands of government agents, as when corruption brought an end to public financing; or private actors, as when price fixing brought a reluctant Congress to regulate rates. Actors certainly pursued their own interests in the course of waging battles to curtail apparent abuses of power, but they did so in the context of arguing that centralized authority was antidemocratic and inefficient.

For now, the key question concerning the origins of public policies is this: Were these policies the inevitable products of the natural economic evolution of the industry? That is, were policy shifts functional responses to industry evolution? Recent studies suggest that they were not. Colleen Dunlavy's (1993) study of Prussian and American rail policies highlights stark cross-national policy differences that had lasting effects on the industry. Gerald Berk's (1994) study of the options the United States faced demonstrates that U.S. policy might have taken an alternative track. In this chapter, the sketches of British rail policy that appear at the end of each historical section highlight how very different policy was even in the country most frequently compared to the United States.

Business Strategy Among Railroads, 1825–1906

Railway strategy was extremely volatile between 1825 and 1906, and policy analysts trace changes to legislation and case law. In the terms of economic sociologists, policy shifts brought about different *varieties of markets* over time (White, 1988; Zelizer, 1988). Writing in 1975, Harry Scheiber characterized the period before 1870 as one of "rivalistic state mercantilism." Regional rivalry produced what I will call an *organic market* between 1825 and 1870; pricing was monopolistic and firm structure was unitary because firms seldom sought mergers. Railroaders described interregional, rather than interfirm, competition as the organizing principle of the modern economy. Writing in the late 1880s, Charles Francis Adams (1893) noted that the industry first changed radically at the beginning of the 1870s, at about the time states stopped aiding railroads, began to regulate prices, and encouraged cartelization. Rate regulation and procartel policies produced what I will call a *cooperative market* between 1871 and 1896; railroads set prices in groups, and firms sought loose business combinations with other railroads. Railroaders argued that price cooperation and interfirm coordination were natural in this industry, because market entry was discouraged by industry characteristics. Writing in the early 1990s, Robert Dawson Kennedy (1991) noted that the industry next began to change at the end of the 1880s, at about the time Washington tried to enforce price competition. Case law enforcing price competition from 1897 produced what I will call a *competitive market* between 1897 and 1906; railroads practiced predatory pricing to destroy their competitors, and they sought formal mergers to create large integrated systems. Railroaders described the industry as naturally monopolistic and depicted consolidation as inevitable because of the industry's high fixed costs.

Local Government Activism and the Organic Market, 1825–1870

Between 1825 and 1870 the U.S. economy was highly localistic. Most firms served local markets exclusively and faced little or no competition from firms in other regions. State and local governments actively promoted economic growth through massive projects to build needed infrastructure and manufacturing enterprises (Callender, 1902; Hartz, 1948; Lipset, 1963). The conception of economic life underlying this public policy regime conflicted with the laissez-faire ideals that then prevailed in Britain. Although Americans eschewed unwanted government meddling with industry, they saw public capitalization of industry as a way for the local community to pursue collective purposes. British ideas about growth, as exemplified in Adam Smith's work, depended on multitudes of small competitive firms in each industry. In the United States, by contrast, the difficulty of transport and the relative isolation of most communities led to a more organic conception of growth. Each community sought to establish at least one rail link, at least one miller, at least one blacksmith. The aim was to create a self-sufficient economy comprising all vital components. The axis of competition was between integrated regional economies rather than between firms within industries (Goodrich, 1949). The theory of macroeconomic growth that emerged was that prosperity would result from the collective, competitive efforts of entire communities.

Early regional economies were isolated for obvious reasons. First, large distances and the high cost of transport made trade difficult. Before the end of the 1860s, the railway system was not sufficiently integrated to facilitate transshipment between regions. Before the first Pacific railroad was opened in 1869, goods exchanged with the West Coast and the Orient traveled by wagon or boat at great cost. Second, the financial system was disarticulated. Before the passage of the National Banking Act, in 1863, the existence of thousands of different bank-issued currencies thwarted interregional trade and finance. Before New York rose as America's finance center in the 1870s, American firms had no central capital market.

Public promotion of railroads initially produced monopolistic pricing, for public promotion led to a proliferation of exclusive routes. Later dualistic pricing became popular, with monopolistic rates for exclusive routes and competitive rates for competitive routes. Railroad experts and economists surmised that dualistic pricing was natural, and that it advantaged all customers by maximizing rail income. Public promotion also favored unitary firm structures, which would allow communities to retain control over the railroads they had sponsored. Railroaders concluded that as part of competitive organic economies, it was natural and efficient for railroads to remain in local hands and to retain their unitary structures.

THE PROMOTIONAL POLICY REGIME

State and local governments played large roles in economic life before 1870. States competed to win business in agriculture, manufacturing, commerce, and transport. Every state with a major port on the eastern seaboard sought to establish a transport route westward that would make it the East's commercial and transport capital. Competitive state mercantilism transformed state and local governments into active entrepreneurs in the pursuit of local development: "The elected official replaced the individual enterpriser as the key figure in the release of capitalist energy" (Lively, 1955, p. 81).

Although regional governments were reticent to introduce controls over private enterprises, they were not at all reluctant to contribute money and in-kind assistance to firms (Shonfield, 1965, p. 303). Like the British, Americans believed in minimizing governmental interference in private affairs, but Americans did not oppose government activism per se, so long as activism displeased no one. As the governor of Massachusetts argued in 1828 of proposed legislation to commission private railroads to the Hudson and to Providence: "Here then is a measure of encouragement to domestic industry within our own control—a system of internal improvement, opposed to no constitutional scruples, *of which no interest can complain*, and by which all interests will be promoted" (General Court of Massachusetts, 1828, pp. 25-26; emphasis added).

The state-business relationship that emerged was highly mutualistic. Government policy was oriented to ensuring the establishment of a diversity of firms to serve every vital function locally. Where demand for glass, beer, twine, or canvas went unfilled, states and localities schemed to attract entrepreneurs who would build manufactories to serve the need (Hartz, 1948). They used financial incentives of all sorts, from stock subscriptions to tax incentives to outright subsidies (Handlin & Handlin, 1947). The railway industry benefited handsomely from this public largess, as states and towns competed with one another to win rail depots that would link them with the world. "No ambitious town could stand idly by and see a new railroad go to a rival place. There was no option but to vote bonds" (Ripley, 1912, p. 38).

Down to about 1870, every major rail project won public subsidies. Estimates of the total governmental contribution toward railroad construction vary, but antebellum public aid may well have exceeded 50% of total outlays (Dunlavy, 1993; Goodrich, 1960). States and localities saw it as their inalienable duty to finance industries that would become the building blocks of local economies. As late as 1871 the Massachusetts Board of Railroad Commissioners would write: "It now seems to be generally conceded that some provision for the construction of a certain amount of railroad facilities is, in this country at any rate, a matter of public charge" (1871, p. viii).

BUSINESS STRAGEGY

Public activism designed to create self-sufficient local economies, by establishing key industries, had important effects on business strategy among railroads. Across industries, this policy regime discouraged the establishment of enterprises that would compete with existing firms, by directing capital to needs that were unmet and sectors that were underdeveloped. In the rail industry, it created an incentive for entrepreneurs to find unserved routes and win public construction aid for them. One result was that most early routes were monopolistic, even routes between major cities, and hence rate making was monopolistic. A second result was that mergers were rare and unitary-form firms remained the norm.

Monopolistic and Dualistic Pricing. Monopolistic pricing was common at first. Down to about 1850, most railroads held service monopolies to all points on their routes and hence could charge what they pleased. Dualistic pricing became popular thereafter. Railroads charged high rates to isolated towns where they held monopolies, but low rates to large cities where they faced competition. Thus a railroad that terminated in two major cities might charge 10 cents a ton for goods shipped from one terminus to the other, but 20 cents a ton for goods shipped only half that distance to an intermediate town. John Blair, president of the Warren Railroad, summed up the new rate prescription in a letter to another railroad president in 1858: "Our duty is to discriminate where we have competition and get our share and meet the trade, and whenever we can and there is not competition make it up—this we must do at every station be it large or small" (quoted in Cochran, 1965, p. 262).

Firm Structure: The Unitary Form. In 1825 the closely held family firm was far and away the dominant corporate form in the United States and throughout the world (Chandler, 1990). Mergers were rare in part because large firms would have demanded managers, and the idea of hiring managers to replace owners in day-to-day affairs was all but untested (Chandler, 1977); in part because mergers that implied joint ownership were incompatible with family control of firms; and in part because the high cost of transport made it difficult to achieve economies of scale via mergers in most sectors. By 1825 some textile firms had achieved fairly large size (Dalzell, 1987), but they grew through internal expansion rather than merger.

Between 1825 and 1870 most railroads retained their original unitary forms in part, then, because there was little precedent for merger. The typical railroad was controlled by a small number of investors or a single family. Two elements of the early policy regime discouraged mergers. First, because public promotion policies generated a proliferation of lines to serve different regions and discouraged the establishment of competing lines, early railroads seldom faced the kinds of direct competition that fostered mergers among rivals. Second, state and local governments that chartered and capitalized railroads treated them as integral parts of the local economy that were vital to manufacturing, agricultural, and commercial interests. Governments, as both shareholders and chartering authorities, resisted proposals to merge railroads, because mergers might take this public good out of local hands. Thus, before the end of the 1860s, when Jay Gould and his Erie associates sought to buy up failing railroads to create an interregional system, mergers remained extremely rare.

THE ECONOMIC PRINCIPLES
DRAWN FROM THE ORGANIC MARKET

These economic conditions produced a vision of economic life that was collaborative, mutualistic, and organic. American states and localities competed as communities and saw their main competitors as other communities that sought to become centers of commerce, transport, and manufacturing. These ideas are evident in early policy discourse. In 1823 a committee of the Pennsylvania legislature proposed that the state inquire into the effects of New York's nearly complete Erie Canal, arguing that unless Pennsylvania sponsored a competing route, "her career of wealth will be less progressive than that of other states, and instead of regaining the high commercial rank she once held, she will be driven even from her present station in the system of the Confederacy" (quoted in Bishop, 1907, p. 172). Individual entrepreneurs perceived their destinies to be linked to the destinies of the communities in which they operated and thus came to see interregional competition as paramount.

The prevalence of dualistic rate structures, in which low long-distance rates coexisted with high short-distance rates, led railroaders to describe as natural and fair rates based on the presence or absence of competition, rather than on distance. They argued that dualistic rates were efficient and thus advantaged all customers. Where business could be increased by dropping rates, it was in the interest of railroads *and all of their customers* to reduce rates. As John Brooks, president of the Michigan Central, pointed out in 1859, railroads would increase their aggregate income by charging low rates on competitive routes. Clients on noncompetitive routes would ultimately benefit from dualistic pricing: "Every possible accommodation should be given to business from competing points. . . . It is neither wrong nor unjust to the people along the line that the foreign traffic should be done at lower rates, provided it is not done at less than cost" (quoted in Cochran, 1965, p. 273). Railroaders did not worry that although dualistic rates might maximize railroad income, they would put certain shippers from isolated regions at a competitive disadvantage. They only saw that monopoly and competitive routes had emerged naturally, and thought it natural that railroads should make the best of both kinds of routes.

Between 1825 and 1870 jointly held firms were popularized, in part as a result of such legal conventions as limited liability law (Coleman, 1990; Creighton, 1990); however, mergers among existing firms remained rare. The organic conception of economic life, in which interregional competition dominated intraindustry competition, led communities to conceive of their railroads as local enterprises built to transport goods and people to a regional metropolis. The idea of combining separate firms did not fit into this conception of economic life. Even where branch lines were built to connect secondary towns with main rail lines, founders—who sometimes included stockholders of the main lines—usually established separate companies to operate the branch lines. The closely held unitary firm continued to be the prototypical corporate form.

BRITAIN, 1825–1870

Were public promotion and the business strategies it produced inevitable? In Britain, policy, strategy, and economic thought were quite different. Parliament provided railroad charters, complete with rights to expropriate private lands, but otherwise remained stridently anti-interventionist (Dobbin, 1994b; Parris, 1965). Because public capital was never part of the calculus of railroad founding, railroaders focused on building railroads that would see healthy returns. They frequently duplicated popular routes that were already being served. In turn, competitors often set prices collaboratively. Long before 1870 railroad pricing had become cooperative on many routes. Long before 1870 railroads had pursued mergers to prevent rate wars. By 1870 British railroad leaders were describing price cooperation and merger as natural in the industry (Chester, 1981, pp. 177-179).

The comparative reliance of U.S. railroads on public financing has often been put down to capital availability. British railroaders, it has been argued, had ready access to capital. In fact, British railroads had little access to bank loans because British industry had financed expansion internally, and therefore London banks had scant experience with long-term industrial loans. When British rail entrepreneurs sought capital for their projects, they frequently had to establish regional stock markets that could attract local investors (Bagwell & Mingay, 1970, p. 28; Gourvish, 1980, p. 17). Although American railroaders had to win public subsidies to attract sufficient capital, British railroaders had to establish new financial institutions.

THE DEMISE OF THE PUBLIC PROMOTION MARKET

This first sort of market came to an end in about 1870, when public policy changed in two important ways. First, local, state, and federal governments foreswore future aid to railroads as a result of widespread corruption in the administration of public aid. Americans took instances of graft as evidence that excessive economic powers had been concentrated in the hands of government. By the end of the 1860s, 14 states had passed constitutional amendments either prohibiting or severely limiting future government aid to railroads and other private corporations; in 1872 the Credit Mobilier scandal tarnished more than a dozen senators and congressmen, and two vice presidents, bringing an end to congressional land grants (Cleveland & Powell, 1909, pp. 237-240; Dunn, 1913, p. 9). Second, most states regulated rates to prevent rate dualism. Americans took rate anomalies as evidence that too much power had been concentrated in the hands of private railroad entrepreneurs. By the end of the 1860s, state railroad commissions had been established across New England to prevent price inequities; by 1871 the Granger movement—farmers and ranchers opposed to rate discrimination against rural regions—began to win commissions to regulate rates across the Midwest and the South (McCraw, 1984, p. 57; Stover, 1970, p. 91). Many of these states regulated prices through short haul/long haul laws, stipulating that railroads could not charge more, in absolute terms, to ship goods short distances than they charged to ship them longer distances *over the same track*. These commissions made illegal the prevailing dualistic pricing strategy of charging low rates for competitive routes and high rates for noncompetitive routes.

Procartel Policies and the Cooperative Market, 1871–1896

THE PRICE REGULATION POLICY REGIME

After about 1870 American railroads faced a new policy regime. Two dramatic changes occurred almost simultaneously: Railroad prices were regulated through antidiscrimination laws, and public financing came to an end.

Meanwhile, state and federal governments began to encourage price fixing. In the 1870s voluntary price fixing was perfectly legal. Federal legislation from 1866, facilitating collaborative management and equipment sharing among railroads, seemed to signal federal acquiescence to railroad cooperation in rate setting (Kennedy, 1991, p. 145). By the mid-1870s states were encouraging price fixing as a remedy for unchecked price wars. Real competition had never existed in the industry, Massachusetts's commissioners argued. The most Massachusetts had seen was "fierce contests and violent fluctuations of very short duration," which destroyed firms but did not reduce rates in the long run (Massachusetts Board of Railroad Commissioners, 1875, p. 41). The commissioners concluded from this that the industry was not naturally competitive. Because interfirm cooperation was inevitable, they reasoned, the public would be best served by government oversight: "[A]n open and reasonable combination would probably be found far less fruitful in abuses than a secret and irresponsible one. One or the other must exist under the circumstances of the case" (Massachusetts Board of Railroad Commissioners, 1875, p. 41). Other states offered similar encouragements to price fixing.

Thus, with one hand state legislatures undermined the dualistic pricing strategy that railroads had come to depend on, and with the other they advocated price fixing to quell the rate wars that had emerged.

BUSINESS STRATEGY

The end of public capitalization made life difficult for the numerous railroads that had routinely returned to governments for new capital infusions. The Baltimore and Ohio, for instance, received $500,000 from Baltimore at its inception in 1827. The B. & O. won another $500,000 from Baltimore in 1828, $500,000 from Maryland in 1833, $3 million in bonds from both Baltimore and Maryland in 1836, $1.5 million from Baltimore in 1839, and $500,000 from Wheeling, West Virginia, by 1853 (Goodrich, 1960, pp. 80-82). After states made public financing unconstitutional in the 1860s and 1870s, railroads could not draw public funds to cover construction costs and operating losses. Meanwhile, the new antidiscrimination laws eliminated railroads' lucrative pricing strategy of offsetting low competitive rates with high monopolistic rates. On top of this, a 3-year economic recession hit America in 1873. Railroads scrambled to find business strategies that would return them to profitability.

C. F. Adams (1893) concludes that between 1869 and 1975, the combined effect of the antidiscrimination laws and the economic downturn produced cutthroat competition and scores of failures among railroads. For the first time, railroads engaged in price wars in the hope of bankrupting their competitors. As the Boston and Albany Railroad's annual report stated in 1875, the recent decline in railroad receipts was "due exclusively to the unprecedented competition that has prevailed during the greater part of the year, by which the rates of transportation to and from the West have been forced to the lowest point known in the annals of railroading" (McCraw, 1984, p. 39).

Cooperative Pricing. One result of the new rate competition was a novel rate-making strategy. As early as the 1850s, the freight agents of competing railroads had fixed prices informally. As physical links between rail lines were perfected and completed during the 1860s, the potential for competition skyrocketed, and railroads found it increasingly difficult to enforce common rates through informal agreements. Before rate regulation, railroads had made up for competitive losses by raising rates on short-distance monopolistic routes. Antidiscrimination law put an end to this by requiring that short-distance rates be lower than long-distance rates. It now became vitally important that railroads not only participate in but also abide by pricing agreements.

By 1874 the recession had caused the volume of rail traffic to decline significantly, sparking increased competition for the traffic that remained. Rates fell to levels that were not remunerative. "This resulted," wrote the Commissioners of Massachusetts, "in what was known as the 'Saratoga Combination' of 1874, through which the managers of the railroad lines attempted not only to establish common rates, but to make those rates binding upon each party to the combination through a central executive organization" (Massachusetts Board of Railroad Commissioners, 1878, p. 65). The enforcement of rates was the key to this strategy. The Saratoga Combination was followed by the Southern Railway and Steamship Association in 1875, the Eastern Trunk Line Association in 1877, and a series of other regional associations (Fink, 1979b). Albert Fink, the mastermind of these associations, insisted that they aimed to achieve public purposes: the "establishment and maintenance of reasonable and non-discriminating transportation tariffs" (Fink, 1979b, p. 22).

Firm Structure: Loose Integration. Unitary firm structure gave way to loose integration in the 1870s for two reasons. First, because pricing agreements were not legally enforceable, cartels collapsed whenever a participant faced a crisis that led him to cut his rates. Closer ties among railroads promised to prevent the breaking of pricing agreements.

Second, the new antidiscrimination laws precluded a common strategy for winning business: rate discrimination against customers of competing firms. Take the case that spurred the establishment of the Rhode Island rate discrimination law. The Boston and Providence railroad conducted the only rail service between those two cities but owned one of many shipping companies connecting Providence with New York. By cutting the rate on Boston-Providence rail service for customers who used their Providence-New York steamboat service, they could win all of the Boston-New York traffic for their steamboat. The B. & P.'s owners won steamboat business not by reducing steamboat rates but by discriminating against the customers of other steamboats wishing to use their rail service. The new law prevented discounting on one leg of a journey to win business on another.

Given these constraints, rail managers hoped that informal integration would help to discipline competing railroads. Pools, whereby railroads apportioned traffic or profits at a predetermined ratio, were the least constraining and most popular form of combination, but railroads soon employed more formal types of combination: joint stockholding arrangements, leasing agreements, holding companies, and trusts (Cochran, 1965, p. 136). Many firms pursued several of these strategies simultaneously. By 1880 virtually all of America's important railroads had at least joined pools that divided traffic or profits.

THE ECONOMIC PRINCIPLES
DRAWN FROM THE COOPERATIVE MARKET

Analysts soon drew the conclusion that although competition among entrepreneurs had been needed in the industry's construction phase, economic realities rendered competition irrational in the next phase. Interfirm cooperation was to be the principle that guided the rail industry. There was no doubt, wrote Massachusetts's Commissioners of Railroads in 1878, that competition "furnished the great stimulus through which a succession of what would otherwise have been looked upon as impossibilities has been accomplished in railroad development," yet there was no denying that this very competition had produced harsh and unjust discrimination (Massachusetts Board of Railroad Commissioners, 1878, p. 78). Although some analysts had expected competition to prevail in the mature rail industry, the commissioners pointed out that recent experiences led to the belief that "uncontrolled competition is but one phase in railroad development and must result in some form of regulated combination"—their term for cooperation under state oversight (Massachusetts Board of Railroad Commissioners, 1878, p. 80).

Railroad entrepreneurs increasingly expressed the belief that price competition could only produce instability, bankruptcy, and ultimately exorbitant rates. As Robert Harris, president of the Northern Pacific, wrote in October of 1887: *"There was never a more fallacious idea than that low rates could best be acquired by competition.* This principle applies to almost all kinds of business but it does not apply to Railroads and other Highways" (quoted in Cochran, 1965, p. 362). For C. F. Adams (1893, p. 26), the theory of competition was "an economic theory misapplied" to the rail industry. "[W]hile the result of other and ordinary competition was to reduce and equalize prices, that of railroad competition was to produce local inequalities and to arbitrarily raise and depress prices" (Adams, 1893, pp. 119-120).

Adams found to be ludicrous the premise, underlying arguments for competition, that new competitors would enter the market should prices be out of line with costs. Those who championed rate competition held the unrealistic belief that "railroads were not monopolies. There was nothing to prevent the organization of new companies to construct parallel and competing lines of road. Here was the remedy through competition." Adams concludes: "the mere statement of it revealed its utter absurdity" (Adams, 1893, p. 130). Market entry was discouraged by two factors. First, the cost of entering a rail market was extremely high. Second, entrepreneurs could expect existing railroads, who invited market entry by charging high rates, to quickly undercut the prices of a new competitor. Moreover, when two viable competitors had been established, they invariably colluded to fix prices, with the knowledge that new competitors were unlikely to emerge.

According to Albert Fink, the mastermind of the early trunk line pricing agreements who has been called the "father of railway economics," the railway industry did not operate under truly competitive conditions. As a result, competition did not produce properly regulated prices. Price regulation could only be achieved by railroad cartels with the force of the law behind them. "A proper distinction should be drawn between healthy competition, regulated by natural laws upon correct principles, and competition which is merely the result of mismanagement. The natural laws of competition do not regulate changes in [railroad] tariffs" (Fink, 1979b, p. 9).

When it came to firm structure, railroad experts concluded that the industry demanded interfirm arrangements for coordinating traffic and stabilizing prices. As Charles Perkins, president of the Chicago, Burlington, and Quincy, wrote in 1879, railroads would naturally group themselves into cooperative systems of some sort. "This law, like other natural laws, may work slowly, but it is the law nevertheless" (quoted in Cochran, 1965, p. 433). C. F. Adams argued that the finite number of competitors on each route; the high costs of entering the market, and the fact that market entry would create overcapacity, overinvestment, and bankruptcy made some sort of collaboration inevitable. "When the number of those performing any industrial work in the system of modern life is necessarily limited to a few, the more powerful of those few will inevitably absorb into themselves the less powerful through trusts, pools, and other arrangements" (Adams, 1893, p. 121). Wherever the number of potential competitors is limited, "the effect of competition is . . . to bring about combination and closer monopoly. The law is invariable. It knows no exceptions. The process through which it works itself out may be long, but it is sure" (Adams, 1893, p. 121). Because the industry was naturally cooperative, government prohibitions against price fixing and integrated management would merely stimulate bankruptcies that would lead the industry toward monopolization.

In this second period, price theory and the theory of the firm changed. The idea that dualistic pricing was natural and just gave way to the idea that collaborative rate making, which would produce rates that were both proportional to distance and stable, was natural in the rail industry. Collaborative pricing took hold in other industries, such as steel and hardware, as well (Chandler, 1990, pp. 72-75). The idea that the unitary railway firm was part of an organic local economy, and was hence inherently independent, gave way to the idea that railway firms were part of a larger market that held many possibilities for competition. Informal integration between railroads in different regions came to be seen as efficient.

THE DEMISE OF THE COOPERATIVE MARKET

Anticartel sentiments ran high in the United States, largely because cartels represented just the sort of concentrated economic control that American state institutions vilified. As a result, the earliest agreements had incited fears of abuse in the public (Adams, 1893, p. 151). The problem, in essence, was that Americans saw economic concentration as inherently evil and as antidemocratic (Dobbin, 1994b, 1994c; McCraw, 1984). "The combination of railroads, it is claimed, is unrepublican,—through it the dynasty of the 'Railroad Kings' is insidiously asserting itself. This argument is of the kind which sets refutatior at defiance" (Adams, 1893, pp. 212-213). The huge powerful firms that dominated the rail industry in the 1880s represented, for Americans, an "evil tampering with the natural order of things. They were not merely economic freaks but also sinister new political forces—powers that had to be opposed in the name of American democracy" (McCraw, 1984, p. 77). The Interstate Commerce Act of 1887 forbade pooling and all forms of price fixing. The Sherman Act of 1890 outlawed trusts and other forms of combination designed to restrain trade.

Although it would be a decade before the Supreme Court ruled the Interstate Commerce Act's antipooling clause to be constitutional, public anticartel fervor and the passage of the Commerce Act marked the beginning of the end of the cooperative market.

BRITAIN, 1871–1896

Was this brief phase of cartelization in the rail industry inevitable? Was its demise inevitable? Between about 1871 and 1896, the American rail industry came to look more like the British, in that it depended on cooperative pricing and informal integration (Williams, 1885, p. 453). Parliament actively encouraged cartelization in the 1850s and 1860s by giving the force of law to cartel agreements. From 1860 Parliament condoned regular national rate-fixing conferences. New legislation in 1888 gave the Railway Commission a formal role in the establishment of common rates (Armitage, 1969; Davies, 1924). British policy differed in that, from the early 1870s, Parliament forbade selected mergers and sent the message that it opposed mergers in general (Bagwell, 1974, p. 164; Cleveland-Stevens, 1915, pp. 59-60). Thus Parliament followed the course C. F. Adams proposed of regulating cartels and discouraging mergers in order to protect the public interest and prevent the rise of monopolies. The British, like their American counterparts, came to see the industry as naturally cooperative and divined economic principles that followed a new cooperative theory that has been dubbed "laissez-collectives-faire" (Grove, 1962, p. 28). In Britain, as in the United States, cartels emerged in a number of industrial sectors, but in Britain the legislature did not subsequently quash cartels to restore price competition. The cooperative rail market survived until Parliament reorganized the industry in 1921.

Antitrust Law and the
Competitive Market, 1897–1906

From 1897, when the Supreme Court upheld the antipooling components of the Interstate Commerce and Sherman acts, relations among railroads changed substantially. Rate associations failed, and railroads were forced to return to price competition to sustain market share. Railroad managers soon articulated a new vision of how the industry would operate. Now that price fixing was outlawed, railroad leaders espoused predatory pricing, or below-cost rates designed to drive competitors from the market. Now that informal integration was outlawed, railway analysts declared the industry naturally monopolistic and prescribed both end-to-end mergers that would create integrated long-distance service and regional mergers that would eliminate local rivals.

THE MARKET-ENFORCEMENT POLICY REGIME

The intent of both the Sherman Act of 1890 and the Commerce Act of 1887 was clearly to prevent "restraints of trade" in order to guard the economic liberties of consumers, competitors, and potential competitors. By outlawing price fixing and pooling agreements that would dampen free price competition, Congress sought to guarantee free and fair trade to all.

Railroads initially sought to circumvent the antipooling clause of the Interstate Commerce Act. In the decade after 1887, the Morgan clan encouraged railroads to adhere to collectively set prices (Cochran, 1965, p. 171). Rather than disbanding, the eastern and southern associations drew up new agreements in the hope of using the act for their own purposes. The Morgans, whose financial empire included substantial railway holdings, claimed that a clause in the act calling for "just and reasonable rates" gave railroads authority to collectively set fair rates (Chandler, 1977, p. 171). In December of 1888, Charles Perkins of the CB & Q proposed that the ICC be given the power to authorize price agreements: "How would it do to provide simply that when two or more railroads wish to form a pool they shall submit the agreement to the Interstate Commission" (Cochran, 1965, p. 199). The proposal failed, but some industry leaders continued to believe that pooling would eventually be deemed constitutional.

Railroaders fought the act for a decade, but the Court held, in *United States v Trans Missouri Freight Association* (166 U.S. 290, 1897) and *United States v Joint Traffic Association* (171 U.S. 505, 1898), that railroad agreements violated the antipooling clause of the Interstate Commerce Act as well as the prohibition against "restraint of trade" in the Sherman Act

(Kennedy, 1991, p. 154; Kolko, 1965; Skowronek, 1982, p. 158). Pooling and price fixing were now unambiguously illegal. Railroad managers soon predicted all-out price wars.

The Supreme Court's decisions had dramatic effects across many industrial sectors. Mergers reached an all-time high in the United States between 1897 and 1902.

BUSINESS STRATEGY

Predatory Pricing. Although many railroaders sought to circumvent the Interstate Commerce Act in the late 1880s, others believed that the intent of the law was perfectly clear and took actions right away to expand market share and capture their competitors. Rate wars reemerged. Charles Perkins wrote to the editor of the *New York Evening Post* on February 25, 1888: "The Interstate Law is responsible for the existing rate war. Pooling, or self-regulation, has been prohibited and nothing provided to take its place" (Cochran, 1965, p. 447). Under the predatory strategy, railroads dropped their rates to levels they hoped would drive their competitors out of business. For a railroad that faced a single rival, the ideal solution was to drive the competitor into bankruptcy and purchase his assets for a fraction of their value. This would leave the first company with a monopoly and with minimal capital obligations.

Firm Structure: The Merger Mania. The incidence of mergers and acquisitions skyrocketed, partly because of predatory pricing but also partly because formal integration became a positive business strategy, not merely an approach to escaping receivership. Annual railroad mergers in the United States had held steady at about 35 a year between 1890 and 1896. Suddenly, in 1897, they jumped to nearly 80 and in 1900 reached nearly 130 (Ripley, 1915, p. 458). The new theory of the firm called for integrated interregional railroads that could monopolize service on key routes. The idea of a self-sustaining system that would not face price competition, either in local or interregional markets, caught on. As Thomas McCraw concludes, of the effect of government efforts to undermine pooling: "Denied the opportunity to pool their traffic, American railroads devised an alternative method of imposing order on chaos. Each of the major lines began to build, purchase, or acquire through merger what one prominent executive called a 'self-sustaining system' " (McCraw, 1984, p. 51).

A number of railroads built systems by constructing new lines that closely paralleled those of their competitors in a particular region, but key financiers such as J. P. Morgan did what they could to promote mergers in place of new construction, which typically produced overcapacity. Morgan's organization was "prepared to say that they will not negotiate, and will do all in their power to prevent negotiation of any securities for the construction of parallel lines" (quoted in Chandler, 1977, p. 171). Morgan and his cronies did not always prevent parallel construction, but they did promote the idea that it was better to buy out potential rivals than to build competing lines. Paradoxically, then, although the Commerce Act was designed to undercut the concentration of power found in the cartel, it actually increased concentration through mergers, for cartels were illegal but mergers that produced monopolies were not, even if they were designed to restrain trade (Fligstein, 1990, p. 35).

THE ECONOMIC PRINCIPLES
DRAWN FROM THE COMPETITIVE MARKET

At the end of the 1880s, American business and political leaders operated without clear principles for guiding economic and policy decisions. As the economist Henry Carter Adams wrote in 1886: "[T]he present generation is without principles adequate for the guidance of public affairs. We are now passing through a period of interregnum in the authoritative control of economic and governmental principles" (1954, p. 66). Before 1870 state and local activism in economic life had generated remarkable progress, but by about 1870 the idea of government activism had been thoroughly discredited by graft. In the 1870s and 1880s governments replaced activism with weak regulation for industries such as banking and railroading, but the result was unprecedented economic concentration that seemed to threaten the foundation of democracy. From the perspectives of government and business alike, both of the familiar strategies had proven disastrous.

From the 1890s, railwaymen explained the industry's peculiarities with ideas about fixed versus marginal costs that had been put forth by Albert Fink. Fink may have been influenced by the marginal revolution inspired by W. S. Jevons, Karl Menger, and Alfred Marshall. Marginal cost theory offered railway analysts an explanation of the industry's rate problems.

Thus, rate theory changed dramatically. Albert Fink's theory of fixed costs in the rail industry was at the heart of his ideas about pricing, competition, and combination. Fink made a clear distinction between the "fixed or inevitable expenses which attach to the operation of railroads, and which are the same whether one or many trains are run over a road" and the (marginal) costs associated with operation (Fink, 1979a, p. 39). "In the consideration of the subject of the cost of railroad transportation it is of the greatest importance to discriminate between the expenditures which vary with the amount of work performed and those which are entirely independent thereof" (Fink, 1979a, p. 39). The failure to comprehend this distinction frequently led railroads to charge below-cost rates unwittingly. A more general problem in the rail industry was that fixed costs were high, and this led troubled firms to set prices below their costs. Instability was inherent in such a system. Fink and his cronies did not blame public policies that prevented dualistic pricing for this problem, as they might well have, for they had come to accept antidiscrimination law as natural.

The enforcement of price competition also led to a new theory of the firm. Faced with competition, railroads must lower rates to just above costs: "If the obtainable rate exceeds cost, no matter how little, it becomes his interest to accept the terms offered. The important question to be decided is what is the minimum cost" (Fink, 1979a, p. 54). Because minimum costs were difficult to calculate, and because troubled railroads faced an incentive to offer below-cost rates, the rational railroad manager would seek to merge with his rivals in order to eliminate the possibility that he would have to compete with below-cost rates. Thus, Fink's economic theory explained why formal integration was desirable. In an industry such as railroading, in which competition can lower prices to unremunerative levels, stability can be achieved only through centralized rate making. Given that rate setting *among* companies was illegal, the only viable alternative was centralized rate setting *within* integrated companies.

Economies of scale distinguished the rail industry from many others, according to Henry Carter Adams. Where economies of scale obtain, enforced competition is destructive and self-defeating (Skowronek, 1982, p. 132). Such industries are inherently monopolistic, and the government can only check their monopolistic tendencies by subjecting them to public controls. Adams's theory of increasing returns to scale explained the inevitability of consolidation.

In sum, in this third period, legislation that had been adopted explicitly to protect economic liberties, rather than to increase efficiency, nonetheless led to a new vision of economic efficiency (Wilson, 1980). Natural selection gradually became the metaphor for macroeconomic efficiency.

BRITAIN, 1897–1906

Was legislation that imposed price competition on the industry inevitable? Americans quickly came to believe that it was. Antitrust discourse soon suggested that procompetition legislation merely reinforced the economic conditions found in the state of nature, yet other countries took very different views of cartels. In Britain, the Railway Clearing House had set rates nationally from the 1840s. By 1872, a member of Parliament reported, "I do not think that at this moment there is a competitive rate existing in the kingdom" (Fink, 1979b, p. 16). In 1888 Britain's Railway and Canal Traffic Act gave the Railway Commission authority to forge national rate agreements among the country's railroads (Dobbin, 1994b). Germany and other Continental nations likewise enforced rate agreements among railroads, rather than treating them as illicit (Chandler, 1990, p. 56).

Historians agree that the business strategies of predatory pricing and formal merger that prevailed after 1897 were stimulated by railway regulation and antitrust law. Alfred Chandler (1990) writes, "If interfirm agreements on rates, allocation of traffic, and pooling of profits had been legally enforceable in the courts, as they were in other countries, a powerful incentive for system-building by acquisition, merger, and new construction would have disappeared" (p. 57). In Britain, different policies eventuated in different business strategies. The combination of (a) antimerger policies, (b) procartel policies, and (c) strict antidiscrimination laws to stop predatory pricing led British railroads not to seek mergers at the turn of the century, but to continue to check competition through pools, cartels, and other sorts of interfirm agreements (Channon, 1983, p. 59). One result was that a cooperative market, like that which emerged in the United States in the 1870s, survived in Britain. A competitive market never arose there. Hence, between 1872, when Parliament began to discourage mergers, and 1921, when Whitehall consolidated railroads into regional monopolies, industry concentration changed little. Britain's largest railroads at the turn of the century held no more than 1,000 miles of track, but American railroads held as much as 10,000 miles (Chandler, 1990, p. 253).

Conclusion

Business strategy among American railroads went through three distinct phases during the 19th century. Pricing was at first monopolistic, then cooperative, then predatory. Firm structure was at first unitary, then informal integration, then formal horizontal and vertical integration. Different economic laws were articulated to accompany each of these strategies. The idea that economic growth and individual prosperity would result from local organic economies actively pursuing progress was articulated during what I have called the organic market that operated between about 1825 and 1870. The idea that intraindustry competition was normally efficient, but that the rail industry constituted an exception because of high entry costs, was articulated during the cooperative market that operated between the early 1870s and the late 1890s. The idea that high fixed prices and economies of scale made the industry naturally monopolistic, and thus that efficiency would be achieved as monopoly was approached, was articulated during the competitive market that operated after about 1897.

Was it public policy that produced these changes over time in the American rail industry, or were these stages inevitable because of the economics of rail transport? Comparisons with the British case suggest that public policy played a key role in shaping business practices and economic ideas. In the first period, American regional governments financed railroads, but British government left entrepreneurs to their own devices. An organic interregional vision of competition emerged in America that never appeared in Britain. In the second period, American governments ended public aid, outlawed dualistic pricing, and encouraged cartels. British policy looked similar. In both settings, cooperative pricing practices and informal integration emerged. In both settings, railway economists dubbed the industry naturally cooperative. In the third period, when the United States outlawed price fixing and *informal* integration, Britain instead promoted price fixing and discouraged *formal* integration. In consequence, the United States saw predatory pricing and mergers, and Britain saw ever-stronger rail cartels. American economists soon dubbed the industry naturally monopolistic, but their British counterparts continued to view it as cooperative.

The history of American rail policy, business strategy, and economic thought underscores important insights from neo-institutional organizational theory. First, public policy played a key role in constituting the economic environment, even when policymakers viewed their actions as merely restorative of natural economic conditions. Whereas most institutional studies have examined changes within the U.S. antitrust, procompetition, policy regime that has been in force since late in the 1800s, by looking at a different slice of history, I have shown that policy shifts can completely alter the ground rules of economic life. Second, new business strategies were constructed under each policy regime, and they came to be embraced by the industry as a whole. Although the diffusion of business strategies has not been the focus here, as it is in many neo-institutional studies, we saw some direct evidence from each period that railroaders actively constructed collective business prescriptions. Third, new policies and the business strategies they generated led to entirely new ideas about economic efficiency. In each period, a new theory emerged to explain the efficiency of macro policy institutions and of micro business strategies simultaneously. In the first period, for instance, the theory held that macroeconomic growth would occur as regional firms banded together and competed with other regions, and microeconomic efficiency would result from collaboration among regional firms in different sectors. Economic ideas, then, were abstracted from experience in each period, and experience was manifestly shaped by industrial policy.

Finally, American rail history reinforces arguments by political institutionalists that public and private institutions become mutually reinforcing over time. Recent studies have shown that policy institutions are reinforced by the private institutions that surround them (Scott, 1994a; Thelen, 1991; Zysman, 1983)—that policy inertia is not a result of internal processes alone. In the railway industry, during each period railroaders adapted to the policy environment by developing business strategies that would operate in tandem with public policies. During each period they also articulated economic theories that made both public policy and business strategy rational. These private-sector processes served to reinforce public policy. The policies of the first two periods were abandoned not because they lacked private-sector reinforcement—in fact, railroads resisted both major changes. Rather, early policies were altered because they appeared to conflict with institutionalized precepts of American democracy, which defined concentrated power as both antidemocratic and inefficient.

Conclusion

Crafting a Wider Lens

W. RICHARD SCOTT

SØREN CHRISTENSEN

THE PRECEDING CHAPTERS DEAL VARIOUSLY with institutional aspects of organizations. Although a number of common themes are apparent—attention to history, to context, to rule systems, to cultural patterns—there are also variety and differences in approach and emphasis. It seems fair to conclude that, at this point in time, institutional theory is more appropriately regarded as a theoretical orientation—as a family of concepts and arguments—than as a tightly integrated, parsimonious theory. In this respect, institutional theory resembles most other theories in the social sciences.

In these concluding comments, we review two broad areas of divergence and discuss one locus of commonality. We begin by considering some of the controversies concerning the origins of institutions. Next, we discuss differing conceptions of institutions, emphasizing normative versus cognitive views. Finally, we consider the importance of examining behavior and structure in context, a perspective deeply ingrained in institutional analysis.

The Origins of Institutions

CHOICE BEHAVIOR

Whether viewed as cognitive or normative systems—as systems of symbols and beliefs or as rule and governance systems—institutions do

302

not "just grow." They must be constructed and maintained as well as adapted and changed. How this is done—by whom and by what processes—is a matter of considerable controversy in the institutions literature generally, and our own contributors reflect this lack of consensus. A principal focus of disagreement concerns how to conceptualize choice behavior: To what extent do actors make choices? When choices are made, what decision models are employed? Where—in what social positions—is discretion located?

Though DiMaggio (1988) is correct in his accusation that early neo-institutionalists in sociology gave insufficient attention to *agency*—the identification of specific actors who are motivated to carry out the actions described—most contributors to this volume take pains to indicate who is taking the action and what interests are at stake. Borum and Westenholz, Garud and Kumaraswamy, Mezias, and Thornton, in particular, identify particular actors and the interests involved in constructing the various institutional arrangements. Although it is obviously useful to attempt to identify specific agents working in varying circumstances, an institutional perspective raises the more fundamental question: Which actors are allowed to act as agents? As Suchman emphasizes, having the capacity to take action is not a natural state, but is socially determined. Who has the power and the right to make choices and to take action is itself institutionally defined.

In addition to the question of who, there is also the question of how choices are made. A number of institutional arguments are at odds with the rational choice model of decision making. Abell lays out the basic elements of this influential model and usefully differentiates stronger (neoclassical economic) from more relaxed (bounded rationality) versions. As Knudsen emphasizes, the latter models are employed by neo-institutional economists, such as Williamson, as important ingredients in their explanation of the emergence of organizational governance systems. Organizations replace markets when decision complexity exceeds individual cognitive capacities, as a way of reducing the costs of managing transactions. Under certain conditions, actors are motivated by their self-interest to construct rule systems that will bind their own and others' behavior. Or, in the weaker functional version, rule systems that more efficiently serve the interests of participants are more likely to be selected: to survive. As noted in our introduction to this volume, rational choice theorists are most likely to embrace a regulative view of institutional forms.

For Abell and other rational choice advocates, actors who follow rules or taken-for-granted routines depart from rational choice—they behave irrationally in not attempting to optimize their own preferences. However, other institutionalists embrace a broader and more socially embedded view of individual choice: Individuals are viewed as social beings attempting to "make sense of"—both in the sense of interpreting and in the sense of constructing—their situations. They are not focused on maximizing utilities but on securing a basis for "practical action" (DiMaggio & Powell, 1991). They are not governed by individualistic *rational* criteria, but rather by a desire to behave *reasonably*, taking into account social rules and personal relationships.

Such analysts, most of whom subscribe to either a normative or a cognitive view of institutional forms, insist that much "irrational" behavior is perfectly reasonable behavior. They emphasize the extent to which choice is constrained and guided by existing beliefs and structural arrangements, and the extent to which the social structure creates new types of incentives and mediates between existing incentives and individual interests. Following rules is quite sensible when activities are interlocked and individual information is circumscribed, as Simon (1957) has long since taught us. Rules and routines often embody accumulated experience, as Nelson and Winter (1982) argue. Rules often protect one's long-term interests against choices, which, in the short run, appear to be of advantage but which sacrifice longer term gains, as both Mouritsen and Skærbæk and Knudsen point out.

More specifically, normative institutionalists substitute what March and Olsen (1989) term a "logic of appropriateness" for an "instrumental logic." Rather than basing decisions on the criteria of narrow interests, individuals are seen as basing their decisions on an awareness of their social role and a recognition of what they are expected to do in a given situation. Social rewards and controls are seen to be as important or more important than economic incentives. Cognitive institutionalists stress the extent to which widely shared belief systems control and canalize individual conceptions of the nature of a situation and, thereby, views of what options are available and what actions are allowed. Wider ideologies and value commitments provide a scaffolding for the construction of common agreements and shared rules—"constitutions"—that provide a basis for the resolution of inconsistencies in members' preferences at a given point in time as well as over time, as Knudsen argues.

If we take an even broader view of the relation between institutional theory and rationality as viewed by sociological analysts, we again observe much variety, but also evolution over time. In the earliest views of neo-institutional scholars, such as that of Meyer and Rowan (1977) and DiMaggio and Powell (1983), institutional logics are depicted as being in opposition to rational (or "technical") criteria of decision making. Institutions are seen as providing an alternative framework for decision making and structural design.

Somewhat later, institutional and rational decision criteria began to be viewed as providing relatively independent bases of organizing, different but not necessarily in conflict (see Scott, 1992, pp. 132-134; Scott & Meyer, 1983, 1991a). Here, organizational actors are viewed as capable of responding to criteria that stress efficiency in producing outcomes (rational criteria) or conformity to prescribed processes (institutional criteria), but the extent to which these criteria are inconsistent is viewed as variable and to be determined by empirical investigation. To conform to institutional criteria may or may not be inconsistent with narrow self-interest or a concern to maximize efficiency.

Even more recently, a growing number of theorists have begun to argue that an institutional framework subsumes a rational perspective (see, e.g., Fligstein, 1990; Friedland & Alford, 1991; Powell, 1991; Scott, 1987; Whitley, 1992a, 1992b). Institutions are viewed as defining the actors and their interests; they are seen to establish the ends for action and the criteria for success. They determine who—which actors—are allowed to have and pursue interests, and what is taken to be evidence of efficiency and of effectiveness. In this more expansive (imperialistic?) institutional version, rational choice becomes a "special case" limited to specific times and situations. This broader view of institutional effects is represented throughout this volume, but particularly in the contributions of Suchman, Mouritsen and Skærbæk, Garud and Kumaraswamy, Karnøe, and Dobbin.

BOTTOM-UP VERSUS TOP-DOWN EXPLANATIONS

Suchman provides an illuminating discussion of the process by which institutions are created. His discussion of problem generation, naming, and cognition followed by response categorization, comparison, theorization, and diffusion helps to clarify the circumstances under which new institutions are likely to be crafted and who—which agents—are more likely to be able to successfully undertake the task. Note that his conception embraces the broader vision of institutions as cognitive and normative frameworks supporting and governing social action—all kinds of social action, including "rational" action.

Suchman also addresses the question, posed above, of the social location of those who construct institutions—whether institution builders operate from the bottom up or the top down (see Scott, 1994b, pp. 73-75; 1995, pp. 140-143). The prevailing assumption guiding earlier studies was that institutions are constructed from the bottom up or locally, that is, by participants working inside the structures they were creating. Such studies might involve either rational or broader social views of choice and decision making. Thus, Williamson's arguments, based on assumptions of bounded rationality, describe how managers and other types of organizational participants attempt to put in place governance structures that will minimize transactions costs (see Williamson, 1975; 1991a). Selznick (1949, 1957) describes the efforts of organizational leaders attempting to construct ideologies (cognitive structures) and normative frameworks that will motivate participants to preserve the distinctive characteristics of their enterprise.

Alternatively, institutions may be constructed from the top down or globally, as actors external to and at higher levels either impose institutional arrangements or provide a limited menu of models from which local designers are expected to choose. DiMaggio's (1983) discussion of how the program designers of the National Endowment for the Arts in the United States led to the creation of public arts councils at the state level and increased structuration of the arts field provides a good illustration of a top-down process.

Depending on a number of conditions identified by Suchman—including the level at which problems are formulated, the nature of communication links, and the "degree of social agency accorded to social units at that level" by existing institutional arrangements—the locus of actors creating institutional forms varies from situation to situation. The contributors to this volume illustrate this diversity.

Lant and Baum and Suchman focus on the actions of actors operating within or at the level of the organizations affected, emphasizing bottom-up processes. Lant and Baum examine and speculate upon the processes by which hotel managers develop shared conceptions of the nature of their business, in particular, who their competitors are and what types of competitive strategies to pursue. These managers are viewed as both responding to cues in their environment and creating this environment as they develop cognitive maps of the industry and their own position within it, based variously on experiences with their socializing institutions, information obtained from their parent companies, travel agents, and interaction with their peers. Suchman emphasizes the role of "information intermediaries": actors whose structural position allows them to observe multiple examples of organizations facing similar sets of problems and attempting varying solutions. In the development of Silicon Valley in California during the 1970s and 1980s, lawyers were in a unique position to garner information and develop and diffuse models of how to structure one's organization.

By contrast, several contributors stress a more top-down perspective, emphasizing the source of cognitive and normative models to be situated in the wider institutional environment. For these analysts, the environment is the source of order. Contrary to Weick's (1979) well-known depiction of the process by which actors within organizations "enact" their environments, we confront here accounts of how environments work to "enact" organizations (see Scott, 1994c). As is the case in the wider institutions literature, our own analysts vary considerably in the extent to which they both attempt to and succeed in identifying the specific environment agents at work.

Christensen and Molin and Thornton, for example, identify quite palpable agents. The origins of the Danish Red Cross, as depicted by Christensen and Molin, are to be found in the actions of delegates to the Geneva Treaty who created the International Red Cross Committee. Denmark during this early founding period was coerced, coaxed, and shamed into creating a localized version of the internationally crafted model. As is often the case when actions are undertaken under duress, for many years the ideology and structure of the Danish Red Cross were decoupled from its actual programs and activities. Thornton views changes in the U.S. publishing industry occurring as a consequence of takeover activities by larger corporate firms. These firms, in the initial wave during the late 1960s, acquired publishing companies in order to diversify their holdings; in a second wave, in the 1980s, the strategy being pursued was one of globalization. In both cases, however, the takeovers were accompanied by changed cognitive and normative rules regarding the nature of the publishing business: A corporate, financial conception challenged and supplanted an earlier book-oriented culture, managed by editors and characterized by small, independent publishing houses. The new beliefs and norms were carried, to a great extent, by a new cadre of top executives and financial officers who moved into publishing organizations at the time of the takeovers.

Mezias also emphasizes top-down processes but provides a more complex picture of multiple environmental agents, often acting in conflict. He details the interactions involving state regulatory agencies—who, in the fragmented environment of the modern state, are often numerous, quasi-independent, and capable of issuing conflicting rules—and professional bodies associated with corporate accounting. He evaluates the effect of the various influence and control mechanisms associated with these environmental agencies on decisions by corporate officers in a diverse set of large corporations to adopt new standards and practices in accounting.

In their analysis of the Royal Danish Theater, Mouritsen and Skærbæk provide an interesting account of the struggle over 200 years to accommodate two different models: rational fiscal administration and the civilizing effects of high culture. Both accounting and art represent highly esteemed values, and each is somewhat antagonistic to the other. The analysts provide a rich historical review of the ways in which these values were represented and expressed by constituencies associated with the theater over many years. However, we obtain a less clear picture of the identity and motivations of environmental agents committed to the preservation and diffusion of these values at the more global level.

Last, several of our contributors employ an interactive model, describing how environmental forces were mediated by organizational agents to arrive at specific structures and practices. This approach is pursued by Borum and Westenholz, Garud and Kumaraswamy, and Dobbin. In recounting the evolution of the Copenhagen Business School, Borum and Westenholz point to a variety of wider societal-level changes that instigated (empowered) one or another constituency of the school to make basic changes in its structure or goals. Garud and Kumaraswamy detail the heavily interactive process by which firms in the computer industry not only compete to meet existing technical standards but also compete to develop new standards. Industry-wide standards provide both a framework within which specific engineers and managers in computer companies operate to produce today's products and a springboard to stimulate the creation of new standards and the next generation of microprocessors. Dobbin depicts the interactions of governmental regulative agents and railway entrepreneurs during the nineteenth century in the United States, as successive policy regimes designed by state officials gave rise to strategic responses from the industry, which in turn stimulated new policies. Far from acting as an "invisible hand" or "free market," the U.S. industrial policy was crafted by agents of the state and modified by the strategies and reactions of agents within the industry.

Institutional Elements

In the introductory chapter to this volume, three types of institutional elements were identified: the regulative, the normative, and the cognitive. Although all existing institutions represent complex combinations of these elements, it is analytically useful to distinguish among them, because the elements activate different mechanisms and are associated with different effects (see discussion and Table 1 in the introductory chapter; see also Scott, 1995). Moreover, many concrete institutional forms are often dominated by one of the three elements, and even when this is not the case, social scientists, because of their theoretical predilections, often privilege one of the three elements over the others in their analyses.

The contributors to the current volume are tilted strongly toward the cognitive pole in their analyses. Of the 10 empirically based chapters, 8 give prominence to the cognitive forces at work. The 8 include those by Baum and Lant, Suchman, Christensen and Molin, Mouritsen and Skærbæk, Thornton, Garud and Kumaraswamy, Karnøe, and Dobbin. To illustrate, Lant and Baum's evidence for the existence of institutional forces in their discussion of the Manhattan hotel industry includes the presence of shared beliefs, cognitive categories, mental models, and managerial perceptions. The effects of these forces are demonstrated by presenting evidence of homogeneous groups of hotels, isomorphism of competitive strategies within groups, and, more generally, a socially constructed cognitive community. Similarly, in his account of the development of an institutional structure in Silicon Valley, Suchman examines evidence regarding problem naming, response categorization, theorized models, and interpretive schemas. The effects of institutional development are observed in the increased standardization of venture financing contracts.

The remaining chapters could be mined to reveal similar assumptions, concepts, and arguments. The chapters by Garud and Kumaraswamy and by Karnøe are somewhat distinctive in that they examine how cognitive institutions frame and shape technical processes. Dobbin's examination of the effects of public policy on business strategies in the railroad industry embraces a cognitive view of policy—policies as conceptual constraints and as ways of thinking.

Two chapters represent a primarily normative view of institutions, although both also give attention to their cognitive components. Borum and Westenholz develop institutional arguments more in line with the early Selznickian conception. This older institutionalism gives more attention to conflicts of interest, to informal structures, to cooptation, to localized sources of power and influence, and to commitment (see DiMaggio & Powell, 1991, p. 13). In this vein, Borum and Westenholz describe a variety of forces shaping the evolution of the Copenhagen Business School but emphasize the existence of "opportunity fields" around the organization whose resources and interests shape the structure of the school through the use of incentives, cooptation, and political and professional pressures.

Mezias describes a relatively full-fledged institutional structure that embraces cognitive, normative, and regulative elements. However, most of his attention is centered on the public regulative apparatus, exercising its fragmented but nevertheless legitimate control attempts, and on the professional accounting bodies, attempting to wield their normative control.

The cognitive analysts stress the importance of unobtrusive controls: of cognitive constraints, taken-for-granted assumptions, and unconscious decision premises guiding behavior. By contrast, control processes are more explicit in the normative and regulatory models: We are more likely to hear about influence attempts, rewards and penalties, and obligatory behavior reinforced both by internalized norms and external surveillance and sanctioning mechanisms.

The Importance of Context

More than any other theoretical paradigm in the social sciences, the institutional perspective emphasizes the importance of the wider social context. The figure tends to be defocalized to stress the centrality of the ground. In many institutional versions, the figure is not simply embedded in, but also penetrated and constituted by, the ground. Organizations (our figures) are seen to be products of their environments (our ground)—not necessarily passive objects, but products shaped by interactions with their context.

Although other theoretical perspectives, such as the contingency, resource dependence, and population ecology approaches, also acknowledge the importance of the environment, the institutional approach calls attention to a wider range of environmental influences. Organizations are recognized to exist in wider fields that can include influences not only in the near vicinity but also operating at distant locations. Organizations are recognized as being affected not only by present influences and pressures but also by past circumstances. Organizations are seen to exist not just as technical systems, exchanging resources, inputs, and outputs, but also as social systems, incorporating actors and relationships. Organizations are seen as being constructed and shaped by cultural systems embodying symbolically mediating meanings. In short, the institutional perspective highlights, in particular, nonlocal, historical, relational, and cultural forces as factors shaping organizations (see Scott, 1983; Scott & Meyer, 1994).

NONLOCAL INFLUENCES

Many of our contributors recognize nonlocal forces as central to the shaping of the organizations under study. For example, Christensen and Molin view the Danish Red Cross as the creation of a international body. Similarly, the Danish National Theater is observed by Mouritsen and Skærbæk to have been created in response to the visits of touring companies from Germany and France, and, more important, from the desire on the part of the Danish elite to demonstrate their civility by participating in the developing European cultural scene. Borum and Westenholz describe how, over time, the Copenhagen Business School was shaped by forces operating at first the national and later the international level. Thornton, in her study of the U.S. publishing industry, examines the influences stemming from corporate agents operating outside the boundaries of publishing in the wider business community, both nationally and globally.

Other chapters focus on domestic influences at the societal or organizational field levels. Mezias emphasizes the role of state agencies and professional associations operating at the national level in the United States in modifying accounting standards affecting corporate financial behavior. Karnøe details the effects of wider state agencies, educational systems, and the culture of engineering to account for differences in U.S. and Danish engineers working on the harnessing of wind power. Dobbin examines the effects of changes in state policy on the strategies of U.S. railway entrepreneurs.

In all these chapters, analysts attend to the reality that organizations are not just the products of their immediate local environments, whether viewed as organization "sets," supplying critical resources or direct competition; as organization "populations," consisting of similarly constituted organizations competing for the same resources; or as organization "communities," consisting of interdependent systems of competing and cooperating units sharing the same locale. Organizations participate in wider arenas of relations and forces, many of them operating at a societal or world-system level.

HISTORICAL INFLUENCES

Zald (1990) points out that history matters for organizations in two important ways. First, as Stinchcombe (1965) first observed, when an organization is founded—the conditions present at the time when the organization comes into existence—has a lasting influence on its structure and mode of operation. This type of imprinting effect is perhaps best exemplified in the present collection in the piece by Mouritsen and Skærbæk on the Danish National Theater. Founded in the late 18th century, the theater has existed uneasily over a 200-year period, attempting to reconcile the demands for representing the values of rational business administration, on one hand, and the high culture on the other.

The second way in which history matters is reflected in the way that organizations develop through time. Each organization displays a distinctive life course; each undergoes transitions and structural transformations at a particular time, in a specific sequence, and subject to particular forces and influences. When effects occur affects how they occur. More and more social analysts are becoming aware of the importance of time-dependent developmental processes in shaping the distinctive nature of organizational forms (see Arthur, 1989; David, 1986). The two chapters that best reflect these concerns of institutional analysts in our collection are those by Christensen and Molin and by Borum and Westenholz. Each details the effects of a series of events and pressures in shaping, on one hand, the Danish Red Cross and, on the other, the Copenhagen Business School. In their analysis of the latter organization, Borum and Westenholz are particularly insistent that the multiple structures of the CBS, each created in response to a distinctive set of influences occurring at a particular time, continue to coexist. Later forms do not erase all traces of earlier ones; rather, they remain present, such that the current structure is a complex synthesis of previous existences.

RELATIONAL INFLUENCES

The institutional persuasion in social science has long insisted on the importance of social structure: on social relationships rather than simply personal attributes, on configuration and arrangements rather than simply aggregation and composition. Such views are particularly characteristic of the older sociological institutionalism, as exemplified in the work of Selznick (1949). The importance of social ties has recently been underlined in the influential essay on social embeddedness by Granovetter (1985), who reminds us that these forces are at work not only in the obviously social systems of families and communities but also in the economic world of buyers and sellers, firms and corporate enterprises.

The importance of the surrounding social structures on organizational structure and performance is well illustrated in the chapters by Thornton, on U.S. publishers, and by Karnøe, on wind power technologies. Publishers were largely insulated from the changing corporate world of multi-divisional companies until the late 1960s, when they became prime take-over targets. Preexisting social relations—among editors and authors, publishers and editors, publishers and publishers—have been transformed by two waves of acquisition activity. Karnøe emphasizes the significance of institutional infrastructures—educational and training institutions, governmental agencies, and the linkages between design and production units—in accounting for differences in the approaches of U.S. and Danish engineers to wind technology.

CULTURAL INFLUENCES

What is new about the new sociological institutionalism is its attention to symbolic forces: to cultural rules and interpretive schema. Institutions are carried not only by social structures but by cultural rules, as we argued in the introductory chapter to this volume. Cultural carriers exhibit distinctive features. As Scott has pointed out, a concern with cultural forces challenges and undercuts the mechanical metaphor of levels of analysis: "The cultural environment is not 'out there' " as a set of independent relational social structures, but is present "within the human mind of the organizational participant" (1994a, p. 97). Cultural values and beliefs are among the most portable of human attributes. They travel through all manner of conveyances, through interpersonal interactions as well as all types of media: print, radio, television, the worldwide net. They do not depend for their diffusion on specific network relationships but flow through a much broader and less constrained set of channels (see Strang & Meyer, 1993).

Cultural influences are represented in many of the studies reported in this volume. From Lant and Baum's analysis of shared field conceptions of hotel operators to Dobbin's examination of cultural premises underlying policy regimes in 19th-century America, one study after another is sensitive to influences stemming from the wider culture.

Concluding Comment

More so than any other theoretical perspective, an institutional view recognizes the value of a wide-angle lens approach to organizations. Distant forces, remote in both space and time, are recognized to be at work in local and current happenings. Research designs are recalibrated to include broader contextual factors and agents. Organizations, which for too long have been viewed as autonomous, rational systems, are again seen in their proper context, being viewed as constituted, constrained, and supported by their social and cultural environments. Organization theorists, who for too long have been isolated from mainstream social science concerns, return to the fold, helping to seek answers to the central and enduring issues of power, of interdependence, of legitimacy, and of meaning.

References

Abell, P. (1991). Is rational choice theory a rational choice of theory? In J. S. Coleman & T. J. Fararo (Eds.), *Rational choice theory: Advocacy and critique*. Newbury Park, CA: Sage.

Abell, P. (1993a). Some aspects of narrative method. *Journal of Mathematical Sociology, 18*, 93-134.

Abell, P. (1993b). *A model of organization culture*. Mimeo, London School of Economics, London, UK.

Abrahamson, E., & Fombrun, C. J. (1992). Forging the iron cage: Interorganizational networks and the production of macro-culture. *Journal of Management Studies, 29*, 175-194.

Abrahamson, E., & Rosenkopf, L. (1993). Institutional and competitive bandwagons: Using mathematical modeling as a tool to explore innovation diffusion. *Academy of Management Review, 18*(3), 487-517.

Abzug, R., & Mezias, S. J. (1993). The fragmented state and due process protections in organizations: The case of comparable worth. *Organization Science, 4*, 433-453.

Adams, C. F., Jr. (1893). *Railroads: Their origin and problems* (rev. ed.). New York: Putnam.

Adams, H. C. (1954). The relation of the state to industrial action. Reprinted in J. Dorfman (Ed.), *Two essays by Henry Carter Adams*. New York: Columbia University Press. (Original work published 1886)

Adams, W., & Brock, J. W. (1982). Integrated monopoly and market power: System selling, compatibility standards, and market control. *Quarterly Review of Economics and Business, 22*(4), 29-42.

Ainslie, G. (1982). A behavioral economic approach to the defence mechanism: Freud's energy theory revisited. *Social Science Information, 21*, 735-779.

Akerlof, G. A. (1990). Interview. In R. Swedberg (Ed.), *Economics. Redefining their boundaries: Conversations with economists and sociologists*. Princeton, NJ: Princeton University Press.

Alchian, A. (1950). Uncertainty, evolution, and economic theory. *Journal of Political Economy, 58*, 211-221.

Alchian, A. A., & Demsetz. H. (1972). Production, information costs, and economic organization. *American Economic Review, 62,* 777-795.

Alexander, J. C. (1987). *Twenty lectures: Social theory since World War II.* New York: Columbia University Press.

Allison, P. D. (1984). *Event history analysis.* Beverly Hills, CA: Sage.

Amburgey, T. L., & Lippert, P. G. (1989). *Institutional determinants of strategy: The legitimation and diffusion of management buyouts.* Working paper, University of Wisconsin.

Amburgey, T. L., & Miner, A. S. (1992). Strategic momentum: The effects of repetitive, positional, and contextual momentum on merger activity. *Strategic Management Journal, 13,* 335-348.

American Hotel and Motel Association. (1992). *Hotel and motel redbook.* New York: American Hotel and Motel Association.

Andersen, O. S. (1990). The planning of change—Some factors that planners keep forgetting. In F. Borum & P. H. Kristensen (Eds.), *Technological innovation and organizational change.* Copenhagen: New Social Science Monographs.

Anderson, P., & Tushman, M. L. (1990). Technological discontinuities and dominant designs: A cyclical model. *Administrative Science Quarterly, 35,* 604-633.

Aoki, M. (1986). Horizontal vs. vertical information structure in the firm. *American Economic Review, 76*(5), 971-983.

Apple/IBM birthday: Users snub star-crossed pairings. (1992, June 29). *Computerworld,* p. 1.

A raft of Sun clones give users new choices. (1991, July 15). *Computerworld,* p. 72.

A risky new architecture for the future. (1985, March). *Digital Design,* pp. 92-98.

Armitage, S. (1969). *The politics of decontrol of industry: Britain and the United States.* London: Weidenfeld and Nicolson.

Arthur, B. (1989). Competing technologies and lock-in by historical events: The dynamics of allocation under increasing returns. *Economic Journal, 99,* 116-131.

Arthur, W. B. (1988). Self-reinforcing mechanisms in economics. In P. W. Anderson, K. J. Arrow, & D. Pines (Eds.), *The economy as an evolving complex system* (pp. 9-32). Redwood City, CA: Addison-Wesley.

A simpler path to computing. (1986, June). *High Technology,* pp. 28-35.

AT&T, SunSPARC interest in new chip design. (1988, January). *Minimicro Systems,* pp. 17-21.

Bagwell, P. S. (1974). *The transport revolution.* London: Routledge.

Bagwell, P. S., & Mingay, G. E. (1970). *Britain and America: A study of economic change, 1850-1939.* London: Routledge & Kegan Paul.

Barley, S. R. (1986). Technology as an occasion for structuring: Evidence from the observations of CT scanners and the social order of radiology departments. *Administrative Science Quarterly, 31,* 78-108.

Barley, S. R., & Kunda, G. (1992). Design and devotion: Surges of rational and normative ideologies of control in managerial discourse. *Administrative Science Quarterly, 37,* 363-399.

Barnard, C. (1962). *The functions of the executive.* Cambridge, MA: Harvard University Press. (Original work published 1938)

Barney, J. B. (1986). Strategic factor markets. *Management Science, 32,* 1231-1241.

Baron, J. N., Dobbin, F. R., & Jennings, P. D. (1986). War and peace: The evolution of modern personnel administration in U.S. industry. *American Journal of Sociology, 92,* 350-383.

Barr, P. S., Stimpert. J. L., & Huff, A. S. (1992, Summer). Cognitive change, strategic action, and organizational renewal. *Strategic Management Journal, 13,* 15-36.

Bartunek, J. M. (1988). The dynamics of personal and organizational reframing. In R. E. Quinn & K. S. Cameron (Eds.), *Paradox and transformation. Toward a theory of change in organization and management* (pp. 137-162). Cambridge, MA: Ballinger.

Baum, J.A.C., & Lant, T. K. (1993). *Cognitive categorization of competitor groups and perceptions of competitive intensity in the Manhattan hotel industry.* Working paper, New York University.

Baum, J.A.C., & Mezias, S. J. (1992). Localized competition and the dynamics of organizational failure in the Manhattan hotel industry, 1898-1990. *Administrative Science Quarterly, 37,* 580-604.

Baum, J.A.C., & Oliver, C. (1991). Institutional linkages and organizational mortality. *Administrative Science Quarterly,* 187-218.

Beckenstein, A. (1979). Merger activity and merger theories: An empirical investigation. *The Antitrust Bulletin, 5* (no. 24, pp. 105-128). Washington, DC: Federal Legal Publications.

Becker, H. S. (1982). *Art worlds.* Berkeley: University of California Press.

Benston, G. J. (1980). *Conglomerate mergers: Causes, consequences, and remedies.* Washington, DC: American Enterprise Institute.

Berger, P. L., & Luckmann, T. (1967). *The social construction of reality: A treatise on the sociology of knowledge.* Garden City, NY: Doubleday/Anchor.

Berk, G. (1994). *Alternative tracks: The constitution of American industrial order, 1865– 1917.* Baltimore: Johns Hopkins University Press.

Berle, A. A., Jr., & Means, G. C. (1932). *The modern corporation and private property.* New York: Macmillan.

Bishop, A. L. (1907). The state works of Pennsylvania. *Transactions, 8,* 147-297.

Boland, R. J. (1982). Myth and technology in the American accounting profession. *Journal of Management Studies, 19,* 109-127.

Boli, J. (1987). Human rights or state expansion? Cross-national definitions of constitutional rights. In G. M. Thomas, J. W. Meyer, F. O. Ramirez, & J. Boli (Eds.), *Institutional structure: Constituting state, society, and the individual* (pp. 133-149). Newbury Park, CA: Sage.

Borgatti, S. P., Everett, M. G., & Freeman, L. C. (1992). *UCINET IV version 1.0.* Columbia: Analytic Technologies.

Brennan, G., & Buchanan, J. M. (1985). *The reason of rules: Constitutional political economy.* Cambridge, UK: Cambridge University Press.

Brint, S., & Karabel, J. (1991). Institutional origins and transformations: The case of American community colleges. In W. W. Powell & P. J. DiMaggio (Eds.), *The new institutionalism in organizational analysis* (pp. 337-360). Chicago: The University of Chicago Press.

Brittain, J. W., & Wholey, D. R. (1988). Competition and coexistence in organizational communities: Population dynamics in electronics components manufacturing. In G. R. Carroll (Ed.), *Ecological models of organizations* (pp. 195-222). Cambridge, MA: Ballinger.

Bruner, J. S. (1951). Personality dynamics and the process of perceiving. In R. R. Blake & G. V. Ramsey (Eds.), *Perception: An approach to personality* (pp. 121-147). New York: Ronald.

Brunsson, N. (1985). *The irrational organization. Irrationality as a basis for organizational action and change.* Chichester, UK: John Wiley.

Burgelman, R. A. (1983). A model of the interaction of strategic behavior, corporate context, and the concept of strategy. *Academy of Management Review, 8,* 61-70.

Burns, L. R., & Wholey, D. R. (1993). The adoption and abandonment of matrix management programs: Effects of organizational characteristics and interorganizational networks. *Academy of Management Journal, 36*, 106-138.

Burrell, G., & Morgan, G. (1979). *Sociological paradigms and organisational analysis.* London: Heinemann.

Burt, R. S. (1987). Social contagion and innovation: Cohesion versus structural equivalence. *American Journal of Sociology, 92*, 1287-1335.

California Energy Commission. (1990). *Annual reports on wind project performance reporting system, 1986-1990.*

Callender, G. S. (1902). The early transportation and banking enterprises of the states in relation to the growth of corporations. *Quarterly Journal of Economics, 17*, 111-162.

Castello, C., & Elliot, D. (1991). Wind behavior research and development and federal wind program cost/performance. *Proceedings, American Wind Energy Association* (TP-253-4673). Washington, DC: American Wind Energy Association.

Chamberlin, E. H. (1962). *The theory of monopolistic competition.* Cambridge, MA: Harvard University Press.

Chandler, A. D., Jr. (1962). *Strategy and structure: Chapters in the history of the American industrial enterprise.* Cambridge: MIT Press.

Chandler, A. D., Jr. (1977). *The visible hand: The managerial revolution in American business.* Cambridge, MA: Belknap.

Chandler, A. D., Jr. (1986). The evolution of modern global competition. In M. E. Porter (Ed.), *Competition in global industries* (pp. 405-448). Cambridge, MA: Harvard Business School Press.

Chandler, A. D., Jr. (1990). *Scale and scope: The dynamics of industrial capitalism.* Cambridge, MA: Harvard University Press.

Chandler, A. D., Jr. (1992a). Organizational capabilities and the economic history of the industrial enterprise. *Journal of Economic Perspectives, 6*(3), 79-100.

Chandler, A. D., Jr. (1992b). Corporate strategy, structure and control methods in the United States during the 20th century. *Industrial and Corporate Change, 1*(2), 263-284.

Channon, G. (1983). A.D. Chandler's "visible hand" in transport history. *The Journal of Transport History, 3*(2), 53-64.

Chester, D. (1981). *The English administrative system, 1780-1870.* Oxford, UK: Clarendon.

Christensen, J. F., Karnøe, P., Larsen, J. N., Lotz, P., & Valentin, F. (1990). *Innovation in small and medium sized companies—Methodology and empirical aspects* (Report No. 1 on dynamic specialization). Copenhagen: Institute for Industrial Research and Social Development, Copenhagen Business School. (in Danish only)

Christensen, J. P. (1986). De Videregående Uddannelser under Forandring: Resultater og Blokeringer [Higher education under change: Results and blockings]. *Politica, 1*, 38-60.

Christensen, S. (1976). Decision making and socialization. In J. G. March & J. P. Olsen (Eds.), *Ambiguity and choice in organizations* (pp. 351-385). Oslo: Universitetsforlaget.

Clark, B. R. (1956). *Adult education in transition.* Berkeley: University of California Press.

Cleveland, F., & Powell, F. (1909). *Railroad promotion and capitalization in the United States.* New York: Longman Green.

Cleveland-Stevens, E. (1915). *English railways: Their development and their relation to the state.* London: George Routledge.

Coase, R. H. (1937). The nature of the firm. *Economica, 4*, 385-405.

Coase, R. H. (1960). The problem of social costs. *Journal of Law and Economics, 3*, 1-44.

Cochran, T. C. (1965). *Railroad leaders 1845–1890: The business mind in action*. New York: Russell & Russell.

Cohen, M. D., March, J. G., & Olsen, J. P. (1972). A garbage can model of organizational choice. *Administrative Science Quarterly, 17*, 1-25.

Cohen, M. D., March, J. G., & Olsen, J. P. (1976). People, problems, solutions and the ambiguity of relevance. In J. G. March & J. P. Olsen (Eds.), *Ambiguity and choice in organizations* (pp. 24-37). Oslo: Universitetsforlaget.

Cohen, W. M., & Levinthal, D. A. (1990). Absorptive capacity: A new perspective on learning and innovation. *Administrative Science Quarterly, 35*, 128-152.

Coleman, J. S. (1974). *Power and the structure of society*. New York: Norton.

Coleman, J. S. (1988). Social capital in the creation of human capital. *American Journal of Sociology* (Suppl. 94), 95-120.

Coleman, J. S. (1990). *Foundations of social theory*. Cambridge, MA: Belknap.

Compaq emerges from ACE with commitment to Intel. (1992, May 4). *Infoworld*, p. 110.

Computer firms, menaced by Microsoft, are planning new effort to unify Unix. (1993, August 31). *Wall Street Journal*, p. B10.

Conlisk, J. (1980). Costly optimisers versus cheap imitators. *Journal of Economic Behavior and Organization, 15*, 1-22.

Constant, E. W. (1980). *The origins of the turbojet*. Baltimore: Johns Hopkins University Press.

Constant, E. W. (1984). Communities and hierarchies: Structure and practice of science and technology. In R. Laudan (Ed.), *The nature of technological knowledge*. Boston: Reidel.

Coser, L. A., Powell, W. W., & Kadushin, C. (1982). *Books: The culture and commerce of publishing*. Chicago: The University of Chicago Press.

Covaleski, M. A., & Dirsmith, M. W. (1988). An institutional perspective on the rise, social transformation, and fall of a university budget category. *Administrative Science Quarterly, 33*, 562-587.

Creighton, A. L. (1990). *The emergence of incorporation as a legal form for organizations*. Doctoral dissertation, Department of Sociology, Stanford University.

Crozier, M. (1964). *The bureaucratic phenomenon*. Chicago: The University of Chicago Press.

Cyert, R., & March, J. G. (1963). *A behavioral theory of the firm*. Englewood Cliffs, NJ: Prentice Hall.

Daft, R. L., & Weick, K. E. (1984). Toward a model of organizations as interpretation systems. *Academy of Management Review, 9*, 284-295.

Dalzell, R. F. (1987). *Enterprising elite: The Boston associates and the world they made*. Cambridge, MA: Harvard University Press.

D'Andrade, R. G. (1984). Cultural meaning systems. In R. A. Shweder & R. A. LeVine (Eds.), *Culture theory: Essays on mind, self, and emotion* (pp. 88-119). Cambridge, UK: Cambridge University Press.

Dannemand Anderson, P. (1993). *En analyse af den teknologiske innovation i Dansk vind-mølleindustri* (An analysis of technological innovation in the Danish wind turbine industry: The role of the test and research center). Unpublished doctoral thesis, Copenhagen Business School.

D'Aunno, T., Sutton, R. I., & Price, R. H. (1991). Isomorphism and external support in conflicting institutional environments: A study of drug abuse treatment units. *Academy of Management Journal, 14*, 636-661.

David, P. (1985). Clio and the economics of QWERTY. *Economic History, 75*, 227-332.

David, P. (1986). Understanding the economics of QWERTY: The necessity of history. In W. Parker (Ed.), *Economic history and the modern economist* (pp. 30-49).

David, P., & Bunn, J. A. (1990). Gateway technologies and network industries. In A. Heertje & M. Perlman (Eds.), *Evolving technology and market structure.* Ann Arbor: University of Michigan Press.

Davidow, W. H., & Malone, M. S. (1992). *The virtual corporation.* New York: HarperCollins.

Davidson, R. (1993, July). In search of wisdom. *WindPower Monthly,* p. 29.

Davies, A. E. (1924). *British railways, 1825-1924. Why nationalization is inevitable.* London: Railway Nationalization Society.

Davis, G. F., Diekmann, K. A., & Tinsley, C. H. (1994). The decline and fall of the conglomerate firm in the 1980s: The deinstitutionalization of an organizational form. *American Sociological Review, 59,* 547-570.

Davis, G. F., & Stout, S. K. (1992). Organization theory and the market for corporate control: A dynamic analysis of the characteristics of large takeover targets, 1980-1990. *Administrative Science Quarterly, 37,* 605-633.

Department of Energy (DOE). (1984). *A five year research plan 1985-1990: Wind energy technology, generating power from the wind* (DOE/CE—T11, UC Category: 60).

Dertouzos, M., Lester, R., & Solow, R. M. (1989). *Made in America: Regaining the productive edge,* the MIT commission on industrial productivity. New York: Harper Perennial.

Dess, G., & Davis, P. (1984). Porter's (1980) generic strategies as determinants of strategic group membership and organizational performance. *Academy of Management Journal, 27,* 467-488.

de Tocqueville, A. (1945). *Democracy in America* (Vols. 1-2) (H. Reeve & P. Bradley, Trans.). New York: Vintage. (Original work published 1835)

de Tocqueville, A. (1955). *The old regime and the French revolution.* Garden City: Doubleday. (Original work published 1856)

Developers race toward unlimited memory. (1992, July 15). *Datamation,* pp. 79-80.

Dhaliwal, D. S., Salamon, G. L., & Smith, E. D. (1982). The effect of owner versus management control on the choice of accounting methods. *Journal of Accounting and Economics, 4,* 41-53.

Digital unveils alpha chip, as open systems competition. (1992, April). *InfoCanada,* pp. 21-22.

DiMaggio, P. J. (Ed.). (1986a). *Nonprofit enterprise in the arts.* Oxford, UK: Oxford University Press.

DiMaggio, P. J. (1986b). Structural analysis of organizational fields: A blockmodel approach. In B. M. Staw & L. L. Cummings (Eds.), *Research in organizational behavior* (Vol. 8, pp. 355-370). Greenwich, CT: JAI.

DiMaggio, P. J. (1988). Interest and agency in institutional theory. In L. G. Zucker (Ed.), *Institutional patterns and organizations: Culture and environment* (pp. 3-21). Cambridge, MA: Ballinger.

DiMaggio, P. J. (1991). Constructing an organizational field as a professional project: U.S. art museums, 1920-1940. In W. W. Powell & P. J. DiMaggio (Eds.), *The new institutionalism in organizational analysis* (pp. 267-292). Chicago: The University of Chicago Press.

DiMaggio, P. J. (1992). Nadel's paradox revisited: Relational and cultural aspects of organizational structure. In N. Nohria & R. Eccles (Eds.), *Networks and organizations: Structure, form, and action* (pp. 118-142). Cambridge, MA: Harvard Business School Press.

DiMaggio, P. J., & Powell, W. W. (1983). The iron cage revisited: Institutional isomorphism and collective rationality in organizational fields. *American Sociological Review, 48,* 147-160.

DiMaggio, P. J., & Powell, W. W. (1991). Introduction. In W. W. Powell & P. J. DiMaggio (Eds.), *The new institutionalism in organizational analysis* (pp. 1-38). Chicago: The University of Chicago Press.

Dobbin, F. (1993). The social construction of the great depression: Industrial policy during the 1930s in the United States, Britain, and France. *Theory and Society, 22*, 1-56.

Dobbin, F. (1994a). Cultural models of organization: The social construction of rational organizing principles. In D. Crane (Ed.), *The sociology of culture: Emerging theoretical perspectives* (pp. 117-153). Oxford, UK: Basil Blackwell.

Dobbin, F. (1994b). *Forging industrial policy: The United States, Britain, and France in the railway age.* New York: Cambridge University Press.

Dobbin, F. (1994c). Railroads. In G. Carroll & M. Hannan (Eds.), *Organizations in industry: Strategy, structure, and selection* (pp. 59-86). New York: Oxford University Press.

Dobbin, F., Edelman, L., Meyer, J. W., Scott, W. R., & Swidler, A. (1988). The expansion of due process in organizations. In L. G. Zucker (Ed.), *Institutional patterns and organizations: Culture and environment* (pp. 71-100). Cambridge, MA: Ballinger.

Dore, R. (1983). Goodwill and the spirit of market capitalism. *British Journal of Sociology, 34*, 459-482.

Dosi, G. (1982). Technological paradigms and technological trajectories. *Research Policy, 11*(3), 147-162.

Dosi, G. (1988). Sources, procedures, and microeconomic effects of innovation. *Journal of Economic Literature, 26*, 1120-1171.

Dosi, G., Teece, D., & Winter, S. G. (1992). Toward a theory of corporate coherence: Preliminary remarks. In G. Dosi, R. Giannetti, & P. A. Toninelli (Eds.), *Technology and enterprise in a historical perspective* (pp. 185-211). Oxford, UK: Clarendon.

Douglas, M. (1990). Converging on autonomy: Anthropology and institutional economics. In O. E. Williamson (Ed.), *Organization theory: From Chester Barnard to the present and beyond* (pp. 98-115). Oxford, UK: Oxford University Press.

Duesenberry, J. (1960). An economic analysis of fertility: Comment. In *Demographic and economic change in developed countries* (pp. 230-240). Princeton, NJ: Princeton University Press.

Dunlavy, C. (1993). *Politics and industrialization: Early railroads in the United States and Prussia.* Princeton, NJ: Princeton University Press.

Dunn, S. O. (1913). *Government ownership of railways.* New York: Appleton.

Durkheim, E. (1961). *The elementary forms of religious life.* New York: Collier Books. (Original work published 1912)

Durkheim, E. (1966). *Suicide.* New York: Free Press. (Original work published 1897)

Durkheim, E. (1982). *The rules of sociological method and selected texts on sociology and its method.* New York: Free Press.

Dutton, J. E., & Jackson, S. E. (1987). Categorizing strategic issues: Links to organizational action. *Academy of Management Review, 12*, 76-90.

Edelman, L. (1990). Legal environments and organizational governance: The expansion of due process in the American workplace. *American Journal of Sociology, 95*, 1401-1440.

Edelman, L. (1992). Legal ambiguity and symbolic structures: Organizational mediation of civil rights law. *American Journal of Sociology, 97*, 1531-1576.

Edwards, C. D. (1955). Conglomerate bigness as a source of power. In National Bureau of Economic Research, *Business concentration and price policy* (pp. 331-359). Princeton, NJ: Princeton University Press.

Eggleston, D., & Stoddard, F. S. (1987). *Wind turbine engineering design.* New York: Van Nostrand Reinhold.

Ellerbrock, M. J., & Wells, G. J. (1983). Tourist and commercial demand for hotel/motel services: An empirical investigation. *Review of Regional Studies* (issue no. 12).

Elsbach, K. D., & Sutton, R. I. (1992). Acquiring organizational legitimacy through illegitimate actions: A marriage of institutional and impression-management theories. *Academy of Management Journal, 35,* 699-738.

Elster, J. (1979). *Ulysses and the sirens.* Cambridge, UK: Cambridge University Press.

Elster, J. (1985). Weakness of the will and the free-rider problem. *Economics and Philosophy, 1,* 231-265.

Elster, J. (1989). *Nuts and bolts for the social sciences.* Cambridge, UK: Cambridge University Press.

EPRI Journal. (1990, June). Palo Alto, CA: Electrical Power Research Institute.

Ergas, H. (1986). *Does technology policy matter.* Brussels: Center for European Policy Studies.

Fallows, J. (1994). *Looking at the sun: The rise of the new East Asian economic and political system.* New York: Pantheon.

Farrell, J., & Saloner, G. (1986). Installed base and compatibility: Innovation, product preannouncements and predation. *American Economic Review, 76,* 940-955.

Farrell, J., & Saloner, G. (1988). Coordination through committees and markets. *Rand Journal of Economics, 19,* 235-252.

Felstiner, W.L.F., Abel, R. L., & Sarat, A. (1980). The emergence and transformation of disputes, naming, blaming, claiming . . . *Law and Society Review, 15,* 631-654.

Ferguson, C. H., & Morris, C. (1993). *Computer wars.* New York: Times Books.

Fink, A. (1979a). Report of the vice president and general superintendent, Louisville & Nashville railroad co., 1873–1974. In A. D. Chandler, Jr. (Ed.), *The railroads: Pioneers in modern management* (pp. 21-67). New York: Arno. (Original work published 1876)

Fink, A. (1979b). Argument before the committee of commerce of the House of Representatives of the United States on the Reagan bill for the regulation of interstate commerce. In A. D. Chandler, Jr. (Ed.), *The railroads: Pioneers in modern management* (pp. 3-55). New York: Arno. (Original work published 1880)

Flamm, K. (1988). *Creating the computer: Government, industry and high technology.* Washington, DC: Brookings Institution.

Flath, D., & Leonard, E. W. (1979). A comparison of two logit models in the analysis of qualitative marketing data. *Journal of Marketing Research, 16,* 533-538.

Fligstein, N. (1985). The spread of the multidivisional form among large firms, 1919-1979. *American Sociological Review, 50,* 377-391.

Fligstein, N. (1987). The interorganizational power struggle: Rise of finance personnel to top leadership in large corporations, 1919–1979. *American Sociological Review, 52,* 44-58.

Fligstein, N. (1990). *The transformation of corporate control.* Cambridge, MA: Harvard University Press.

Fligstein, N., & Brantley, P. (1992). Bank control, owner control, or organizational dynamics: Who controls the large modern corporation? *American Journal of Sociology, 98,* 230-307.

Fligstein, N., & Markowitz, L. (1993). Financial reorganization of American corporations in the 1980s. In W. J. Wilson (Ed.), *Sociology and the public agenda* (pp. 185-206). Newbury Park, CA: Sage.

Florida, R., & Kenney, M. (1990). *The breakthrough illusion: Corporate America's failure to move from innovation to mass production.* New York: Basic Books.

Fogelson, J. H. (1978). The impact of changes in accounting principles on restrictive covenants in credit agreements and indentures. *Business Lawyer, 10,* 769-787.

Fombrun, C. J., & Zajac, E. (1987). Structural and perceptual influences on intraindustry stratification. *Academy of Management Journal, 30,* 33-50.

Frank, H. F. (1985). *Choosing the right pond.* New York: Oxford University Press.

Frank, R. (1988). *Passions within reasons: The strategic role of the emotions.* New York: Norton.

Frankfurt, H. (1971). Freedom of the will and the concept of a person. *The Journal of Philosophy, 68*(1), 5-20.

Friedland, R., & Alford, R. R. (1991). Bringing society back in: Symbols, practices, and institutional contradictions. In W. W. Powell & P. J. DiMaggio (Eds.), *The new institutionalism in organizational analysis* (pp. 232-266). Chicago: The University of Chicago Press.

Gabel, H. L. (1987). Open standards in the European computer industry: The case of X/OPEN. In H. L. Gabel (Ed.), *Product standardization and competitive strategy* (pp. 91-123). New York: Elsevier Science.

Galaskiewicz, J. (1991). Making corporate actors accountable: Institution-building in Minneapolis-St. Paul. In W. W. Powell & P. J. DiMaggio (Eds.), *The new institutionalism in organizational analysis* (pp. 293-310). Chicago: The University of Chicago Press.

Galaskiewicz, J., & Burt, R. S. (1991). Interorganizational contagion in corporate philanthropy. *Administrative Science Quarterly, 36,* 88-105.

Galaskiewicz, J., & Wasserman, S. (1989). Mimetic and normative processes within an interorganizational field: An empirical test. *Administrative Science Quarterly, 34,* 545-579.

Gambling on RISC. (1986, June 1). *Datamation,* pp. 86-92.

Garfinkel, H. (1967). *Studies in ethnomethodology.* Englewood Cliffs, NJ: Prentice Hall.

Garrad, A. (1988, April). The future needs: Close cooperation between mathematicians and manufacturers. *WindPower Monthly,* pp. 22-25.

Garud, R., & Kumaraswamy, A. (1993a). Changing competitive dynamics in network industries: An exploration of Sun Microsystems' open systems strategy. *Strategic Management Journal, 14*(5), 351-369.

Garud, R., & Kumaraswamy, A. (1993b). *Economies of substitution in technological systems.* NYU working paper.

Garud, R., & Rappa, M. (1994). A socio-cognitive model of technology evolution: The case of cochlear implants. *Organization Science, 5*(3), 344-362.

Geertz, C. (1973). *The interpretation of cultures.* New York: Basic Books.

Geertz, C. (1983). *Local knowledge: Further essays in interpretive anthropology.* New York: Basic Books.

General Court of Massachusetts. (1825–1922). *Acts and resolves of the general court of Massachusetts.* Boston: State Printers.

Gerschenkron, A. (1962). *Economic backwardness in historical perspective.* Cambridge, MA: Harvard University Press.

Gerstner's new vision for IBM. (1993, November 15). *Fortune,* pp. 119-126.

Giddens, A. G. (1976). *New rules of sociological method.* New York: Basic Books.

Giddens, A. G. (1979). *Central problems in social theory: Action, structure and contradiction in social analysis.* Berkeley: University of California Press.

Giddens, A. G. (1984). *The constitution of society.* Berkeley: University of California Press.

Giddens, A. G. (1990). *The consequences of modernity.* Cambridge, MA: Polity.

Gifford, A., Jr. (1991). A constitutional interpretation of the firm. *Public Choice, 68,* 91-106.

Gipe, P. (1995). *Wind energy comes of age.* New York: John Wiley.

Glasberg, D. S., & Schwartz, M. (1983). Ownership and control of corporations. *Annual Review of Sociology, 9,* 1-18.

Golbe, D., & White, L. (1988). A time-series analysis of mergers and acquisitions in the U.S. economy. In A. Auerback (Ed.), *Corporate takeovers: Causes and consequences*. Chicago: The University of Chicago Press.

Golding, E. W. (1955). *The generation of electricity by wind power*. London: Spon Publishers.

Goodrich, C. (1949). The Virginia system of mixed enterprise: A study of state planning of internal improvements. *Political Science Quarterly, 64*, 355-387.

Goodrich, C. (1960). *Government promotion of American canals and railroads 1800-1890*. New York: Columbia University Press.

Gould, S. J., & Lewontin, R. (1979). The spandrels of San Marcos and the Panglossian paradigm: A critique of the adaptionist program. In E. Sober (Ed.), *Conceptual issues in evolutionary biology* (pp. 252-270). Cambridge, MA: Bradfords.

Gourvish, T. R. (1980). *Railways in the British economy: 1813-1914*. London: Macmillan.

Granovetter, M. (1985). Economic action and social structure: The problem of embeddedness. *American Journal of Sociology, 91*, 481-510.

Granovetter, M., & Swedberg, R. (Eds.). (1992). *The sociology of economic life*. Boulder, CO: Westview.

Grove, J. W. (1962). *Government and industry in Britain*. London: Longman.

Gundelach, P. (1988). *Sociale Bevægelser og Samfundsændringer* [Social movements and societal changes]. Aarhus, Denmark: Politica.

Hagerman, R. L., & Zmijewski, M. E. (1979). Some economic determinants of accounting policy choice. *Journal of Accounting and Economics, 1*, 141-161.

Hall, P. A. (1986). *Governing the economy: The politics of state intervention in Britain and France*. New York: Oxford University Press.

Hall, P. A. (1993). Policy paradigms, social learning and the state: The case of economic policy-making in Britain. *Comparative Politics, 25*, 275-297.

Hall, R. L., & Hitch, C. J. (1939). Price theory and business behavior. *Oxford Economic Papers, 2*, 12-45.

Handlin, O., & Handlin, M. F. (1947). *Commonwealth: A study of the role of government in the American economy: Massachusetts, 1774-1861*. Cambridge, MA: Harvard University Press.

Hartz, L. (1948). *Economic policy and democratic thought: Pennsylvania, 1776-1860*. Cambridge, MA: Harvard University Press.

Haunschild, P. R. (1994). Interorganizational imitation: The impact of interlocks on corporate acquisition activity. *Administrative Science Quarterly, 38*(4), 564-592.

Hayes, R., Wheelwright, S., & Clark, K. (1988). *Dynamic manufacturing: Creating the learning organization*. New York: Free Press.

Healy, P. M. (1985). The effect of bonus schemes on accounting decisions. *Journal of Accounting and Economics, 7*, 85-108.

Henderson, R. M., & Clark, K. (1990). Architectural innovation: The reconfiguration of existing product technologies and the failure of established firms. *Administrative Science Quarterly, 35*, 9-30.

Hennessy, J. L., & Patterson, D. A. (1989). *Computer architecture: A quantitative approach*. San Mateo, CA: Morgan Daufman.

Herman, E. S. (1981). *Corporate control, corporate power*. New York: Cambridge University Press.

Hickson, D. J., Pugh, D. S., & Pheysey, D. C. (1971). Operations technology and organization structure: An empirical reappraisal. *Administrative Science Quarterly, 16*, 378-397.

High RISC factors. (1986, April 16). *Computerworld*, pp. 45-47.

Hirsch, P. M. (1972). Processing fads and fashions: An organization-set analysis of cultural industry systems. *American Journal of Sociology, 77*, 639-659.

Hirsch, P. M. (1975). Organizational environments and institutional arenas. *Administrative Science Quarterly, 20*, 327-344.

Hirsch, P. M. (1985). The study of industries. In S. B. Bacharach & S. M. Mitchell (Eds.), *Research in the sociology of organizations* (Vol. 4, pp. 271-309). Greenwich, CT: JAI.

Hirsch, P. M. (1986). From ambushes to golden parachutes: Corporate takeovers as an instance of cultural framing and institutional integration. *American Journal of Sociology, 91*, 800-837.

Hirschi, T. (1969). *Causes of delinquency*. Berkeley: University of California Press.

Hirschman, A. O. (1984). Against parsimony: Three ways of complicating some categories of economic discourse. *Bulletin: The American Academy of Arts and Sciences, 37*, 11-28.

Hodgson, G. M. (1988). *Economics and institutions: A manifesto for a modern institutional economics*. Philadelphia: University of Pennsylvania Press.

Hodgson, G. M. (1993). *Economics and evolution: Bringing life back into economics*. Cambridge, MA: Polity.

Holland, J. H., Holyoak, K. J., Nisbett, R. E., & Thagard, P. R. (1986). *Induction: Processes of inference, learning, and discovery*. Cambridge: MIT Press.

Holthausen, R., & Leftwich, R. (1983). The economic consequences of accounting choice. *Journal of Accounting and Economics, 5*, 77-117.

Hotel Association of New York City. (1992). *Membership roster: Officers, directors, membership*. New York: Author.

How Intel and Motorola missed the Sun rise. (1987, November). *Electronic Business*, pp. 32-34.

HP gathers some allies for PA-RISC. (1992, April 6). *Computerworld*, pp. 41+.

Huey, J. (1993, November). How McKinsey does it. *Fortune*, pp. 56-81.

Huff, A. S. (Ed.). (1990). *Mapping strategic thought*. Somerset, NJ: John Wiley.

Huff, A. S., & Schwenk, C. R. (1990). Bias and sensemaking in good times and bad. In A. S. Huff (Ed.), *Mapping strategic thought* (pp. 89-108). Somerset, NJ: John Wiley.

Hughes, T. P. (1989). *American genesis: A century of invention and technological enthusiasm 1870-1970*. New York: Viking Penguin.

Imai, K-I., Nonaka, I., & Takeuchi, H. (1985). Managing the new product development process: How Japanese companies learn and unlearn. In K. B. Clark, R. Hayes, & C. Lorenz (Eds.), *The uneasy alliance: Managing the productivity-technology dilemma* (pp. 337-375). Boston: Harvard Business School Press.

Jarrell, G. A. (1988). On the underlying motivations for corporate takeovers and restructurings. In G. Libecap (Ed.), *Corporate reorganization through mergers, acquisitions, and leveraged buyouts: Supplement 1. Advances in the study of entrepreneurship, innovation, and economic growth* (pp. 13-41). Greenwich, CT: JAI.

Jensen, H. (1931). *De danske Stænderforsamlingers historie 1830-1848* [The history of the Danish pre-constitutional debates, 1830-1948]. Copenhagen: H. Schultz Forlag.

Jensen, M. C., & Meckling, W. H. (1976). Theory of the firm: Managerial behavior, agency costs, and ownership structure. *Journal of Financial Economics, 3*, 305-360.

Jensen, M. C., & Ruback, R. S. (1983). The market for corporate control: The scientific evidence. *Journal of Financial Economics, 2*, 5-50.

Jepperson, R. L. (1991). Institutions, institutional effects and institutionalism. In W. W. Powell & P. J. DiMaggio (Eds.), *The new institutionalism in organizational analysis* (pp. 143-163). Chicago: The University of Chicago Press.

Jørgensen, T. B., & Melander, P. (1992). *Livet i Offentlige organisationer* [Life in public organizations]. Copenhagen: DJFs Forlag.

Jørgensen, U., & Karnøe, P. (1994). The Danish wind turbine story: Technical solutions to political visions. In A. Rip, T. Misa, & J. Schot (Eds.), *Managing technology in society: New forms for the control of technology*. San Diego: Academic Press.

Joy, W. (1990, June). Keynote speech at the Design Automation Conference, Orlando, FL.

Junge-Jensen, F. (1992). Den nye tid [The new epoch]. In O. Lange (Ed.), *Kampen for en højere Læreanstalt* [The struggle for an institution of higher education] (pp. 80-87). Copenhagen: Handelshøjskolens Forlag.

Kahneman, D., Slovic, P., & Tversky, A. (Eds.). (1982). *Judgement under uncertainty: Heuristics and biases.* Cambridge, MA: Cambridge University Press.

Karnøe, P. (1990). Technological innovation and industrial organization in the Danish wind industry. *Entrepreneurship & Regional Development, 2,* 105-123.

Karnøe, P. (1991). *Danish wind turbine industry a surprising international success: On innovations, industrial development and technology policy.* Copenhagen: Samfundslitteratur. (In Danish)

Karnøe, P. (1993). *Approaches to innovation in modern wind energy technology: Technology policies, science, engineers and craft traditions* (Publication No. 334). Stanford, CA: Stanford University, Department of Economics, Center for Economic Policy Research.

Katz, M. L., & Shapiro, C. (1985). Network externalities, competition, and compatibility. *American Economic Review, 75,* 424-440.

Katzenstein, P. (1985). *Small states in world markets: Industrial policies in Europe.* Ithaca, NY: Cornell University Press.

Kennedy, R. D., Jr. (1991). The statist evolution of rail governance in the United States, 1830–1986. In J. L. Campbell, J. R. Hollingsworth, & L. N. Lindberg (Eds.), *Governance of the American economy* (pp. 138-181). New York: Cambridge University Press.

Klecka, W. R. (1980). *Discriminant analysis.* Beverly Hills, CA: Sage.

Knight, F. (1956). *On the history and method in economics.* Chicago: The University of Chicago Press.

Knoke, D. (1990). *Political networks: The structural perspective.* Cambridge, MA: Cambridge University Press.

Knudsen, C. (Ed.). (1989). *Institutionalismen i samfundsvidenskaberne* [Institutionalism in the social sciences]. Copenhagen: Samfundslitteratur.

Knudsen, C. (1993a). Equilibrium, perfect rationality and the problem of self-reference in economics. In U. Mäki, B. Gustafsson, & C. Knudsen (Eds.), *Rationality, institutions and economic methodology* (pp. 133-170). London: Routledge.

Knudsen, C. (1993b). Modelling rationality, institutions and processes in economics. In U. Mäki, B. Gustafsson, & C. Knudsen (Eds.), *Rationality, institutions and economic methodology* (pp. 265-299). London: Routledge.

Kolko, G. (1965). *Railroads and regulation 1877–1916.* Princeton, NJ: Princeton University Press.

Kotz, D. M. (1978). *Bank control of large corporations in the United States.* Berkeley: University of California Press.

Kranakis, E. (1989). Social determinants of engineering practice: A comparative view of France and America in the nineteenth century. *Social Studies of Science, 19,* 5-70.

Krasner, S. D. (Ed.). (1983). *International regimes.* Ithaca, NY: Cornell University Press.

Krasner, S. D. (1984). Approaches to the state: Alternative conceptions and historical dynamics. *Comparative Politics, 17,* 223-246.

Krasner, S. D. (1988). Sovereignty: An institutional perspective. *Comparative Political Studies, 21,* 66-94.

Kreps, D. M. (1990). *A course in microeconomic theory.* New York: Harvester Wheatsheaf.

Kristensen, P. H. (1988). Virksomhedsperspektiver på industripolitikken: Industrimodernister og Husmænd [Industrial policy from different perspectives of the firm: Industrial modernists and smallholders]. *Politica, 3.*

Kristensen, P. H. (1990). Denmark's concealed production culture, its socio-historical construction and dynamics at work. In F. Borum & P. H. Kristensen (Eds.), *Technological innovation and organizational change* (pp.165-188). Copenhagen: New Social Science Monographs.

Kristensen, P. H. (1992). Strategies against structure: Institutions and economic organization in Denmark. In R. Whitley (Ed.), *European business systems: Firms and markets in their national contexts* (pp. 117-136). London: Sage.

Kristensen, P. H. (1994). Strategies in a volatile world. *Economy and Society, 23*(3), 305-334.

Kuhn, T. S. (1962). *The structure of scientific revolutions.* Chicago: The University of Chicago Press.

Lane, C. (1992). European business systems: Britain and Germany compared. In R. Whitley (Ed.), *European business systems: Firms and markets in their national contexts* (pp. 64-97). London: Sage.

Lange, O. (Ed.). (1992). *Kampen for en højere Læreanstalt* [The struggle for an institution of higher education]. Copenhagen: Handelshøjskolens Forlag.

Langlois, R. N. (1986). *Economics as a process: Essays in the new institutional economics.* Cambridge, UK: Cambridge University Press.

Langlois, R. N. (1992). External economies and economic progress: The case of the microcomputer industry. *Business History Review, 66,* 1-50.

Langlois, R. N., & Robertson, P. L. (1992). Networks and innovation in a modular system: Lessons from the microcomputer and stereo component industries. *Research Policy, 21,* 297-313.

Latour, B., & Woolgar, S. (1979). *Laboratory life: The social construction of scientific facts.* Beverly Hills, CA: Sage.

Laudan, R. (1984). *The nature of technological knowledge.* Boston: Reidel.

Layton, E. (1974). Technology as knowledge. *Technology and Culture, 15,* 31-41.

Layton, E. (1976). American ideologies of science and engineering. *Technology and Culture, 17,* 688-701.

Lazonick, W. (1992). Controlling the market for corporate control: The historical significance of managerial capitalism. *Industrial and Corporate Change, 1*(3), 445-488.

Leftwich, R. (1981). Evidence of the impact of mandatory changes in accounting principles on corporate loan agreements. *Journal of Accounting and Economics, 3,* 3-36.

Leone, R. A. (1986). *Who profits?: Winners, losers, and government regulation.* New York: Basic Books.

Levinthal, D. A., & Fichman, M. (1988). Dynamics of interorganizational attachments: Auditor-client relations. *Administrative Science Quarterly, 33,* 345-369.

Levitt, B., & March, J. G. (1988). Organizational learning. *Annual Review of Sociology, 14,* 319-340.

Levitt, B., & Nass, C. (1989). The lid on the garbage can: Institutional constraints on decision making in the technical core of college-text publishers. *Administrative Science Quarterly, 34,* 190-207.

Lewin, K. (1951). *Field theory in social psychology.* New York: Harper.

Lieberson, S. (1992). Einstein, Renoir and Greeley: Some thoughts about evidence in sociology. *American Sociological Review, 57,* 115.

Lindberg, L. N., & Campbell, J. L. (1991). The state and the organization of economic activity. In J. L. Campbell, J. R. Hollingsworth, & L. N. Lindberg (Eds.), *Governance of the American economy* (pp. 356-395). New York: Cambridge University Press.

Lipset, S. M. (1963). *The first new nation: The United States in historical and comparative perspective.* New York: Norton.

Lively, R. A. (1955). The American system: A review article. *The Business History Review,* 29, 81-96.

Mäki, U., Gustafsson, B., & Knudsen, C. (Eds.). (1993). *Rationality, institutions and economic methodology.* London: Routledge.

Manhattan Classified Directory (Yellow Pages). (1992). New York: NYNEX Information Resources Company.

Manne, H. G. (1965). Mergers and the market for corporate control. *Journal of Political Economy, 73,* 110-120.

March, J. G. (1981a). Decisions in organizations and theories of choice. In A. H. Van de Ven & W. F. Joyce (Eds.), *Perspectives on organizational design and behavior* (pp. 205-244). New York: Wiley Interscience.

March, J. G. (1981b). Footnotes to organizational change. *Administrative Science Quarterly, 26,* 563-577.

March, J. G., & Olsen, J. P. (1976). *Ambiguity and choice in organizations.* Oslo: Universitetsforlaget.

March, J. G., & Olsen, J. P. (1984). The new institutionalism: Organizational factors in political life. *American Political Science Review, 78,* 734-749.

March, J. G., & Olsen, J. P. (1989). *Rediscovering institutions: The organizational basis of politics.* New York: Free Press.

March, J. G., & Olsen, J. P. (1994). Institutional perspectives on governance. In H-U. Derlin, U. Gerhardt, & F. Scharpf (Eds.), *Systemrationalität und Partialinteresse: Festschrift für Renate Mayntz* [Collective rationality and member interests] (pp. 249-270). Baden-Baden: Nomos Verlagsgesellschaft.

March, J. G., & Simon, H. A. (1958). *Organizations.* New York: John Wiley.

Markus, H., & Zajonc, R. B. (1985). The cognitive perspective in social psychology. In G. Lindzey & E. Aronson (Eds.), *Handbook of social psychology* (3rd ed.) (Vol. 1, pp. 137-230). New York: Random House.

Marris, R. (1964). *The economic theory of managerial capitalism.* London: Macmillan.

Marshall, A. (1920). *Principles of economics: An introductory volume* (8th ed.). London: Macmillan.

Massachusetts Board of Railroad Commissioners. (1870s). *Annual report of the railroad commissioners.* Boston: Commonwealth of Massachusetts.

Maurice, M., Sorge, A., & Warner, M. (1980). Societal differences in organizing manufacturing units. *Organization Studies, 1,* 59-86.

McClelland, E. F. (1990). *Rationality and dynamic choice: Foundational explorations.* Cambridge, UK: Cambridge University Press.

McCraw, T. K. (1984). *Prophets of regulation.* Cambridge, MA: Harvard University Press.

McGee, J., & Thomas, H. (1986). Strategic groups: Theory, research, and taxonomy. *Strategic Management Journal, 7,* 141-160.

McKelvey, B. (1982). *Organizational systematics: Taxonomy, classification, evolution.* Berkeley: University of California Press.

Mead, G. H. (1934). *Mind, self, and society.* Chicago: The University of Chicago Press.

Melicher, R. W., Ledolter, J., & D'Antonio, L. J. (1983, August). A time series analysis of aggregate merger activity. *Review of Economics and Statistics, 65,* 423-430.

Melicher, R. W., & Rush, D. F. (1974, March). Evidence on the acquisition-related performance of conglomerate firms. *Journal of Finance, 29,* 141-149.

Mergerstat Review. (1989-1991). Schaumburg, IL: Merrill Lynch Business Brokerage and Valuation.

Merton, R. K. (1938). Social structure and anomie. *American Sociological Review, 3,* 672-682.

Meyer, J. W. (1986). Social environments and organizational accounting. *Accounting, Organizations and Society, 11*, 345-356.

Meyer, J. W. (1994). Rationalized environments. In W. R. Scott & J. W. Meyer (Eds.), *Institutional environments and organizations: Structural complexity and individualism* (pp. 28-54). Thousand Oaks, CA: Sage.

Meyer, J. W., Boli, J., & Thomas, G. M. (1987). Ontology and rationalization in the western cultural account. In G. M. Thomas, J. W. Meyer, F. O. Ramirez, & J. Boli (Eds.), *Institutional structure: Constituting state, society, and the individual* (pp. 12-37). Newbury Park, CA: Sage.

Meyer, J. W., & Rowan, B. (1977). Institutionalized organizations: Formal structure as myth and ceremony. *American Journal of Sociology, 83*, 340-363.

Meyer, J. W., & Rowan, B. (1983). The structure of educational organizations. In J. W. Meyer & W. R. Scott (Eds.), *Organizational environments: Ritual and rationality* (pp. 68-84). Beverly Hills, CA: Sage.

Meyer, J. W., & Scott, W. R., with Rowan, B., & Deal, T. E. (1983). *Organizational environments: Ritual and rationality.* Beverly Hills, CA: Sage. (Updated edition in 1992)

Mezias, S. J. (1987). *Technical and institutional sources of organizational practices: The case of a financial reporting method.* Unpublished doctoral thesis, Graduate School of Business, Stanford University.

Mezias, S. J. (1990). An institutional model of organizational practice: Financial reporting at the Fortune 200. *Administrative Science Quarterly, 35*, 431-457.

Mezias, S. J., & Chung, S. (1989). *Decision making and public policy: A study of the financial accounting standards board.* University of Manchester: Financial Executives Research Foundation.

Milgrom, P., & Roberts, J. (1992). *Economics, organization and management.* Englewood Cliffs, NJ: Prentice Hall.

Miller, P., & Rose, N. (1990). Governing economic life. *Economy and Society, 19*(1), 1-31.

Mills, C. W. (1940). Situated actions and vocabularies of motive. *American Sociological Review, 5*, 904-913.

Ministry of Cultural Affairs. (1978). Det Konglige Teater—En fremtid som hele landets teater. Betænkning 872 fra Udvalget on Det Konglige Teaters målsætning [The Royal Theater: A future as the theater of the whole country] (Report 872). Copenhagen: Committee on the Objective of the Royal Theater, Ministry of Cultural Affairs.

Mintzberg, H. (1979). *The structuring of organizations.* Englewood Cliffs, NJ: Prentice Hall.

Mintzberg, H. (1983). *Structure in fives: Designing effective organizations.* Englewood Cliffs, NJ: Prentice Hall.

Mintzberg, H. (1987). Five P's for strategy. *California Management Review, 30*, 11-24.

Moe, T. M. (1984). The new economics of organizations. *American Journal of Political Science, 28*, 739-777.

Moe, T. M. (1990). The politics of structural choice: Toward a theory of public bureaucracy. In O. E. Williamson (Ed.), *Organization theory: From Chester Barnard to the present and beyond* (pp. 116-153). New York: Oxford University Press.

Mohr, L. B. (Ed.). (1982). *Explaining organizational behavior: The limits and possibilities of theory and research.* San Francisco: Jossey-Bass.

Monsen, R., & Downs, A. (1965). A theory of large managerial firms. *Journal of Political Economy, 73*, 221-236.

Montgomery, C., & Wernerfeldt. B. (1988). Tobin's q and the importance of focus in firm performance. *American Economic Review, 78*, 246-250.

Montias, J. M. (1986). Public support for the performing arts in Europe and the United States. In P. J. DiMaggio (Ed.), *Nonprofit enterprise in the arts* (pp. 287-319). Oxford, UK: Oxford University Press.

Moore, G. (1979). The structure of the national elite network. *American Sociological Review, 44,* 673-692.

Mouritsen, J. (1994). Rationality, institutions and decision making: Reflections on March and Olsen's "Rediscovering institutions." *Accounting, Organizations and Society,* pp. 193-211.

Mowery, D. C., & Rosenberg, N. (1989). *Technology and the pursuit of economic growth.* Cambridge, UK: Cambridge University Press.

Mueller, D. C. (1977). The effects of conglomerate mergers: A survey of the empirical evidence. *Journal of Banking and Finance, 1,* 315-347.

Neiiendam, R. (1953). Rigsdagen og Det Kongelige Teater—1849–1949 [The parliament and the royal theater]. In *Den Danske Rigsdag 1849–1949, Bind V* [The Danish Parliament 1849-1949, Vol. 5] (pp. 599-689). Copenhagen: Statsuiiuisteriet (The Prime Ministers Department).

Neisser, U. (1976). *Cognition and reality: Principles and implications of cognitive psychology.* San Francisco: Freeman.

Neisser, U. (1987). *Concepts and conceptual development: Ecological and intellectual factors in categorization.* Cambridge, MA: Cambridge University Press.

Nelson, D. (1980). *Frederick W. Taylor and the rise of scientific management.* Madison: University of Wisconsin Press.

Nelson, R. L. (1959). *Merger movements in American industry, 1895–1956.* Princeton, NJ: Princeton University Press.

Nelson, R. L. (1966). Business cycle factors in the choice between internal and external growth. In W. Alberts & J. Segall (Eds.), *The corporate merger* (pp. 52-70). Chicago: The University of Chicago Press.

Nelson, R. R. (1992). Why firms differ, and how does it matter? *Strategic Management Journal, 12,* 61-74.

Nelson, R. R., & Winter, S. G. (1982). *An evolutionary theory of economic change.* Cambridge, MA: Belknap.

Nelson, V. (1984, March/April). A history of the SWECS industry in the U.S. *Alternative Sources of Energy, 66,* 20-23.

Neter, J., & Wasserman, W. (1974). *Applied linear statistical models.* Homewood, IL: Irwin.

New York Convention and Visitors Bureau. (1992). *The New York hotel guide.* New York: Author.

New York Convention and Visitors Bureau. (1992). *New York City tour package directory.* New York: Author.

Niskanen, W. A. (1971). *Bureaucracy and representative government.* Chicago: Aldine-Atherton.

Noble, D. F. (1984). *Forces of production: A social history of industrial automation.* New York: Knopf.

North, D. C. (1990). *Institutions, institutional change and economic performance.* Cambridge, UK: Cambridge University Press.

Norusis, M. J. (1990). *SPSS base system user's guide.* Chicago: SPSS, Inc.

OEEC. (1953). *Wind power: Technical papers presented to the wind power working committee.* Paris/London: Organization for Economic Cooperation and Development.

Oliver, C. (1991). Strategic responses to institutional processes. *Academy of Management Review, 16,* 145-179.

Orlikowski, W. J. (1992). The duality of technology: Rethinking the concept of technology in organizations. *Organization Science, 3*, 398-427.

Orrù, M., Biggart, N. W., & Hamilton, G. G. (1991). Organizational isomorphism in East Asia. In W. W. Powell & P. J. DiMaggio (Eds.), *The new institutionalism in organizational analysis* (pp. 361-389). Chicago: The University of Chicago Press.

Orton, J. D., & Weick, K. E. (1990). Loosely coupled systems. A reconceptualization. *Academy of Management Review, 15*, 203-223.

Oswald, A. (1993). *Following behavior in social and economic settings.* London: Center for Economic Performance, London School of Economics.

Parris, H. (1965). *Government and the railways in nineteenth century Britain.* London: Royal Institute of Public Administration.

Parsons, T. (1951). *The social system.* Glencoe, IL: Free Press.

Parsons, T. (1960). *Structure and process in modern societies.* Glencoe, IL: Free Press.

Payne, J. W. (1976). Task complexity and contingent processing in decision making: An information search and protocol analysis. *Organizational Behavior and Human Performance, 16*, 366-387.

Payne, J. W., Laughhunn, D., & Crumm, R. (1981). Translation effects of gambles and aspiration level effects in risky choice behavior. *Management Science, 26*, 1039-1060.

Penrose, E. T. (1955). Limits to the growth and size of firms. *American Economic Review, Papers and Proceedings,* 531-543.

Penrose, E. T. (1959). *The theory of the growth of the firm.* Oxford, UK: Oxford University Press.

Perrow, C. (1986). *Complex organizations: A critical essay* (3rd ed.). New York: Random House.

Pethokoukis, J. M. (1994, August 22). Sparks from takeovers set sectors ablaze. *Investor's Business Daily,* p. 1.

Pfeffer, J. (1972). Merger as a response to organizational interdependence. *Administrative Science Quarterly, 17*, 382-394.

Pfeffer, J. (1981). *Power in organizations.* Marshfield, MA: Pitman.

Pfeffer, J. (1982). *Organizations and organization theory.* Boston: Pitman.

Pfeffer, J., & Salancik, G. R. (1978). *The external control of organizations.* New York: Harper & Row.

Piore, M. J., & Sabel, C. F. (1984). *The second industrial divide: Possibilities for prosperity.* New York: Basic Books.

Polanyi, K. (1944). *The great transformation: The political and economic origins of our time.* New York: Rinehart.

Politiken. (1994, March 23). (Danish newspaper)

Popkin, P. (1979). *The rational peasant.* Berkeley: University of California Press.

Porac, J. F., & Thomas, H. (1990). Taxonomic mental models in competitor definition. *Academy of Management Review, 15*, 224-240.

Porac, J. F., & Thomas, H. (1994). Cognitive categorization and subjective rivalry among retailers in a small city. *Journal of Applied Psychology, 79*, 64-66.

Porac, J. F., Thomas, H., & Baden-Fuller, C. (1989). Competitive groups as cognitive communities: The case of Scottish knitwear manufacturers. *Journal of Management Studies, 26*, 397-416.

Porter, M. E. (1979, May). The structure within industries and companies' performance. *Review of Economics and Statistics,* 214-227.

Porter, M. E. (1980). *Competitive strategy: Techniques for analyzing industries and competitors.* New York: Free Press.

Powell, W. W. (1988). Institutional effects on organizational structure and performance. In L. G. Zucker (Ed.), *Institutional patterns and organizations: Culture and environment* (pp. 115-136). Cambridge, MA: Ballinger.

Powell, W. W. (1991). Expanding the scope of institutional analysis.In W. W. Powell & P. J. DiMaggio (Eds.), *The new institutionalism in organizational analysis* (pp. 183-203). Chicago: The University of Chicago Press.

Powell, W. W., & DiMaggio, P. J. (Eds.). (1991). *The new institutionalism in organizational analysis*. Chicago: The University of Chicago Press.

Powell, W. W., & Friedkin, R. (1987). Organizational change in nonprofit organizations. In W. W. Powell (Ed.), *The nonprofit sector—A research handbook* (pp. 180-194). New Haven, CT: Yale University Press.

Prahalad, K., & Hamel, G. (1990). The core competence of the corporation. *Harvard Business Review, 68*(3), 79-91.

Prelec, D., & Herrnstein, R. J. (1991). Preferences or principles: Alternative guidelines for choice. In R. J. Zeckhauser (Ed.), *Strategy and choice* (pp. 318-340). Cambridge: MIT Press.

Rabinowitz, L., Kelley, H. H., & Rosenblatt, R. M. (1966). Effects of different types of interdependence and response conditions in the minimal social situation. *Journal of Experimental Social Psychology, 2*, 169-197.

Rask, E. (1980). *Trolden med de tre hoveder* [The troll with three heads]. Sted: Udgiver.

Ravenscraft, D. J., & Scherer, F. M. (1987). *Mergers, sell-offs, and economic efficiency*. Washington, DC: Brookings Institution.

Reger, R. K., & Huff, A. S. (1993). Strategic groups: A cognitive perspective. *Strategic Management Journal, 14*, 103-124.

Reid, S. R. (1968). *Mergers, managers and the economy*. New York: Free Press.

Rieppel, O. (1990). Structuralism, functionalism, and the four Aristotelian causes. *Journal of History of Biology, 23*, 291-320.

Ripley, W. Z. (1912). *Railroads, rates and regulation*. New York: Longman Green.

Ripley, W. Z. (1915). *Railroads, finance and organization*. New York: Longman Green.

RISC chip vendors vie for third-party support. (1988, May 30). *Infoworld*, p. 31.

RISCy business. (1990, November 17). *The Economist*, p. 93.

Ritzer, G. (1975). *Sociology: A multiple paradigm science*. Boston: Allyn & Bacon.

Ronen, N. J., & Sadan, S. (1981). *Smoothing income numbers*. Reading, MA: Addison-Wesley.

Rosch, E. (1978). Principles of categorization. In E. Rosch & B. Lloyd (Eds.), *Cognition and categorization* (pp. 28-48). Hillsdale, NJ: Lawrence Erlbaum.

Rosenberg, N. (1982). *Inside the black box: Technology and economics*. Cambridge, UK: Cambridge University Press.

Rosenberg, N. (1992). Science and technology in the twentieth century. In G. Dosi, R. Giannetti, & P. A. Toninelli (Eds.), *Technology and enterprise in a historical perspective* (pp. 63-96). Oxford, UK: Clarendon.

Rosenberg, N., & Steinmüeller, W. E. (1988, May). Why are Americans such poor imitators? *American Economic Review, 78*(2), 229-234.

Rumelt, R. P. (1974). *Strategy, structure, and economic performance*. Cambridge, MA: Harvard University Press.

Rumelt, R. P. (1984). Towards a strategic theory of a firm. In R. B. Lamb (Ed.), *Competitive strategic management* (pp. 566-570). Englewood Cliffs, NJ: Prentice Hall.

Sabel, C. F. (1982). *Work and politics: The division of labor in industry*. Cambridge, UK: Cambridge University Press.

Sabel, C. F. (1993, March). *Learning by monitoring*. Unpublished manuscript, MIT.

Salamon, G. L., & Smith, E. D. (1979). Corporate control and managerial misrepresentation of performance. *The Bell Journal of Economics, 10*, 319-328.

Saviotti, P. P., & Metcalfe, J. S. (1991). Present development and trends in evolutionary economics. In P. P. Saviotti & J. S. Metcalfe (Eds.), *Evolutionary theories of economic and technological change. Present status and future prospects* (pp. 1-30). Chur, Switzerland: Harwood Academic Publishers.

Scheiber, H. N. (1975). Federalism and the American economic order, 1789–1910. *Law and Society Review, 10*, 57-118.

Scheiber, H. N. (1981). Regulation, property rights, and definition of "the market": Law and the American economy. *The Journal of Economic History, 41*, 103-109.

Schelling, T. C. (1984). The intimate contest for self-command. In T. C. Schelling (Ed.), *Choice and consequences: Perspectives of an errant economist* (pp. 57-82). Cambridge, MA: Harvard University Press.

Scherer, F. M., & Ross, D. (1990). *Industrial market structure and economic performance* (3rd ed.). Princeton, NJ: Houghton Mifflin.

Schmitter, P. (1990). Sectors in modern capitalism: Models of governance and variation in performance. In R. Brunetta & C. Dell'Aringa (Eds.), *Labour relations and economic performance* (pp. 3-39). London: Macmillan.

Schotter, A. (1981). *The economic theory of social institutions.* Cambridge, UK: Cambridge University Press.

Schumpeter, J. A. (1942). *Capitalism, socialism and democracy.* London: Unwin.

Scott, M. B., & Lyman, S. M. (1968). Accounts. *American Sociological Review, 33*, 46-62.

Scott, W. R. (1983). The organization of environments: Network, cultural, and historical elements. In J. W. Meyer & W. R. Scott (Eds.), *Organizational environments: Ritual and rationality* (pp. 155-175). Beverly Hills, CA: Sage.

Scott, W. R. (1987). The adolescence of institutional theory. *Administrative Science Quarterly, 32*, 493-511.

Scott, W. R. (1992). *Organizations: Rational, natural, and open systems* (3rd ed.). Englewood Cliffs, NJ: Prentice Hall. (Original work published 1981)

Scott, W. R. (1994a). Institutional analysis: Variance and process theory approaches. In W. R. Scott & J. W. Meyer (Eds.), *Institutional environments and organizations: Structural complexity and individualism* (pp. 81-99). Thousand Oaks, CA: Sage.

Scott, W. R. (1994b). Institutions and organizations: Toward a theoretical synthesis. In W. R. Scott & J. W. Meyer (Eds.), *Institutional environments and organizations: Structural complexity and individualism* (pp. 55-80). Thousand Oaks, CA: Sage.

Scott, W. R. (1994c). Conceptualizing organizational fields: Linking organizations and societal systems. In H-U. Derlien, U. Gerhardt, & F. W. Scharpf (Eds.), *Systemrationalitat und partialinteresse* [Systems rationality and partial interests] (pp. 203-221). Baden-Baden: Nomos-Verlagsgesellschaft.

Scott, W. R. (1995). *Institutions and organizations.* Thousand Oaks, CA: Sage.

Scott, W. R., & Meyer, J. W. (1983). The organization of societal sectors. In J. W. Meyer & W. R. Scott (Eds.), *Organizational environments: Ritual and rationality* (pp. 129-153). Beverly Hills, CA: Sage.

Scott, W. R., & Meyer, J. W. (1991a). The organization of societal sectors: Propositions and early evidence. In W. W. Powell & P. J. DiMaggio (Eds.), *The new institutionalism in organizational analysis* (pp. 108-140). Chicago: The University of Chicago Press.

Scott, W. R., & Meyer, J. W. (1991b). The rise of training programs in firms and agencies: An institutional perspective. In B. M. Staw & L. L. Cummings (Eds.), *Research in organizational behavior* (Vol. 13, pp. 297-326). Greenwich, CT: JAI.

Scott, W. R., & Meyer, J. W. (Eds.). (1994). *Institutional environments and organizations: Structural complexity and individualism.* Thousand Oaks, CA: Sage.

Seely, B. (1993, April). Research, engineering, and science in American engineering colleges: 1900–1960. *Technology and Culture, 34*(2), 344-386.

Selznick, P. (1949). *TVA and the grass roots.* Berkeley: University of California Press.

Selznick, P. (1957). *Leadership in administration: A sociological interpretation.* New York: Harper & Row.

Selznick, P. (1992). *The moral commonwealth. Social theory and the promise of community.* Berkeley: University of California Press.

Selznick, P., with the collaboration of Nonet, P., & Vollmer, H. M. (1969). *Law, society and industrial justice.* Berkeley: Russell Sage.

Sen, A. (1977). Rational fools: A critique of behavioral foundations of economic theory. *Philosophy of Public Affairs, 6,* 317-344.

Series5 caches in 65 MIPS. (1989, October). *Computer Technology Review,* p. 16.

SGI vows to keep MIPS chip "open." (1992, March 23). *Infoworld,* pp. 29+.

Shepsle, K. A. (1986). Institutional equilibrium and equilibrium institutions. In H. Weisburg (Ed.), *Political science: The science of politics* (pp. 51-82). New York: Agathon.

Shepsle, K. A., & Weingast, B. (1987). The institutional foundations of committee power. *American Political Science Review, 81,* 85-104.

Shonfield, A. (1965). *Modern capitalism.* London: Oxford University Press.

Simon, H. A. (1957). *Administrative behavior* (2nd ed.). New York: Macmillan. (Original work published 1945)

Simon, H. A. (1962). The architecture of complexity. *Proceedings of the American Philosophical Society, 196,* 467-482.

Singh, J. V. (Ed.). (1990). *Organizational evolution: New directions.* London: Sage.

Six SPARC-based machines a shocking experience. (1991, September). *UNIX Review,* pp. 47-61.

Sjöstrand, S-E. (1992). On the rationale behind "irrational" institutions. *Journal of Economic Issues, 26*(4), 1007–1040.

Skærbæk, P. (1992). Implementering af økonomistyring. In T. B. Jørgensen & P. Melander (Eds.), *Livet i offentlige organisationer* [Life in public organizations] (pp. 249-275). Copenhagen: DJFs Forlag.

Skinner, B. (1953). *Science and human behavior.* New York: Random House.

Skowronek, S. (1982). *Building a new American state: The expansion of national administrative capacities: 1877–1920.* Cambridge, UK: Cambridge University Press.

Sneath, P.H.A., & Sokal, R. R. (1973). *Numerical taxonomy.* San Francisco: Freeman.

Solbourne targets Sun with systems price cuts. (1991, December 16). *Computerworld,* p. 6.

Sorge, A. (1991). Strategic fit and the societal effect: Interpreting cross-national comparisons of technology, organizations and human resources. *Organization Studies, 12*(2), 161-190.

Steiner, P. O. (1975). *Mergers: Motives effects policies.* Ann Arbor: University of Michigan Press.

Steuer, M. (1989). *Culture and optimality* (STICERD discussion paper). London: London School of Economics.

Stinchcombe, A. L. (1965). Social structure and organizations. In J. G. March (Ed.), *Handbook of organizations* (pp. 142-193). Chicago: Rand McNally.

Stoddard, F. (1986). *The California experience.* Paper presented at a conference of the Danish Association of Wind Turbine Manufacturers.

Stoddard, F. (1990, September 23-28). *Wind turbine blade technology: Decade of lessons learned.* World Renewable Energy Congress, Reading, England.

Stover, J. F. (1970). *The life and death of the American railroad.* New York: Oxford University Press.

Strang, D., & Meyer, J. W. (1993). Institutional conditions for diffusion. *Theory and Society, 22,* 487-511.

Strotz, R. H. (1956). Myopia and inconsistency in dynamic utility maximization. *Review of Economic Studies, 23,* 165-180.

Suchman, M. C. (1991). *On the role of law firms in the structuration of Silicon Valley.* Paper presented to the annual meetings of the American Sociological Association, Cincinnati, OH.

Suchman, M. C. (1994). *On advice of counsel: Law firms and venture capital funds as information intermediaries in the structuration of Silicon Valley.* Unpublished doctoral dissertation, Department of Sociology, Stanford University.

Suchman, M. C., & Eyre, D. P. (1992). Military procurement as rational myth: Notes on the social construction of weapons proliferation. *Sociological Forum, 7,* 137-161.

Summers, P. (1992, November). *Wind energy research takes flight: DOE unveils plans for the nation's most advanced user facility for wind research.* National Renewable Energy Laboratory.

Taiwan's PC makers at the workstation crossroads. (1991, April 8). *Electronic Business,* pp. 63-66.

Teece, D. (1980). Economies of scope and the scope of the firm. *Journal of Economic Behavior and Organization, 1,* 233-247.

Teece, D. (1982). Towards an economic theory of the multiproduct firm. *Journal of Economic Behavior and Organization, 3,* 39-63.

Thaler, R. H., & Shefrin, H. M. (1981). An economic theory of self-control. *Journal of Political Economy, 89,* 392-406.

Theater Commission of 1933. (1934). *Betænkning afgivet at Teaterkommissionen af 1933* [Report from the theater commission of 1933]. Copenhagen: Ministry of Cultural Affairs.

Thelen, K. (1991). *Union of parts: Labor politics in postwar Germany.* Ithaca, NY: Cornell University Press.

Thelen, K., & Steinmo, S. (1992). Historical institutionalism in comparative politics. In S. Steinmo, K. Thelen, & F. Longstreth (Eds.), *Structuring politics: Historical institutionalism in comparative analysis* (pp. 1-32). New York: Cambridge University Press.

The microprocessor marketing wars. (1989, July 10). *Electronic Business,* pp. 28-36.

The revolutionary: Computer maker aims to transform industry and become a giant. (1988, March 18). *Wall Street Journal,* pp. 1+.

Thomas, G. M., & Meyer, J. W. (1984). The expansion of the state. *Annual Review of Sociology, 10,* 461-482.

Thornton, P. H. (1993). *From craft house to corporate enterprise: Acquisition growth of the college publishing industry.* Unpublished doctoral dissertation, Department of Sociology, Stanford University.

Thornton, P. H. (1994). *The evolution of organizational fields: Institutional and organizational change in the college publishing industry, 1958 to 1990s.* Paper presented at the annual meetings of the American Sociological Association, Los Angeles.

Thresher, R., & Dodge, D. (1990). Wind technology today. Chapter 4 in an unknown book. The authors are manager and director, respectively, at U.S. National Renewable Energy Laboratory.

Thurow, L. (1992). *Head to head: The coming economic battle among Japan, Europe and America.* New York: Morrow.

Tolbert, P. S. (1988). Institutional sources of organizational culture in major law firms. In L. G. Zucker (Ed.), *Institutional patterns in organizations* (pp. 101-113). Cambridge, MA: Ballinger.

Tolbert, P. S., & Zucker, L. G. (1983). Institutional sources of change in the formal structure of organizations: The diffusion of civil service reform, 1880-1935. *Administrative Science Quarterly, 28,* 22-39.

Touma, W. R. (1993). *The dynamics of the computer industry: Modeling the supply of workstations and their components.* Norwell, MA: Kluwer.

Towards faster, simpler computers. (1985 August). *IEEE Spectrum,* pp. 38-45.

Tushman, M. L., & Anderson, P. (1986). Technological discontinuities and organizational environments. *Administrative Science Quarterly, 31,* 439-465.

Tushman, M. L., & Rosenkopf, L. (1992). Organizational determinants of technological change: Toward a sociology of technological evolution. In B. Staw & L. L. Cummings (Eds.), *Research in organizational behavior* (Vol. 14, pp. 311-347). Greenwich, CT: JAI.

Ulrich, D., & McKelvey, B. (1990). General organizational classification: An empirical test using the United States and Japanese electronics industries. *Organization Science, 1,* 99-118.

Utterback, J. M., & Abernathy, W. J. (1975). A dynamic model of process and product innovations. *OMEGA, 3,* 639-656.

Van de Ven, A. H., & Garud, R. (1994). The co-evolution of technical and institutional events in the development of an innovation. In J.A.C. Baum & J. Singh (Eds.), *Evolutionary dynamics of organizations* (pp. 425-443). New York: Oxford University Press.

Vanberg, V. (1992). Organizations as constitutional systems. *Constitutional Political Economy, 3,* 223-253.

Vibæk, J., & Kobbernagel, J. (1980). *Foreningen til Unge Handelsmænds Uddannelse 1880-1980* [The Society for the Education of Young Merchants 1880-1980]. Copenhagen: Nyt Nordisk Forlag Arnold Busck.

Vincenti, W. (1990). *What engineers know and how they know it.* Baltimore: The Johns Hopkins University Press.

von Hayek, F. A. (1948). *Individualism and economic order.* Chicago: The University of Chicago Press.

Wallace, A.F.C. (1961). *Culture and personality.* New York: Random House.

Watts, R. L., & Zimmerman, J. L. (1978). Towards a positive theory of the determination of accounting standards. *The Accounting Review, 53,* 112-134.

Watts, R. L., & Zimmerman, J. L. (1986). *Positive accounting theory.* Englewood Cliffs, NJ: Prentice Hall.

Weber, M. (1968). *Economy and society* (G. Roth & C. Wittich, Eds.). New York: Bedminister Press. (Original work published 1924)

Weber, M. (1952). *The Protestant ethic and the spirit of capitalism.* New York: Scribner. (Original work published 1904-1905)

Weick, K. E. (1979). *The social psychology of organizing* (2nd ed.). Reading, MA: Addison-Wesley. (Original work published 1969)

Weicker, R. P. (1990, December). An overview of common benchmarks. *Computer,* pp. 65-75.

Wernerfeldt, B. (1984). A resource-based view of the firm. *Strategic Management Journal, 5,* 171-180.

Wheelwright, S. (1987). Restoring competitiveness in U.S. manufacturing. In D. Teece (Ed.), *The competitive challenge: Strategies for industrial innovation and renewal* (pp. 83-100). New York: Harper & Row.

White, H. C. (1988). Varieties of markets. In B. Wellman & S. D. Berkowitz (Eds.), *Social structures: A network approach* (pp. 226-260). New York: Cambridge University Press.

White, H. C. (1992). *Identity and control*. Princeton, NJ: Princeton University Press.

Whitley, R. (1992a). *Business systems in East Asia: Firms, markets and societies*. London: Sage.

Whitley, R. (Ed.). (1992b). *European business systems: Firms and markets in their national contexts*. London: Sage.

Williams, F. S. (1885). *Our iron roads: Their history, construction, and administration* (6th ed.). London: Bemrose.

Williamson, O. E. (1964). *The economics of discretionary behavior*. Englewood Cliffs, NJ: Prentice Hall.

Williamson, O. E. (1967). Hierarchical control and optimum firm size. *Journal of Political Economy, 75*, 123-138.

Williamson, O. E. (1975). *Markets and hierarchies: Analysis and antitrust implications*. New York: Free Press.

Williamson, O. E. (1981). The modern corporation: Origins, evolution, attributes. *Journal of Economic Literature, 19*, 1537-1568.

Williamson, O. E. (1985). *The economic institutions of capitalism: Firms, markets, relational contracting*. New York: Free Press.

Williamson, O. E. (1988). Mergers, acquisitions, and leveraged buyouts: An efficiency assessment. In G. Libecap (Ed.), *Corporate reorganization through mergers, acquisitions, and leveraged buyouts: Supplement 1. Advances in the study of entrepreneurship, innovation, and economic growth* (pp. 55-79). Greenwich, CT: JAI.

Williamson, O. E. (1990). The firm as a nexus of treaties: An introduction. In M. Aoki, B. Gustafsson, & O. E. Williamson (Eds.), *The firm as a nexus of treaties*. London: Sage.

Williamson, O. E. (1991a). Comparative economic organization: The analysis of discrete structural alternatives. *Administrative Science Quarterly, 36*, 269-296.

Williamson, O. E. (1991b). Economic institutions: Spontaneous and intentional governance. *Journal of Law, Economics and Organizations, 7*, 159-187.

Williamson, O. E. (1993). Transaction cost economics and organizational theory. *Industrial and Corporate Change, 2*, 107-156.

Wilson, J. Q. (Ed.). (1980). *The politics of regulation*. New York: Basic Books.

WindPower Monthly. (1986, November). Exhaustive research and development in Japan now moving upwards to megawatt scale, pp. 10-11.

Winter, S. G. (1988). On Coase, competence and corporation. *Journal of Law, Economics and Organizations, 4*, 163-180.

Wren, D. (1987). *The evolution of management thought* (3rd ed.). New York: John Wiley.

Wrong, D. H. (1961). The oversocialized conception of man in modern sociology. *American Sociological Review, 26*, 183-193.

Wyckoff, D. D., & Sasser, W. E. (1981). *The U.S. lodging industry*. Lexington, MA: D. C. Heath.

Zald, M. N. (1986). The sociology of enterprise, accounting and budget rules: Implications for organizational theory. *Accounting, Organizations and Society, 11*, 327-340.

Zald, M. N. (1990). History, sociology and theories of organization. In J. J. Jackson (Ed.), *Institutions in American society: Essays in market, political and social organizations* (pp. 81-108). Ann Arbor: University of Michigan Press.

Zald, M. N., & Denton, P. (1963). From evangelism to general service: The transformation of the YMCA. *Administrative Science Quarterly, 8*, 214-234.

Zalewski, B. (1992). *The history of the Danish Red Cross*. Unpublished manuscript for a doctoral dissertation, Copenhagen Business School.

Zelizer, V. A. (1988). Beyond the polemics on the market: Establishing a theoretical and empirical agenda. *Sociological Forum, 4*, 614-634.

Zmijewski, M. E., & Hagerman, R. L. (1981). An income strategy approach to the positive theory of accounting standard setting/choice. *Journal of Accounting and Economics, 3*, 129-149.

Zucker, L. G. (1977). The role of institutionalization in cultural persistence. *American Sociological Review, 42*, 726-743.

Zucker, L. G. (1983). Organizations as institutions. In S. B. Bacharach (Ed.), *Research in the sociology of organizations* (Vol. 2, pp. 1-47). Greenwich, CT: JAI.

Zucker, L. G. (Ed.). (1988). *Institutional patterns and organizations: Culture and environment*. Cambridge, MA: Ballinger.

Zysman, J. (1983). *Governments, markets, and growth: Financial systems and the politics of industrial change*. Ithaca, NY: Cornell University Press.

Commissionary Reports

Betænkning fra det i Henhold til Lov af 7. aug. 1922 nedsatte Byggeudvalg vedrørende det Kgl. Teater [Report on the Building Committee Concerning the Royal Theater Settled on the Law of 7 August 1922]. (1923). Copenhagen: Ministry of Cultural Affairs.

Betænkning fra Spareudvalget vedrørende Det kgl. Teater [Report from the Committee on Economizing Regarding the Royal Theater]. (1922). Copenhagen: Ministry of Cultural Affairs.

Betænkning om optrædendes engageringsforhold [Report on wage conditions for artists]. (1967). Copenhagen: Ministry of Cultural Affairs.

Betænkning afgivet af Udvalget vedrørende Det Kongelige Teaters bygnings- og driftsforhold. Betænkning nr. 712 [Report given by the Committee on the Royal Theater's Building Conditions. Report no. 712]. (1974). Copenhagen: Ministry of Cultural Affairs.

De af folketinget valgte Statsrevisorer [The auditors of public accounts appointed by Parliament]. (1976). Beretning om undersøgelser inden for Det Kongelige Teaters regnskabsområde. [Report on the investigations into the Royal Theater's statements of account]

De af folketinget valgte Statsrevisorer [Parliament-Elected Auditors of Public Accountants]. (1988). Beretning om Det Kongelige Teaters driftsudgifter og -indtægter i årene 1983–1985. Beretning fra rigsrevisor fremsendt til Folketinget i henhold til § 18, stk. 1, i lov om revisionenen af statens regnskaber m. m. [Report on the examinations within the accounting area of the Royal Theater]

Den Danske Rigsdag, 1849–1949, Bind V [The Danish Parliament, 1849–1949, Vol. 5]. (1953). J.H. Schultz Forlag.

Det Kongelige Teaters handlingsplan 1990–1992 [The business plan of the Royal Theater, 1990–1992]. (1989). Copenhagen: The Board of Directors of the Royal Theater.

En undersøgelse af fleksibiliteten i løn-og ansættelsesforholdene på Det Kongelige Teater [An investigation of the wage and employment relationships of the Royal Theater]. (1988). Copenhagen: Ministry of Cultural Affairs.

Kommissions Betænkning om det kongelige Teater og Kapel [The Commission's report on the Royal Theater and Orchestra]. (1897).

Organisationsudvikling på Det Kongelige Teater [Organizational development at the Royal Theater]. (1989). Copenhagen: Administrations-og Personaledepartementet [Treasury Department].

Rapport om Det Kongelige Teaters organisatoriske og økonomiske forhold afgivet til kultur-ministeren d. 8. juni 1988 [Report on the organizational and economic conditions submitted to the Minister of Cultural Affairs 8 June 1988]. (1988).

Rapport vedrørende vurdering af Det Kongelige Teaters aktivitetsstyrings-og regnskabs-systemer [Report regarding the appraisal of the activity-steering and accounting systems]. (June, 1988). Copenhagen: Ministry of Cultural Affairs.

Rapport om Videreudvikling af Det Kongelige Teaters Økonomi-og aktivitetsstyring. Fra Styregruppen vedrørende Videreudvikling af Det Kongelige Teaters Aktivitetsstyrings-og regnskabssystem [Report on the development of the accounting system at the Royal Theater. From the Committee on the Further Development of the Accounting System at the Royal Theater]. (December, 1989).

og bilagsrapport [Supplementary report].

Rigsrevisionen [The public auditors]. (1989). Rapport om Det Kongelige Teaters konomi i 1989. [Report on the economy of the Royal Theater in 1989]

Teatrene i Danmark. (1961). Betænkning nr. 278 afgivet af den af regeringen den 26. januar 1954 nedsatte teaterkommission. [Report on the further development of the accounting and activity-steering of the Royal Theater. From the Steering Group of the Activity-Steering and Accounting System, December, 1989]

Author Index

Subject Index

About the Contributors

Peter Abell is the director of the Interdisciplinary Institute of Management at the London School of Economics. He was formerly a professor of Sociology at Surrey University and Birmingham University, both in the United Kingdom. His main recent publications are *The Theory of Comparative Narratives* and *Rational Choice Theory*, for which he was the editor.

Joel A. C. Baum is an Associate Professor in the Division of Management and Economics at the University of Toronto, Scarborough Campus. Previously, he was an Associate Professor at the Stern School of Business at New York University. Current research includes studies of managers' (mis)understandings of competitive processes, spatial evolution, and the dynamics of chain affiliation in the Manhattan hotel industry (with Theresa K. Lant, Heather A. Haveman, and Paul L. Ingram, respectively). He recently coedited, with Jitendra V. Singh, *Evolutionary Dynamics of Organizations*. He has published in such academic journals as *Administrative Science Quarterly, American Journal of Sociology, American Sociological Review, Organization Science, Social Forces,* and *Social Science Research*. He serves on the editorial board of *Administrative Science Quarterly*.

Finn Borum is a Professor of Organization Theory and Development at the Institute of Organization and Industrial Sociology, Copenhagen Business School. He has authored and coauthored several books on organizational analysis, change, conflict, and power.

Søren Christensen is Senior Associate Professor at the Copenhagen Business School. He is the director of the Scandinavian Consortium for Organizational Research, which has a research facility at Stanford University in California. He has published books on decision making, organizational culture, and project leadership. His current research interests involve a study of the nonprofit sector in Denmark from a comparative perspective.

Frank Dobbin is an Associate Professor of Sociology at Princeton University. His book, *Forging Industrial Policy: The United States, Britain, and France in the Railway Age*, investigates the emergence of distinct national industrial policy paradigms. He is, with Timothy Dowd, analyzing how policy shifts affected business strategy and notions of efficiency among 300 early U.S. railroads. He is also, with John Sutton, analyzing how civil rights law shaped the human resource management revolution in organizations.

Raghu Garud is an Associate Professor of Management and Organizational Behavior at the Stern School of Business, New York University. His teaching and research explore interactions among technological change, firm strategies, and organizational designs. He teaches a course on the management and assessment of technologies. He is currently coediting a book titled *Technological Entrepreneurship: Oversights and Foresights*.

Peter Karnøe is an Associate Professor at the Institute of Organization and Industrial Sociology, Copenhagen Business School. His current interest is in studying engineering practices from a social constructionist perspective. He is a member of the Center for Interdisciplinary Studies in Technology Management, and co-leader of the Group of Business Systems Research and Economic Sociology at the Institute of Organization and Industrial Sociology.

Christian Knudsen is an Associate Professor at the Institute of Industrial Economics and Strategy at the Copenhagen Business School. He is coeditor of *Rationality, Institutions, and Economic Methodology*.

Arun Kumaraswamy is a Ph.D. candidate in Strategic Management at the Stern School of Business, New York University. His research interests include investment strategy and competitive dynamics in high-technology industries. He has published several papers on these and related topics. He is currently working on his dissertation, which uses a real options perspective to understand high-tech firms' investments in R&D.

Theresa K. Lant is an Associate Professor of Management at the Stern School of Business, New York University. She joined NYU after receiving her Ph.D. in 1987 from Stanford University's Graduate School of Business. She is interested in exploring how micro-level processes influence macro-level phenomena. Her current research projects include a study of the relationships among managers' cognitive maps of competitive relationships, the development of competitive groups, and actual competitive dynamics. She is representative-at-large for the Organization and Management Theory Division of the Academy of Management.

Stephen J. Mezias in an Associate Professor of Management at the Stern School of Business, New York University. He received his M.S. in statistics and his Ph.D. in organizational behavior from Stanford University. Recent publications have appeared in *Administrative Science Quarterly, The Journal of Economic Behavior and Organization, Organization Science,* and *Strategic Management Journal.*

Jan Molin is an Associate Professor at the Copenhagen Business School's Institute of Organization and Industrial Psychology. He is affiliated with the Copenhagen Foundation of Applied Research. He has published books on organization theory, mergers and acquisitions, postmodernism in organizational sociology, and scientific paradigms from a systems theory perspective. His current research involves a study of nonprofit organizations from an institutional perspective.

Jan Mouritsen is a Professor of Management Accounting at the Copenhagen Business School. He is interested in the organization, technology, and methods of modern accounting. His work is oriented toward the role of calculation and visibility in organizations and society.

W. Richard (Dick) Scott is Professor in the Department of Sociology, with courtesy appointments in the Graduate School of Business, the School of Education, and the School of Medicine, at Stanford University. He also serves as the founding director of the Stanford Center for Organizations Research. He is the author or coauthor of many scholarly articles and about a dozen books, including most recently, *Organizations: Rational, Natural and Open Systems; Institutional Environments and Organizations: Structural Complexity and Individualism* (with John Meyer and associates); and *Institutions and Organizations.* He is a past fellow of the Center for Advanced Study in the Behavioral Sciences and was the recipient, in 1988, of the Distinguished Scholar Award from the Management and Organization Theory Division of the Academy of Management. He currently serves on the governing board of the Commission on Behavioral and Social Sciences and Education of the National Research Council, National Academy of Sciences. He is presently studying the evolution of the field of medical care organizations in the San Francisco Bay Area, from World War II to the present.

Peter Skærbæk is an Assistant Professor of Accounting at the Copenhagen Business School. He received his Ph.D. in public sector accounting. He has been particularly interested in the application of accounting theory within the performing arts.

Mark C. Suchman is an Assistant Professor of Sociology and Law (by courtesy) at the University of Wisconsin-Madison. He holds an A.B. from Harvard University, a J.D. from Yale Law School, and both an M.A. and a Ph.D. in Sociology from Stanford University. His current research employs theories from the sociology of organizations and the sociology of law in order to examine the role of law firms and venture capital funds in the development of California's Silicon Valley. Recent publications include "Military Procurement as Rational Myth: Notes on the Social Construction of Weapons Proliferation," coauthored with Dana P. Eyre, in *Sociological Forum*, and "Invention and Ritual: Notes on the Interrelation of Magic and Intellectual Property in Preliterate Society," in the *Columbia Law Review*.

Patricia H. Thornton received her Ph.D. from Stanford University. She is an Assistant Professor of Sociology at Duke University and teaches in the Markets and Management Program. Her research focuses on institutional analyses of change in entrepreneurial organizations and industries. Her current research investigates how macro environments penetrate and change micro culture and structure.

Ann Westenholz is an Associate Professor at the Institute of Organization and Industrial Relations, Copenhagen Business School. Her interest is in workplace democracy in general and she has, in the past 20 years, been involved in research concerning, for example, semiautonomous working groups, workers' representation on boards of directors, and worker-managed and worker-owned firms. She is currently involved in a project on how and why employee representatives are constituted as strategic actors in their firm.

Printed in the United States
By Bookmasters